Golden Leaves and Burned Books:
Religious Reform and Conflict in the Long
European Reformation

GOLDEN LEAVES AND BURNED BOOKS:
Religious Reform and Conflict in the Long European Reformation

Edited by
Teemu Immonen and Gabriele Müller-Oberhäuser

CULTURAL HISTORY — KULTTUURIHISTORIA 16

Published by the Finnish Society for Cultural History, Finland
ISBN 978-952-68776-4-8 (PRINT)
ISBN 978-952-68776-5-5 (PDF)
ISSN 1458-1949

Finnish Society for Cultural History
c/o Cultural History
20014 University of Turku
https://kulttuurihistoria.net/

Cover Henri Terho

Cover photo Teemu Immonen: Saint Radegund, stained glass (detail), the Church of Sainte-Radegonde, Poitiers.

Layout Päivi Valotie
Printed by BoD, Hamburg.

VERTAISARVIOITU
KOLLEGIALT GRANSKAD
PEER-REVIEWED
www.tsv.fi/tunnus

CONTENTS

Introduction

Teemu Immonen and Gabriele Müller-Oberhäuser

During the late medieval and early modern period, Europe witnessed a continuous series of religious reform movements. The phenomenon was not new. After all, the idea of reform had been central to Christianity from very early on, and in some ways reform is the essence of Christianity. To a degree, medieval society in its entirety was based on the same idea. Throughout the period, the concept of the return to and the renewal of a past considered exemplary formed an essential motive behind the activities of both religious and lay communities. For those who held power, the past offered a legitimate justification for the current situation by explaining how things were meant to be as they were and as they had always been. Likewise, the past could serve as an image of the ideal order, the golden age against which those looking for a change evaluated the present, in their eyes an inferior and corrupted age. It is against this background that the reformers typically sought to justify their demands. For them, the present appeared as a departure from the exemplary past and the only chance of redemption was in a return to authentic models it represented.

From the eleventh century and especially the thirteenth century onwards, an ever increasing number of people became involved in the religious and social debates, which were tightly interwoven. The development of trade and cities, as well as the expansion of the European cultural sphere were accompanied by a growing social mobility and a rise in the number of people involved in literary communication. The many social changes and the emergence of new social groups claiming participation and influence in society inspired different reform movements. Throughout the religious world of the Middle Ages, the emerging groups inevitably had to justify their place in society in religious terms. Religious discussion and debate were essential to both the creation of identities of these new social groups and the re-creation or remodelling of the identities of the established religious communities. In these processes, books and other forms of written communication played a dominant role, for communities as well as for their individual members.

Concentrating on religious reform and the Reformation, the essays of this volume mainly cover the period from the Later Middle Ages to the sixteenth century, though some contributions also consider earlier reform processes in the High Middle Ages as well as some developments in the seventeenth century. Making use of the concept of the 'Long Reformation'[1] as a frame for these essays with their different temporal *foci* implies a reference to more recent approaches to religious reforms and the Reformation with regard to continuity and discontinuity between the later Middle Ages and the Reformation, thus allowing for earlier influential processes of religious reform before the Reformation as well as for different types of reformation in Europe during the sixteenth century[2] and even later. This volume addresses various forms of textual and, in the case of book decoration, also pictorial communication in various processes of reform in Europe, thus giving special attention to the important relationship between text and image in manuscripts and printed books.

The chapters reflect on the use of books in religious reform movements and their impact on lay people and monastic communities, an impact which could be positive or negative, integrative and supportive or causing controversy and conflict. For those committed to religious renewal, books were the necessary and often enthusiastically welcomed vehicles for the transmission of religious reform concepts and for establishing

[1] Wallace 2004; Tyacke 1998.
[2] Wallace 2004, 2, 4–8 on the debate about religious camps, confessions, multiple reformations.

and consolidating new communities. In addition to texts, also the materiality of the books and the images on their leaves and covers were involved in the process. The mere existence of a material book offered a visual place of origin, a container, and a point of reference for the words that constituted the message; the object provided a tangible form for the message. The images, for their part, both added to the prestige of the books and contributed to the interpretation of their contents.

Books dedicated to the distribution and propagation of ideas of religious reform also met with severe opposition and negative reactions. Attempts to hinder or reverse religious reform verbally and textually in the form of controversial oral, written or printed material, are manifest indicators of conflicts over reform in the religious field. Consequently, books could become objects of literary censorship, not only on the textual level by refuting and banning them, but also in the form of attacks on books as material objects that often led to their mutilation or even to their complete destruction, as is most evident in book burning rituals. At the same time they could incriminate and endanger their owners and users and play an essential part in the persecution of 'heretics'.

The inherent tension in the title of this collection of essays, 'Golden Leaves and Burned Books', signifies the two extremes in assessing and evaluating the function of books in the transmission of ideas of religious reform. Based on different views of the value of books for transmitting knowledge or for supporting religious beliefs and new ways of leading a good life pleasing to God, we find two opposing attitudes, of veneration on the one hand and of condemnation on the other. In the eyes of those in favour of reform, books could be appreciated as a highly valued *trésor*, textually with a precious content and possibly also materially in their shape and decoration, whereas those trying to suppress them or simply opposed to their content might consider books as poison, as infectious, devilish and definitely dangerous.

Thus, while concentrating on literary (and pictorial) communication processes in the religious field, the authors of the present book make use of various approaches, mainly from cultural history and book history. Their contributions are based on source material and case studies relevant to the topic of religious reform in mainland Europe, predominantly from Germany, France and Spain, but also from England. One objective of the authors is to place book history in the broader context of cultural history, these two 'histories' being strongly connected by their emphasis on inter-disciplinarity. This implies a commitment to more recent attempts at redefining book history as it has developed as a discipline since the 1980s, its beginnings (among others) represented by the works of Robert Darnton[3] and Donald F. MacKenzie.[4] It is a discipline that now often aims to reach beyond Darnton's 'communications circuit' with its interconnected phases of the 'life course of the book' through production, distribution and reception, by placing the book more specifically within the context of "human history, including the history of culture".[5]

The authors of the present volume consider a book at the same time a product of a culture and an argument in a discussion about reforming a culture. With the concept of culture, we refer to the field of human activity in general as it appears in a particular temporal context determined by historical circumstances. We are particularly indebted to the French tradition of cultural history represented by the Annalists[6] and to Michel Foucault's ideas concerning the "archaeology of knowledge"[7]. Essential with regard to the present volume is the notion popularized by the French that the deeds of man take place in a reality constructed on different time layers and discourses of which humans themselves are only partially conscious. These do not dictate human activity but they do provide the premises within which human activity can take place. A book employs cultural heritage to revolutionize and/or transform the present.

The era discussed in this volume, from the fourteenth to the sixteenth century, was one in which there was a far-reaching media change, often even called the 'first media revolution', with the arrival of the printing press in the middle of the fifteenth century. Research

---

[3] Darnton 1982; Darnton 2007.
[4] McKenzie 1986.
[5] Raymond 2017, 295; Howsam 2014; Howsam 2006; for a recent approach based on the core concepts of materiality, sociality/sociability and space in book history see Bellingradt and Salman 2017.
[6] See, especially, Braudel 1958.
[7] Foucault 1972.

on the change from 'script to print' was fundamentally stimulated by Elizabeth Eisenstein's inspiring, and also in some respects provocative, study *The Printing Press as an Agent of Change. Communications and Cultural Transformations in Early-Modern Europe*[8] of 1979. In a work of almost 800 pages, she discussed the impact of the new technology of book production on Western intellectual and cultural life, on the Renaissance, on the Reformation and on natural science. Her book can be considered the starting point of modern print culture studies, beyond traditional book history.[9] It was especially her view of the inextricable connection between the Reformation and the printing press with its relevance for the changes in literary communication within the religious field of early modern Europe that had a far-reaching influence on further research. Among the many consequences of her work in later research, the debate on differences and continuities between the scribal culture of the Middle Ages and early modern print culture was in no small measure triggered by criticism from medievalists who argued convincingly that in many fields of literary communication there were more aspects of continuity than clear-cut rupture and 'revolution': for example, regarding the supposed opposition between the shifting (and corrupt) texts produced in the *scriptorium* and the typographical fixity guaranteed by the printing shop.

In more recent research, the refusal to see the change from script to print as one of an abrupt substitution of manuscripts by printed books is predominant. It is accompanied by concepts of a more complex relation between various types of literary communication from the Later Middle Ages to early modern times.[10] Firstly, speech, that is oral modes of communication of any sort, had a huge importance in medieval times,[11] and even in early modern times it still played an indispensable role, often being more important for transmitting knowledge and religious reform ideas than books. Secondly, the continuing relevance of manuscript

---

[8] Eisenstein 1979; for the most comprehensive response to and criticism of Eisenstein see Johns 1998, and for Eisenstein's reaction to her critics Eisenstein 2005.

[9] Baron et al. 2007 1–12.

[10] Walsham and Crick, 2004, 1–26.

[11] Clanchy 1993.

production, even in the improved conditions of a well-established print culture, has been emphasized in research on the sixteenth and seventeenth centuries. While literary communication by manuscript in a print culture was mainly a matter of choice, for example, to have manuscripts circulate only among the initiated and the chosen few or to hand over a manuscript as a unique presentation copy in search of patronage, very often this form of communication was also chosen under pressure and in case of danger of censorship or persecution so that manuscripts circulated underground to avoid detection and punishment.[12]

In concentrating on the theory and practice of religious reform with respect to the forms and the degrees of involvement of the religious orders and the secular clergy as well as laypeople, the interest in the impact of the changing processes of communication on these groups also implies a stronger emphasis on the reception phase of the communications circuit, on reading books[13] or on hearing books read aloud as part of an audience,[14] as well as on the use of books,[15] thus allowing for different ways of reception with special regard to varying levels of literacy, first of all among the laity.

The history of medieval and early modern literacy and its role in the formation of shared identities has been well studied from many different viewpoints.[16] James Thompson's *The Literacy of the Laity in the Middle Ages* (1960) was an early important study on the dispersion of literacy, although its scope did not reach beyond the upper social classes and it concerned only the period before 1300. More recently, the discussion about the diffusion of literacy to specific groups, such as knights and

---

[12] Marotti and Bristol 2000; Love 1998, 3–137.

[13] Towheed 2011; Towheed and Owens 2011.

[14] For the concept of "a history of audiences as a broader kind of reading history allowing for reception processes beyond the act of reading" see Rose 2002, 3.

[15] Sherman 2008; Pearson 2008.

[16] For recent surveys, see, for example Mostert and Adamska 2014; Bubalo 2014.

women, has brought interesting results.[17] From the 1980s, scholars of medieval and early modern literacy have become increasingly interested in the function of literacy instead of focusing solely on the ability to read. On the one hand, recent studies have blurred the dichotomy between literate and illiterate; there existed different kinds of literacy and the needs of the people resorting to literary material varied greatly.[18] On the other hand, perhaps more importantly for the present book, the focus of the research has moved towards 'interpretive', 'imagined', and 'textual communities'.[19]

Stanley Fish originally coined the concept of 'interpretive communities' to explain how texts are interpreted in a cultural context. Fish was not interested in the veracity of the texts but in the ways that social interaction affects reading and how the community of readers produces new meanings for established texts.[20] Benedict Anderson, for his part, was interested in the formation of national identities. He argued that a nation is a socially constructed community, and therefore 'imagined' by people who consider themselves to be part of this community, which encompasses both the living, the dead and those yet to be born. This concept is equally useful to describe a religious community, as Tjamke Snijders has pointed out.[21]

Brian Stock's 'textual communities' were communities united by a shared set of texts considered essential and by a shared interpretation of these texts. For Stock, the crucial factor for the development of such a community was not necessarily the level of literacy of the members of the group or a written version of a text, but an individual who, having mastered the text, interpreted it to the community, thus reforming the group's thought and action.[22] Stock's study belonged to a tradition which reaches back to Maurice Halbwachs and his influential work

---

[17] For the knights, see Aurell 2017 (2011); Johnston 2014. For nuns, see Blanton et al 2013; Blanton et al. 2013; Blanton et al. 2018. For the literate women in Quattrocento Florence, see Kaborycha 2012.

[18] See, Gee 2014 (1990) and articles in Blanton et al. 2013.

[19] Fish 1980; Anderson 2003 (1983); Stock 1983.

[20] Fish 1980, 147–174. For example Roger Chartier has developed Fish's ideas. See, Chartier 2007.

[21] Anderson 2003 (1983); Snijders 2015, 146.

[22] Stock 1983, 90.

On Collective Memory[23]. The role of memory, the past as a rhetorically constructed foundation of a group's identity, has been the focus of these studies,[24] which have developed into a complex area of research known as cultural memory studies, with important distinctions such as that between communicative and cultural memory proposed by Jan Assmann.[25] To arouse interest and a response among their audience as well as transmitting facts and intellectual ideas, the texts appealed to emotions, too. The emotional and affective nature of reading and listening to texts read aloud has been studied by Mary Carruthers and Mark Amsler, among others.[26]

The essays in this volume build on earlier research yet offer a novel viewpoint on the history of books. The intention is to contribute new aspects to the discussion of the complex relationship between book history and cultural history in research on the development of the religious field from the Later Middle Ages to the Reformation of the sixteenth century. The essays combine the studying of texts and the discussion of books as material objects. The approach demands attention to the external features of books, their decoration and the forms of writing, all of which add to the meaning of the texts. In addition, the focus on material aspects allows the tracing of the distribution of reforms even when narrative sources remain silent. These features are discussed over the long term and concern an area which covers Western Christendom.

While all the essays in this collection illustrate this central topic of forms of communicating religious reform, they have nevertheless different *foci*, especially with regard to the relationship between reform groups and the aspects of individual and social identity, of integration and conflict.

Part I focuses on books and the creation of 'us-ness'. Päivi Räisänen's article, *Books and reading among rank-and-file Anabaptists in the 16th and early 17th centuries*, explores the role of lay reading practices and ideas of religious and social reform among one of the most contested

---

[23] Halbwachs 1992 (1950).
[24] Fentress and Wickham 1992; Geary 1994; Hen and Innes 2000; Innes 2000; McKitterick 2004.
[25] Assmann 2010; Assmann 1992.
[26] Carruthers 1998; Amsler 2011.

proponent groups of the German Reformation(s), the Anabaptists. Bible study groups have been identified as a key context for forming specifically Anabaptist perspectives in Zurich, Switzerland, where one of the first Anabaptist groups emerged among the radicalized students of Ulrich Zwingli in the early 1520s. The author's focus, however, is on later groups in the German Empire. She places the scattered source evidence (e.g. interrogation protocols) in the broader context of social and cultural practices of early modern reading and communication. The article discusses, firstly, what texts circulated among the Anabaptists and which were produced by them. Apart from the Bible, the author focuses on three types of texts central for Anabaptist life and self-understanding, namely prophesies, song-books and martyrologies. Secondly, the author analyses the use of these texts, emphasizing social practices. Not only were texts read aloud, but they were also discussed, memorized, copied, modified, and sung, whether by one person or in company. The author argues that these practices not only helped to spread Anabaptist ideas, but also actively moulded both individual and collective identities.

The objective of Marika Räsänen's article, *Books of golden rays and ripped folios: Thomas Aquinas's book-relics in religious reforms*, is the cult of one of the major medieval scholars, Thomas Aquinas. The author focuses on Thomas's image as the saintly author whose books symbolized the true Catholic faith and which were the physical evidence of the reformer himself. Räsänen analyses how Thomas's image as the holder of the truth, often presented through books radiating gold on altar panels, was created and recreated in iconography, hagiography, and liturgy from the end of the fourteenth to the seventeenth century. She tracks the changes in the imaginary of Thomas holding a book from the times of the Great Western Schism, which caused division among the Dominican Order, through the conflict between protestant movements and the Catholic Church, which raised the profile of Thomas the Reformer to new heights.

In her article on *Good examples for the sisters: books about St Birgitta of Sweden and the reform of Dominican nuns in Teutonia*, Meri Heinonen analyses the spread of Birgittine texts within observant Dominican convents in Teutonia. The approach is based primarily on the existence of Birgittine manuscripts in the libraries of Dominican female houses, but also on the known interaction between the male and female houses of the Dominican Order and between the Dominicans and Birgittines. The author also asks why the observant Dominicans, both friars and nuns, were interested in Birgitta and suggest that the canonized saint Birgitta enhanced the credibility of Catherine of Siena (1347–1380), who was not canonized until 1461 but had been considered a definitive example of reform-mindedness within the order already long before the reforms occurred.

In *The pictorial hagiography of Saint Radegund and the Capetian religious reform in late thirteenth-century Poitiers* Teemu Immonen discusses the role of manuscript 252 of the Médiathèque François-Mitterrand of Poitiers in the Capetian religious reform in Poitou. The manuscript survives in a mutilated form, its illuminated pages having been ripped out, probably in the 19th century. The contents of the illuminations can be deduced, however, from different surviving pictorial sources. Central to the article is the question of how the illustrations within the book covers of MS 252 were expected to promote the Capetian religious reform policy. The illuminations of the manuscript can be viewed by only a limited audience at a time. Thus, the article explores the limits and the potentials of manuscript illumination in the propagation of a religious ideology.

The essays in Part II on the marking of the borders between 'us' and 'them' contribute to the dialectic between religious groups and the outer world. The focus of Reima Välimäki's article, *Old errors, new sects: the Waldenses, Wyclif and Hus in fifteenth-century manuscripts* is the Hussites, who represented the major heresy and the cause of an ecclesiastical and political crisis in fifteenth-century Bohemia. The article explores how the "old" heretical movement of the Waldenses was used to categorise, label and undermine the programme and doctrine of the Hussites. The fifteenth-century Catholic authors, including some of the most prominent figures of their day, saw connections between the earlier Waldensian heresy and the Wycliffite and Hussite movements they encountered. The old and new heresies were also compared at a very tangible level on the leaves of the manuscripts. Välimäki examines how treatises against Waldenses, especially those written in the 1390s during the last major persecution of German Waldenses, were combined in the fifteenth-century manuscripts with texts refuting Wyclif, Hus and their followers. The author demonstrates how polemical treatises and compilations produced from them were not only propaganda but also ways of discernment, categorisation and knowledge. In other words, they were tools to re-arrange a disturbed spiritual geography by placing the new movements in the continuum of heresy.

Thomas Devaney's article, *Countering the 'heretics': miracle books and Marian devotion in early modern Spain*, examines the illustrated miracle books of the shrine of Nuestra Señora de la Cabeza and other shrines to argue that, in the late sixteenth and early seventeenth century, they functioned both to ensure the continued popularity of the shrines and to disseminate an understanding of veneration of images as a means of countering the Protestant threat. Spanish Catholics had long accorded sacred images a central role in their devotions. "Miracle books," or compilations of the wondrous healings and other prodigies that had occurred at particular shrines, had been common for centuries. Their popularity increased dramatically in the first half of the sixteenth century, as printing allowed far more believers access to these texts than had previously been possible. In the aftermath of the Protestant reformations, however, and especially after the Council of Trent, holy images acquired additional meanings. In response to reports of Protestant rejection of "superstitious" practices, spiritual authorities such as Teresa de Ávila advocated the veneration of images as a means of opposing heresy. The author therefore emphasizes that miracle books did more than simply recount tales of marvellous cures and conversions; they characterized romerías as front lines in a battle to strengthen the hearts of the people and to eradicate heresy.

In his article, *Between pilgrimage and reform: Bernhard of Breidenbach's travelogue to the Holy Land (1486) as printed paradigm, moral guidebook and mirror of princes*, Stephan Schröder discusses one of the first printed travelogues, the pilgrimage report of Bernhard of Breidenbach (c. 1434/40–1497). The report was a great success at the time of its publication in 1486. The text was reprinted twelve times up to 1522 and translated into several languages. The attraction of Breidenbach's report was in part a result of the general popularity of travel and pilgrimage reports in the late Middle Ages, but the success of the book also resulted from the lavish and large-sized woodcuts produced by the Dutch painter Ehrhart Reuwich, who was specifically engaged to accompany Breidenbach on his journey. The comprehensive travelogue enabled Breidenbach to present himself as an expert on the history of the Holy Land and the world overseas. The author notes, however, that Breidenbach also used the pilgrimage report as a vehicle to support reform efforts in the Empire. Breidenbach even included some harsh-sounding advice for the future emperor Maximilian I, on whom many people had built high hopes for change. Since Breidenbach made an effort to present the book at the time of the coronation of Maximilian as German king in Frankfurt in spring 1486, these passages are of special significance. The article thus reads Breidenbach's work not only in the context of the Holy Land pilgrimage, but as a mirror for princes and medium of propaganda within the political disputes of Imperial Reform.

Part III focuses on action and counteraction in the context of book censorship, with an emphasis on conflicts that include the use of violence, either spoken, written or printed, or even physical, against the books themselves or against their owners and readers.

In her article, *The role of pamphlets in church controversies in late medieval England*, Eva Schaten examines the role of pamphlets during church controversies. Posting rolls and single sheets in the entrance area of churches was an effective way to address the town population, frequently employed by both secular and ecclesiastical authorities. But the space was also appropriated by dissidents, who posted lists of demands for church reform, slanderous poems, or even calls to join a rebellion. The deliberate provocation of posting these writings in a place normally reserved for official announcements added fuel to the controversy and aggravated the conflict, often resulting in hastily issued proclamations to stop the posting of further pamphlets and to identify the perpetrators. These mostly ineffective countermeasures drew even more attention to the controversy, showing that well-placed pamphlets could be a very efficient propaganda tool.

In her article, *Physical and verbal violence: persecuted Protestant communities during the reign of Mary I (1553–1558)*, Gabriele Müller-Oberhäuser investigates the severe persecution of Protestant communities in England under Queen Mary I. Against the general background of Mary's Catholic restoration policy and in the context of diverse forms of violence used against persons, which often involved torture and executions, and against material objects like books by means of censorship (including the utter destruction of books by burning), this article focuses on the relationship between forms of physical and non-physical violence. The latter is particularly observable in the use of language in interrogations and trials of 'heretics'. The author includes a closer examination of the role of Edmund Bonner, bishop of London, in the Marian re-Catholization process and in the prosecution and persecution of Protestants. The study leads to a reconsideration of the negative image of 'bloody Bonner' (and 'bloody Mary' too), which is mainly (though not exclusively) based on John Foxe's later *Book of Martyrs* (first edition 1563). In the light of more recent and often controversial discussions in research about the complex processes of religious change and reform in sixteenth-century England, the author takes into account different concepts of 'reformation' in the wider European context of religious renewal.

In her article, *Concepts of violent language in inner-Protestant controversies in Elizabethan England*, Sarah Ströer considers how the early puritan reformers of the 1560s and 1570s used language violently and how the Established Church reacted to them. Perhaps more so than in other epochs, Renaissance people were aware of language and of how it was used. This heightened awareness was a by-product of the re-orientation to classical antiquity and especially of the reception of Ciceronian texts. Language was seen as the ability that defined humanity, distinguished humans from (other) animals, and eloquent language was the mark of the civilized gentleman. At the same time, the normative literature of the time knew a strong ethical code concerning the use of language. Authors were aware of the dangers of 'wrong' language use and even viewed language as having the power to cause injury, analogous to physical violence. These concepts of language have important implications for the study of the religious controversies of the time, in which the contributors often attacked each other with the use of written words. Questions arise as to which circumstances made a certain language use inappropriate and unacceptable.

Bibliography

Amsler, Mark: *Affective Literacies: Writing and Multilingualism in the Late Middle Ages*. Late Medieval and Early Modern Studies 19. Brepols, Turnhout 2011.

Anderson, Benedict: *Imagined Communities: Reflections on the Origin and Spread of Nationalism*. 13th edn. Verso, London 2003. (Orig. 1983)

Assmann, Jan: Communicative and Cultural Memory. *A Companion to Cultural Memory Studies*. Eds. Astrid Erll and Ansgar Nünning. De Gruyter, Berlin, New York 2010, 109–118.

Assmann, Jan: *Das kulturelle Gedächtnis: Schrift, Erinnerung und politische Identität in frühen Hochkulturen*. Beck, Munich 1992.

Aurell, Martin: *The Lettered Knight: Knowledge and Behaviour of the Aristocracy in the Twelfth and Thirteenth Centuries*. Central European University Press, Budapest 2017. (Orig. *Le chevalier lettré: Savoir et conduite de l'aristocratie aux XIIe et XIIIe siècles*. Fayard, Paris 2011)

Baron, Sabrina Alcorn, Eric N. Lindquist and Eleanor Shevlin (eds): *Agent of Change: Print Culture Studies after Elizabeth Eisenstein*. University of Massachusetts Press, Amherst 2007.

Bellingradt, Daniel and Jeroen Salman: Books and Book History in Motion: Materiality, Sociality and Spatiality. *Books in Motion in Early Modern Europe: Beyond Production, Circulation and Consumption*. New Directions in Book History. Eds. Daniel Bellingradt, Paul Nelles and Jeroen Salman. Palgrave Macmillan, Houndmills 2017, 1–11.

Blanton, Virginia, Veronica O'Mara, and Patricia Stoop (eds.): *Nuns' Literacies in Medieval Europe: The Hull Dialogue*. Medieval Women: Texts and Contexts 26. Brepols, Turnhout 2013.

Blanton, Virginia, Veronica O'Mara, and Patricia Stoop (eds.): *Nuns' Literacies in Medieval Europe: The Kansas City Dialogue*. Medieval Women: Texts and Contexts 27. Brepols, Turnhout 2015.

Blanton, Virginia, Veronica O'Mara, and Patricia Stoop (eds.): *Nuns' Literacies in Medieval Europe: The Antwerp Dialogue*. Medieval Women: Texts and Contexts, 28. Brepols, Turnhout 2018.

Braudel, Fernand: Histoire et Sciences sociales: La longue durée. *Annales: Histoire, Sciences Sociales*. 13.4/1958, 725–753.

Bubalo, Đorđe: *Pragmatic Literacy in Medieval Serbia*. Utrecht Studies in Medieval Literacy 29. Brepols, Turnhout 2014.

Carruthers, Mary: *The Craft of Thought: Meditation, Rhetoric, and the Making of Images, 400–1200*. Cambridge University Press, Cambridge 1998.

Chartier, Roger: The Order of Books Revisited. *Modern Intellectual History* 4.3/2007, 509–519.

Clanchy, Michael T.: *From Memory to Written Record: England 1066–1307*. 2nd ed. Blackwell, Oxford and Cambridge 1993.

Darnton, Robert: What is the History of Books? *Daedalus* 111.3/1982, 65–83.

Darnton, Robert: 'What is the History of Books?' Revisited. *Modern Intellectual History* 4.3/2007, 495–508.

Eisenstein, Elizabeth L.: *The Printing Press as an Agent of Change: Communications and Cultural Transformations in Early-Modern Europe*. Cambridge University Press, Cambridge 1979.

Eisenstein, Elizabeth L.: Afterword: Revisiting the Printing Revolution. *The Printing Revolution in Early Modern Europe*. 2nd ed. Cambridge University Press, Cambridge 2005, 313–358.

Fentress, James, and Chris Wickham: *Social Memory*. Blackwell, Oxford 1992.

Fish, Stanley: *Is There A Text in This Class? The Authority of Interpretive Communities*. Harvard University Press, Cambridge MA and London 1980.

Foucault, Michel: *The Archaeology of Knowledge*. Transl. A. M. Sheridan Smith. Pantheon Books, New York 1972. (Orig. *L'archéologie du savoir*. Gallimard, France 1969)

Geary, Patrick: *Phantoms of Remembrance: Memory and Oblivion at the End of the First Millennium*. Princeton University Press, Princeton 1994.

Gee, James: *Social Linguistics and Literacies: Ideology in Discourses*. 4rd ed. Routledge, New York 2014. (1. ed. 1990)

Halbwachs, Maurice. *On Collective Memory*. Ed. and transl. Lewis A. Coser. University of Chicago Press, Chicago 1992. (Orig. *La Mémoire collective*. Presses Universitaires de France, Paris 1950)

Hen, Yitzhak, and Matthew Innes (eds.): *The Uses of the Past in the Early Middle Ages*. Cambridge University Press, Cambridge 2000.

Howsam, Leslie: *Old Books & New Histories: An Orientation to Studies in Book and Print Culture*. University of Toronto Press, Toronto 2006.

Howsam, Leslie: The Study of Book History. *The Cambridge Companion to the History of the Book*. Ed. Leslie Howsam. Cambridge University Press: Cambridge 2014, 1–13.

Innes, Matthew: Introduction: Using the Past, Interpreting the Present, Influencing the Future. *Using the Past in the Early Middle Ages*. Eds. Yitzhak Hen and Matthew Innes. Cambridge University Press, Cambridge 2000, 1–8.

Johns, Adrian: *The Nature of the Book: Print and Knowledge in the Making*. University of Chicago Press, Chicago and London 1998.

Johnston, Michael: *Romance and the Gentry in Late Medieval England*. Oxford University Press, Oxford 2014.

Kaborycha, Lisa: Brigida Baldinotti and Her Two Epistles in Quattrocento Florentine Manuscripts. *Speculum* 87.3/2012, 793–826.

Love, Harold: *The Culture and Commerce of Texts: Scribal Publication in Seventeenth-Century England*. University of Massachusetts Press, Amherst 1998. (1st ed. 1993)

McKenzie, Donald F.: *Bibliography and the Sociology of Texts*. The Panizzi Lectures 1985. The British Library, London 1986.

McKitterick, Rosamond. *History and Memory in the Carolingian World*. Cambridge University Press, Cambridge 2004.

Marotti, Arthur F. and Michael Bristol (eds.): *Print, Manuscript, Performance. The Changing Relations of the Media in Early Modern England*. Ohio State University Press, Columbus Ohio 2000.

Mostert, Marco and Anna Adamska (eds.): *Uses of the Written Word in Medieval Towns: Medieval Urban Literacy II*. Utrecht Studies in Medieval Literacy 28. Brepols, Turnhout 2014.

Pearson, David: *Books as History: The Importance of Books Beyond Their Texts*. The British Library, London 2008.

Raymond, Joad: Matter, Sociability and Space: Some Ways of Looking at the History of Books. *Books in Motion in Early Modern Europe: Beyond Production, Circulation and Consumption. New Directions in Book History*. Eds. Daniel Bellingradt, Paul Nelles and Jeroen Salman. Palgrave Macmillan, Houndmills 2017, 289–295.

Rose, Jonathan: A Preface to a History of Audiences. *The Intellectual Life of the British Working Classes*. Yale University Press, New Haven and London 2002, 1–11.

Sherman, William H.: *Used Books: Marking Readers in Renaissance England*. University of Pennsylvania Press, Philadelphia, 2008.

Snijders, Tjamke: *Manuscript Communication: Visual and Textual Mechanics of Communication in Hagiographical Texts from the Southern Low Countries, 900–1200*. Utrecht Studies in Medieval Literacy 32. Brepols, Turnhout 2015.

Stock, Brian: *The Implications of Literacy: Written Language and Models of Interpretation in the Eleventh and Twelfth Centuries*. Princeton University Press, Princeton, New Jersey 1983.

Thompson, James Westfall: *The Literacy of the Laity in the Middle Ages*. Burt Franklin, New York 1960.

Towheed, Shafquat: Introduction. *The History of Reading*. Vol. 3: *Methods, Strategies, Tactics*. Eds. Rosalind Crone and Shafquat Towheed. Palgrave Macmillan, Houndmills 2011, 1–12.

Towheed, Shafquat and W. R. Owens: Introduction. *The History of Reading*. Vol. 1, *International Perspectives, c. 1500–1990*. Eds. Shafquat Towheed and W.R. Owens, Palgrave Maxmillan, Houndmills 2011, 1–12.

Tyacke, Nicholas: Introduction: Re-Thinking the "English Reformation". *England's Long Reformation 1500–1800*. Ed. Nicholas Tyacke. University College Press, London 1998, 1–32.

Wallace, Peter G.: Introduction. *The Long European Reformation: Religion, Political Conflict, and the Search for Conformity, 1350–1750*. Palgrave Macmillan, Houndmills 2004, 1–21.

Walsham, Alexandra and Julia Crick: Introduction. *Script, Print and History*. Eds. Alexandra Walsham and Julia Crick. Cambridge University Press: Cambridge 2004, 1–26.

I
BOOKS AND THE CREATION OF 'US-NESS'

Books and reading among rank-and-file Anabaptists in the sixteenth and early seventeenth centuries

Päivi Räisänen-Schröder

Introduction[1]

Argula von Grumbach (1492–1554), a Bavarian noblewoman and "the first lay Protestant theologian,"[2] remembered reading a German-language Bible, a gift from her father at the age of ten, as a formative event in her life. Bible reading not only rewarded her intellectually, but spiritually and emotionally: "Ah, but what a joy it is when the spirit of God teaches us and gives us understanding, flitting from one text to the next!"[3] Similarly, although in a socially much humbler milieu, the bookbinder Jörg (Georg) Frell (b. 1530) described how his artisan father took great pains to pay for the Bible he bought for his eldest son in 1540. Like Argula, Jörg refers to the overwhelming joy of reading the Bible,

[1] This article has been written with the financial support of the Academy of Finland (project number 1275246).

[2] See http://www.luther2017.de/en/wiki/women-move-the-church-since-luthers-time/argula-von-grumbach-i-have-not-written-womens-gossip-to-you/ (retrieved 12 April 2016).

[3] Grumbach 1995, 86.

a divine pleasure and need (*begyrt unnd freüdt*) that had lost none of its intensity over the years.[4]

The early years of the Reformation(s) in Germany, until the Peasants' War of 1524–1525, were a time of active lay participation in the overall quest for social, political and moral reform.[5] The Gospel, the living Word of God, was at the heart of the reform agenda of the early evangelicals, who, in the early 1520s, could not yet be neatly categorised as Lutherans, Zwinglians, Anabaptists, or the like. Their common goal was to improve the church and society, although ideas about how this could or should be achieved varied extremely.[6] Many thought, like Luther, that they were living in the end times, or dreamt of the dawn of a new, better age: "waking from slumber" or "light replacing darkness"[7] were consequently metaphors frequently used in reform-oriented popular texts and images. Such powerful images and arguments for reform that many found appealing both intellectually and emotionally were provided above all by Scripture, which became increasingly accessible to laypeople in vernacular translations and more affordable printed books[8] and pamphlets.[9] At the same time, as Andrew Pettegree has concluded, "the search for answers to these troubling questions allowed the market

---

4 "Aber alle zyt unnd wyl was unns kurtz, nu das wyr die bibel überkäment. Ein söliche begyrt unnd freüdt hatend wyr zu der bibel. Unnd die begyrt unnd freüdt hat uns der herr gott nit genomen, sunder in unns je lenger ye meer gemeeret, das ich uff den hüttigen tag kein größere freüdt unnd kurtzwil uff erden hab, dan läsen in der heilligen und göttlichen gescbrifften." Rageth and Vasella 1942, 459. On Frell's spirituality, see Peduzzi 2007. For similar reading examples from Protestant England, see Ryrie 2013, 270–281.

5 Gawthrop and Strauss 1984, 34–38, 42; Matheson 1995, 45; Zitzlsperger 2003, 379–380.

6 On the laypeople's different reform goals, see Edwards 1994, 3, 5–6; Chrisman 1996, 15; Pettegree 2010, 102.

7 Pettegree 2010, 129.

8 The term 'books' here refers not only to printed books, but also "manuscripts and ephemeral matters," Cambers 2011, 7. See also Howsam 2015, 2–6.

9 Edwards 1994, 1–2, 15; Matheson 2000, 28, 40–43, 46–47; Pettegree 2010, 101–102, 104, 130. See also Peduzzi 2007, 68.

for religious books to grow exponentially", as "[p]rinters and booksellers eagerly embraced the opportunity to reach a new book-buying public."[10]

Both von Grumbach and Frell later actively sought to change the world for the better, using insights and arguments they had developed from their biblical readings and discussions about the will of God as revealed in the Holy Scripture. Von Grumbach wrote a series of pamphlets in 1523 and 1524, achieving a remarkable number of almost 30,000 printed copies. However, her public voice silenced after 1524.[11] Frell, a Swiss Anabaptist, on the other hand, fought for his cause a generation later, but in equally or even more difficult circumstances in terms of laypeople's opportunities for participating in religious and social reform. From an Anabaptist perspective, and also in statements by many laypeople not clearly belonging to this officially heretical group, the need for reform had not diminished although new churches had emerged. In the Bible they could find arguments as to why this was so and what should be changed.[12]

Thanks to the printing press, contributions to the debate could be detached from time and place more easily than ever before.[13] At the same time, heated discussions were held in daily life, and on the local level: among family, friends, neighbours and colleagues, that is, in networks that have been framed by scholars as the "interpretative community".[14] Books figured in these debates in many roles, for instance as carriers of ideas, as valued, detested, or even forbidden artefacts, and inspiring discussion topics. They provided models for orientation and identification. And yet, if we only focus on books – especially printed ones – we will get too narrow an idea of the many communication modes of the era. Books only became meaningful when interpreted in a certain cultural and social context, and books were an integral part of a hybrid field of textual, oral, aural and visual communication. This broad spectrum of interaction was also the setting for the spread (or

---

[10] Pettegree 2010, 129.

[11] On Argula von Grumbach, see e.g. Matheson 1995; Zitzlsperger 2003.

[12] A frequently used argument was 1 Cor. 5:7 and Mt. 7:17 (a bad tree cannot bear good fruit and *vice versa*).

[13] See e.g. Matheson 2000, 26–27.

[14] See e.g. Chartier 2007, 518.

rejection) of Reformation ideas. Peter Matheson has noted aptly that in the early Reformation, "poet, artist, musician, printer and pamphleteer allied with preacher so that, in Luther's words, the Gospel was not only preached, but painted, sung, and – we might add – rhymed."[15]

This article explores lay reading practices and ideas of religious and social reform in a very specific, yet significant, lay setting, among the Anabaptists in southwest Germany, in the Duchy of Württemberg. Anabaptism has been called the "most important of the grass-roots movements of reform in the sixteenth century"[16] and the study of Anabaptist reading patterns can give us clues to the practices and meanings of reading in the early modern period, also on a more general level. However, Anabaptism was not just a religious movement, but also a social and political one, as these dimensions cannot be separated in a premodern context. In protesting against the official church, Anabaptists also protested against the secular authorities, as state and ecclesiastical power increasingly intertwined with the new church orders emerging in the 16th century.

In the following, I will first outline the social context and main text types of Anabaptist reading, before exploring what books were confiscated from Anabaptists in Württemberg and people suspected as such from the late 16th century onwards, a period that has long been overlooked in Anabaptist research. The last part of this article is dedicated to rank-and-file Anabaptists' Bible reading and their uses of biblical arguments in conflict situations, be it within the village or – as is more commonly registered in the sources – with the authorities. The sources of this study consist mainly of ecclesiastical interrogation protocols and reports, complemented by some letters by Anabaptists. The material calls for cautious use due to its magisterial bias, but can yield important insights into how books were viewed and used by different people and parties, and in what settings their contents were discussed.[17] This article therefore aims to broaden our understanding of

---

[15] Matheson 2000, 25.

[16] Snyder 1991b, 385.

[17] The methods developed by historical criminology on how to read court protocols critically have proven useful for analysis. From this huge body of research, see e.g. Davis 1987; Simon-Muscheid & Simon 1996; Sabean 1998; Schwerhoff 1999.

the role of reading among laypeople of the 16th century who were trying to adapt to the changing world around them, and, sometimes, be part of that change that continued right up to the end of the 16th century. This is a new, yet fruitful approach to understanding Anabaptism beyond the traditional perspective of the early leaders, their books and teachings.

Towards a history of reading practices

In the quest for a new religious and social order, reading and books played an important role that still needs to be explored in detail, especially for the extremely heterogenous Anabaptist groups and individuals. Scholarship has by now recognised religious books and religious reading as central objects of Western church history as it has increasingly turned away from traditional perspectives on the churches as institutions towards a social and cultural history of the believers.[18] Within the interdisciplinary field of book history, there has been a shift from the study of book production, the book market, ownership of books, and other classical but more economic and structural analyses, towards a history of reading or a "history of audiences".[19]

What exactly is meant by the history of reading (or, more narrowly, reader response criticism), varies to such an extent that a recent survey has characterised it as "less […] a field than a battleground."[20] I advocate a relatively broad understanding of reading as a social and cultural practice. Following Jeroen Blaak, who has studied the role of books and reading in everyday life in the 17th and 18th centuries, a cultural-historical approach to the history of reading

> focuses on reading behaviour; it studies the way books were used. The key questions here are the how, where, when and why of reading,

[18] Bödeker et al. 1991, 13–14. On the uses, see Bödeker et al. 1991, 15–19.
[19] Rose 1992. See also Price 2004, 311–312; Blaak 2008, 4–7. Research on the printing industry and book market continues to flourish, see e.g. Pettegree 2010.
[20] Price 2004, 304.

questions seeking to describe the interaction between book and reader. In studies of reading behaviour, the book is seen as a cultural rather than an economic product, which shifts attention away from groups of consumers to the diverse meanings that books may have had for different people.[21]

Although most work on the history of reading has been done on modern readers, interest in early modern audiences has been on the rise.[22] For instance, increasingly 'secular' reading – in the context of the rise of the novel in the 18th century, for example – has fascinated scholars.[23] On the other hand, the reading practices of religious groups, especially English revivalists such as the Puritans, have been studied over the last few years.[24] Dutch Protestant readers in the 17th and 18th centuries have also come under scrutiny.[25] In German, there is less current research on early modern reading when it comes to the lower strata of society, whereas elite book cultures have attracted more attention.[26] To find German studies concerning the Reformation from a book-historical perspective, one has, for the most part, to go back to the rich body of research devoted to pamphlets and propaganda, popular culture and lay participation in religious reform, especially in the 1980s and 1990s.[27]

As for book-historical approaches within Anabaptist studies, Bible study groups have been identified by Arnold Snyder as a key context for forming specifically Anabaptist perspectives in Zurich, Switzerland, where one of the first Anabaptist groups emerged among radicalised

---

[21] Blaak 2008, 10.
[22] Ryrie 2013, 270.
[23] See, with further references, Price 2004, 312.
[24] See e.g. Snook 2005; Colclough 2007; Simpson 2009; Cambers 2011; Narveson 2012. Further, Ryrie 2013 integrates reading within a larger framework of 'being Protestant' in early modern Britain.
[25] See, with further references, e.g. Blaak 2002; Baggerman and Dekker 2009; Blaak 2008.
[26] See e.g. Shevchenko 2007; Bepler and Meise 2010; Buchhester 2015.
[27] The body of research is too vast to quote here. See e.g. Köhler 1981; Scribner 1981; Goertz 1987; Scribner 1987; Edwards 1994; Chrisman 1996. For a recent contribution, see Kaufmann 2016.

students of Ulrich Zwingli in the early 1520s.[28] Snyder has placed a lot of emphasis on the complex interplay between the written or printed word and the oral culture of the 16th century, and he remains one of the few scholars who have touched upon Anabaptist reading practices. Otherwise, book-historically inspired research on Anabaptists is surprisingly rare and has largely focused on individual authors, genres, or on the production and spread of specific works, mostly by leading Anabaptist thinkers.[29]

The latest contributions to this strand of research come from Kat Hill and Martin Rothkegel. While Kat Hill's study of Anabaptist printing has drawn attention to the personal networks of the people involved in printing and selling Anabaptist books, arguing that there was a profitable market for Anabaptist books that went beyond the confined circles of religious radicals, the question of readership and reception remains largely unanswered. However, she makes the important point that we should not think of Anabaptist or radical printing as marginal, but as an integral part of the early Reformation printing industry and book market.[30] Martin Rothkegel, for his part, has recently written extensively about the practicalities of distributing radical literature during the Reformation.[31] Contrary to Hill, he considers Anabaptist book culture to be highly clandestine. Rothkegel's study focuses on selected prints, their authors and printers. His short depiction of Anabaptist reading communities is heavily dependent on their charismatic leaders who, according to Rothkegel, had the authority to orchestrate what was read in a certain group and how.[32] This stands in contrast to the more dynamic model of exchange that is suggested by Snyder's research.

To look at reading practices of rank-and-file Anabaptists is therefore a novel approach to understanding Anabaptism in its local historical context. Like Snyder, I argue that the local community and experience of conflict was central to shaping common Anabaptist views in dialogue

---

[28] Snyder 1991a; Snyder 1991b.
[29] See e.g. Fluri 1953; Rempel 2007; Zorzin 2008b; Zorzin 2010; Leu 2012; Hill 2015.
[30] Hill 2015.
[31] Rothkegel 2016.
[32] Rothkegel 2016, 216.

with their peers, neighbours and both secular and ecclesiastical magistrates. I will here attempt a first geographically confined case study of the southwest German Duchy of Württemberg. Württemberg officially turned Lutheran in 1534, and soon became known for its well-organised church and school systems.[33] Anabaptism was a prohibited and punishable form of religiosity, even though death sentences were not executed under Lutheran rule. Instead, a system of control was established with regular parish visitations; one of their tasks was to single out suspicious religious behaviour in the villages. People labelled as headstrong Anabaptists were in danger of losing their property and being expelled from the duchy. Despite government measures, a small but persistent Anabaptist minority survived in some parts of the duchy well into the early 17th century, as long as they were tolerated by the community around them.[34]

Reading, reform and conflict in Anabaptist life

In all other 16th-century churches, regardless of their denomination, Anabaptists were viewed as heretics and treated accordingly. The close link between heresy and reading has been pointed out in research many times. Robert W. Scribner, for one, described heresy as

> knowledge become dangerous [...] because it has got out of control, especially when so persistently held that it challenges hierarchy and the ideological coherence that constitutes hegemony: the prime character-istic of a heretic is always stubbornness.[35]

---

[33] Brecht 1967, 9; Gawthrop and Strauss 1984, 36. On the rank-and-file Anabaptists as a long-neglected field of study, see Goertz 1996; Räisänen 2011, 32.

[34] On Anabaptists in Württemberg, see Clasen 1965; Räisänen 2011; Räisänen-Schröder 2016.

[35] Scribner 1994, 278. See also Rubin 1991, 332.

Literacy and vernacular reading were thus important triggers of potentially dangerous knowledge.[36] As for Reformation ideas, initially also considered as potentially radical and dangerous, "the majority of laymen and of half-educated persons undoubtedly acquired their views from life experiences and from social conflict, from the Bible, and from casual conversations with like-minded persons."[37] It may even be that oral and written forms of communication interacted especially in terms of religious themes.[38] Further, as Arnold Snyder has claimed, the "oral/aural medium [...], was radically egalitarian: women and men of all social stations could and did communicate new ideas primarily in conversation with one another."[39] Other scholars have pointed to the opportunities for "distance learning" for women and laymen provided by the young print industry.[40] Mark Edwards has emphasised how printing

> undermined central authority because it encouraged the recipients of the printed message to think for themselves about the issues in dispute, and it provided the means – printed Bibles especially – by which each person could become his or her own theologian.[41]

Lay men and women participated actively in contemporary debates, using all media and communication forms known and available to them. It has to be remembered that already in the decades before the Reformation, there had been both a broad lay interest in religious reform and demand for vernacular devotional texts; discussing and reading about religion was nothing new in itself.[42]

Arnold Snyder has underlined in his study on the early Zurich Anabaptists, how vernacular reading and interpreting the Bible "could

---

[36] Scribner 1994, 278. See also Tomkowiak 1991, 194–196.

[37] Laube 1988, 23.

[38] Blaak 2008, 342. See also Pettegree 2010, 102.

[39] Snyder 1996b, 6.

[40] Matheson 2000, 27.

[41] Edwards 1994, 3, 7. The print market offered a broad variety of religious arguments during the early Reformation, see e.g. Pettegree 2010, 102.

[42] Chrisman 1996, 11; Blaak 2008; 1–2; Corbellini and Hoogvliet 2013, 521.

not help but sharpen social and political conflict."[43] Similar positions have been taken by other scholars. Miriam Usher Chrisman, for example, has argued in her analysis of over 300 lay pamphlets from the early 16th century that

> [a]lthough all the writers espoused faith against works and the primacy of Scripture, the lay pamphlets expose the differences between the ranks, revealing the issues in dispute, the presence of mutual antagonisms and distrust, and the continuation of old patterns of suspicion and fear.[44]

In other words, Bible reception was essentially shaped by the social surroundings in which the reading took place. Early Reformation slogans, such as the priesthood of all believers, were interpreted against the experience one had accumulated and could observe in daily life. As Chrisman states, the laity's "perception of the Reformation was influenced by the realities of their own lives. They interpreted the new ideas in terms of their social aspirations, the political conflicts in which they were involved, and their individual search for a deeper spirituality."[45] This explains the at times confusing plethora of interpretations; it was not at all uncommon to arrive at opposing conclusions on an issue based on a reading of the Holy Book. What was shared was the quest for reform, be it on an individual, local or larger societal scale.

In the lower social ranks, interpretations tended to accentuate the injustices observed within church and society, the most obvious example here being the lists of grievances gathered by dissatisfied peasants striving for more local autonomy in the years prior to the Peasants' War.[46] The sharp social criticism – in extreme cases even the willingness of some Anabaptist groups to use force to implement a better Christian society – is the reason why religious radicals were so feared by many contemporaries, and especially the governing elites. No matter how small the rebellious circles may have been, their threat to

---

[43] Snyder 1991b, 378, 380.
[44] Chrisman 1996, 8.
[45] Chrisman 1996, 14. See also Edwards 1994, 5–6.
[46] See e.g. Stayer 1991.

society was conceived as real.[47] Once Lutherans started building their own churches, their magistrates soon developed a vision of adequate reading for the common people along the lines expressed by Luther in the wake of the Peasants' War, arguing that common people should restrict their readings mainly to an authorised catechism.[48]

In Württemberg, as elsewhere, the authorities tried to prevent the circulation of heretical books in the duchy, because they saw a clear connection between dangerous reading and rebellion. Ducal ordinances defined forbidden books and renewed the official guidelines in 1558, 1563 and 1593. Any text that contradicted the Augsburg Confession was forbidden. Local bailiffs and pastors were obliged to observe and report cases of suspicious reading, distribution of forbidden texts or similar alarming activities in their area.[49] Yet, as Kat Hill has noted, censorship was rarely a straightforward process.[50] Württemberg authorities knew well how hard it was to find and confiscate forbidden literature.

Anabaptist texts and their circulation

For dissenting religious groups such as the Anabaptists, which had to be careful not to attract too much attention, and whose members at times lived far apart from their like-minded peers, literature came to play an important role in the shaping and upholding of religious identity and a sense of group belonging. Further, when larger gatherings were impossible, religious texts could replace sermons as means of religious education and edification. Moreover, texts could be employed for persuading possible converts or for apologetics.[51] Different groups may also have resorted to different production and circulation strategies, depending on their situation and goals, as Alejandro Zorzin has

---

[47] Goertz 1986, 36.
[48] Gawthrop and Strauss 1984.
[49] Clasen 1965, 47. The ducal ordinances are printed in QGT I, 237–238, 669, 1038.
[50] Hill 2015, 110–111.
[51] Rothkegel 2016, 202, 209.

demonstrated for the early Swiss Brethren.[52] This calls, then, for careful case studies, if we want to get a more precise picture of the how and when of Anabaptist reading on the local level.

Generally, Anabaptists were keen Bible readers and as such part of the early Reformation enthusiasm for vernacular Bible translations and commentaries. They rejected infant baptism as not grounded in the Scriptures, and replaced it by believer's baptism, which they understood as the original, early Christian practice. This interpretation was based on a close reading of Mark 16:16: "The one who believes and is baptised will be saved." The passage indicated to most Anabaptists the correct order of first faith and only then baptism. The Bible version preferred by the Anabaptists was the Froschauer Bible, named after the Zurich printer Christoph Froschauer. According to Adolf Fluri, Froschauer Bibles were especially "popular because of the clear type, pictorial decoration, and popular language".[53] To some Anabaptists it was important that the Bible did not have any pictures of saints, as these were conceived as idolatrous. Trying to buy such a book was at times considered proof of a heretical mindset.[54] Further, many preferred the New Testament to the Old.[55] For the easier understanding of Scripture, Anabaptists could use concordances that explained key issues in subject order. Concordances allowed access to biblical contents even without the possession of an actual Bible and could be used as a "theological and spiritual compendium" and read aloud at gatherings. Further, a compendium enabled easy memorisation of biblical arguments.[56]

Lay Anabaptists produced and consumed theological texts of various sorts beyond the Bible and biblical concordances. Following Kat Hill, Anabaptist literature can be roughly categorised into "translations and commentaries (mainly of biblical texts), theological tracts, and songs and hymns."[57] Their popularity varied at different times. Biblical

---

[52] Zorzin 2008a; Hill 2015, 84. For a variety of different strategies, see also Rothkegel 2016.
[53] Fluri 1953; Leu 2012.
[54] Snyder 1996a, 34. For late medieval examples, see Rubin 1991, 332.
[55] Perduzzi 2007, 67.
[56] Snyder 2001, x.
[57] Hill 2015, 102.

translations and commentaries made up the bulk of Anabaptist prints, and were produced especially in the 1520s, whereas songbooks and hymnals dominated Anabaptist printing in the following decades.[58] Even though printing may have been a more viable option than has been thought so far, the majority of works written by Anabaptists circulated only in manuscript form.[59]

Robert Friedmann has characterised Anabaptist writings generally as "at once confessional (doctrinal), devotional, and also polemical", but never "scholarly and academic" in the manner of the major reformers such as Luther, Zwingli or Calvin, who developed a more systematical theological approach. In essence, Anabaptist writings were, regardless of literary genre, "testimonies of faith".[60] Among the most popular was Menno Simons' (1496–1561) *Fundament der christlichen Kirche*, published first in 1539. In this work Simons both attacked his adversaries and outlined his confession that Christ is the sole foundation of Christian faith.[61] Readers may have found comfort in those parts where Simons dealt with the anxieties of the few (and always persecuted) true Christians.

Access to Anabaptist writings varied. Hutterite chronicles, produced by the Anabaptists settled in Moravia, were for the eyes of community members only, which led the Jesuit Christoph Andreas Fischer to complain in 1606 that the Hutterites "keep their books so secret, that only one out of a thousand gets to read them."[62] Other visitors from outside experienced suspicion from the Hutterites, too; usually non-Hutterites were allowed to see only songbooks or in some cases the doctrinal *Rechenschaft* by the Hutterite leader Peter Riedemann

---

[58] Hill 2015, 102–104.

[59] Claus-Peter Clasen has estimated that only 76 works of Anabaptist origin appeared in print in south and central Germany, Switzerland and Austria before 1618. Kat Hill, on the contrary, states that in the course of the 16th century, "71 printers produced 278 works in a total of 29 towns across Germany." Clasen 1972, 349; Hill 2015, 84. On the relationship between manuscript and printed books, see Ezell 2015.

[60] See e.g. Friedmann 1956.

[61] Cf. 1 Cor. 3:11.

[62] Quoted in Friedmann 1965, 94. On printed and manuscript literature among Hutterites, see e.g. Rauert 1999; Seebass 2011.

(1506–1556).[63] Indeed, Hutterite literary influences were not entirely confined to their Moravian settlements. The Hutterites engaged in active missionary work all over German-speaking Europe, sending missionaries regularly to their former homelands to visit families, deliver letters and gifts, and proselytise. Hymnals and other small books were carried on these travels and songs were also sung while on the road.[64]

Many of the missionaries came to Württemberg, like the former shoemaker Paul Glock (d. 1585), who was caught and held captive at Hohenwittlingen castle for nineteen years. Glock spent his time writing songs and doctrinal treatises, singing, and engaging in active discussions with both his fellow prisoners and his overseers. He described regular reading and singing as a spiritual pastime that was "sometimes merry (*frölich*), sometimes sad (*traurig*), changeable as mountain weather."[65] This close link between reading/singing and different emotions needs more study; at this point, it gives us a powerful clue about the meanings of these activities to the people who performed them (we remember the joy of Bible reading as expressed by Argula von Grumbach and Jörg Frell at the beginning of this article).

Books confiscated from Württemberg Anabaptists

Although it does not reveal exactly what and how was read, or indeed what emotions the reading may have evoked or helped to control, information about books confiscated from open or suspected Anabaptists gives us an idea of what texts circulated in the area. As was already pointed out, German Bibles were read by Anabaptists too, but these were not forbidden books and therefore not confiscated. Further, the confiscated volumes were just the tip of the iceberg, as the authorities themselves were well aware. In Württemberg, texts confiscated from potential Anabaptists were usually songbooks, theological writings or

---

[63] Rothkegel 2000, 59.
[64] Chudaska 2010. On Hutterite mission, Schlachta 2000.
[65] Letter from Paul Glock to Peter Walpot, 23 February 1576, QGT I, 463–465.

letters to or from other Anabaptists. Altogether the information about books confiscated remains relatively vague, as a magisterial comment from 1598 states. During a thorough investigation in Urbach, a large parish known for its many Anabaptists, the authorities reported having confiscated five books:

> From Jakob Greiner in Walkersbach the *Fundament*, from Leonhard Mayer's wife, born Greiner, a printed and a handwritten songbook,[66] from Jakob, son of Alexander Faut, a songbook, from young Jerg Luipold a songbook. There are without doubt more Anabaptist books like these in this place, but we have not been able to find out anything more from such devious (*verschlagen*) people.[67]

Although almost no titles are given in the protocols, songbooks were clearly identified as Anabaptist and confiscated.[68]

The title that is mentioned most often from the late 16th century onwards was Menno Simons' *Fundament der christlichen Kirche*, often with its shortened title *Fundamentbuch* or *Fundament*. Between 1582 and 1614, ten people in Württemberg were accused of being in possession of the work, as Table 1 shows.[69]

[66] Or, possibly, a book that was partly printed and partly handwritten? The source is not entirely clear on this.

[67] Protocol of the inspection in Urbach, 3 June 1598, HStAS A282/3094c Nr. 14, 26r–27v.

[68] There is one notable exception to this rule regarding Schwenckfeldian books that were confiscated in Cannstatt in 1544. The reporting pastor of Cannstatt named the titles and gave a detailed account of the contents of all six books that were found. QGT I, 91–94.

[69] The information is drawn from Gustav Bossert's printed source edition (QGT I). In cases from the Schorndorf district analysed in my dissertation, I have provided the original quotes and archival signatures. Visitation protocol (henceforth: Vis.prot.) of Pleidelsheim 1582, QGT I, 542; Vis.prot. of Horrheim 1583, QGT I, 560; Vis.prot. of Großheppach 14 August 1584, QGT I, 584–585; interrogation protocol of Gall Schnaitman of Fellbach 1596, QGT I, 682–683; Prot. of the inspection in Urbach, 3 June 1598, HStAS A282/3094c Nr. 14, 55v; Vis.prot. of Geradstetten, spring and autumn 1608, LKAS A26/466 II, 107v–108r, QGT I, 800; Report of Spezialis and bailiff in Schorndorf, 11 September 1614, HStAS A63/78; Vis. prot. of Beutelsbach 1605, HStAS A282/1122, 16–17.

Table 1. Persons in possession of Menno Simons' Fundamentbuch in Württemberg.

Name	Place	Occupation, if known	Type of aquisition, if known	Year of confiscation
Caspar Hun	Pleidelsheim	beadle (*Büttel*)	borrowed	1582
Matthias Hebler	Horrheim	?	bought second-hand	1583
Peter Ehrenpreis	Illingen	son of village mayor	?	1583
Maria Schmid (née Greiner)	Großheppach	wife of village court member	?	1584
Gall Schnaitmann	Fellbach	weaver	?	1596
Abraham Faut, Jr	Urbach	tailor	borrowed	1598
Jakob Greiner	Walkersbach	glass-maker	?	1598
Matthias Schätzlin	Beutelsbach	cooper	?	1605
Hans Vetter	Geradstetten	?	received as payment for work	1608
Hans Seifer	Geradstetten	?	received as a gift	1614

This small sample from one of the most densely-populated areas in 16th-century central Europe does not allow for generalisations on a larger scale.[70] However, a few things are striking, such as the occupations or

[70] On the population numbers, see e.g. Landwehr 2000, 42.

social standing of the book owners (artisans or people from the leading families in the village). One of the persons, Caspar Hun, was, strictly speaking, not an owner, but had borrowed the book "from a weaver in Besigheim."[71] The other cases point to other, quite typical, early modern modes of book acquisition: buying second-hand and receiving either as gifts or as payment for something, in this case work. We do not know whether any of the persons listed in the table actually bought the *Fundamentbuch* directly from a bookseller; perhaps it was safer and easier to use existing networks of like-minded people, as with the borrowing of incriminating texts.[72]

Of the persons mentioned, only Abraham Faut was reported to have owned another book, an unspecified Anabaptist songbook.[73] Maria Schmid stands out as the only woman mentioned. She was born into the longstanding Anabaptist Greiner family in and around Walkersbach. By 1584, she had had come into conflict with the authorities so often that she was ordered to be chained to her home. However, her husband, a member of the local court, set her free on a regular basis. Further, he was the one who read the *Fundamentbuch* aloud to her, although the protocol is specific about her being the actual owner of the book, not her husband.[74] Unfortunately, in none of the other cases is anything mentioned about how the confiscated book was actually used. Only with Gall Schnaitmann is there a small hint that he may have been carrying the book with him when he was caught and imprisoned.[75] The authorities sought to scold and instruct the people caught having a forbidden book, and then confiscate it. Consequently, there was no need to record bibliographical information in more detail.

In only few cases did the authorities remark on the effects of forbidden reading as far as they could observe them during interrogations. The

[71] Vis.prot. of Pleidelsheim 1582, QGT I, 542.

[72] Vis.prot. of Horrheim 1583, QGT I, 560; Prot. of the inspection in Urbach, 3 June 1598, HStAS A282/3094c Nr. 14, 55v.

[73] Prot. of the inspection in Urbach, 3 June 1598, HStAS 282/3094c Nr. 14, 55v.

[74] Vis.prot. of Großheppach 14 August 1584, QGT I, 584. On chained Ana-baptist women, see Kobelt-Groch 1990/91.

[75] Interrogation protocol of Gall Schnaitman of Fellbach, 1596, QGT I, 682–683.

interrogators noted that reading the *Fundamentbuch* had clearly had an impact on Gall Schnaitmann's dissenting views, for example on Christology.[76] With Matthias Hebler of Horrheim, on the other hand, the authorities "could not notice that he would have absorbed any error over time" (*nicht gespürt, dass er nach der Zeit etwas Irrtums gefasst*). Nevertheless, Hebler had to hand over his book to the interrogators and a close eye was kept on him.[77]

The popularity of the *Fundamentbuch* is altogether significant, because Menno Simons, the leader who gave the Mennonites their name, gathered followers mainly in northern Germany and the Netherlands. Thus Württemberg's rank-and-file Anabaptists read doctrinal literature across geographical and doctrinal borders that have often been assumed to have been rather strict. Some even read and distributed writings by both Anabaptist authors and the Spiritualist Caspar von Schwenckfeld (1490–1561). The boldest ones did this during the Lutheran sermons, with the clear purpose not only of reading a religious text of their own choice, but of openly challenging and even ridiculing the pastor in front of the parishioners.[78]

After Simons' *Fundamentbuch*, songbooks were the next most frequently confiscated type of Anabaptist book in Württemberg. Unfortunately, the copies confiscated (let alone those that were not) have not survived, and consequently individual books cannot be checked for comments, annotations, augmentations or the like. As for the songbooks confiscated in Württemberg, we can only guess about their precise contents. Presumably they were of either Swiss or Hutterite origin, although a mixing of traditions and overstepping strict group boundaries is not unlikely.

Most of the confiscated hymnals were found in Urbach and nearby Walkersbach, where an active and tightly-knit network of Anabaptists existed from the second half of the 16th century onwards. The inquiring authorities learnt in May 1598 that Konrad Anckelin, a local

---

[76] Interrogation protocol of Gall Schnaitman of Fellbach, 1596, QGT I, 683.

[77] Vis.prot. of Horrheim 1583, QGT I, 560.

[78] Vis.prot. of Walkersbach, spring and autumn 1577, LKAS A26/466 I, 204r, 218v; report of Spezialis in Dettingen 1596, QGT I, 681; report on Anabaptists in Stuttgart and Heslach 1563, QGT I, 1048.

councilman, had bought his children "the Anabaptist songbook".[79] Also young Abraham Faut, mentioned above for owning the *Fundamentbuch* and an Anabaptist songbook, lived in Urbach. It was recorded that Faut had learnt and sung the song of the martyred Jörg Wagner out of his hymnal. In the case of the next Urbacher, Leonhart Zehender, interrogated during the same thorough investigation of the parish in spring 1598, we get a glimpse of how books were handed down from one trusted person to the next. Jörg Faut, a well-known Anabaptist (who had also lent a copy of the *Fundamentbuch* to Jerg Luipold in the same village), had passed on an Anabaptist songbook "acquired by Basti Faut's stepdaughter Katharina, the deceased Anabaptist woman" to Zehender. Jerg Luipold was a neighbour of Jörg Faut and clearly discussed reading matters with him. Abraham Faut, Leonhard Zehender and Anna Mayer (née Greiner), who owned both a handwritten and printed hymnal, all agreed in the end to hand the books in their possession over to the authorities.[80]

If Jörg Faut was an active distributor of Anabaptist ideas in Urbach, the same can be said for Peter Ehrenpreis in Illingen. Ehrenpreis, son of the local mayor and thus of notable social standing, was known to possess a *Fundamentbuch* as early as 1583.[81] Most records about him, however, are dated to the late 1590s.[82] In between, he had spent some time in Moravia, presumably at some Hutterite community where he had received adult baptism. In 1585 he was caught in Illingen and imprisoned for a while in Maulbronn. At this point, the investigating authorities already treated him as a headstrong Anabaptist.[83] However, Ehrenpreis agreed to attend Lutheran services, if released, and seems to have kept his promise at least until 1588.[84] Sometime before February

---

[79] Prot. of the inspection in Urbach, 30 May 1598, HStAS A282/3094c Nr. 6, 102r.

[80] Prot. of the inspection in Urbach, 3 June 1598, HStAS A282/3094c Nr. 14, 53r, 54r, 55v.

[81] Vis.prot. of Horrheim 1583, QGT I, 560.

[82] Report of pastor of Illingen, 2 August 1596, QGT I, 687–688.

[83] Vis.prot. of Illingen, 1585, QGT I, 598.

[84] Vis.prot. of Illingen, 1586, QGT I, 616; Vis.prot. of Illingen, 1587, QGT I, 631–632; Vis.prot. of Illingen, 1588, QGT I, 637.

1592, he left his wife and child behind and went to Strasbourg, but apparently returned soon thereafter. Four years later he was back in Illingen and had made plans to move with his family to Moravia, as a dismissed maid from his household alerted the authorities.[85]

As far as the present study is concerned, the most interesting information about Peter Ehrenpreis comes from the correspondence between the local pastor and the leading churchmen of the duchy in the summer of 1596. Ehrenpreis was well-known for his dissenting views in Illingen, but also protected by his family members and friends, so the authorities had a hard time proving their suspicions about him.[86] During their inquiries, the abbot of Maulbronn learnt from Ehrenpreis' servant girl that Ehrenpreis often used to read aloud to his household members from a New Testament.[87] Further, Peter Ehrenpreis and his like-minded wife rarely bothered to show up at the Lutheran services, and never when the catechism was explained at noon. Even before, when Ehrenpreis still attended the midday services, he left whenever the pastor touched on subjects that displeased him – such as the Lutheran teachings on the sacraments – or when children were baptised. He had changed his seat to one where the pastor could not see Ehrenpreis and judge if he was present or not. On Sundays, it was suspected that he and his wife went to Anabaptist gatherings in nearby villages or woods, as they were not seen in church. Last but not least, Peter Ehrenpreis was in the habit of singing Anabaptist songs aloud when working in his vineyards or elsewhere. What the authorities were most troubled about was that Ehrenpreis was very popular and respected among the villagers for his outwardly modest lifestyle and these songs. The pastor of Illingen had no hope of winning him over to the Lutheran Church and wished that Ehrenpreis would go back to Moravia before he could convert others in Württemberg.[88]

Peter Ehrenpreis obviously did not care if somebody overheard him singing Anabaptist songs, perhaps quite the contrary. He was keen on

---

[85] Vis.prot. of Knittlingen, February 1592, QGT I, 1111; Report from Illingen, 5 July 1596, QGT I, 1118.

[86] QGT I, 687–691.

[87] Report of abbot Holder of Maulbronn, 30 July 1596, QGT I, 689.

[88] Report of pastor of Illingen, 2 August 1596, QGT I, 687–688.

discussing religious matters, as he did especially with his brother-in-law, Castolus Weisser.[89] We do not exactly know what songs he sang, but it seems that the practice was recurring and well-known. Considering his ties to Moravia, he may have sung Hutterite songs. Perhaps he, too, like Abraham Faut in Urbach, sang about the fate of a steadfast martyr like Jörg Wagner? Or did he prefer songs that covered more dogmatic ground? Judging by the popularity of his songs among the villagers, and from the widespread interest in martyrs in early modern religiosity, I am inclined to assume the first.[90] After all, Hutterite martyr songs "emphasised the martyrs' exemplariness" and were thus, according to Ursula Lieseberg, "an effective educational tool" both for the singer(s) and the potential audience.[91] Apart from dealing with the possibility of martyrdom in one's own life and "honouring the executed, the poems encouraged the Brethren to stand up in the same way for Hutterite convictions in a hostile world."[92] But instead of going back to Jörg Wagner, who had died in 1527, Ehrenpreis may have resorted to one of the newer Hutterite martyr songs that were written in growing numbers from about 1582 to 1592. They have been characterised as highly schematic, with an emphasis on the execution and death of the martyrs. These lengthy descriptions were enriched with stories about miracles before, during or after the martyr's death, a feature that is missing in martyr songs from other Anabaptist groups. Also the didactic emphasis on the exemplary role of the martyrs is most emphatic in the Hutterite songs.[93]

Singing Anabaptist songs – as well as reading, carrying around, borrowing or hiding songbooks – provides an excellent example of the hybrid forms and uses of written/printed texts and oral/aural forms of communication in the early modern era. They could easily be used together. Further, songs were designed to be remembered easily, so the leap from a written/printed page to everyday usage, also in non-literate

---

[89] Report of pastor of Illingen, 2 August 1596, QGT I, 687–688.
[90] On the popularity of martyrs, see e.g. Burschel 2004; Freeman 2007, 4–5. On Hutterite martyr songs, see Lieseberg 1993.
[91] Lieseberg 1993, 324.
[92] Lieseberg 1993, 324.
[93] Lieseberg 1993, 329–334.

circles, was relatively small.[94] Within Protestantism, often conceived as the most 'bookish' of Christian confessions, hymnals lead us to see the more spiritual and emotional side of the piety that was strongly focused on the word of God, the Gospel. Alec Ryrie's observations on British Puritans also ring true for 16th and early 17th century Anabaptists. According to Ryrie,

> psalms were ubiquitous in early modern Protestant devotion: said or sung in church, in the family, in conference, and in private prayer; read, transcribed, paraphrased, memorised. Protestant devotion was, we might say, psalmic, and the psalms' themes therefore helped to define the vocabulary of Protestant piety. Those themes are distinctive. A great many of the psalms allude, in the first person, to situations of pressing danger, and in particular to the scorn and malice of enemies. [...] [T]he psalms' threats and dangers were easily interpreted allegorically. Devotees might be daily encouraged to think of, for example, their backache or their money troubles as an assault from spiritual enemies: that is, as crises and as persecution.[95]

Württemberg's Anabaptists were used to living with the constant threat of being discovered or reported, although the immediate danger varied according to situation (for instance, the goodwill of neighbours or the ability of the parish pastor to act on dissenters).[96] Singing martyr songs in particular could provide a channel for dealing with the fears and other feelings evoked by living on the margins. They may, however, also have further reinforced the sense of being persecuted Christians, unlike the 'lax and worldly' Lutherans.

Songbooks are regularly mentioned in letters between Anabaptists. Often, just like other artefacts, they were sent from one person to

[94] However, contemporary pamphlets and bible concordances could also be written with an illiterate audience in mind, leaning heavily on the spoken word. See Rössing-Hager 1981; Snyder 2001, x.
[95] Ryrie 2013, 423.
[96] For a more thorough analysis of the Württemberg Anabaptists and their treatment, see Räisänen 2011.

another accompanied with a letter.[97] These songbooks could be either handwritten or printed. This is almost all that is known to us about the materiality and bibliographical side of these books. The most important Anabaptist songbooks in German, whether printed or manuscript, can be traced to the Swiss Brethren or the Hutterites. The confiscated songbooks are, if at all, only specified as "Anabaptist" or "sectarian". The oldest printed copy survives from 1583, entitled *Ausbund etlicher schöner christlicher Gesäng*, and is preserved in Munich.[98] However, we know of earlier prints both of this title from the early 1570s and the slightly older *Ein schön gesangbuechlein Geistlicher lieder* from the 1560s.[99] This scant survival of songbooks may be due to the fact that they were heavily used and thus simply wore out. The active use of the songbooks can also be seen in the many modifications of the song texts that vary from copy to copy or edition to edition.[100]

As was common practice, the Anabaptist songbooks did not include any notation but only referred to well-known melodies, often secular, popular tunes.[101] As with the music, authorship was not restricted to Anabaptists only, but other suitable texts (such as those of Sebastian Franck) could be included, although the majority of identified songwriters belonged to some Anabaptist circle.[102] Women also wrote songs, even though most of the songs in these books are by men. Martina Bick has further noted that the *Ausbund* has a considerable number of songs about martyr women.[103]

The intended audience was broader than just the immediate community. The 1583 *Ausbund* even offered itself to any true Christian regardless of denomination. It argued that people cannot judge what religion is true, only God can.[104] This may well have been an attempt to

---

[97] See e.g. the letters of Matthias Binder to Leonhart Reisst, 2 September 1573, QGT I, 373–374; Paul Glock to Peter Walpot, Easter 1569, QGT I, 1098.

[98] *Ausbund* 1583.

[99] Burschel 2004, 118–120, 126–128.

[100] Burschel 2004, 124–125; Lieseberg 1993, 324. See also Lieseberg 1998, 40–129.

[101] Friedmann 1956; Gregory 2007, 489–490. *Ausbund* 1583, 76.

[102] Friedmann 1956.

[103] Bick 2013.

[104] *Ausbund* 1583, foreword [no pagination].

make the book look more innocent to potential sellers, owners and users. However, the choice of medium – print – also indicates that the book was aimed at a larger, presumably also more heterogeneous audience, both in terms of geography and religious views, than a manuscript song collection could ever reach. This point is underscored by the observation of Bick that many of the 16th century Anabaptist songs were framed in rather general Christian terms, touching on themes such as thanksgiving, pleas to the Almighty or songs of lamentation.[105]

The contents encompass a broad variety of songs that have been categorised by scholars as doctrinal, missionary, biblical, historical and martyr songs. It has been noted that epic songs are especially frequent, that is, long narrative songs for example about incarceration, martyrdom or biblical events. They may have been used less during Anabaptist services than in more informal gatherings, or during work or travel.[106] The case of Peter Ehrenpreis has already been analysed. Further examples from other areas could broaden the picture, such as the case of Anna Jansz of Rotterdam (1509/10–1539). According to a later narrative about her, she eventually lost her life because of her bold use of Anabaptist hymns. Her singing was recognised as heretical by fellow travellers who shared a boat with Anna, leading to her being reported, caught, incarcerated and interrogated, and finally – as she would not recant – executed in 1539.[107]

Bible reading and biblical argument in conflict situations

The examples at the beginning of this article point to an individual reading of the Bible. However, both Argula von Grumbach and Jörg Frell did not leave it at that. Rather, they discussed their private readings with others, and presumably also read together with their like-minded peers. Von Grumbach, for instance, referred to an anonymous group of women she read with.[108] It is therefore not possible to neatly divide

[105] Bick 2013.
[106] Chudaska 2010.
[107] Packull 1996, 341.
[108] Grumbach 1995, 27.

reading practices into 'private' or 'individual' as opposed to 'collective' or 'communal'. Instead, we should think of a mix of reading modes, depending on what was read, where and when. As Jeroen Blaak has pointed out, early modern readers varied their reading strategies, but not according to genre, adapting them flexibly to the given situation.[109]

Bible circles existed in Württemberg, too, although the sources only offer glimpses into them. It is hard to estimate their degree of organisation and durability. Still, the practice of gathering around a Bible to read, listen and discuss recurs in the sources. One such group may have been organised around Melchior Greiner, a glass-maker from Walkersbach who was an active member of the Swiss Brethren. His powerful reading and interpretation of Bible passages made a lasting impact on a young maid named Anna from the village of Großengartach around 1582. Anna admitted that she was very impressed by Greiner's take on a sinner's repentance,[110] something that many Württemberg Anabaptists claimed to miss in the daily lives of the Lutherans around them.[111] These gatherings seem to have been relatively open both to converts, whether actual or potential, and curious neighbours. Some visitors later claimed to attend them only in order to receive news from their relatives who had moved to Moravia.[112] In some instances, even the local pastors were invited to join. Whereas the reading session that the maid Anna participated in was open to both sexes, women also discussed religious matters and biblical interpretations among themselves. Anna Marx of Urbach was even accused of running a "heretical school" for the women in her area.[113] The seamstress Gertrud Schöpperlin from Winterbach combined work and mission on her travels up and down the Rems

---

[109] Blaak 2002, 74.

[110] Hearing of Anabaptists in Großengartach, 5 March 1586. QGT I, 606–607.

[111] Based on their reading of Matt. 18:15–18, the Anabaptists generally preferred stricter church discipline and a harsher ban practice than the Lutherans.

[112] Report of Abbot Holder of Maulbronn, 30 July 1596, QGT I, 690–691.

[113] List of grievances by the pastor in Urbach, 1598. HStAS A282/3094c, f. 84r.

river valley and was known to have instructed several other women in Anabaptist ideas.[114]

Three young men in the village of Knittlingen near Maulbronn were suspected of reading the German Bible and "other books" together in 1575. One of them, the journeyman Jacob May, was singled out as the main culprit who claimed to interpret Scripture better than the local pastor. He was in the habit of sitting with his back toward the pulpit, sneering openly at the pastor's sermons. According to the pastor, the young man made no secret of his Anabaptist outlook.[115] Here, as in the similar cases quoted above, the authorities directly linked vernacular reading to subversive behaviour and dissenting religious views.

Often the gatherings at which the Bible was read and discussed took place in private homes. The Greiner household was well-known for opening their home to like-minded people, many of them relatives.[116] Also private reading was practised within one's own four walls,[117] where it was safest, as was copying and writing texts that could arouse magisterial suspicion. In the case of Thomas Hägen, a literate barber or shearer from the small town of Göppingen, who dedicated his time to writing and copying Anabaptist texts, these activities were betrayed to the authorities in 1597. Hägen's family lived on the upper floor of a townhouse and the neighbours, hostile to Hägen's religious views and sharp tongue, easily heard that he had entertained visitors late in the evenings. Obviously in this case, the close proximity to unsympathetic neighbours also betrayed forbidden literary activities at home, by way of daily observation and gossip.[118]

In the countryside, domestic doings were perhaps easier to hide, although also here one had to be very careful to keep a secret, as local news travelled fast. It seems, rather, that most of the Anabaptists counted on their neighbours not to tell on them, and that officially forbidden

[114]Vis.prot. of Schorndorf, 7 April 1602, HStAS A281/1120, 6–7; Vis.prot. of Beutelsbach, spring 1616, LKAS A26/466 II, 174v.

[115]Vis.prot. of Knittlingen, autumn 1575, LKAS A26/466 I, 126v.

[116]See e.g. vis.prot. of Walkersbach, autumn 1577, LKAS A26/466 I, 218r–220r.

[117]See e.g. vis.prot. of Pleidelsheim 1582, QGT I, 542.

[118]QGT I, 694–695.

activities, like secret conventicles and the distribution of Anabaptist literature, were conducted half in the open. We have to assume, therefore, that at least in rural Württemberg, Anabaptists shared enough common cultural, religious and customary ground with their neighbours not to be reported to the authorities all too easily.[119]

When defending their dissenting views, be it in daily village life or in front of the authorities, many suspect Anabaptists resorted to the most powerful rhetorical weapon at their disposal, the word of God. Paul Glock, the already mentioned shoemaker-turned-missionary, for instance, provided his examiners in 1563 with a lengthy handwritten declaration of his faith, carefully argued with citations from the Holy Book.[120] More often than not, however, these quotations were performed live and only a fraction of them is known to us, namely when instances of biblical argument were noted by the pastors or scribes in their documentations of a case.

It is striking how well-versed illiterate laypeople in Württemberg presented themselves in front of the authorities. The peasant woman Anna Leins of Bartenbach, for one, replied "it is written in the Holy Scriptures that one has to work, and who does not work should not eat," when confronted in May 1581 with the fact that she had freed herself from the chains the authorities had – literally – put on her after deciding that she was a headstrong Anabaptist who should be kept indoors.[121] When Barbara Bauer was questioned in 1620 for her dissenting conduct, she referred to "chapter six in John's Gospel" when defending her views on the Eucharist. She admitted that "she could not read herself, but had learnt these things from her mother." It is also noteworthy how patiently the interrogating theologians explained what they saw as the correct interpretation of this passage to Bauer.[122]

---

[119] See also Räisänen-Schröder 2016.

[120] Paul Glock's letter to Leonhard Lanzenstil in Moravia 7 June 1563, QGT I, 1079.

[121] Cf. 2 Thessalonians 3:10. Report on Anna Leins 5 May 1581, HStAS A282/3087, Nr. 13.

[122] Report of Schorndorf's Spezialis and bailiff about Anabaptists in Urbach, 9 August 1620, HStAS A282/3094a, Nr. 26.

Other women also related that although they were not literate themselves, they had people at hand who could read Scripture aloud to them (as we have already seen in several cases above).[123] "Although her mother does not go to church," Barbara Halt testified in 1620, she "has the Bible read to her at home." To further underscore the conformity of this activity with official norms, the daughter described what Christian virtues her mother was teaching to her children: "She instructs us not to swear, to believe in God and to be kind to people." Her brothers confirmed this practice.[124]

As Barbara Halt's testimony shows, firstly, Bibles were read together with household members. Secondly, the lines between reading, worship and discussion appear blurred rather than clear-cut. Thirdly, Halt's statement suggests that domestic Bible reading could be used as an attempt to obscure forbidden activities when questioned by hostile authorities. This was the case both for Anabaptists and followers of the Spiritualist Caspar von Schwenckfeld, at least in southwestern Germany. Interestingly, Caroline Gritschke has argued that the right to read what texts they wanted and the freedom to discuss religious subjects were among the things on which lay Schwenckfelders were least willing to compromise, although they were quite flexible on other, even doctrinal, issues.[125]

Church leaders had called for lay Bible reading – how could they now reprimand simple people for doing as they were told? "I am not an Anabaptist simply because I have been reading the Epistle of James," claimed Jörg Banholtz, for instance, in a heated debate with the pastor of Urbach in 1620.[126] The conflict had started with Banholtz' critique of the pastor's use of the Bible, as he inquired why the pastor had not

---

[123] See e.g. the case of Maria Niesmüller, vis.prot. of Beutelsbach, autumn 1617, LKAS A26/466 II, 195v.

[124] Report of Schorndorf's Spezialis and bailiff about Anabaptists in Urbach, 9 August 1620, HStAS A282/3094a, Nr. 26.

[125] Gritschke 2006, 334.

[126] Report of pastor in Urbach, 24 June 1620, HStAS A282/3094a, Nr. 25. See also the following report of Schorndorf's Spezialis and bailiff about Anabaptists in Urbach, 9 August 1620, HStAS A282/3094a, Nr. 26. The Bible passage is about enduring trials and persecution patiently, a passage that may well have comforted religious nonconformists under pressure.

considered chapters one to three in the Book of James when interrogating and instructing the children of the nonconforming Halt family in the same parish. This Bible passage would have shown, according to Banholtz, that the Halt children had not given any incorrect answers. In a letter to his superiors, the frustrated pastor recounted how the situation escalated into an outright fight about Bible reading, Banholtz dismissing the pastor's explanation (which is not spelled out) "defiantly" (*trotzig*). Banholtz then continued: "Is the Epistle of James not just as much the Word of God than the letters of the apostle Paul?" And consequently: "If James' letter should not have the same authority as Paul's, why don't we throw it out of the Bible altogether?"[127] The pastor was highly upset about the debacle, most of all because it undermined his authority in front of his catechism pupils, who would in turn surely inform other parishioners about the incident. He feared the rise of a "greater tumult" (*größerer tumult*) in a village that was, even well into the 17th century, hardly confessionalised to the degree the authorities wished for.[128]

In these arguments the Holy Book stood in the centre, quite literally. The Urbach pastor described how he had a German Bible open in front of him on the table. He used it to show the dissenting parishioners the passages he was quoting from so that they would "see that it was not only my opinion, but rather that of the Holy Spirit". He read out "four or five short verses" to demonstrate that the Lutheran interpretation had a true biblical foundation that was "clear as daylight", proving, consequently, that the dissenters were in the wrong.[129]

Reading the Bible could indeed be a subversive act and the authorities would have preferred that lay people restrict their reading to a suitable Lutheran catechism (Zwinglian catechisms were confiscated in Württemberg whenever they were found).[130] Accordingly, it was

---

[127] Report of pastor in Urbach, 24 June 1620, HStAS A282/3094a, Nr. 25; report of Schorndorf's Spezialis and bailiff about Anabaptists in Urbach, 9 August 1620, HStAS A282/3094a, Nr. 26.

[128] Report of Schorndorf's Spezialis and bailiff about Anabaptists in Urbach, 9 August 1620, HStAS A282/3094a, Nr. 26. On the huge debate in German research about confessionalisation, see e.g. Schmidt 1992 with further references.

[129] Report of pastor in Urbach, 24 June 1620, HStAS A282/3094a, Nr. 25.

[130] Vis.prot. of Schmiden, autumn 1573, LKAS A26/466 I, 11r.

mentioned with approval if former dissidents complied with reading the catechism as instructed.[131] A controlled reading of the catechism was one important step in establishing the official Lutheran Church and indicates how little the authorities wanted to risk that laypeople came to unwanted conclusions by reading the Scriptures without approved theological guidance. Therefore it was the task of the local pastors to instruct their young parishioners regularly in the Christian norms outlined in the catechism. The goal was to learn the text by heart and, proceeding to the next level, to obtain "a good Christian understanding" of the contents. Further, the teaching methods should, ideally, be gentle enough not to raise any resistance, but rather to foster a joy of studying the word of God.[132]

Conclusions

This article has examined social practices of reading among Württemberg's rank-and-file Anabaptists, both men and women. In this case study, Anabaptist reading, understood broadly and including both individual and collective uses of texts, had two main purposes. Intellectually, the text was to equip their readers/hearers with biblical arguments strengthened by the authority of God's word in conflict situations. Emotionally and spiritually, reading was to foster the sensibility of belonging to the few – and persecuted – true Christians and to provide comfort, patience and strength in the face of life's trials and conflicts. Reading was flexibly adapted to the situation, and solitary reading was never an isolated activity, but always connected to the reader's social context. More often than not, what was perhaps read alone was later discussed in company. Singing was another flexible activity that could provide comfort and strength in times of loneliness, but also had a strong communal dimension. These practices not only

[131] Vis.prot. of Bittenfeld, 1610, LKAS A26/466 II, 130r.
[132] *Confessio Virtembergica* 1559, HStAS A63/24, 63v–64r.

helped to spread Anabaptist ideas, but also actively sought to shape both individual and collective identities.

There was a clear continuity of lay reading and communication modes before and after the often-declared watershed of 1525. Even though participation in the more public debates may have become more restricted, and authorities pressed for approved catechisms as the main religious reading material for the unschooled, reading, discussing and singing did not end – or probably even diminish – on the grassroots level. Nor did the yearning for a better Christian society cease, as can be seen by the criticism brought forward by Württemberg's rank-and-file Anabaptists decades after the official introduction of the Lutheran Reformation.

Further, the scribal culture remained vital in persecuted and underground groups. In this context, the ability to memorise the contents of a written/printed page was crucial, when being in possession of the book itself could be incriminating. Thematically-organised Bible concordances and hymnals were especially suited to this purpose, and both in use among lay Anabaptists. Menno Simons' popular *Fundamentbuch* was carefully kept by those who could afford it and deliberately borrowed or given only to like-minded and trusted persons.

In sum, the findings from Württemberg support the claims that orality and vernacular reading interact in the Reformation context, as well as recent book-historical insights into reading as a dynamic social process of actively selecting and shaping the material in a given historical setting. Moreover, this geographically-confined exploration of Anabaptist reading practices, shows how it is both necessary and possible to go beyond the traditional book-historical questions of authorship, genre, book production and marketing towards the history of reading practices.

Bibliography

Archival sources

Hauptstaatsarchiv Stuttgart (HStAS)
A63: Religions- und Kirchensachen
A281: Kirchenvisitationsakten. Superintendenz Maulbronn, Amt Schorndorf, 1602–1605
(Büschel 1120–1122)
A282: Kirchenrat: Verschlossene Registratur
Nebenrubrik 34: Wiedertäufer (Büschel 3084–3096)

Landeskirchliches Archiv Stuttgart (LKAS)
A1: Synodus-Protokolle (Visitationsberichte)
A26: Allgemeine Kirchenakten
Bd. 466 I: Sectarii I (1573–1578)
Bd. 466 II: Sectarii II (1608–1620)

Printed sources

Ausbund 1583. Ausbund etlicher schöner Christlicher Geseng, [s.n], [s.l.] 1583. *Bayerische Staatsbibliothek Online*, urn:nbn:de:bvb:12-bsb10207712-6 (retrieved 14 April, 2016).
Bossert, Gustav (ed.): *Quellen zur Geschichte der Wiedertäufer*. Vol. 1, *Herzogtum Württemberg*. M. Heinsius Nachfolger, Leipzig 1930. (QGT I)
Grumbach, Argula von: *Argula von Grumbach: A Woman's Voice in the Reformation*. Ed. Peter Matheson. T & T Clark, Edinburgh 1995.
Friedmann, Robert (ed.): *Die Schriften der Huterischen Täufergemeinschaften: Gesamtkatalog ihrer Manuskriptbücher, ihrer Schreiber und ihrer Literatur 1529–1667*. Österreichische Akademie der Wissenschaften, Vienna 1965.
Seebaß, Gottfried (ed.): *Quellen zur Geschichte der Täufer*. Vol. 18, *Katalog der hutterischen Handschriften und der Drucke aus hutterischem Besitz in Europa*, ed. Matthias H. Rauert and Martin Rothkegel. Gütersloher Verlagshaus, Gütersloh 2011.

Research literature

Baggerman, Arianne and Rudolf Dekker: *Child of the Enlightenment: Revolutionary Europe Reflected in a Boyhood Diary*. Brill, Leiden and Boston 2009.
Bepler, Jill and Helga Meise (eds.): *Sammeln, Lesen, Übersetzen als höfische Praxis der Frühen Neuzeit: die böhmische Bibliothek der Fürsten Eggenberg im Kontext der Fürsten und Fürstinnenbibliotheken der Zeit*. Harrassowitz, Wiesbaden 2010.
Bick, Martina: Liederdrucke der Täufer. *Mennonitisches Lexikon (MennLex)*. Vol. 5, vol. 2, *Geschichte, Kultur, Theologie*. Eds. Hans-Jürgen Goertz et al. 2013. http://www.mennlex.de/doku.php?id=top:liederdrucke (retrieved 14 April 2016).
Blaak, Jeroen: Autobiographical Reading and Writing: The Diary of David Beck (1624). *Egodocuments and History: Autobiographical writing in its social context since the Middle Ages*. Ed. Rudolf Dekker. Verloren, Hilversum 2002, 61–87.
Blaak, Jeroen: *Literacy in Everyday Life: Reading and Writing in Early Modern Dutch Diaries*. Brill, Boston et al. 2008.

Bödeker, Hans-Erich, Gérald Chaix and Patrice Veit: Der Umgang mit dem religiösen Buch in der frühen Neuzeit. Anmerkungen zum Forschungsthema. *Der Umgang mit dem religiösen Buch: Studien zur Geschichte des religiösen Buches in Deutschland und Frankreich der frühen Neuzeit*. Eds. Hans-Erich Bödeker, Gérald Chaix and Patrice Veit. Vandenhoeck & Ruprecht, Göttingen 1991, 13–24.

Brecht, Martin: *Kirchenordnung und Kirchenzucht in Württemberg vom 16. bis zum 18. Jahrhundert*. Calwer Verlag, Stuttgart 1967.

Buchhester, Dörthe: *Die Familie der Fürstin: Die herzoglichen Häuser der Pommern und Sachsen im 16. Jahrhundert: Erziehung, Bücher, Briefe*. Peter Lang, Frankfurt am Main 2015.

Burschel, Peter: *Sterben und Unsterblichkeit: Zur Kultur des Martyriums in der frühen Neuzeit*. Oldenbourg, Munich 2004.

Cambers, Andrew: *Godly Reading: Print, Manuscript and Puritanism in England, 1580–1720*. Cambridge University Press, Cambridge 2011.

Chartier, Roger: The Order of Books Revisited. *Modern Intellectual History* 4/2007, 509–519.

Chrisman, Miriam Usher: *Conflicting Visions of Reform: German Lay Propaganda Pamphlets, 1519–1530*. Humanities Press, New Jersey 1996.

Chudaska, Andrea: Lieder der Hutterer. Mennonitisches Lexikon (MennLex). Vol. 5, vol. 2, *Geschichte, Kultur, Theologie*. Eds. Hans-Jürgen Goertz et al. 2010. http://www.mennlex.de/doku.php?id=top:lieder-der-hutterer (retrieved 14 April 2016).

Clasen, Claus-Peter: *Die Wiedertäufer im Herzogtum Württemberg und in benachbarten Herrschaften: Ausbreitung, Geisteswelt und Soziologie*. Kohlhammer, Stuttgart 1965.

Clasen, Claus-Peter: *Anabaptism: A Social History, 1525–1618. Switzerland, Austria, Moravia, South and Central Germany*. Cornell University Press, Ithaca and London 1972.

Colclough, Stephen: *Consuming Texts: Readers and Reading Communities, 1695–1870*. Palgrave Macmillan, New York 2007.

Corbellini, Sabrina and Margriet Hoogvliet: Artisans and Religious Reading in Late Medieval Italy and Northern France (ca. 1400–ca. 1520). *Journal of Medieval and Early Modern Studies* 43/2013, 521–544.

Davis, Natalie Zemon: *Fiction in the Archives: Pardon Tales and their Tellers in Sixteenth-Century France*. Stanford, CA, Stanford University Press 1987.

Edwards, Mark U.: *Printing, Propaganda, and Martin Luther*. University of California Press, Berkeley 1994.

Ezell, Margaret J.M.: Handwriting and the Book. *The Cambridge Companion to the History of the Book*. Ed. Leslie Howsam. Cambridge University Press, Cambridge 2015, 90–106.

Fluri, Adolf: Froschauer Bibles and Testaments [1953]. *Global Anabaptist Mennonite Encyclopedia Online (GAMEO)*. http://gameo.org/index.php?title=Froschauer_Bibles_and_Testaments&oldid=122489 (retrieved 12 April 2016).

Freeman, Thomas S.: Over Their Dead Bodies: Concepts of Martyrdom in Late-Medieval and Early-Modern England. *Martyrs and Martyrdom in England, c. 1400–1700*. Eds. Thomas S. Freeman and Thomas F. Mayer. Boydell, Woodbridge 2007, 1–34.

Friedmann, Robert: Doctrinal Writings of the Anabaptists [1956]. *Global Anabaptist Mennonite Encyclopedia Online (GAMEO)*. http://gameo.org/index.php?title=Doctrinal_Writings_of_the_Anabaptists&oldid=121015 (retrieved 12 April 2016).

Gawthrop, Richard and Gerald Strauss: Protestantism and Literacy in Early Modern Germany. *Past & Present* 104/1984, 31–55.

Goertz, Hans-Jürgen: Das Täufertum als religiöse und soziale Bewegung. *Die Täuferbewegung – L'anabattismo: Tagung zum 450. Todestag Jakob Huters (1536–1986)*. Ed. Christoph von Hartungen. Bolzano, Praxis 3 1986, 21–37.

Goertz, Hans-Jürgen: *Pfaffenhaß und groß Geschrei: Die reformatorischen Bewegungen in Deutschland 1517–1529.* Beck, Munich 1987.

Goertz, Hans-Jürgen: Die 'gemeinen Täufer': Einfache Brüder und selbstbewusste Schwestern. *Querdenken: Dissens und Toleranz im Wandel der Geschichte, Festschrift zum 65. Geburtstag von Hans R. Guggisberg.* Ed. Michael Erbe. Palatium-Verlag, Mannheim 1996, 289–303.

Gregory, Brad S.: Anabaptist Martyrdom: Imperatives, Experience, and Memorialization. *A Companion to Anabaptism and Spiritualism, 1521–1700.* Eds. John D. Roth and James M. Stayer. Brill, Leiden 2007, 467–506.

Gritschke, Caroline: *'Via Media': Spiritualistische Lebenswelten und Konfessionalisierung: Das süddeutsche Schwenckfeldertum im 16. und 17. Jahrhundert.* Akademie, Berlin 2006.

Hill, Kat: Anabaptism and the World of Printing in Sixteenth-Century Germany. *Past & Present* 226/2015, 79–114.

Howsam, Leslie: *Old Books and New Histories: An Orientation to Studies in Book and Print Culture.* University of Toronto Press, Toronto 2006.

Howsam, Leslie: The Study of Book History. *The Cambridge Companion to the History of the Book.* Ed. Leslie Howsam. Cambridge University Press, Cambridge 2015, 1–13.

Kaufmann, Thomas (ed.), *Reformation und Buch: Akteure und Strategien frühreformatorischer Druckerzeugnisse.* Wiesbaden, Harrassowitz 2016.

Kobelt-Groch, Marion: Frauen in Ketten: "Von widertauferischen weibern, wie gegen selbigen zu handlen". *Mennonitische Geschichtsblätter* 47–48/1990–1991, 49–70.

Köhler, Hans-Joachim (ed.): *Flugschriften als Massenmedium der Reformationszeit: Beiträge zum Tübinger Symposion 1980.* Ernst Klett, Stuttgart 1981.

Landwehr, Achim: *Policey im Alltag: Die Implementation frühneuzeitlicher Policeyordnungen in Leonberg.* Klostermann, Frankfurt am Main 2000.

Laube, Adolf: Radicalism as a Research Problem in the History of Early Reformation. *Radical Tendencies in the Reformation: Divergent Perspectives.* Ed. Hans J. Hillerbrand. Sixteenth Century Journal Publishers, Kirksville 1988, 9–23.

Lieseberg, Ursula: The Martyr Songs of the Hutterite Brethren. *Mennonite Quarterly Review* 67/1993, 323–336.

Lieseberg, Ursula: *Die Lieder des Peter Riedemann: Studien zum Liedgut der Täufer im 16. Jahrhundert.* Peter Lang, Frankfurt am Main 1998.

Leu, Urs: Froschauer-Bibeln. *Mennonitisches Lexikon (MennLex).* Vol. 2, *Geschichte, Kultur, Theologie.* Eds. Hans-Jürgen Goertz et al. 2012. http://www.mennlex.de/doku.php?id=top:froschauer-bibeln (retrieved 12 April 2016).

Matheson, Peter: *The Imaginative World of the Reformation.* T&T Clark, Edinburgh 2000.

Narveson, Kate: *Bible Readers and Lay Writers in Early Modern England: Gender and Self-Definition in an Emergent Writing Culture.* Ashgate, Farnham 2012.

Packull, Werner O.: Anna Jansz of Rotterdam. *Profiles of Anabaptist Women: Sixteenth Century Reforming Pioneers.* Eds. C. Arnold Snyder and Linda Huebert Hecht. Wilfried Laurier University Press, Waterloo Ont. 1996, 336–351.

Peduzzi, Nicole: Der Gantnerhandel im Licht des Verfolgungsberichts des Bündner Buchbinders Georg Frell. *Zwingliana* 34/2007, 61–94.

Pettegree, Andrew: *The Book in the Renaissance.* New Haven, Yale University Press 2010.

Price, Leah: Reading: The State of the Discipline. *Book History* 7/2004, 303–320.

Rageth, Simon and Oskar Vasella (eds.): Die Autobiographie des Täufers Georg Frell von Chur. *Zwingliana* 7/7/1942, 444–469.

Räisänen, Päivi: *Ketzer im Dorf: Visitationsverfahren, Täuferbekämpfung und lokale Handlungsmuster im frühneuzeitlichen Württemberg.* UVK, Constance 2011.

Räisänen-Schröder, Päivi: Appeal and Survival of Anabaptism in Early Modern Germany. *Lived Religion and Temporal Change in Northern Europe c. 1300–1700.* Ed. Sari Katajala-Peltomaa and Raisa Maria Toivo. Brill, Leiden & New York 2016, 104–127.

Rauert, Matthias H.: Die 'Brüder-Schreiber' in Mähren: Zur kollektiven Historiographie der Hutterischen Täufer. *Mennonitische Geschichtsblätter* 56/1999, 103–138.

Rempel, John D. Anabaptist Religious Literature and Hymnody. *A Companion to Anabaptism and Spiritualism, 1521–1700.* Eds. John D. Roth, and James M. Stayer. Leiden, Brill, 2007, 389–424.

Rose, Jonathan: Rereading the English Common Reader: A Preface to a History of Audiences. *Journal of the History of Ideas* 53/1992, 47–70.

Rössing-Hager, Monika: Wie stark findet der nicht-lesekundige Rezipient Berücksichtigung in den Flugschriften? *Flugschriften als Massenmedium der Reformationszeit: Beiträge zum Tübinger Symposion 1980.* Ed. Hans-Joachim Köhler. Ernst Klett Verlag, Stuttgart 1981, 77–137.

Rothkegel, Martin: The Hutterian Brethren and the Printed Book: A Contribution to Anabaptist Bibliography. *Mennonite Quarterly Review* 74/2000, 51–85.

Rothkegel, Martin: 'Den Brüdern um zwei Pfennig leichter dann den Auswendigen': Distributionsbedingungen radikalreformatorischer Milieuliteratur. *Reformation und Buch: Akteure und Strategien frühreformatorischer Druckerzeugnisse.* Ed. Thomas Kaufmann. Wiesbaden: Harrassowitz 2016, 199–219.

Ryrie, Alec: *Being Protestant in Reformation Britain.* Oxford University Press, Oxford 2013.

Sabean, David W.: Village Court Protocols and Memory. *Gemeinde, Reformation und Widerstand: Festschrift für Peter Blickle zum 60. Geburtstag.* Eds. Heinrich Richard Schmidt, André Holenstein, and Andreas Würgler. Tübingen, bibliotheca academica Verlag 1998, 3–23.

Schlachta, Astrid von: 'Searching Through the Nations': Tasks and Problems of Sixteenth-Century Hutterian Mission. *Mennonite Quarterly Review* 74/2000, 27–49.

Schmidt, Heinrich Richard: *Konfessionalisierung im 16. Jahrhundert.* Oldenbourg, Munich 1992.

Schwerhoff, Gerd: *Aktenkundig und gerichtsnotorisch: Einführung in die Historische Kriminalitätsforschung.* Tübingen, edition diskord 1999.

Scribner, Robert W.: *For the Sake of Simple Folk: Popular Propaganda for the German Reformation.* Cambridge University Press, Cambridge 1981.

Scribner, Robert W. (ed.): *Popular Culture and Popular Propaganda in Reformation Germany.* Hambledon Press, London 1987.

Scribner, Robert W.: Heterodoxy, Literacy and Print in the Early German Reformation. *Heresy and Literacy, 1000–1530.* Eds. Peter Biller and Anne Hudson. Cambridge University Press, Cambridge 1994, 255–278.

Shevchenko, Nadezda: *Eine historische Anthropologie des Buches: Bücher in der preußischen Herzogsfamilie zur Zeit der Reformation.* Vandenhoeck & Ruprecht, Göttingen 2007.

Simon-Muscheid, Katharina and Christian Simon: Zur Lektüre von Gerichtstexten: Fiktionale Realität oder Alltag in Gerichtsquellen? *Arbeit – Liebe – Streit: Texte zur Geschichte des Geschlechterverhältnisses und des Alltags, 15. bis 18. Jahrhundert.* Eds. Dorothee Rippmann, Katharina Simon-Muscheid, and Christian Simon. Basel, Verlag des Kantons Basel-Landschaft 1996, 17–39.

Simpson, James: *Burning to Read.* Harvard University Press, Cambridge Mass. 2009.

Snook, Edith: *Women, Reading, and the Cultural Politics of Early Modern England.* Ashgate, Aldershot 2005.

Snyder, C. Arnold: Biblical Text and Social Context: Anabaptist Anticlericalism in Reformation Zürich. *Mennonite Quarterly Review* 65/1991a, 169–191.

Snyder, C. Arnold: Orality, Literacy, and the Study of Anabaptism. *Mennonite Quarterly Review* 65/1991b, 371–392.

Snyder, C. Arnold: Agnes Linck from Biel. *Profiles of Anabaptist Women: Sixteenth-Century Reforming Pioneers.* Eds. C. Arnold Snyder and Linda A. Hubert Hecht. Wilfrid Laurier University Press, Waterloo Ont. 1996a, 32–37.

Snyder, C. Arnold: Introduction. *Profiles of Anabaptist Women: Sixteenth-Century Reforming Pioneers.* Eds. C. Arnold Snyder and Linda A. Hubert Hecht. Wilfrid Laurier University Press, Waterloo Ont. 1996b, 1–15.

Snyder, C. Arnold: Preface. *Biblical Concordance of the Swiss Brethren 1540.* Ed. C. Arnold Snyder. Pandora Press, Kitchener 2001.

Stayer, James M.: *The German Peasants' War and Anabaptist Community of Goods.* McGill–Queen's University Press, Montreal 1991.

Tomkowiak, Ingrid: Geplagte Priester, verwilderte Gemeinden: Aspekte von Popularität in Bauernpredigten. *Der Umgang mit dem religiösen Buch: Studien zur Geschichte des religiösen Buches in Deutschland und Frankreich der frühen Neuzeit.* Eds. Hans Erich Bödeker, Gérald Chaix, and Patrice Veit. Vandenhoeck & Ruprecht, Göttingen 1991, 194–220.

Zitzlsperger, Ulrike: Mother, Martyr and Mary Magdalene: German Female Pamphleteers and their Self-Images. *History* 88/2003, 379–392.

Zorzin, Alejandro: Reformation Publishing and Anabaptist Propaganda: Two Contrasting Communication Strategies for the Spread of the Anabaptist Message in the Early Days of the Swiss Brethren. *Mennonite Quarterly Review* 82 (2008a), 503–516.

Zorzin, Alejandro: Peter Schöffer d. J. und die Täufer. *Buchwesen in Spätmittelalter und Früher Neuzeit: Festschrift für Helmut Claus zum 75. Geburtstag.* Ed. Ulman Weiß. Bibliotheca academica, Epfendorf am Neckar 2008b, 179–213.

Zorzin, Alejandro: Ludwig Hätzer als täuferischer Publizist (1527–1528). *Mennonitische Geschichtsblätter* 67/2010, 25–49.

Internet Sites

http://www.luther2017.de/en/wiki/women-move-the-church-since-luthers-time/argula-von-grumbach-i-have-not-written-womens-gossip-to-you/ (retrieved 12 April 2016).

Books of golden rays and ripped folios: Thomas Aquinas's book-relics in religious reforms

Marika Räsänen

Introduction[1]

In medieval and early modern art one of the most common attributes of Thomas Aquinas is a book in his lap or arms. The book is usually open and often the text is readable. The earliest known representation of this type of image is in an altar panel of Simone Martini, a Sienese painter, which was finished in 1320.[2] The commissioners of the panel were the Dominicans of Pisa, who presumably gave good instructions to the painter on what they wanted the altarpiece to look like. Thomas Aquinas is in a central position in the predella, and moreover, he is represented with a halo. However, in 1320 he was not yet canonized.

[1] I would like to express my gratitude to my colleagues in Münster and Turku who have commented on my text and helped me to go further. I am also grateful to anonymous readers whose remarks improved the text significantly. I owe special thanks to Philip Lane whose diligent reading gave to the text its present form.
[2] The panel, called *Madonna and Child and Saints*, belongs nowadays in the collections of the Museo nazionale di san Matteo, Pisa.

Image 1. *Madonna and Child and Saints*, detail, Museo nazionale di san Matteo, Pisa.

In the surviving Italian public art of that period representation of saint-candidates, especially with the halo, which normally signified a canonized saint, was rare.[3] To include Thomas among the established saintly figures was certainly the choice of the local friars, not the artist, and they must have deliberated on the iconographical setting.

Besides the halo, what else seems to have been important to the friars when portraying Thomas Aquinas in their new altar panel? The image in the predella is a half-length portrait of a man wearing the simple black and white Dominican habit. Although he has the halo, the most prominent and radiant element in the scheme is the huge book that he holds open with both hands, the text facing viewers of the image. On the open pages of the book are written these words from Proverbs: "For my mouth shall speak truth; and wickedness is an abomination to my lips."[4] They form the opening of Thomas's *Summa contra gentiles,* which leaves us in no doubt that the man depicted is Thomas Aquinas. Golden rays of light emanate from the book, or perhaps from the text, so thickly that the margins around the text appear to be painted gold. The black cape is parted by the sleeves of Thomas's arms holding the book, so that the tunic is visible below it and just visible as a triangle of cloth above it. The tunic is white, but here the triangle-shaped piece is transformed to gold by the rays in front of it, implying a connection between the text and Thomas's breast or heart. The book appears to be the central focus of the image, almost as if Thomas's main purpose in being there is to hold it. The rays from the book's pages almost cover him, assimilating him with it and perhaps suggesting that his sainthood derives from it.

In this paper, I ask what the significance of Thomas's book for his cult in general was, and more particularly for his cult as a reformer in the Order of Preachers. In contemporary discussion as well as in hagiographical texts, Thomas Aquinas's fame was partly anchored to his

---

[3] Cannon 1982, 73 and passim.
[4] Translation King James Bible [KJB], Proverbs 8:7. The inscription/Vulgate version: "Veritatem meditabitur guttur meum et labia mea detestabuntur [impium]."

works which were "illuminating" the world.[5] An open book soon became one of his attributes in pictorial representations. Thomas was perceived as a person who brought enlightenment to the world, a reformer, that is, a person who sustains the Catholic faith by his writings. From this perspective, I find it interesting to focus on the roles of books as pictorial or physical representations of Thomas in images of him. Because of the scarcity of sources, to understand the importance given to bound books as objects of veneration and instruments of reform the paper covers a wide time span from the late medieval to the Early Modern Era.

Thomas's writings addressing the metaphysical explanation of existence were vitally important for his saintly reputation and image in the centuries following his death.[6] In turn, the books began to acquire their own holiness from Thomas's sainthood, becoming valuable and meaningful as objects, not only as texts. Alison Frazier has briefly discussed the assimilation of a holy person to his physical representations, and stated that manuscripts could assimilate 'historical saints, saintly narrative, physical book, and saintly relic' in humanist Italy.[7] This stratification of significance of manuscripts comes out strikingly in Thomas's case when one studies both images of beautiful volumes (in

---

[5] When Thomas died, "the sun has withdrawn its splendour", was how the Faculty of Arts of the University of Paris expressed its reaction to Thomas's death in a letter sent to the General Chapter of the Dominican Order on 2 May 1274. See the letter in Latin Laurent 1937, 583–586. The English translation by Foster 1959. William of Tocco, who wrote Thomas's first Life ca. 1323, was explicit on the importance of Thomas's writings: he describes Thomas as a star who enlightened the world by his books, see William of Tocco, *Ystoria sancti Thome de Aquino*, cap. 2.

[6] The connection between Thomas's writings and his saintly reputation is generally noted but rarely properly analysed. A classic study by M.-D. Chenu 1950, on understanding of Thomas's production, partly explains the connection between the writings and sainthood. See also Torrell 1993. From early on, when anyone discussed Thomas's sainthood, they tended to emphasize Thomas's publications. The phenomena can be grasped, for example, from the testimony Bartholomew of Capua gave in the canonization hearings and Thomas's early *Vitae*. See *Processus canonizationis S. Thomae, Neapoli* (1319), 386–389; Ptolemy of Lucca, *Historia Ecclesiastica nova*; Bernard Gui, *Legenda sancti Thomae Aquinatis*.

[7] Frazier 2005, 7.

Pisa and Rome) and mutilated, real books inside reliquaries (in Naples, Salerno and Aversa). Thomas's writings were understood as an organic part of his holiness, so that books or part of books written by him were considered holy objects, relics. Although the relic-utility of Thomas's autographs is clear, when they became venerated in themselves is not so clear.[8] However, when analysing images (both pictorial and textual) representing Thomas's writings in the context of his cult, we can grasp medieval perceptions of books and images such as the one described above hint that the books were also understood as saintly relics.[9]

The relic nature of books and other forms of gathered texts or text fragments in the Middle Ages is remarkably understudied.[10] However, the idea of texts bearing a supernatural power is perhaps as old as writing itself, and we know that textual amulets were used in pre-Christian Europe. Among the most valuable studies on textual relics is Don C. Skemer's book *Binding words*, which discusses the practice of wearing amulets with written words on, a habit that can be defined both magical and/or religious.[11] Alan Boureau comes to similar conclusions in his excellent article on early prints and their uses for magical and Christian worship.[12] Paul Bertrand takes a slightly different approach that

[8] For some remarks on the relic utility of St Francis's autographs, see Bertrand 2006, 373; Boureau 1989, 18.

[9] My suggestion comes close to Heffernan's, according to which medieval hagiographical texts, including such books as saints's *Lives*, had two vital objectives: they had to respond to the specific community's traditional understanding of a holy person and they had to "establish the text itself as a document worthy of reverence, as a relic". Heffernan gives examples from throughout the Middle Ages of the ways in which *Lives* and miracle collections were placed on injured or infected parts of the body, curing the sufferer immediately. Heffernan 1988, 35.

[10] Relics and relic practices have been the subject of numerous studies during recent decades, but these studies rarely concern representative relics such as clothes and other possessions of a holy person or things that had touched him/her. When some classical studies of relics present lists of types of representative relics, they do not usually mention books. Among the classics, see Herrmann-Mascard 1975.

[11] Especially on textual relics and debates on their uses, see Skemer 2006, 50–58.

[12] Boureau 1989.

emphasizes canonically accepted ways to consider the manuscripts and shorter texts as sacred relics.[13] All these studies are extremely important but they can only address a few of the manifold issues surrounding the uses of books and written pieces as power objects. Book-relics, as well as other representative relics, are still in need of much more detailed and varied study than there has been so far.[14] The present paper offers a rather broad view on how to understand the material significance of Thomas's books. The topic is challenging, especially given the scarcity of source material from the Middle Ages: possibly the fine distinction between superstitious and doctrinally correct relic practices has led to avoidance of the topic and the omission of descriptions of the uses of Thomas's texts as relic-objects in medieval or early modern documents.[15] So far Thomas's autographs as holy relics have received special attention in the publications of Théry in the 1930s and Boyle in the 1990s.[16] However, these two scholars focus more on the issues of identification, provenience and reconstruction of the mutilated manuscripts than on questions of their nature as relics in the past.

To understand the primary significance of Thomas's texts and books to the Dominicans from a material viewpoint, it is necessary to read the acts of the General Chapters of the Order of Preachers (i.e. Dominicans).[17] A very useful source for remarks on book-relics associated with Thomas is the collection of *Libri* in the General Archives of the Order of Preachers in Rome. The collection contains dozens of large volumes, each of them conserving hand copied documents, histories and inventories of Dominican houses, most collected in the seventeenth

---

[13] Bertrand 2006.

[14] A good example of the possibilities offered by study of these themes is an article by Éric Palazzo on books as relics in ecclesiastic treasuries, see Palazzo 1997.

[15] Regarding the silence on "unsuitable" practices at a saint's tomb where the relics were kept, possibly regarded as superstitious in the Early Middle Ages, and official documents which omitted those practices, see Redon and Gélis 1984.

[16] See the bibliography (Boyle 2000a and Théry 1931abc).

[17] I have used the digital copy of Monumenta Ordinis fratrum Praedicatorum Historica (hereafter MOPH).

and eighteenth centuries.[18] I have read the descriptions of the movable chattels of numerous Italian convents to gain an understanding of the value given to Thomas's manuscripts and other belongings and to analyse the practices connected to them. The Libri is also a promising source of material to explore the relic utility of manuscripts and other representative objects in connection to Dominican saints in the worldwide context of the Early Modern period. Besides this documentary material, I concentrate on the perception of books in the Dominican hagiography and iconography. In this study, hagiography and iconography are considered as two sides of one coin: following the concept of Birgitte Cazelles, the hagiography consists of "verbal and visual documents commemorating the saints".[19] Words and images are media through which the Dominicans represented their thoughts, doctrine and identity.[20] The images of Thomas's books are considered to reflect the Dominican theology and identity of the period, in both of which the veneration of Thomas's doctrine gained an important place.

Study-books and book-collections

Thomas's texts as physical objects attracted contemporary attention immediately after his death. The first institution expressing its interest

[18] Manuscript series of the Dominican history, namely Libri or Monumenta Annalium Ordinis Praedicatorum, containing 44 volumes from the 15th century onwards and conserved at the Dominican General Archives in Rome (AGOP). The catalogue of the Libri is published by Koudelka 1968 and 1969, see the bibliography.

[19] Cazelles 1991, 1. In the same book with Cazelles, Magdalena Carrasco analyses pictorial hagiography in an illustrative way as a source of history and spirituality: Carrasco 1991.

[20] Dominican figurative art and theology, as well as art and politics of the Order, are examined in several recent or relatively recent studies; among those I have found important and useful Cannon 2013, Gerbron 2010 and 2016, Palazzo 2016. More widely on the theme of how to read visual images and relics as representations of the Early Modern worldview, see Dillenberger 1999, and on reading of medieval images, Belting 1996.

in Thomas's works appears to have been the University of Paris. The Faculty of Arts sent a letter to the General Chapter of the Dominicans asking that Thomas's corpse and some of his writings be sent to Paris after the Master's death in 1274. In exchange, the letter promised to keep the teacher's memory alive. The content of the letter expresses the affection, even devotion, the Faculty felt towards the great Master and his bones. The tone of the letter is perhaps more practical when it addresses Thomas's writings: it asks, almost demands, that all those works (and similar works) Thomas had started to write when he was last teaching in Paris be returned to the Faculty. It apparently considered itself as the rightful owner of the texts because Thomas had contributed to their work while he belonged to the personnel of the University.[21]

We do not know how the Dominican Order reacted to the demands of the University, as no reply has survived. However, we can guess the answer to the first request: the Dominican Order could not donate the Faculty the bones because Thomas had died at a Cistercian house, not a convent of the Order. There are acts of the Dominican General Chapters from a few years later that conserve interesting documentary material telling us how the administrative level of the Order reacted to Thomas's literary heritage.[22]

The first General Chapters that treated Thomas's intellectual work were organized in Milan in 1278 and in Paris in 1279 and 1286.[23] The acts gave admonitions not to criticize Thomas's writings but only to

---

[21] Laurent 1937, 583–586. The letter was sent by the rector of the University and all the masters teaching in the Faculty of Arts. The significance of the letter from the viewpoint of the Faculty of Arts is discussed, for example, in Kretzmann and Stump 1993, 13–14.

[22] It is useful to know that the Dominicans are considered to have had a special relationship with their books from the very beginning of the Order. Studies were valued highly in the Order, and in consequence it emphasized the necessity to own books, both on a personal and a communal level: see Hinnebusch 1973, 191–230.

[23] For Milan 1278, see MOPH 3, 199, for Paris 1279 and 1286, 204 and 235.

promote them.[24] The General Chapter of Zaragoza in 1309 gave the first orders concerning Thomas's texts specifically as objects.[25] First it demands that lectors and sub-lectors read and teach using Thomas's works. Next, it insists that the teachers had to guide students to do the same. Then, the acts discuss the circumstances when students were allowed to sell their books. Most significantly, they were forbidden to sell only two types of books under any circumstances – those containing Thomas's texts and the Bible.[26] In the General Chapter of Bologna in 1315, Thomas's book-objects received detailed attention, so much so that later Chapters did not return to the issue. The acts of Bologna give instructions on how to make books available in convents and how to make sure that the convents owned all the texts written by Thomas.[27]

Thus, the Dominican Order forcefully promoted Thomas's doctrine and his writings inside the community of the friars, but the fame of his philosophical or theological works diffused far beyond the walls of the convents. Outside Dominican circles, Pope John XXII (1316–1334) was one of Thomas's early admirers. It may also have been John who provided the initiative for Thomas's canonization. John's liking for Thomas's doctrine is widely recognized by scholars. From Thomas's writings, the pope found support for his temporal power in his dispute with the Emperor, and, probably even more importantly, for the defence of the

[24] Étienne Tempier, a bishop of Paris, issued a condemnation of over 200 propositions, including some from Thomas's works, in 1277. The same year Albert the Great arrived in Paris to defend Thomas's doctrine. The first steps taken by the General Chapters to defend Thomas were very likely a reaction to Tempier's act and other criticism of Thomas's doctrines. See Torrell 1993, 436–453.

[25] From here on, I will use the word 'book' rather freely to indicate the physical objects containing Thomas's writings. As my approach does not include traditional manuscript studies, questions concerning, for example, binding and whether the object was a compilation of several gatherings and different texts with a cover or not or just a single libellus, are not considered in this paper.

[26] MOPH 4, 38–40. See also Torrell 1993, 453.

[27] MOPH 4, 83–84. The order to own and observe Thomas's entire literary corpus was applied especially in those communities with a studium generale or convents with a master of theology.

orthodox faith and the Roman Church against heresy.[28] Impressively, surviving eye-witness records tell us how the pope gave public sermons in the streets of Avignon during the festivities anticipating Thomas's canonization. In one speech, John praised the Order of Preachers and Thomas, saying that Thomas had illuminated the Church more than anyone since the apostles and the first doctors.[29] In the official canonization bull *Redemptionem misit*, issued on July 1323, the pope gave detailed testimony to the holiness of Thomas's life, also praising more moderately his intellectual work.[30] In other sources John's interest in Thomas's texts is more explicitly described, and it appears that he sought to collect them for his library in the Avignon Palace.[31]

The letter of the University of Paris does not tell us whether Thomas's books were perceived purely as tools for teaching and learning or as something more besides, possibly as a symbol of Thomas's presence in the academic community. However, the acts of the Dominican Order give us a clearer picture of their value. As communal and individual property, his books were tools to teach and study, but they became more than utility objects: the Dominicans pronounced Thomas's works infallible and sacred in a similar manner to the Bible. The presence of theological and philosophical books in the Dominican convents was of axiomatic value, but Thomas's were regarded as an exceptionally important contribution to the Christian knowledge of God and Christ. As such, they were a part of the spiritual treasure of the convent and

[28] Torrell 1993, 321–324; Le Brun-Gouanvic 1996, 7–9; Räsänen 2017, 45–48.

[29] *Récit anonyme*, 514.

[30] *Redemptionem misit*, 523.

[31] Horst 2002, 6; Mandonnet 1923, 27–28; Torrell 1993, 466.

were kept well-guarded in chests.[32] From John XII's statement we can grasp the significance given to Thomas as one who belonged to the same exalted group as the apostles and Church fathers. By doing so, the Pope underlined Thomas's ability to guide the Church, which was being accused of having become corrupted, back to its untarnished origins, the age of the apostles. This image of Thomas as the successor of the apostles was actively used by later reformers.[33]

Representing the book of the golden margins and reform

After reading the acts of the General Chapter, we need not be surprised that Thomas holds the radiant book in his hands in Simone Martini's painting: the books of the Dominican master represent knowledge comparable to the Bible. If we left things here, however, one of Thomas's most common attributes would remain only partially explained. The discussion of the significance of a book in Thomas's hands, or in his lap in comparable pictures, must be considered in the cultural context in which the depiction was born. By examining different representations,

---

[32] It is easy to get acquainted with Thomas's vast production on the Internet site of Corpus Thomisticus: http://www.corpusthomisticum.org/iopera. html. Surviving manuscript copies of *Summa Theologiae* (over 600 according to Boyle) testify to the enthusiasm the work encountered among the Dominicans and laity in the Middle Ages. As Leonard Boyle reminds us, the parts of *Summa* circulated independently and they had their own identity. The best surviving – and the most popular – part seems to have been *Secunda secundae*, see Boyle 2000a, 85. Tommaso Kaeppeli has studied the Dominican libraries in Italy and managed to reconstruct parts of medieval collections. Thomas's texts seem to have been widely diffused as the Acts suggested to us: however, only two autographs are mentioned, see Kaeppeli 1966. Also in general on books as a part of memory and treasure of Church, see Palazzo 1997. On the definition of treasure in the medieval Church, see Cordez 2016, 19–46.

[33] Thomas was an important model in many respects to such Florentine reformers as Giovanni Dominici, Fra Angelico, and Antonino of Florence. On the relationship between the last and Thomas, see Howard 2013.

in the following pages I seek to understand both written and pictorial representations of books in hagiographical material.

William of Tocco's *Life* of Thomas, *Ystoria sancti Thome de Aquino* is often taken as a logical starting point when considering Thomas Aquinas's hagiographical image. It is true that William was already writing the *Ystoria* when Simone Martini's panel was ordered, but the panel was finished in 1320, whereas the *Ystoria* was completed only in 1323.[34] Although copies of early versions of the *Ystoria* presumably started to circulate among the Dominicans before the canonization, they are hardly likely to have been the source for the Dominicans of Pisa.[35] Besides this chronological problem, William does not represent Thomas so much as an author as a humble friar, often troubled by the Sacred Scripture, again making *Ystoria* an improbable model for Simone Martini.[36] In *Ystoria*, then, the image of Thomas as a writer and book-producer is subdued, although, as Agnes Dubreil-Arcin argues, the model of the scholar is detectable in William's text.[37]

To understand better the context of the book with the golden margins and its meaning, I propose that we should study other contemporary sources. The southern Italian oral tradition and Ptolemy of Lucca's *Historia ecclesiastica nova*, in which he gives a short *Life* of Thomas, are especially interesting. I start with an analysis of the oral tradition, which was recorded in writing for the first time by the papal inquisitors and notaries in Naples in 1319.[38] The second round of hearings of the

[34] William had presumably started to collect memories of Thomas even before the official canonization process began and later he was appointed as a pro-curator of the case: see esp. Torrell 1993, 466–469. The first stage of the work was presented to the pope in 1318, and the fourth and the last redaction was finished in 1323, see Le Brun-Gouanvic 1996, 16, 68–76. On the value of William's work to other hagiographical texts written in connection to Thomas's medieval cult, see Räsänen 2017, esp. p. 205.

[35] On the manuscript tradition of *Ystoria*, see Kaeppeli 1975, 166–167, and Le Brun-Gouanvic 1996, 61–80.

[36] In these situations, Thomas received visions, in which, for example, the apostles Peter and Paul helped him to explain difficult passages, see William of Tocco, *Ystoria sancti Thome de Aquino*, cap. 31.

[37] Dubreil-Arcin 2011, 82.

[38] *Processus canonizationis S. Thomae, Neapoli* (1319). See Räsänen 2017, passim.

witnesses to Thomas's life and post-mortem miracles was organized in Fossanova in 1321.[39]

When seeking counterparts for the representation of Thomas in Simone Martini's predella, one testimony stands out. In Naples in 1319, a Dominican friar, Anthony of Brescia, gave a testimony that Albert of Brescia, a famous Dominican theologian, had seen a vision in which St Augustine declared Thomas his equal in doctrinal purity but his better in the purity of flesh. In the vision there were two persons, one wearing the vestments of a bishop and another the Dominican habit. The latter had a crown and vestments ornamented with precious jewels, two halos and a great shining jewel on his chest. According to Albert, Augustine clarified the symbolism of the vision by saying that the precious jewels represented the numerous books that Thomas had written.[40]

If we compare the vision to Simone Martini's predella, we notice that Thomas does not carry the jewel on his chest, but both the chest and the whole central part of his body is covered by the shining book and golden rays. The radiant book possibly replaced the jewel on the chest and made visible the books mentioned in the vision. If we take a wider look at the predella, we notice that the saints are grouped in pairs; only the central part is divided into three, the theme of *Man of Sorrow* being at the centre and St Mary and St John the Apostle at the sides. To the right of St John the first pair of saints are St Thomas and St Augustine. The pair gives us good reason to suggest that the imposing vision of Albert of Brescia was the inspiration for the representation of the book in Simone Martini's predella. That the vision had a powerful effect is clear from the fact that Albert of Brescia's testimony appeared in *Ystoria* and other hagiographies without much editing.[41] Similarly, it became an impressive final part of the Matin lections of the liturgy for

---

[39] *Processus canonizationis S. Thomae, Fossanova* (1321). See Räsänen 2017, passim.

[40] *Processus canonizationis S. Thomae, Neapoli* (1319), cap. LXVI: "Qui lapides pretiosi libros multos et opera scripture sue que composuit significant."

[41] William of Tocco, *Ystoria sancti Thome de Aquino*, cap. XXII; Bernard Gui, *Legenda sancti Thomae Aquinatis*, cap. LI.

Thomas's *dies natalis* on 7 March and one of the themes of Dominican sermons for the same day.[42]

Joanna Cannon has recently studied the panel and interpreted the messages transmitted by the chorus of biblical saints together with two canonized Dominican saints, St Dominic and St Peter Martyr, and not yet canonized Thomas. Cannon's interpretation is fine and multilayered and she emphasizes the significance of the panel for the Dominican identity through several themes central to the vocation of the Order.[43] However, I would have expected the analysis of Thomas's vicinity to the *Man of Sorrow* to be more central, although she returns to the theme of the connection between Thomas and Christ's body when discussing the case of a lost panel of the Orvietan polyptych. In the case of the Orvietan polyptych, Cannon stresses Thomas's role in composing the Corpus Christi office in 1264 and the possibility that the Dominican art reflected the contemporary discussion of Thomas's composition before he was canonized.[44] Considering the early date of the production of the predella of Simone Martini, Thomas's presence and the golden margin book is understandable through the master's theology and texts, clearly highly esteemed among the well educated friars. However, in my view, Thomas's halo becomes understandable only through the *Man of Sorrow* and his interpretation of the Corpus Christi office and other Eucharistic writings.

Officially, the Dominicans started to promote Thomas's authorship of the Corpus Christi liturgy rather late: the first acts of the General Chapters on the matter were published in 1322, although the re-establishment of the feast started in 1318.[45] The earliest and most commonly surviving of the written sources on Thomas's role in writing

---

[42] The ninth lection for Thomas Aquinas's feast: see Räsänen 2017, appendix. On sermons, see for example Vincent Ferrer's cycle *de sanctis*. On the vision and its implications, see the interesting article of Hall 1985.

[43] Cannon 2013, 147–150.

[44] Cannon 2013, 150–152. On Thomas's role in composing Corpus Christi, there is a vast bibliography. A very accurate study on the theme of the Eucharist that covers far more than just Thomas's participation in reshaping the Corpus Christi liturgy is Rubin 1991.

[45] Räsänen 2016.

of the Office is Ptolemy of Lucca's *Historia ecclesiastica nova*, probably finished by 1316:

> [Thomas Aquinas] composed the Office of Corpus Christi at Urban's demand, which was the second that he had made at Urban's request. He did this completely, both including the readings for the whole office, for both day and night, as well as for the Mass, and for everything to be sung that day. If we look closely at the author's words in the History, almost all the figures from the Old Testament seem to be included in this Office, adapted in a splendid and unique style to the sacrament of the Eucharist.[46]

Other early hagiographical texts, including William's *Ystoria*, are more cursory on the matter. Ptolemy clearly considered the office important among Thomas's works. In general, Ptolemy, being a former student of Thomas Aquinas himself, concentrates on describing his master mostly from the perspective of his intellectual career, not forgetting to mention how he received heavenly help in certain situations. Ptolemy's confidence in Thomas's abilities was so great that he declared him supreme among modern teachers in every subject.[47] To emphasize Thomas's intellectual authority, Ptolemy gives a long list of titles written by Thomas, meant to be complete.

I propose that the interpretation of the golden margin book should be made in the context of promoting Thomas's activity in writing the Corpus Christi liturgy. The book's golden radiating rays represent the truth of Christ's body.[48] It truly materializes the incarnation of Christ on parchment.[49] Moreover, the book, together with the opening verse, "For

---

[46] Ptolemy of Lucca, *Historia ecclesiastica nova*, 566. Translation from Rubin 1991, 186.

[47] Ptolemy of Lucca, *Historia Ecclesiastica nova*, 589.

[48] A much later source from the beginning of the seventeenth century describes Thomas's corpse as radiating the divinity of the holy sacrament ("Corps Glorieux que – – rayonné de la Divinité de ce S. Sacramenta"). In this much earlier case, indeed, I would confirm that the radiating element is Christ's body. See Lavaur 1628, 20–21.

[49] On object, living material such as parchment and representation, see Baschet 2008, 25–64.

my mouth shall speak truth", seems to attach God's voice to Thomas's body. The opening verse is from the *Summa contra gentiles*, and not from the Corpus Christi liturgy or the Eucharist treatises as one might expect. Thomas had handled the Eucharistic theme abundantly in his writings, but the Corpus Christi was the only liturgy that was approved by the pope while Thomas was living. In a sense, that work was canonized before the canonization of Thomas himself.[50] In the predella, Thomas was placed on the right side of St Augustine, a figure of great importance to the Dominican Order. St Augustine had handled the Eucharist in his works and according to the Dominican tradition of the famous vision, he had declared Thomas's doctrine equal to his own. Both the vision and the predella suggest that by following Thomas's doctrine, it was possible to return to the original Church and the age of the apostles, Church Fathers and early martyrs, all of whom are represented in this art work. From the birth of their Order, the Dominicans had promoted themselves as the new apostles. By preaching, they corrected those who had chosen an erroneous path. Thus, the panel must be interpreted as a propagation of the Order and its future saint, who was a perfect follower of Christ – more perfect that St Augustine himself. The idea of Thomas as the follower of Christ and the one to lead Christians back to the purity of the early Church seems to have been dear to the later reformers. As Cyril Gerbron has noted, the radiant book in Thomas's hands again

[50] Interestingly, Joanna Cannon has proposed that Simone Martini also painted for the convent of Orvieto an altar panel with the representation of Thomas Aquinas slightly after the Pisa in 1320/21. If Cannon is correct, the lost panel would have presented Thomas as equally sized to other, officially (canonized) saints – which would have been exceptional, but not impossible. The commissioner of the panel was Trasmondo Monaldeschi, an admirer of Thomas's doctrine, and a person who was a very active promoter of Thomas's cult in the town. See Cannon 2013, 150 and Cannon 1982, 83, 87. It is worth noting that Thomas also wrote *Contra gentiles* in the Umbrian town. Locally in Orvieto, Thomas's authorship of the Corpus Christi liturgy was more strongly emphasized than in the Dominican Order in general or any-where else, see Räsänen 2016, and the forthcoming article A. I would stress that such an exceptional panel would have been possible to execute only in Orvieto, and the active, close contacts between the central Italian convents would have been in the background when establishing the very young cult of Thomas Aquinas in Pisa or elsewhere.

took a prominent role in the art of Fra Angelico.[51] Fra Angelico was a Dominican friar who gave his support to the famous reformers of the Order such as Giovanni Dominici and Antonino of Florence.

The radiant book draws the spectator's attention to it and highlights more the sacred nature of its texts than the man who holds it. The golden rays cover Thomas's breast; bathing it in gold just as they make the book golden. The depiction of the golden margin book emphasizes Thomas's works as treasures, something we saw already expressed in the Acts of the Order. Moreover, I would suggest that the image assimilates the book and Thomas, the assimilating element being the golden colour emerging from the text of the book. The book, as well as its author Thomas, were sanctified by the sacred scripture he put on the parchment by the guidance of God. Thus the predella image makes a strong case that Thomas should be canonized. Clearly, Thomas's books had an important doctrinal and affective role in the Dominican community from very early on.

Venerating Thomas's books

Only a couple of years after the above image was painted, the Dominicans of Pisa ordered a new altar panel in which Thomas was depicted following the same principal idea as in the earlier panel. This time, however, Thomas, canonized more or less at the same time when the panel was finished, was the protagonist of the work, again with his books. The panel is called the *Triumph of St Thomas Aquinas*. The painting was formerly attributed to Francesco Traini, but nowadays to Lippo Memmi. In this painting Thomas has not just one book, but five in his lap. It is worth noting that the five books are far from unique in this panel painting, but there are Christ himself with the closed book, Moses with the plaques of law (not exactly a book), St Paul, all four Evangelists with the books as well as Aristotle and Plato with books. All of them and their books are depicted as sources of wisdom for Thomas:

[51] Gerbron 2010, 230–237. See also his book 2016.

Image 2. *Triumph of St Thomas Aquinas*, Santa Caterina of Pisa.

golden rays descend from them to Thomas's head. There is one book upside down. It belongs to Averroes. The Andalusian polymath is in a position that symbolizes his inferiority: He is cast down by the strength of the saint's writings, specifically by Thomas' *Summa contra gentiles*, which is the most prominent book in the altar panel.[52] The painting glorifies Thomas, his wisdom shines, his words diffuse as rays and inspire the people at the bottom edge of the panel. Among them are religious folk and clergymen, even lay men of high status. In this panel Thomas is principally a mediator of knowledge to an educated audience.[53]

It seems to me that in this panel Thomas's books are depicted as objects to be venerated, perhaps even as relics. Below I will analyse the books as a physical extension of Thomas's mind and body and as the activation of his presence through his texts. The Memmi panel shows in greater detail than the panel discussed above why Thomas' scripture had to be taken as sacred: Thomas's books were a synthesis of divine annunciation and learned knowledge of the ancient philosophers and earlier Christian authors. This depiction contrasts strongly with the 'official' hagiography, William of Tocco's *Ystoria*, presented above. William was particularly careful to show Thomas's writings as a product of divine guidance, and in this sense unique.[54] In the Memmi panel, the books on Thomas's lap are emphatically his works and they transmit the essence and truth of God and his apostles. Bernard Gui, a famous inquisitor, wrote a new *Life* of Thomas Aquinas a couple of years after the canonization and realization of the Memmi panel. He was more interested in Thomas's writings than William. Bernard proclaims,

---

[52] Cannon 2013, 150. The way in which Averroes is depicted below Thomas's feet is probably also commenting on the theory of one shared intellect forcefully opposed by Thomas Aquinas, the theme of which was still under a lively discussion in the beginning of the fourteenth century.

[53] The panel is still in the custody of its original community, the Dominicans of Santa Caterina of Pisa. On the basic information and detailed interpretation of the altar panel, see Polzer 1993.

[54] According to William, Thomas also received a reward for his faithfulness as a follower when the crucifix speaks: "Thomas, you have written well of me, what would you have from me for your reward?" Thomas answered: "Lord, nothing else but you." Following this vision Thomas wrote several texts: these are the third part of *Summa theologiae*, on Christ's Passion, Resurrection and the sacrament of the Eucharist. On another occasion, a Christ figure appeared and spoke of Thomas's notes on the Eucharist. This time, the assurance was more specific: "You have written well of the sacrament of my body." See William of Tocco, *Ystoria sancti Thome de Aquino*, cc. 34 and 52. Colledge 1974, 23.

among other things, that "This is not the place to describe at length the errors which the razor edge of Thomas's mind has cut off at their root; enough to say that the errors and follies of unbelievers have never, to this day, met with so terrible an adversary as the author of the *Summa contra Gentiles*."[55] With this sentence, Bernard seems to articulate the same as the Memmi panel, in which Thomas is depicted sitting inside a round form with a noteworthy resemblance to the iconography of *Maiestas Domini*, referring to Christ's task as lawgiver or judge. The impression of *Maiestas Domini* becomes stronger when one reads the beginning of *Genesis* from another book on Thomas's lap "In the beginning God created the heaven and the earth. And the earth was without form, and void", and from the third book "Beholding the contents of the old and new Law by careful study we…".[56] The people below Thomas receive his doctrine, represented as rays coming from his books. Among the rays are written sentences "Teacher of the Gentiles in faith and verity" and "Here he found the entire way of discipline".[57] The panel conveys strongly the idea of the beginning of a new era for the Christian people under the rule, law and guidance of St Thomas.

The books in the Memmi panel appear as venerated objects. They are depicted individually with their own independent characters, which makes it possible to recognise them easily, even to read them without difficulty as their open pages are turned towards the spectator. The composition gives an idea of an altar table on which the books are piled. The most central is *Summa contra Gentiles*, which radiates golden light. Below the people admire and honour Thomas with his books, as one can see from their gazes and gestures. Both Polzer and Cannon have read later *Annales* of the convent of Pisa and they affirm that an altar dedicated to Thomas as well as the Memmi panel were activating a very lively cult at the Dominican convent. According to Cannon, the panel was in the area which was accessible only to the

---

[55] The translation from Foster 1959, 35.

[56] Transliterations of the texts from the book-images are from Polzer 1993, 38–39. Translations KJB.

[57] *Doctor gentium in fide et veritate* and *Hic adinvenit omnem viam discipline*. Transliterations are from Polzer 1993, 39. The first sentence is from the Epistle of Paul to Timothy 2,7, but the source of the second was unknown to Polzer.

friars, but despite this it seems to have been the object through which the laity prayed for miracles. Cannon argues persuasively that the lay people knew the image well enough to venerate it and donate many wax figures to it as *Annales* reports.[58] When one takes into consideration the way in which the books on Thomas's lap are depicted and how the people venerate them in the painting, it seems very probable that in Pisa Thomas's presence was emphasized with the texts he had written. The books were likely used to promote his saintly cult just as body part relics did in other places.

In fact, there is other surviving written evidence of the devotional uses of Thomas's texts; especially interesting is a legend written after the translation of Thomas's relics to Toulouse. It explains that the Dominican Master Elias Raymundus, who did not yet have the rights to Thomas's body, ordered that every week a mass should be sung to Thomas and principal lectors of the Dominican convents had to read *Epistolas* of Peter and Paul and bachelors *Summa contra gentiles*.[59] I propose that the mass and reading of Thomas's writings aloud functioned as common prayers to transfer the relics into Dominican possession. In medieval understanding when the saint was present, it was hoped that he or she would mediate the supplicant's prayers to God. Reading the texts written by Thomas activated his presence and power in the same way that bodily relics did when a supplicant had them next to him/her.[60]

If the Memmi panel strongly suggests that Thomas's books had achieved a relic-like status in rituals, the composition in the Carafa Chapel in Santa Maria sopra Minerva, the Dominican church in Rome, makes this status, in my view, absolutely clear. First, there are several books depicted in the paintings of the Chapel commissioned by Cardinal Oliviero Carafa in 1488.[61] One of the themes of the paintings is the *Triumph of St Thomas*, which had become quite common in late

---

[58] Polzer 1993; Cannon 2013, 150.

[59] Toulouse, MS 610, p. 13.

[60] On the Office of Thomas dies natalis as an activation process when the Dominicans did not possess the Saint's body, see Räsänen 2017.

[61] The painter was famous Filippino Lippi whose role as well as other aspects of the decoration has been abundantly studied. For further reading, and especially regarding Thomas's image in Lippi's paintings, see Norman 1993.

medieval Italian art after the Memmi panel.[62] However, according to
Polzer, the overall message of the composition highlights Thomas's role
as a mediator of God's truth and interpreter of sacred and classical texts
more than the Memmi panel.[63] In Pisa Thomas's figure resembles *Maiestas
Domini*, and in Rome he also sits on the cathedra, or throne, but there he
is depicted in the same way and more or less in the same perspective as
others around him. He has a book in his hand, which says, "I will destroy
the wisdom of the wise", referring to the false wisdom of malice.[64] The
personification of theology points to the lunette of a building, partly a
chapel or shrine, where one can see an open book located in the tondo.
At the centre of the lunette of the chapel-like construction, the book in
the tondo is in the position (the apse) where the *Maiestas Domini* usually
was in medieval Italy. The book in the tondo is *Summa contra gentiles*, as
shown again by the words we can see.[65] The image in Rome, like the two
images discussed above, emphasizes the nature of Thomas's book as the
word of God and even an embodiment of God. Placed high in the tondo
in the lunette, in the place often reserved for representations of God,
Christ and his mother, the book has a special meaning. It can be seen as
a symbol of the Holy Church. In a sense the representation of the book
was comparable to the *Maiestas Domini* theme, which provided the link
between Thomas and the very essence of God already noticeable in the
Memmi panel in Pisa. In sum, in Renaissance Rome Thomas's book
was elevated to the position previously occupied only by biblical figures,
Church Fathers and early martyrs.[66] The book in the tondo (and the
very similar-looking book in his hand) represents Thomas himself, the
presence of his sainthood and the wisdom in his texts. The book is the
embodiment of Thomas, the object of veneration, even of the cult.

It was probably in Renaissance Rome that Thomas's book became
an object of open veneration and consequently understood as the relic

[62] For a good general analysis of the context and message of this particular
fresco, see Geiger 1982.
[63] Polzer 1993.
[64] *Sapientiam sapientium perdam*, I Corinthians 1,19. See Polzer 1993.
[65] Polzer 1993, 50.
[66] On Thomas's cult in general in Renaissance Rome, see O'Malley 1974 and
1981.

that most fully represented him. However, if we read Williams's *Ystoria* carefully we can recognize that it did attribute some kind of relic nature to Thomas's book. At one point William describes how the saint's hand transmitted saintly wisdom to the sacred book and how the hand remained worthy to write numerous works for the Christians with texts that led them to divine knowledge: "The hand which with the finger of intelligence opened the book in a spiritual way to the one who sat to the right of the throne."[67] Interestingly, the passage links the book and its text to Thomas's hand, which was the only body-part relic in Dominican possession at the time when the text was written.[68] Indeed, this is one of the rare passages in which William places emphasis on Thomas's activity as a writer, which gave holiness to Thomas's body. His explanation of why Thomas's book should have been considered a relic is, it appears, material: because the letters and words were a continuation of his hand and fingers, and because his saintly hand transmitted the power of God to the parchment.[69] The text echoes medieval views that saints' belongings and all material items connected to a saint's body, even after death, were considered representative relics. In fact, *Ystoria* gives us good reason to believe that Thomas's texts, at least in those cases when they were believed to have been written by the saint himself, were

---

[67] William of Tocco, *Ystoria sancti Thome de Aquino*, cap. 70: "illum librum in spiritu digito intellectus aperuit quem de dextera sedentis in throno."

[68] The hand-relic was first given to Thomas's sister Teodora, the Countess of Sanseverino, in 1288 and it was later relocated to the Dominican convent of Salerno where it has since remained. See more in Räsänen 2017, 216–217.

[69] William was not the only one who was interested in the relic nature of Thomas's hand. Later, for example, a famous reformer, Antoninus of Florence (1389–1459), visited the hand-relic in Naples and described its miraculous appearance. See an early testimony on the hand's special value from *Processus canonizationis S. Thomae, Neapoli* (1319), XLVI and Antonino de Florencia, *Tertia pars historiarum* CXCIIIv. On St Thomas as the model for Antoninus, the famous reformer of Renaissance Florence, see Cornelison 2012, 22.

perceived and used as relics. [70] Possibly the use of books as relics began at the same time when the body-parts acquired their official status as relics, that is, from the day of canonization.

I would argue that William emphasized Thomas's hand because it was one of the rare body-part relics in the public possession of the Dominicans, and his writings because they were written by the very same hand. Equating the hand-arm-relic with the written text may thus have resulted from the situation when William wrote, when the Dominicans did not possess Thomas's corpse or other significant bone relics. So they seem to have started to venerate and use Thomas's books and parts of books as they normally used bodily relics. They had plenty of Thomas's books: a special category of the text-relics, Thomas's autographs, were circulating in some numbers, for example in southern Italy.[71] A further factor that enabled Thomas's books to achieve a status equal to that of

---

[70] A similar idea of the veneration of a book emerges from Alison Knowles Frazier's book, *Possible Lives*. Frazier illustrates a case in Milan some decades before the painting project in the Carafa Chapel started. Cardinal Brada da Castiglione was searching for material in relation to the reunification of the eastern and western churches in the library of St Thecla. He found a manuscript which was allegedly an autograph of St Ambrose, the Church Father and patron saint of the city. Milanese people got wind of the cardinal's departure from the city and his intention to bring the manuscript with him. The people rose up and prevented the theft of the manuscript; moreover, according to a contemporary eye-witness, they came close to killing the cardinal because they suspected that he had mutilated the manuscript by splitting it into pieces and was prepared to steal some of the bodily relics of Ambrose as well. Frazier indicates the several ways in which the contemporary perception of the book equated with the perception of relics in the minds of most people, including the most educated, in the fifteenth century. The book, together with St Ambrose's bodily remains, was a vital part of their identity and cultural heritage in Milan and by their act they defended the Milanese way of living and self-understanding. See Frazier 2005, 1–7.

[71] Some surviving sources give an idea that the places where Thomas had been working possessed some of his autographical writings and they may have been donated by them to other places. One example is mentioned in the article of Kaeppeli, in which he describes how one autograph manuscript was transported from Naples to Bergamo by two Dominican friars in 1354. The manuscript was conserved in the Dominican Library of Bergamo until the end of the 18th century, and then moved to the Vatican Library (nowadays Vat. lat. 9850), see Kaeppeli 1966. See also Taurisano 1924.

the body parts as relics may be that the books achieved a prominent role in the Dominican art of reform in medieval and Early Modern Italy. One of the most impressive examples of art works that praise Thomas's books and reform is in the Carafa Chapel in Rome, as described above. The reform spirit and power of the books was perceivable not only from pictorial representations but three-dimensional objects, the books and their fragments as we will see in the next section.

The cult of autograph books in Naples, Salerno and Aversa

Thomas's cult increased in popularity during the fifteenth century. The popularity seems to have grown especially in connection with the Church reforms but also in lay piety.[72] Thomas's fame as a reformer and warrior against heretics were the most likely reason for the flourishing of his relic cults, including those of both body-parts and book-relics in Early Modern Europe. Indeed, in Naples Thomas was elevated to take a place among the old saintly protectors of the town in 1605. His promotion was due to his orthodox doctrine, clearly defined by Pope Clement VIII (1592–1605). The Pope reminded people of the divine nature of Thomas's scripts and affirmed that with the help of the prayers of the new protector, powerful and merciful God would make all the bad things good and satisfying.[73] Thomas's ability to combat heresy was considered important in the turbulent period when protestant movements were sweeping the Catholic cities. The same phenomenon, Thomas's newly recognized power and his elevation to the ranks of the saintly protectors, is identifiable in several European towns at the same time.[74] In addition to the image of the active soldier of Christ, Thomas

---

[72] Räsänen, forthcoming article A.

[73] Ancient saints were Ianuarius, Athanasius, Asprenus, Agrippinus, Severus, Eusebius and Anellus. The bull of Pope Clement VIII on elevation is copied in the Acts of the General Order of Preachers, see MOPH 11, 187–188.

[74] For example, according to a Toulousan advocate, Thomas's glorious body prevented heresy from entering the city and threatening the Holy Sacrament. Thomas's Eucharistic writings were believed to enforce his power against heresies, see Lavaur 1628.

retained his meditative side. In his orthodox faith, he was the perfect model of how to turn to God's help in prayer and contemplation.

Thomas's presence among the Patron Saints of Naples took material form in his arm relic, previously lodged at the Dominican convent of San Domenico, but now translated in a silver casket to the high altar of the city Cathedral.[75] The translation took place on 20 January 1605, and in connection with the act Pope Clement emphasized the power of the arm against heresy.[76] The capacity of the arm to illustrate the sacred scripture and overthrow heresy had been a feature of William's and Bernard's *Vitae*, as noted above. In Naples, the precious arm-relic received a new feast day: Pope Paul V (1605–1621) gave detailed orders for its annual celebrations on 19 January. The festivities, as Paul promised, would be a part of the compensation for Thomas's protection against pestilence, famine, war and other disasters.[77]

When the arm relic was translated to the cathedral of Naples, it appears that the Dominican friars kept a part of it for themselves. Surprisingly, this piece of the arm-relic remains in the background, almost as if it no longer existed, when studying the inventories and other sources from Early Modern Naples. It is the relic-book which takes a prominent role. Liber A at the Dominican General Archives in Rome gives a schematic list of statues that contain a relic at the sacristy of the convent of the Dominicans and among them is a statue representing

---

[75] This arm-relic arrived in Naples from Toulouse in 1372. The relic donation seems to have been some kind of compensation to the Neapolitan friars, who had to give up their desire to have Thomas's body in the custody of the local convent. See Douais 1903 for the document of the relic donation in 1372, and Räsänen 2017 on the early history of Thomas's relics (ca. 1274–1372).

[76] AASS, Martii I, 741: "partem dexteri ejus brachii, quo scribente profligavit haereses et sacras litteras illustravit." MOPH 11, 189.

[77] The bull is edited in the Acts of the General Order of Preachers, see MOPH 11, pp. 192–193. Besides the arm relic in Naples, in Salerno the hand was forcefully promoted among the laity in the seventeenth century as part of the cult of the body-part relic. According to Théry 1931c, 319, on 22 April 1662, Gonzales visited Salerno where he "retira du reliquaire où elle était enfermée la main de s. Thomas, pour la faire vénéreraux magistrats de Salerne, et afin commémorer ce pieux souvenir, institua une fête speciale."

St Thomas which includes a piece of his arm bone.[78] The same document describes in a much more detailed manner Thomas's former cell, which was transformed into a chapel and where the mass was celebrated. There were several reliquaries in the chapel, one being a large and well executed silver and gilded copper ostensory. According to the description, it contained a book written in St Thomas's own hand.[79] Nowadays this manuscript, once in the ostensory, is kept among the other manuscripts from the Dominican convent at the National Library of Naples (MS I. B. 54). The famous book is Thomas's copy on commentaries of Albert the Great on the works of pseudo-Dionysis.[80]

One of the earliest mentions of the cult of Thomas's book-relic in Naples comes from the editor of the collection of saints' lives, *Acta sanctorum*, tome I of March, which was printed in 1668. The Bollandist Daniel Papebroch describes how he himself participated in Thomas's feast day festivities and venerated his relics some years earlier:

> Moreover, there is a holy altar in the cell of Saint Thomas (transformed as a chapel). On the altar lies a book on Dionysus's celestial hierarchy

[78] AGOP, XIV, Liber A pars II, f. 535r: "Di più vi sono diverse statue famosissime – – altra di S. Tommaso d'Aquino, dove si conserva il suo braccio, di palmi." See also Koudelka 1968.

[79] AGOP, XIV, Lib. A pars II, f. 412v: "il volume scritto di proprio pugno da S. Tomaso sopra il trattato che fas[?] Dionisio de Coelesti Hierarchia, e tutto questo è di argento, e rame indorato."

[80] We know only a little about the early history of the manuscript. It was copied by Thomas himself when he was Albert's student in the years 1245–1252. The manuscript belonged to the Dominican house of San Domenico Maggiore in Naples from Thomas' own days there. The hypothesis is that Thomas carried the manuscript to his home convent and left it there when he himself travelled around Europe. When the convent was suspended, the manuscript was transported with the rest of the convent's library to the Biblioteca nazionale at the beginning of the nineteenth century. One of the first mentions is by Caracciolo from his Napoli Sacra (1624), in which he describes San Domenico Maggiore: "In questo famoso tempio se serba il braccio dell'Angelico Dottor San Tomaso... In oltre vedesi un libro scritto dal detto Santo sopra san Dionigi De Coelesti Hierarchia." For a detailed description of the manuscript, see Théry 1931b, 15–54. On the history of the ms., see Boyle 2000b, 123 and more generally on the history of Dominican manuscripts in Naples, Kaeppeli 1966, 30–53.

which Thomas has written by his own hand. In the year of 1661 in Naples, on Thomas' feast day [on 7 March], we have honored each of these monuments.[81]

According to Papebroch, the focus of the friars' veneration was Thomas's autograph manuscript and the cell itself. For a religious and scholarly inclined person, the veneration of the place where Thomas studied and wrote some of his most famous texts seems natural, as does devotion to the book.

Interestingly, it was not only Dominicans and scholars who were attracted by Thomas's manuscript in Naples. G. Théry, who has studied Thomas's Neapolitan autograph, has remarked that several seventeenth-century travel guides described Thomas's cell as a place worth visiting where one could see Thomas Aquinas's book.[82] Théry also refers to other interesting early modern sources from the seventeenth to early nineteenth centuries and cites them frequently. According to these sources, Thomas's book relic was continuously venerated in his chapel. An eighteenth-century source, for example, describes the festivities of Thomas's feast day on 7 March, saying that the book in the ostensory was displayed at the altar, candles illuminated it and the Neapolitans came to venerate it.[83] According to Vincenzo Maria Perrotta and his *Descrizione storica della Chiesa e del monistero di s. Domenico Maggiore di Napoli*, printed in 1828, the mass was celebrated in the chapel every day, but Thomas's feast day was an exceptional event: many foreign priests arrived in the city to visit and venerate Thomas's cell, and because of the pilgrims "the famous manuscript of Saint Thomas was unveiled for the veneration of the faithful".[84] Théry's citation suggests that the relic-book

---

[81] AASS, Martii I, 739. "Est praeterea cella S. Thomae piissimum sacellum commutate ubi et liber supra Dionysium de coelesti hierarchia, propria S. Thomae manu conscriptus, habitus. Nos ipsi anno MDCLXI Neapoli in festo S. Thomae existentes, singula ista monumenta venerati sumus."

[82] Théry 1931b, 18–19. According to the guides, numerous Neapolitans visited Thomas's chapel on his feast day.

[83] Théry 1931b, 22.

[84] Perrotta 1828, 136: "esponevasi alla venerazion de' fedeli il celebre manoscritto di s. Tommaso."

was no longer kept on the altar of the chapel but moved to a safer place and presented to the faithful only on special occasions.

Another illustrative example comes from Aversa, not far from Naples. A source describes how the Dominican convent of the town conserved

> a book with the second volume of the sentences written by Thomas' own hand as a precious relic. On 7 March [1720], on the day which was dedicated to angelic doctor Thomas Aquinas, a feast especially for the book is organized in the Dominican church.[85]

Based on this record, all the students of the town arrived in a procession to listen to the divine office and the sermon in the saint's honour. They also offered a big white candle as a gift to the saint.[86] Interestingly, the above quotation emphasizes that the liturgical feast was given explicitly for the book, which would therefore have been the central object of veneration on that day.

Reading Théry's words, it is difficult to say whether the first Neapolitan guide books are referring to Thomas's autograph more as a curiosity object than as a relic for a larger audience. Step by step, the book seems to have become an important relic of lay devotion. The practices of veneration of the book-relics are similar to those for the saintly bones, which certainly was a good strategy to emphasize the nature of the books to anyone who was not yet aware of their relic value. Seemingly, Thomas's book had become popular and famous, and possibly to emphasize its preciousness it was moved from the altar to a

---

[85] AGOP, Liber GGG, pars II, f. 682v–683r: "In questo medesimo luogo conservasi anco[ra] come preziosa reliquia un libro, che contiene l'esposizione sopra il secondo libro delle Sentenze, scritto di propria mano del nostro Angelico Dottore S. Tomaso di Aquino, per il quale libro li 7 marzo, giorno dedicato al santo, si fa in questa chiesa, particolar festa."

[86] AGOP, Liber GGG, pars II, f. 682v–683r. In his article in 1931c, 326, footnote, Théry adds that the manuscript in question was the third part of Thomas's *Sentences*. When Théry wrote his text the manuscript was conserved in the Vatican Library, nro. 9851. In addition, Kaeppeli gives a shelfmark Vat. lat. 9851: see Kaeppeli 1966, 9. According to Uccelli, the manuscript was a gift from Charles d'Anjou to the convent of Aversa.

safer place. If this removal was done, its purpose was also very likely to protect the manuscript from relic thieves and other collectors.

There are examples of the autographs being broken up to increase the number of relics, just as it happened with saints' corpses. Théry read this as a sign that Thomas's autographs had the same success as the body-part relics, to the point that there were fears of Thomas's books being destroyed completely. Leonard Boyle has stated that the autograph manuscript at San Domenico had been plundered for souvenirs and relics from the sixteenth century onwards. Another example of a book which was split up to the point of being lost is in the Museo del Duomo of Salerno.[87] At the beginning of the 1930s, at the time when Théry studied the manuscript, it was conserved in one side chapel of San Tommaso d'Aquino, the Salernitan Dominican church. In the Chapel, it was inside the altar, behind bars and inside a reliquary.[88] The manuscript consisted of 65 folios, and according to Théry, the division had happened before 1662, when a general vicar Antonio Gonzales foliated it.[89] In any case, in 1693 the Dominican Master General ordered that this and other reputed authographs in the area of Naples be shown respect: "by no pretext or argument shall any folios or parts of folios from the manuscripts be taken away."[90] The order's main purpose was probably to conserve the manuscripts as complete as possible, but it may also have been intended to prevent a dubious practice that sometimes led to magical uses of parchment pieces as amulets.[91]

Ecclesiastics in Catholic areas apparently saw Protestant heresy as the biggest threat to Early Modern people. They forcibly promoted the cult of Thomas Aquinas, who was presented as the greatest opponent of

---

[87] Boyle 2000b, 124.

[88] Théry 1931c, 311.

[89] Théry 1931c, 312, 318, 319.

[90] "ne quocumque praetextu aut ratione folia, aut folium quodlibet, aut partes folii ex iisdem manuscriptis aut extrahant aut extrahere permittant". Théry 1931c, 335, seems to think that the manuscript at the San Tommaso of Salerno was not in fact Thomas's autograph, but that the Dominican master had just added single words here and there. It is also important to remember that in Milan people rioted when they thought the cardinal had stolen and ripped up St Ambrose's autograph, see the footnote 70.

[91] On this practice, see Skemer 2006.

all kinds of heretical ideas.[92] In southern Italy, where there were some body-part relics, all pieces from different parts of Thomas's arms and hands, his autographs became very important as they were seen as the continuation of the part of the body that acted against heresy. The above description of religious and lay veneration of Thomas's book in his chapel in San Domenico Maggiore closely resembled the descriptions of the festivities organized to celebrate Thomas's body part relics. It is plausible that both religious and lay people perceived Thomas's manuscripts as a very functional (and material, as they were a physical embodiment of God's truth) remedy for the threat posed by heretics. Although the laity fervently venerated Thomas's autographed texts, some practices, like for example the translation of the relic-arm in the main church of Naples or the festivities organized by the governors of Salerno for the local arm-relic, hint that the bones remained the main focus of lay piety. At the same time, the sources strongly indicate that the Dominican friars of southern Italy were even more orientated to veneration of the book-relics than Thomas's bones. It would be interesting, if difficult, to study whether the pieces cut from Thomas autographs were used especially as portable and personal relics to protect the owner from sins of heresy.[93] I presume that in the sixteenth and seventeenth centuries Thomas's writings were read aloud publicly in churches everywhere in the Catholic realms to promote not only his cult but the (counter-) Reformation. This is a topic that would be interesting to explore further in the future.

---

[92] Thomas's image as the persistent adversary of heretics seems to have been one reason why he was selected as the Protector of the confraternity of the book printers and binders in Rome in 1600. The confraternity was founded to control the profession and book circulation. Obviously, the purpose of the supervision was to prevent the spread of the seditious printed material of the Protestants, see *Statuti* 1674.

[93] In the case of St Francis's autograph, brother Leon (the thirteenth century) is said to have carried the manuscript with him all the time. In the fifteenth century, Abbess Eustochia of Messina was buried with the books that allegedly belonged to St Claire. The book was presumably used for her protection in death as well in life. See Bertrand 2006, 373–374. Talismanic uses of all types of relics were, and still are, common.

Conclusion

The books as material objects or their representations in art were perceived as Thomas's embodiment and presence in those places where they were presented. These books or pieces of parchment were understood as holy objects, relics, as they were an extension of Thomas's sacred right arm and the fruit of the writer's achievement as a voice of God and his holies. It seems that the books were more than just contact relics, being regarded as continuations of the body, just like body part relics. They were also an incarnation of Christ, interpreted by Thomas. Thomas was a special author as he had close contact to his subject, that is Christ; and the subject himself had approved some of Thomas's texts. In his closeness, Thomas belonged in the same reality as Christ and his followers, the apostles. From this perspective, he was very natural choice for the early reformers to emphasize as a model for all Christians.

My contention is that Thomas's autographs were used alongside his body-part relics and in a similar way in a much earlier period and on a larger scale in observant reform than we can demonstrate with the surviving sources. I have managed to find solid evidence of this kind of practice only from the post-medieval period and in connection with the Catholic reformation. In the seventeenth century Thomas's autographs appear to have a prominent position among the other relics in the area of Naples. There are presumably many reasons for the success of the book relics. From the viewpoint of the ongoing Church reform, the fact that the books contained doctrinally solid material probably helped to sustain the reform effectively. The books described the ideal world, the world that the reform was intended to realise. In addition, the widespread criticism of the saints and their relics by protestant movements was a serious challenge to the Catholic party. In this situation, books that were approved as genuinely written by a saint who had indisputably been flesh and blood, and who could not be represented as a remote and imagined personification from ancient times, and who was a relatively respected master even among the Catholics' adversaries, were perceived as the perfect relics.

Bibliography

Archival and manuscript sources

Rome, Archivio Generale dell'Ordine dei Predicatori (AGOP), XIV
    Liber A, pars I
    Liber GGG, pars II
Toulouse, Bibliothèque municipale
    MS 610

Printed sources

Acta Sanctorum (AASS), Martii I. Victor Palme, Paris and Rome 1865.

Antonino de Florencia: *Tertia pars historiarum domini Antonini archipresulis flore[n]tini [...]*. Iacobi Myt, Lyon 1527.

Bernard Gui: *Legenda sancti Thomae Aquinatis: Thomae Aquinatis vitae fonts praecipuae*. Ed. Angelico Ferrua O.P.. Edizioni domenicani, Alba 1968, 129–195.

Douais, S.G. Mgr.: *Les reliques de Saint Thomas d'Aquin: Textes originaux*. Librairie Vve CH. Poussielgue, Paris 1903.

Foster, Kenelm: *The Life of Saint Thomas Aquinas: Bibliographical Documents*. Longmans, London 1959.

Laurent, Marie-Hyacinthe (ed.): *Documenta*. Fontes Vitae S. Thomae Aquinatis, VI. *Revue Thomiste* 1937.

Lavaur M. J.: *Don du Corps de S. Thomas d'Aquin & sa Translation à la Ville de Tolose*. Traduit de latin en francois par M. J. Lavaur avocat Tolosain. A Tolose Chez I. Boude et N. D'Estey. Prés le college de Foix 1628.

Monumenta Ordinis fratrum Praedicatorum Historica (MOPH). Istituto Storico Domenicano (Rome) & Digitale Bibliothek Spezial.

Processus canonizationis S. Thomae, Fossanova (1321). Fontes Vitae S. Thomae Aquinatis, 5. Ed. Marie-Hyacinthe Laurent, *Revue Thomiste*, 1911, 409–510.

Processus canonizationis S. Thomae, Neapoli (1319). Fontes Vitae S. Thomae Aquinatis, 4. Ed. Marie-Hyacinthe Laurent, *Revue Thomiste* 1911, 265–407.

Ptolemy of Lucca: *Historia ecclesiastica nova*. Ed. Ottavio Clavuot, MGH SS, 39. Hahnsche Buchhandlung, Hannover 2009.

Récit anonyme. Fontes Vitae S. Thomae Aquinatis, 5. Ed. Marie-Hyacinthe Laurent. *Revue Thomiste* [1911].

Redemptionem misit, Bulle de canonisation de saint Thomas d'Aquin, Avignon, 18 Juillet 1323. Fontes Vitae S. Thomae Aquinatis, 5. Ed. Marie-Hyacinthe Laurent, *Revue Thomiste* [1911], 519–530.

Statuti della venerab. compagnia et vniversità de' librari di Roma sotto l'invocatione de S. Tomaso d'Aquino [...]. Stamperia di Giuseppe Coruo e Bartolomeo Lupardi, Rome 1674.

William of Tocco: *Ystoria sancti Thome de Aquino de Guillaume de Tocco*. Ed. Claire Le Brun-Gouanvic. Pontifical Institute of Mediaeval Studies, Toronto 1996.

Research literature

Baschet, Jérôme: *L'iconographie médiévale*. Paris 2008.

Belting, Hans: *Likeness and Presence: A History of the Image before the Era of Art*. Transl. Edmund Jephcott. University of Chicago Press, Chicago 1996.

Bertrand, Paul: Authentiques de reliques: authentiques ou reliques? *Le Moyen Age* 112.2/2006, 363–374. DOI 10.3917/rma.122.0363

Boyle, Leonard E., O.P.: The Setting of the "Summa theologiae" of Saint Thomas. *Facing History: A Different Thomas Aquinas*. With an Introduction by Jean-Pierre Torrell O.P.. Féderation international des instituts d'études médiévales, Louvain-la-Neuve 2000a. [First published in The Etienne Gilson Series 5. Pontifical Institute of Mediaeval Studies, Toronto 1982]

Boyle, Leonard E., O.P.: *Facing History: A Different Thomas Aquinas*. With an Introduction by Jean-Pierre Torrell O.P.. Féderation international des instituts d'études médiévales, Louvain-la-Neuve 2000b. [First published in *Littera, sensus, sententia: Studi in onore del Prof. Clemente J. Vansteenkiste O.P.*. Ed. Abelardo Lobato. Studia Universitatis S. Thomae in Urbe, 33. Massimo, Milan 1991, 117–134]

Boureau, Alain: Franciscan Piety and Voracity: Uses and Strategems in the Hagiographic Pamphlet. *The Culture of Print: Power and the Uses of Print in Early Modern Europe*. Ed. Roger Chartier. Princeton University Press, Princeton 1989, 15–58.

Cannon, Joanna: Simone Martini, the Dominicans and the Early Sienese Polyptych. *Journal of the Warburg and Courtauld Institutes* 45/1982, 69–93.

Cannon, Joanna: *Religious Poverty, Visual Riches: Art in the Dominican Churches of Central Italy in the Thirteenth and Fourteenth Centuries*. Yale University Press, New Haven CT and London 2013.

Carrasco, Magdalena: Sanctity and Experience in Pictorial Hagiography: Two Illustrated Lives of Saints from Romanesque France. *Images of Sainthood in Medieval Europe*. Ed. Renate Blumenfeld-Kosinski and Timea Szell. Cornell University Press, Ithaca 1991, 33–66.

Cazelles, Brigitte: Introduction. *Images of Sainthood in Medieval Europe*. Ed. Renate Blumenfeld-Kosinski and Timea Szell. Cornell University Press, Ithaca 1991, 1–17.

Chenu, Marie-Dominique: *Introduction a l'étude de Saint Thomas d'Aquin*. Institut d'études médiévales, Montréal and Paris 1993 (orig. 1950).

Colledge, Edmund: The Legend of St Thomas Aquinas. *St Thomas Aquinas 1274–1974: Commemorative Studies*, 1. Pontifical Institute of Mediaeval Studies, Toronto 1974, 13–28.

Cordez, Philippe: *Trésor, mémoire, merveilles: Les objects des églises au Moyen Âge*. L'histoire et ses représenatations, 11. Éditions de l'École des hautes études en sciences sociales, Paris 2016.

Cornelison, Sally J.: *Art and the Relic Cult of St Antoninus in Renaissance Florence*. Ashgate, Farnham and Burlington 2012.

Dillenberger, John: *Images and Relics: Theological Perceptions and Visual Images in Sixteenth-Century Europe*. Oxford University Press, New York and Oxford 1999.

Dubreil-Arcin, Agnes: *Vies de saints, légendes de soi: l'écriture hagiographique dominicaine jusqu'au Speculum sanctorale de Bernard Gui (1331)*. Brepols, Turnhout 2011.

Frazier, Alison Knowles: *Possible Lives: Authors and Saints in Renaissance Italy*. Columbia University Press, New York 2005.

Geiger, Gail L.: Filippino Lippi's Triumph of Saint Thomas Aquinas. *Rome in the Reneissance: The City and the Myth*. Medieval and Renaissance Texts and Studies. Center for Medieval & Early Renaissance Studies, Binghamton, N.Y. 1982, 223–236.

Gerbron, Cyril: Des images comme miroirs pour l'observance dominicaine en Toscane (1420–1450). *Mélanges de l'École française de Rome – Moyen Âge* 122.1/2010, 211–238.

Gerbron, Cyril: *Fra Angelico: Liturgie et mémoire*. Études Renaisantes, 18. Brepols, Turnhout 2016.

Hall, Edwin: "Aureola super Auream": Crowns and related symbols of Special Distinction for Saints in Late Gothic and Renaissance Iconography. *Art bulletin* 67.4/1985, 589–590.

Heffernan, Thomas: *Sacred Biography: Saints and their Biographers in the Middle Ages*. New York, Oxford University Press 1988.

Herrmann-Mascard, Nicole: *Les reliques des saints: Formation coutumiere d'un droit*. Klincksieck, Paris 1975.

Hinnebusch, William A.: *The History of the Dominican Order*. Vol. 2. Alba House, New York 1973.

Horst, Ulrich, O.P.: *The Dominicans and the Pope: Papal Teaching Authority in the Medieval and Early Modern Thomist Tradition*. Transl. James D. Mixon. University of Notre Dame Press, Notre Dame, Indiana, 2002.

Howard, Peter: *Aquinas and Antoninus: A Tale of Two Summae in Reneissance Florence*. Etienne Gilson series 35. Pontifical Institute of Medieval Studies, Toronto 2013.

Kaeppeli, Tommaso: Antiche biblioteche domenicane in Italia. *Archivum Fratrum Praedicatorum* 36/1966, 6–80.

Kaeppeli, Thomas O. P: *Scriptores Ordinis Praedicatorum Medii Aevi*, II. Rome 1975.

Koudelka, Vladimir J.: Il Fondo Libri nell'archivio generale dell'ordine domenicano, Liber A–Liber Z. *Archivum Fratrum Praedicatorum* 38/1968, 99–147.

Koudelka, Vladimir J.: Il Fondo Libri nell'archivio generale dell'ordine domenicano, II. Liber AA–Liber MMM. *Archivum Fratrum Praedicatorum* 39/1969, 173–217.

Kretzmann, Norman, and Eleonore Stump (eds.): *The Cambridge Companion to Aquinas*. Cambridge University Press, Cambridge UK 1993.

Le Brun-Gouanvic, Claire: *Édition critique de l'Ystoria sancti Thome de Aquino de Guillaume de Tocco*. Pontifical Institute of Mediaeval Studies, Toronto 1996.

Mandonnet, Pierre: La canonisation de Saint Thomas d'Aquin. *Mélanges thomistes*. Le Saulchoir, Kain 1923, 1–48.

Norman, Diana: In Imitation of Saint Thomas Aquinas: Art, Patronage and Liturgy within a Renaissance Chapel. *Renaissance Studies* 7/1993, 1–42.

O'Malley, John: Some Renaissance Panegyrics of Aquinas. *Renaissance Quarterly* 27.2/1974, 174–192.

O'Malley, John: The Feast of Thomas Aquinas in Renaissance Rome. *Rivista di storia della chiesa in Italia* 35.1/1981, 1–27.

Palazzo, Éric: Le livre dans les trésors du Moyen Age: Contribution à l'histoire de la Memoria médiévale. *Annales. Histoire, Sciences Sociales* 52.1/1997, 93–118.

Palazzo, Éric: *Peindre c'est prier: Anthropologie de la prière chrétienne*. Cerf, Paris 2016.

Perrotta, Vincenzo Maria: *Descrizione storica della chiesa, e del monistero di S. Domenico Maggiore di Napoli*. Dai Torchi di Saverio Giordano, Naples 1828.

Polzer, Joseph: The "Triumph of Thomas" Panel in Santa Caterina, Pisa: Meaning and Date. *Mitteilungen des Kunsthistorischen Institutes in Florenz* 37.1/1993, 29–70.

Redon, Odile and Gélis, Jacques: Pour une étude du corps dans les récits de miracles. *Culto dei santi, istituzioni e classi sociali in età preindustriale*. Eds. Sofia Boesch Gajano and Lucia Sebastiani. Japadre, Aquila and Rome 1984, 563–572.

Rubin, Miri, *Corpus Christi: The Eucharist in Late Medieval Culture*. Cambridge University Press, Cambridge UK 1991.

Räsänen, Marika: The Cult of St Thomas Aquinas, Reform and the Laity in Late Medieval Italy. *Modus Vivendi: Religious Reform and Laity in Late Middle Ages* (forthcoming, A).

Räsänen, Marika: The Memory of St Thomas Aquinas in Orvieto in the late Middle Ages. *Relics, Identity and Memory in Medieval Europe*, Eds. Marika Räsänen, Gritje Hartmann, and Earl Jeffrey Richards. Europa Sacra, 21. Brepols, Turnhout 2016, 285–317.

Räsänen, Marika: *Thomas Aquinas' Relics as Focus for Conflict and Cult in Late Middle Ages: The Restless Corpse*. Amsterdam University Press, Amsterdam 2017.

Skemer, Don C.: *Binding Words: Textual Amulets in the Middle Ages*. The Pennsylvania State University Press, University Park 2006.

Taurisano, Innocenzo: Discepoli e biografi di S. Tommas, *Tommaso d'Aquino O.P.: Miscellanea storico-artistica*. A. Manuzio, Rome 1924, 111–186.

Théry, G.: Le petit reliquaire du couvent de San Domenico Maggiore contenant une page autographe de s. Thomas. *Archivum Fratrum Praedicatorum* 1/1931a/vqi 1, 336–340.

Théry, G.: L'autographe de s. Thomas conserve à la biblioteca nazionale de Naples. *Archivum Fratrum Praedicatorum* 1/1931b, 15–86.

Théry, G.: Le manuscript de Salerne contenant le commentaire de s. Thomas sur les Physiques. *Archivum Fratrum Praedicatorum* 1/1931c, 311–335.

Torrell, Jean-Pierre O.P.: *Initiation à saint Thomas d'Aquin: Sa personne et son oeuvre*. Editions Universitaires, Fribourg 1993.

Good examples for the sisters: books about St Birgitta of Sweden and the reform of Dominican nuns in Teutonia

Meri Heinonen

In 1397 a reformed Dominican house for nuns was established in Schönensteinbach in Alsace. The convent was a former Augustinian house, which became the first Observant convent for female Dominicans in the Teutonia province – it was also one of the first Observant female houses in the Order of Preachers anywhere. Schönensteinbach was therefore a special community, whence nuns were later sent to other convents to reform them. The convent was dedicated to St Birgitta of Sweden, who had been canonized only a few years earlier in 1391. The naming of the Dominican house after Birgitta at a time when no Birgittine monastery had been established in Teutonia province or any other German speaking areas seems rather unexpected.[1] The Dominican friar, reformer and chronicler of the order, Johannes Meyer, who completed his history of Schönensteinbach in his *Buch der Reformacio Predigerordens* in 1468, explains that the dedication was the work of Pope Boniface IX, who had also canonized Birgitta.[2]

---

[1] On the Birgittine monasteries in German areas see Montag 2000, 106–107; Montag 1968, 4–7.

[2] Johannes Meyer, *Das Buch der Reformacio Predigerordens.*

The importance of Birgitta to the German Dominicans was not restricted to the Schönensteinbach dedication. In 1968 Ulrich Montag suggested in his book *Das Werk der heiligen Birgitta von Schweden in oberdeutscher Überlieferung* that together with the Birgittine Order, the Dominicans were the main mediators of Birgitta's works and Birgittine texts in the German vernacular.[3] The interaction between the Dominicans and Birgittines in the German context has been discussed surprisingly little since Montag's work.[4] In this essay I attempt to remedy this situation somewhat by canvassing the spread of Birgittine books within the Observant Dominican female houses and studying more closely the relationship between Saint Birgitta and the Dominican reform, especially in Teutonia. Why did Birgitta become popular in the Dominican Order and what value did she have for the Dominicans as a promoter of the Observant reform? I base my approach on the presence of Birgittine manuscripts in the libraries of Dominican female houses, but I also suggest why the library of St Katharina in Nuremberg seems to have been at the centre of many Birgittine texts and consider the ties that may have connected Saint Birgitta to the Order of Preachers, as well as how books about Birgitta were used to create and maintain a relationship between these two orders.

Saint Birgitta and the Dominicans

Birgitta of Sweden (1302/3–1373) was in many senses a typical later medieval female saint, although her background was perhaps more aristocratic than that of most female saints and mystics of the time. Birgitta's father, Birger Petersson, was a knight, a lawspeaker [*lagman*] and a councillor of state, as was her husband Ulf Gudmarsson whom

---

[3] Montag 1968, 94.

[4] In the Italian sphere the connection between St. Birgitta and the Dominicans has been under more study. See e.g. Roberts 2008, 81–94 where she discusses the influence of Birgitta to Chiara Gambacorta and the first observant Dominican female house San Domenico in Pisa. See also Zarri 2013, 71–72, 75 and Debby 2004, 509–526.

she married in 1316 at the age of thirteen. Her husband's office meant that he travelled Sweden with the king and his court, and as a result Birgitta came to know practically the whole upper class of the country. Although Birgitta had had religious interests earlier, her life changed dramatically when she was widowed in 1344. After this she started to act more openly in a fashion typical of late medieval religious women. She first moved closer to the Cistercian monastery of Alvastra, whose sub-prior (later prior) Peter of Alvastra acted as her confessor together with Master Mathias of Linköping. They also began to record Birgitta's Revelations in the second half of the 1340's. Like many other women saints, Birgitta gained much of her reputation through her mystical/prophetic experiences and harsh ascetic practices.[5]

In 1349 Birgitta travelled to Rome. Her objective was to visit the holy city during the year of the *jubileo* in 1350 and to acquire papal approval for her Rule of the Order of Saint Savior. Birgitta claimed to have received the Rule directly from Christ in one of her revelations.[6] In Rome she gained the reputation of a holy woman and she actively called on the pope to return from Avignon to the Holy City. Birgitta was obviously highly skilled in networking and she established connections with the Roman and Italian religious and secular elite. She never returned to Sweden in her lifetime, dying in Rome in 1373, and some time later her corpse was removed to Vadstena. Three years earlier, in 1370, the pope had accepted Birgitta's Order, though it was to follow the Augustinian Rule – not that of Birgitta - but in 1378 Birgitta's Rule was accepted as a sort of constitution for the Order of St Savior. In these tasks of papal approval Birgitta and the Birgittines received help from Alfonso Pecha, a former bishop of Jaén, with whom Birgitta had become close in the late 1360's in Rome.[7]

Birgitta's order was rather original, and it is no wonder that it was not accepted immediately. The Birgittine monastery was in practice a double monastery, where the friars served nuns and worked under the

---

[5] On Birgitta's life see e.g. Sahlin 2001, 13–19; Salmesvuori 2014, 25–27.
[6] About the background of Birgitta's Rule and her revelations see Morris 2015, 111–112. Morris suggests that the Rule was really a product of a lifetime, not just a single revelation that was written down.
[7] McGinn 2012, 193–194; Salmesvuori 2014, 15.

authority of the abbess, though the sexes were strictly separated from each other and lived in their own convents.[8] According to Birgitta's Rule each convent should have had 13 priests and 4 deacons to serve 60 nuns.[9] Although the order seemed to be a reasonable answer to the problem which several women's communities had confronted (including Dominicans) when the nuns often lacked the services of friars or monks who should have said the daily masses, heard nuns' confessions and distributed the Eucharist, the organization of Birgittine monasteries was not accepted by all: already during the fifteenth century some brethren inside the order opposed the leading role of the abbesses.[10] Even though double monasteries had existed before, they were a rarity during the Late Middle Ages and a leading role for an abbess was in itself exceptional.

While in Italy, Birgitta had developed a close relationship with some Dominicans in high places. Raymond of Capua, the confessor of Catherine of Siena and later the writer of her *Legenda maior,* and the Dominican order's master general from 1380 onwards, knew her personally. It has been suggested that Raymond possibly considered his own protégée Catherine as some sort of follower of Birgitta and there is evidence of common interest and cooperation between the supporters of both women. Soon after Birgitta's death, Alfonso Pecha interviewed Catherine of Siena, probably encouraged by Pope Gregory XI, who had had a great interest in Birgitta.[11] It is even possible that it was Raymond of Capua who had advised him to do this.[12]

Later in the same year, 1374, Catherine was asked to come to Florence to the General Chapter of the Dominicans, and Thomas Luongo has suggested that it was planned to launch Catherine's career as a political

---

[8] Bridget Morris argues that the order's houses were not in fact double monasteries because the brothers and nuns lived in separated houses and were never to meet each other in person except on rare and special occasions such as at the deathbed of a nun. See, Morris 2015, 114–115.

[9] Birgitta of Sweden, *Revelations*, vol. 4, 134.

[10] On the problems within the Dominican Order see Heinonen 2016. On the problems within the order see e.g. Lamberg 2007, 289–293; Morris, 2015, 117.

[11] Luongo 2006, 56–57.

[12] Constant Mews, unpublished article manuscript.

visionary and the second Birgitta on this occasion.[13] Direct contact between the supporters of Birgitta and those of Catherine continued for several years. Alfonso Pecha donated a book about Birgitta to Chiara Gambacorta, the patron and foundress of San Domenico in Pisa. San Domenico was the first Italian reformed Dominican female convent, where a series of predellas to depict the life of St. Birgitta and a panel concerning the Nativity according to the Vision of Saint Birgitta were painted. In addition to Chiara, another admirer of Birgitta was Giovanni Dominici, who was closely associated with the reform in San Domenico and observance in general.[14]

In his *vita maior* of Catherine Raymond of Capua mentions that Pope Urban VI had an idea to send Catherine of Siena together with Birgitta's daughter Catherine of Sweden on a mission to Joanna of Naples, who supported the antipope Clement VII. According to Raymond, he himself advised the pope not to follow this plan because he was worried about the dangers of the trip. The plan was cancelled, even though Catherine of Siena criticized Raymond for being too protective.[15] The making of the plan, however, is evidence of the common interests and shared goals among the supporters of Birgitta and Catherine of Siena and their involvement in papal politics. Birgitta, Catherine and the Dominicans in Germany and Italy had all been interested in the pope's return to Rome. During the Great Western Schism they again found common ground in supporting the Roman pope. As will be shown later, the Dominican faction that stayed loyal to the Roman obedience was also active in the Observant reform and seems to have connected Birgitta to the objectives of the reform, although her status and fame were not exclusively positive.

Before her death Birgitta had given Alfonso Pecha the task of editing her Revelations so that they could be translated into other languages. Alfonso did this, but eliminated the most controversial parts in the process. In addition, he participated in the compilation of Birgitta's *vita* and played an important role in the canonization of the saint, which took place less than twenty years after her death, in 1391 during the

---

[13] Luongo 2006, 58.
[14] Roberts 2004, 84, 90.
[15] Raimondo da Capua, *Legenda maior*, III:11–12, 364.

reign of Pope Boniface IX.[16] Unusually, Birgitta was canonized twice more, in 1415 by the council pope John XXIII and again in 1419 by Martin V. This was partly due to the Great Western Schism that had affected also the canonization procedures, but also because Birgitta's sanctity and her orthodoxy were challenged after the first canonization; even after three canonizations, at the Council of Basel, her *Revelations* were debated, but finally deemed to be orthodox in 1436.[17]

Birgitta's revelations had been questioned already during her lifetime and tested by a panel including several bishops and theologians. As a result, a testimony written by Master Matthias underlining the authenticity of Birgitta's experiences was included in most of the texts that discussed her and her *Revelations*. As Nancy Caciola has noted, it may be that Birgitta's eagerness to get involved in papal politics and the fact that pope's return to Rome had led to the Great Schism raised doubts about Birgitta's sanctity and the authenticity of her revelations.[18] Also, many representatives of the Church, especially those who supported the Observant reform, had rather negative attitudes towards the mystical spirituality of women. Birgitta's fame spread rapidly after her death but she remained a controversial saint

In many respects Birgitta was a typical later medieval female saint, but she was not a likely candidate to promote observance among the Dominican nuns. She did call for Church reform, but her lifestyle was not that of a reformed nun.[19] She was not a reclusive but a public figure, and active in Church politics. She practised harsh asceticism and had mystical visions. In other words, she was almost the antithesis of an ideal Observant nun, whose most important qualities were remaining enclosed, sharing the liturgy with other nuns and avoiding private and excessively severe devotional exercises. However, Birgitta's qualities resembled those of Catherine of Siena (or vice versa). Catherine was an important figure for the Dominicans: after her death she became the model for the Observant nuns and her *vita* spread to Observant

---

[16] Salmesvuori 2014, 15; Sahlin 2001, 29–31.
[17] See Caciola 2003, 277–291; Sahlin 2001, 161–168.
[18] Caciola 2003, 291–319.
[19] Morris 2012, 12–13.

female houses.[20] The connection and similarity between the two saints was obviously meaningful for the Dominicans.

The importance of Catherine of Siena in Dominican reform was partly that in 1380 her former confessor Raymond of Capua became the master general of the part of the Dominican Order that remained obedient to the papacy in Rome. Raymond was an eager promoter of the Observant reform and in 1388 in the general chapter of Vienna he ordered that every province should have at least one convent for the reform-minded friars. The first reformed convent of Teutonia province was established in Colmar in 1389 and eight years later the female house of Schönensteinbach was founded.[21] Raymond spent the last years of his life in Germany. He came to Nuremberg in 1396 to support the reform of the local Dominican friary and after that he travelled in the German-speaking provinces, but he died three years later in Nuremberg. Around the same time Raymond's *Vita* of Catherine was translated into German in the same area.[22] However, it is possible that Raymond did not promote only Catherine for the German friars and nuns. He had known Birgitta personally and considered her an important figure and even an example or precursor of Catherine, so he may well have had good words to say about the saint in Nuremberg. This is especially likely because the Schönensteinbach convent was dedicated to Birgitta while Raymond was staying in the area.

St Birgitta and the texts of Dominican observance

The idea that Raymond of Capua presented Birgitta as a positive model for the nuns and friars is supported by a *Sendbrief* (a sort of open letter) that its editors Ulla Williams and Werner Williams-Krapp have

---

[20] See e.g. Huijbers 2015, 123–128. See also Brakmann 2011, 27.

[21] On the reform in the Dominican Order in Teutonia in general, Hillenbrand 1989, 219–270. See also von Heusinger 2000; Hinnebusch 1973, II, 369–372.

[22] Concerning the German translation of Catherine's *vita* see Brakmann 2011; Hamburger 2004, 4–5.

named *Sendbrief zur wahren Heiligkeit Birgittas von Schweden* ('A Letter concerning the True Holiness of Birgitta of Sweden'). The *sendbrief* was written in Nuremberg in about 1420, some twenty years after Raymond's death. Its audience was probably nuns and it warned against mystical spirituality and experiences, but at the same time it presented Birgitta of Sweden as a true mystic and an exemplary saint. The letter is known in only one manuscript from the Augustinian convent of Pillenreuth some six kilometres from Nuremberg. The convent had very close ties to the Dominican convent of St Katharina in Nuremberg and there is known to have been an exchange of books between the two houses. This book distribution may have occurred because Dominican friars of Nuremberg acted as confessors in both places.[23] It is therefore likely that the Dominicans had given the book to Pillenreuth and the same letter was possibly sent to nuns in St Katharina before its reform. The editors have suggested that a local Dominican friar wrote the letter, which would strengthen the argument that Dominican friars were responsible for it ending up in Pillenreuth. Among other things the *Sendbrief* heavily emphasises that one should always be obedient to priests and confessors, introducing Saint Birgitta as a good religious woman because she had acted under the guidance and control of her confessors.[24]

Although this letter could have been written from the perspective of almost any Dominican friar, its local context is important to take into consideration. As noted, the convent of the Dominican Friars of Nuremberg had been reformed in 1396, but the attempt to reform the female house of St Katharina in the town in the same year had failed utterly in the face of resistance from the nuns, who resolutely and openly refused to follow the orders of their superiors. According to Johannes Meyer, the nuns even physically attacked the friars who, armed with the pope's bull, tried to enclose their convent.[25] Even though Meyer's narrative states that the convent of St Katharina was enclosed after friars had made a second attempt and had thrown flour in the faces of nuns,

[23] Werner Williams-Krapp, 2011,
[24] Williams and Williams-Krapp 2004a, 214–217; Williams-Krapp 2011, 193–195.
[25] Meyer, *Buch der Reformacio* IV:5, 12.

the observance was not rooted in St Katharina until 1428/9, when a new and successful attempt to reform the convent was made by the Dominicans at the request of the city council. [26] In such a situation, where nuns had openly questioned the authority of friars and even the pope, the sending of a letter underlining the importance of obedience and the eminence of the Church's representatives would have been entirely understandable.

We also have some other evidence that the friars of Nuremberg had tried to promote the reform with the help of books and letters. The library of St Katharina grew enormously after the reform in 1428 and by the end of the sixteenth century it contained over 700 manuscripts, whereas only 46 had been held by the convent before the reform. We know that of these 46 books at least one double binding of *Der Heiligen Leben* came to the library between the failed reform attempt and the successful one.[27] However, it is possible that some other books that consist of pastoral and devotional material such as the German legend of Saint Catherine of Siena, texts by Marquard von Lindau, and a German translation of Gertrude of Helfta's *Legatus divinae pietatis* were also donated to the convent in the early fifteenth century and that the goal of these donations was to promote the idea of reform. Among the manuscripts that belonged to the convent before 1428 was Eberhard Mardach's *Sendbrief von wahrer Andacht*. Eberhard Mardach was the prior of the Nuremberg Dominican convent before his death in 1428 and the content of his letter, which was written after the failed reform attempt, is reminiscent of the *Sendbrief* that discussed Birgitta. It similarly expressed mistrust in the mystical experiences of women and criticized those who did not follow the rules of the order and their superiors.[28] This increases the likelihood that books and letters were used to promote the reform for the nuns of St Katharina before 1428 and that Dominicans actively underlined the values of Observance while also stressing the importance of obedience.

26 Meyer, *Buch der Reformacio* IV:5, 12–13; Willing 2004, 19–25.
27 Willing (ed.) 2012, LXXII.
28 Williams-Krapp 2011, 191–195; Williams and Williams-Krapp 2004b. See also Poor 2004, 140–141.

If the anonymous letter was indeed written by a Dominican Friar from Nuremberg, it shows that the friars had a positive interest in Birgitta even before the first Birgittine house was established in southern Germany and that her *fama* was used to promote the goals of the Observant reform. The interest in Birgitta of Sweden was probably further developed after the first Birgittine house in southern Germany was founded by Birgittine monks in the early 1420's in Gnadenberg, circa 35 kilometres from Nuremberg. The first nuns entered Gnadenberg some 15 years later, in 1438. Although there is no direct evidence that the brothers and later nuns of Gnadenberg had direct contact with the Nuremberg Dominicans and exchanged books, the St Katharina house's role as a centre for the distribution of Birgittine texts suggests that there might have been some contacts between these two orders in the Nuremberg area.[29] The positive attitude to Birgitta among the Dominicans of Nuremberg was probably strengthened when nuns from Schönensteinbach, which was dedicated to Birgitta, came to reform St Katharina in 1428.

Dominican observance and the Rule of Birgitta

The first translation of Birgittine texts into High German was done soon after the founding of Schönensteinbach, in Gnadenberg in the early 1430's. It included Birgitta's Rule and the revelations associated with it. Ulrich Montag points out that the translation kept the first person narrative by Jesus and was therefore not meant for use within the Birgittine Order but to explain the Rule and order for outsiders. Without the nuns the Rule in the vernacular was probably not needed in Gnadenberg, and the Rule as it was used within the order (Jesus speaking in the third person) was translated only sometime between 1440 and 1450, that is, after the arrival of nuns in Gnadenberg.[30]

[29] Montag 1968, 135, 193, 198.
[30] Montag 2000, 108–109; Montag 1968, 128–134.

The Birgittine Rule according to this "outsider" version is in the library of St Katharina. The Rule and the revelations explaining it belong to a miscellany manuscript whose parts are dated to different periods. The copy of the Rule was written in St Katharina and if Karin Schneider's identification of the watermark is correct this part of the manuscript would date to the 1430s or early 1440s or thereabouts, in which case it would be an early copy of the Rule.[31] This would mean that the Observant Dominican nuns following the Rule of St Augustine, like the Birgittines, copied constitutions of another order soon after the reform of their own convent. Having the rules of other orders was not unheard of, and the presence of the copy in the library shows that nuns in St Katharina were interested in the Rule of Birgitta or that it was presented them because they could benefit from reading and perhaps copying it. The Birgittine Rule was not, however, placed in library section H, which included the Rules and constitutions of the Dominican Order, but category M (treatises). This was perhaps because it was part of a miscellany that included many other devotional texts, or because it was considered a text worth reading and meditating upon.[32] The Rule of Pseudo-Jerome to Eustochium was also placed in category M in St Katharina's library.[33] The placing of Rules in the category of treatises followed the old monastery habit of keeping copies of Rules of other orders to be read for meditative purposes.[34]

The Birgittine Rule spread to other Dominican reform convents too. Sister Margaret Mändlin copied the Rule with the accompanying revelations in the Observant Dominican convent of Altenhohenau in ca. 1500.[35] We know that five nuns from St Katharina had reformed Altenhohenau in 1465 and the library catalogue of St Katharina mentions that Sister Apollonia Imhoff, who was one of these nuns, had taken a Life of Saint Birgitta with her when she left for Altenhohenau.[36] It is therefore possible that the nuns brought with them a copy of the Rule to

---

[31] Nuremberg, Stadtbibliothek, MS Cent VI 57; Schneider 1965, 189–191.

[32] MBK III/3, 626.

[33] MBK III/3, 624.

[34] For earlier practices, see, for instance, Immonen 2016, 525–527.

[35] Schneider 1996, 43–45.

[36] MBK III/3, 62.

aid the reform and that this was the manuscript that was later copied. The alternative is that the book was later loaned from St Katharina or some other convent to be copied. Whatever the case, the copying of the Rule shows clearly that interest in Birgitta and her Rule was not restricted to Nuremberg but extended to other Dominican houses as well, indicating that the Dominican Order was active in promoting Birgitta as a model of reform for nuns or that nuns themselves considered the Rule of Birgitta useful. This can be understood by looking the content of the texts in the revelations that were related to the Rule.

Birgitta's Rule and the revelations that accompanied it have a strong message that highlights the reform. The Rule opens with an allegory of a king whose vineyard had been spoiled after several good years. The king not only wants to plant a new vineyard and guard it properly but to renew other vineyards that have been dry and unproductive for a long time so that they will bring good harvests as they did when they first bore fruit. This rhetoric of reform and renewal is the very same the Dominicans used themselves when reforming their own order; they wanted to return to the original and superior state that had been lost. Indeed, in the Revelations Christ explicitly says that the vineyards that had dried up were religious orders that had once been fruitful and useful but were now in a poor state. So he wants to plant a new vineyard - the Birgittine Order.[37] Birgitta, however, did give credit to others religious orders and considered it possible to make them fruitful again; for the Observant Dominicans, who concurred with the gist of Birgitta's message, it must have been more than welcome.

In addition to the reform message the Rule of Birgitta also included advice the Dominican reformers appreciated. In the prologue of the Rule Christ tells his bride Birgitta to take care of the vineyard and underlines the importance of obedience, leaving the world, and forsaking one's own will.[38] These were also the themes the Observant Dominicans emphasized in the case of the nuns; obedience and enclosure were considered marks of the nuns' return to the original purity and it seems that for Observant Dominicans enclosure was the guarantee of nuns'

---

[37] The Rule of the Savior in Birgitta of Sweden, *Revelations*, vol. 4, 124.
[38] The Rule of the Savior in Birgitta of Sweden, *Revelations*, vol. 4, 124–125.

obedience and therefore also an outer mark of their reform.[39] As noted above, the very same objectives were underlined in the letters that were written by the Observant Dominican friars for the nuns, in which the enclosing of St Katharina was seen as a mark of nuns' reform.

Other Birgittine texts in the Dominican houses

The Rule of Birgitta was not the only text related to the saint that spread in the Dominican female houses in Teutonia. There is evidence that some parts of Birgitta's Revelations, not just those that were connected to her Rule, were translated and distributed among the Dominican female houses even before Nicolaus Koch, a monk from Gnadenberg, translated the entire Revelations of Birgitta into German around 1470. The library of St Katharina, for instance, had several manuscripts that include excerpts from the Revelations of Birgitta, and many of them predate the year 1470. One of the earliest is a manuscript that Kunigund Schreiberin brought with her when she entered the convent in 1428. The book includes chapters 24–27 from Book II of Birgitta's Revelations together with some treatises and Pope Urban IV's bull about the feast of *Corpus Christi*.[40] These chapters of Revelations discuss the allegory of the three houses of the bride of Christ and use drink, meat, clothes and tools to demonstrate the spiritual virtues that a bride should have.

Kunigund was the widow of a wealthy Nuremberg citizen, Nicholas Schreiberin, who had been a member of the city council and belonged to the patrician families of the town. Nicholas died in 1428 and in the same year his widow Kunigund expressed a wish to enter the reformed Dominican convent of Schönensteinbach. However, her desire, and that of other wealthy widows, to be accepted into reformed Dominican convents led the members of the city council to ask the Dominicans to reform the convent of St Katharina in Nuremberg. As stated above, this

[39] See Heinonen 2013.
[40] Nuremberg, Stadtbibliothek, MS Cent VI 43h; Schneider 1965, 102–104.

reform was more successful than the first attempt and the fortune of Kunigund greatly assisted in the process.[41]

Kunigund was an important supporter not only of St Katharina's reform but of the Observant reform in general, and Karin Schneider has suggested that she probably knew personally the Dominican reformer Johannes Nider, the prior of Nuremberg Dominican convent from 1427. Kunigund owned a copy of *24 goldenen Harfen* ('24 Golden Harps' written by Nider, which is one of the oldest known.[42] The medieval library catalogue of St Katharina mentions Nider's book and calls him "unser erwirdiger, lieber vater, maister Johannes Nyder selig."[43]

In addition to the extract from Birgitta's Revelations and Nider's brand new book, Kunigund brought to the convent a German translation of the *vita* of Catherina of Siena known as *Ein geistlicher Rosengarten*. As we have seen, this was not the first copy of the text in St Katharina, as the convent had owned a translation before the reform.[44] However, the ownership of Catherine of Siena's German *vita* further underlines Kunigund's close relationship with reform-minded Dominicans as well as the connection between Birgitta and Catherine. The names of these two saints stand out in the long list of books owned by Kunigund, as few of them are explicitly written by or about women.

Another laywoman who brought a large number of books to St Katharina, in this case at least 24, was Katharina Tucher, who entered the convent as a lay sister in 1440.[45] Among her books was a manuscript that included a short extract from Birgitta's Revelations (book III, 32) and also prayers attributed to Birgitta.[46] Another early copy including extracts from the Revelations of Birgitta (mainly from Books IV and VI) was donated to nuns of St Katharina by the former prior of the Nuremberg Dominican convent, Georg Falder-Pistoris, who died in 1452. He also gave the nuns a German Rituale, a German translation of Humbert of Romans' interpretation of the Rule and a German version

[41] Simon 2012,3 n 8.
[42] Schneider 1983, 77.
[43] Willing (ed.) 2012, 508.
[44] Hamburger 2004, 5.
[45] Willing (ed.) 2012, XXVIII
[46] Nuremberg, Stadtbibliothek, MS Will II 19.8; Schneider 1965, 416–424.

of Thomas a Kempis' Imitation of Christ.[47] Like some others, this donation seems to have been linked to the reform with its emphasis on following of the Order's Rule and encouraging nuns to concentrate on liturgy and reading of pastoral works.

In addition to these exerpts from Birgitta's Revelations, the library of St Katharina had at least two other manuscripts that included selections from the Revelations, one of them certainly written in the convent after the 1428 reform.[48] Extracts from the Revelations of Birgitta were therefore known in St Katharina already in the first but especially in the second half of the fifteenth century. That the name of Birgitta is mentioned even in small sections of her Revelations and that excerpts from them were translated into German before the entire Revelations had been published in vernacular proves that Birgitta had a high reputation and her work was considered worth consulting. It is probable that her three canonizations from 1391 onwards raised interest in her life and works and spread her *fama*.

In addition to Birgitta's general fame and the similarity of her ideas concerning the reform and its realization to those of the Dominicans, the Order of Friars Preacher might have had other reasons for interest in Birgitta. As noted, Birgitta was considered a predecessor of Catherine of Siena, who was strongly associated with the reform in the Dominican Order. I have suggested that the interest in Birgitta was transmitted by Raymond of Capua, who had known her and was active in the reform of Dominican Order, especially in the Nuremburg area. Furthermore, the supporters of Birgitta and Catherine had shared similar interests in church politics.

There is good reason to accept that the Dominican Order favoured Birgitta and propagated her achievements to strengthen the status of Catherine of Siena. Unlike Birgitta, Catherine was not canonized shortly after her death, so for many years her saintliness was not as well established as Birgitta's, whose first canonization occurred as early as 1391. Catherine of Siena was declared a saint long after the

---

[47] Nuremberg, Stadtbibliothek, MS Cent. VI.46–47; Schneider 1965, 152–154; Willing (ed.) 2012, XXV.
[48] ZB, MS D 231; Nuremberg, Stadtbibliothek, MS Cent VII, 22.

schism, in 1461 when the Observant reform had already reached its peak in Teutonia. The investigations and questioning of witnesses for Catherine's canonization process had started in 1411 and 1416, but it was 50 years before she was declared a universal saint.[49] The positive result of Birgitta's canonization may have been seen as a precedent for Catherine's canonization and the Dominican propagation of Birgitta's *fama* was probably intended to make it so, as well as encouraging the veneration of Catherine during her canonization process, which would in turn make a positive outcome to the process more likely. The positive pairing of Birgitta of Sweden and Catherine of Siena can be seen in Johannes Meyer's *Buch der Reformacio Predigerordens,* in whose third book he introduces the lives of nuns in Schönensteinbach much in the same way as the sister-books written by Dominican nuns in the first half of the fourteenth-century had done. At the beginning of this book Meyer discusses how one can know that revelations and experiences are from God and not from the devil, giving seven marks that can help in identifying the source of them as deriving from God. He concludes that all the (seven) marks are true regarding the holy ladies Saint Birgitta and Saint Catherine of Siena and other true friends of God. It seems that he wanted to reassure his readers that both Birgitta and Catherine received their revelations and experiences from God, not from the evil spirit. However, after this he compares Catherine and Birgitta to the nuns of Schönensteinbach, about whom he is to write.[50]

I have earlier suggested that although Meyer belonged to the Observant reformers, who have often been described as hostile to the mystical spirituality of women, he did understand the needs of nuns and could approach their mystical experiences and miracles with approval. This usually occurred in cases when the experiences had been reported and confirmed by confessors or other priests.[51] In this respect, of course, Meyer followed a line similar to the writer of the *Sendbrief* that discussed Birgitta. The most important thing was obedience.

---

[49] Concerning the canonization of St Catherine of Siena, see Krafft 2013, 25–45.

[50] Johannes Meyer, *Buch der reformacio,* III:3, 59–61.

[51] Heinonen 2013, 255.

When comparing Catherine and Birgitta to the Observant nuns Meyer seems to accept a certain amount of mystical spirituality among the nuns as well, but at the same time he gives Birgitta a status similar to the Order's own saint and the ultimate model of observance, Catherine. It is probable that giving a positive image of Birgitta and Catherine together was not Meyer's own inspiration, but had its roots in the way these two saints were considered in the Order. Very often a similar pairing of Catherine and Birgitta had been made in a negative sense by those who questioned the mystical experiences of women. Presenting them together in a positive light challenged these accusations while framing them both as positive and good models who had had mystical experiences but who had also remained under the control of their confessors. In this way Birgitta was used both as a good example and as a positive proof of the Catherine of Siena's sanctity. In addition, the books about Birgitta were used to promote obedience and acceptance of the reform among the nuns, first in St Katharina in Nuremberg and later in other communities.

We know that St Katharina played a major role in transmitting copies of Birgittine texts to other convents. A good example is a manuscript that is nowadays in Badische Landesbibliothek in Karlsruhe.[52] It is a collection of works that have in common the figure of Birgitta. The manuscript includes a sample of Birgitta's Revelations probably written in Schönensteinbach before the mid-fifteenth century. The other part of the manuscript consists of several other Birgittine texts, namely *Leben und Wunderwerke St Birgitten*, *Bürde der Welt*, *Die drei Birgittenfeste*, a short legend of Birgitta, and a Latin prayer for Birgitta with a German translation. This part had been given to the nuns of Schönensteinbach by the Nuremberg nuns and was probably written in St Katharina.[53]

Of these texts, *Leben und Wunderwerke St. Birgitten* at least belonged to the library of St Katharina in the early fifteenth century. The oldest known copy of the text was written there, probably in the second quarter of the fifteenth century. It is part of a book that also included the life

---

[52] BLB, MS St. Peter perg. 42.
[53] Heinzer and Stamm 1984, 101–103.

of Saint Ursula and the 11,000 virgins.[54] Ulrich Montag considers Nuremberg the point of origin for the High German transmission of this particular work, as all other known versions of the texts are somehow connected to Nuremberg and St Katharina. For instance, a manuscript that is nowadays in Zürich Zentralbibliothek includes, together with an extract of *Leben und Wunderwerke*, 23 sermons that were given by eleven different friars in St Katharina in 1482–1487 and written down by the nuns.[55]

St Katharina probably acquired the book, including the *Leben und Wunderwerke St. Birgitten,* from Anna Imhoff (born Schürstab). She gave nine books to the convent and lived in its vicinity before her death. Among the books she donated, according to the medieval library catalogue, was a "Life of St Birgitta", probably referring to the *Leben und Wunderwerke.*[56] Anna Imhoff was buried in the convent in 1440 but she never became a community member, unlike two of her daughters and one granddaughter. This granddaughter, Apollonia, is the aforementioned nun who took the book that included "The Life of St Birgitta" with her to the convent of Altenhohenau in 1465.[57] As in the case of Birgitta's Revelations, it is worth noting that *Leben und Wunderwerke* circulated in lay circles in the Nuremberg area as well as among the Dominicans. The laywomen read books about Birgitta or at least extracts from her Revelations and knew her by name and fame.

Birgitta's close circle or even Birgittines had not written these aforementioned texts although they were based on Birgitta's *Revelations* and on the *vita* about her, but they had a German origin. A cleric from Bamberg, Johannes Tortsch, wrote two books about Birgitta in the early fifteenth century: the first, *Onus mundi*, was translated into German and abbreviated with the name *Bürde der Welt,* while Tortsch's *Legenda sancta Birgitte* came to be known in the vernacular as *Leben und Wunderwerke St. Birgitten.* These vernacular copies circulated in the Dominican convents, but no copy is known from the Birgittine

[54] Nuremberg, Stadtbibliothek, MS Cent. VI43f; Schneider 1965, 96–98.
[55] Montag 1968, 193; ZB, Cod, D 231
[56] MBK III/3, 622.
[57] Schneider 1983, 80; Schneider 1975, 217–218.

monasteries. It seems that Birgittines had difficulties in accepting these two books that had been written by someone outside their own order. Dominicans, on the other hand, had no such reservations, and the distribution of the books in Dominican houses further strengthens the argument that Dominican nuns were interested in Birgitta and/or that she was offered as a model for them. For instance, a manuscript now in Berlin (Staatsbibl. mgq 189) which includes both above-mentioned texts and a short *vita* of Birgitta in German, originates from the Dominican female house of St Nicolas in Undis in Strassbourg, which had been reformed in 1431 by the nuns from Schönensteinbach and Unterlinden – the manuscript itself dates to the mid-fifteenth century and belongs to the time after the reform.[58]

As these examples indicate, Birgitta and texts related to her had a close connection to the Dominican reform in the Province of Teutonia. The convent of St Katharina in Nuremberg had played a central role as the distributor of Birgittine texts, both those written and translated within and outside the Birgittine Order. It is nevertheless important to note that extracts from the Revelations of St Birgitta and *Leben und Wunderwerke* were also included in books that had originally belonged to the laity. At least in the Nuremberg region, the fame and importance of Birgitta spread to lay people, especially women, who had religious interests. As a wife and a mother Birgitta may have been a more approachable role model for laywomen with religious ambitions than virgin saints such as St Catherine of Siena. From the Dominican viewpoint, more important was probably the possibility to use Birgitta and stories related to her to promote the observance in female houses.

Conclusion

The question of whose interests Birgitta served within the Observant Dominicans is a difficult one. As the examples I have presented show, Dominican Observant friars may have used Birgitta as a model of true

---

[58] Montag 1968, 74–75.

observance in the form of obedience and subordination to the guidance of confessors. Birgitta was considered a reformer calling all orders to a better life, but also a predecessor of Catherine of Siena and proof of her sainthood. In this sense she might have been important for those in the order who wanted to promote the reform and its goals and the importance and sainthood of Catherine of Siena. However, it is even more difficult to know how the nuns in the Dominican convents read the texts telling of the life and revelations of Birgitta. The evidence of the spread of Birgittine texts does show that Dominican nuns (and even laywomen who associated themselves with the Order of Preachers) were interested in Birgitta. It is also clear that the dissemination of texts connected to her were related to the successful reforms in the Dominican female houses.

From a modern perspective Birgitta seems to have been a woman who did what she wanted and acted rather independently, although most of the texts discussed above underlined her obedience and subordination to the will of her confessors. For medieval nuns Birgitta may have been a role model who was an example of active participation, but at the same time she was approved by the friars. She showed the possibilities open to religious women but also the limits to their authority and freedom of action.

Birgitta never appeared in the official liturgy of the Dominican Order, but her name was added during the fifteenth century to several litanies in the processionals that belonged to the Dominican female house in Unterlinden, some thirty to forty kilometres north of Schönensteinbach.[59] Unfortunately I have not been able to find any liturgical manuscripts from Schönensteinbach that inform us about devotion to Birgitta in the monastery that was dedicated to her, but as patron of the house she was almost certainly remembered there. This possible liturgical presence of Birgitta in the Observant Dominican female houses is something that should be studied in the future to get a better idea of her meaning and presence there. The examples presented above provide sufficient evidence that there was a close connection between Birgitta and the Dominican observance. The roots of this connection may lie in Raymond of Capua's

---

[59] See Meyer 2006.

personal relationship with Birgitta, but he was not the only one fascinated by her. Chiara Gambacorta and Giovanni Dominici were among the admirers of the saint in the Italian branch of the Dominicans and both were strong promoters of Observant reform. Furthermore, church political interests connected Birgittines and Observant Dominicans of the Roman obedience. Nevertheless, Raymond's presence in southern Germany and Nuremberg at the end of fourteenth century probably explains why St Katharina became such an important centre for the distribution of Birgittine texts in the Dominican Order and especially its female branch.

Bibliography

Manuscripts

Karlsruhe, Badische Landesbibliothek (BLB)
   MS St. Peter perg. 42
Nuremberg, Stadtbibliothek
   MS Cent VI 57
   MS Cent VII, 22
   MS Will II 19.8
Zurich, Zentralbibliothek Zürich (ZB)
   MS D 231

Printed sources

Birgitta of Sweden: *The Revelations of St. Birgitta of Sweden.*
Vol. 3. *Liber Caelestis, books VI–VII.* Ed. Bridget Morris, transl. Denis Searby. Oxford University Press, Oxford 2012.
Vol. 4. *The Heavenly Emperor's Book to Kings, The Rule and Minor Works.* Ed. Bridget Morris, transl. Denis Searby. Oxford University Press, Oxford 2015.
Meyer, Johannes: *Das Buch der Reformacio Predigerordens. Herausgegeben von Benedictus Maria Reichert.* Quellen und Forfchungen zur Gefchichte des Dominikanerordens in Deutschland, 2–3. Eds. Paulus von Loe and Benedictus Maria Reichert. O. Harrassowitz, Leipzig 1908–1909.
Raimondo da Capua: *Legenda maior.* Ed. Silvia Nocentini. Edizioni di Galluzzo, Florence 2013.

Secondary literature

Bischoff, Bernhard and Paul Ruf (eds.): *Mittelalterliche Bibliothekskataloge Deutschlands und der Schweiz*. III/3. *Bistum Bamberg*. C.H. Beck, Munich 1969 (MBK).

Brakmann, Thomas: *'Ein Geistlicher Rosengarten': Die Vita der heiligen Katharina von Siena zwischen Ordensreform und Laienfrömmigkeit im 15. Jahrhundert*. Untersuchungen und Edition. Peter Lang, Frankfurt am Main 2011.

Caciola, Nancy: *Discerning Spirits: Divine and Demonic Possession in the Middle Ages*. Cornell University Press, Ithaca 2003.

Debby, Nirit Ben-Aryeh. The Images of Saint Birgitta of Sweden in Santa Maria Novella in Florence. *Renaissance Studies* 18/2004, 509–526.

Hamburger, Jeffrey F.: Un jardin de roses spirituel: Une vie enluminée de Catherine de Sienne. *Art de l'enluminure* 11/2004, 2–75.

Heinonen, Meri: Between Friars and Nuns: The Relationships of Religious Men and Women in Johannes Meyer's Buch Der Reformacio Predigerordens. *Oxford German Studies* 42.3/2013, 237–258.

Heinonen, Meri: Men in the Communities of Dominican Nuns – Sister-Books Discussing Priests and Friars. *Journal of Religious History* 40.4/2016, 589–609.

Heinzer, Felix and Gerhard Stamm: *Die Handschriften von St. Peter im Schwarzwald*. Vol. 2. *Die Pergamenthandschriften*. Die Handschriften der Badischen Landesbibliothek in Karlsruhe, 10.2. Harrassowitz, Wiesbaden 1984.

von Heusinger, Sabine: *Johannes Mulberg OP (+1414): Ein Leben im Spannungsfeld von Dominikanerobservanz und Beginenstreit*. Akademie Verlag, Berlin 2000.

Hillenbrand, Eugen: Die Observantenbewegung in der deutschen Ordensprovinz der Dominikaner. *Reformbemühungen und Observanzbestrebungen im spätmittelalterlichen Ordenswesen*. Ed. Kaspar Elm. Duncker & Humblot, Berlin 1989, 219–270.

Huijbers, Anne: 'Observance' as Paradigm in Mendicant and Monastic Order Chronicles. *A Companion to Observant Reform in the Late Middle Ages and Beyond*. Eds. James Mixson and Bert Roest. Brill, Leiden and Boston 2015, 111–145.

Hinnebusch, William: *The History of the Dominican Order*. 2 vols. Alba House, New York 1973.

Immonen, Teemu: De generibus monachorum. The Reading of the First Chapter of the Rule of St Benedict in Monte Cassino under Abbot Desiderius. *Sodalitas. Studi in memoria di Faustino Avagliano*. Eds. Mariano Dell'Omo, Federico Marazzi, Fabio Simonelli, and Cesare Crova. Miscellanea Cassinese, 86. Pubblicazioni Cassinesi, Montecassino 2016, 523–534.

Lamberg, Marko: *Jöns Budde. Birgittalaisveli ja hänen teoksensa*. SKS, Helsinki 2007.

Luongo, Thomas F.: *The Saintly Politics of Catherine of Siena*. Cornell University Press, Ithaca 2006.

Mews, Constant, unpublished article manuscript.

Meyer, Christian: *Collections d'Alsace, de Franche-Comté et de Lorraine*. Vol. I. *Colmar, Bibliothèque municipale*. Catalogue des manuscrits notés du Moyen Âge conservés dans les Bibliothèques publiques de France. Brepols, Turnhout 2006.

McGinn, Bernard: *The Varieties of Vernacular Mysticism, 1350–1550*. Crossroads Publishing, New York 2012.

Montag, Ulrich: *Das Werk der heiligen Birgitta von Schweden in oberdeutscher Überlieferung*. C. H. Beck, Munich 1968.

Montag, Ulrich: The Reception of St Birgitta in Germany. *The Translation of the Works of St Birgitta of Sweden into Medieval European Vernaculars*. Eds. Bridget Morris and Veronica O'Mara. Brepols, Turnhout 2000, 106–116.

Morris, Bridget: Introduction in *The Revelations of St. Birgitta of Sweden. Liber Caelestis, books VI–VII.* Translated by Denis Searby and edited by Bridget Morris. Oxford University Press, Oxford 2012.

Morris, Bridget: Introduction in *The Revelations of St. Birgitta of Sweden.* Vol. 4, *The Heavenly Emperor's Book to Kings, The Rule and Minor Works.* Edited by Bridget Morris, translated by Denis Searby. Oxford University Press, Oxford 2015.

Poor, Sara S.: *Mechthild of Magdeburg and Her Book: Gender and the Making of Textual Authority.* University of Pennsylvania Press, Philadelphia 2004.

Roberts, Ann: *Dominican Women and Renaissance Art: The Convent of San Domenico of Pisa.* Ashgate, Aldershot 2008.

Sahlin, Claire Lynn: *Birgitta of Sweden and the Voice of Prophecy.* Boydell, Rochester 2001.

Salmesvuori, Päivi: *Power and Sainthood: The Case of Birgitta of Sweden.* Palgrave Macmillan, New York 2014.

Schneider, Karin: *Die deutschen mittelalterlichen Handschriften. Beschreibung des Buchschmucks Heinz Zirnbauer. Die Handschriften der Stadtbibliothek Nürnberg.* Vol. 1. Harrassowitz, Wiesbaden 1965.

Schneider, Karin: Beziehungen zwischen den Dominikanerinnenklöster Nürnberg und Altenhohenau im ausgehenden Mittelter: Neue Handschriftenfunde. *Würzburger Prosastudien II. Untersuchungen zur Literatur und Sprache des Mittelalters. Kurt Ruh zum 60. Geburtstag.* Ed. Peter Kesting. Wilhelm Flink Verlag, Munich 1975, 211–218.

Schneider, Karin: Die Bibliothek des Katharinenklosters in Nürnberg und die städtische Gesellschaft. *Studien zum städtischen Bildungswesen des späten Mittelalters und der frühen Neuzeit. Bericht über Kolloquien der Kommission zur Erforschung der Kultur des Spätmittelalters 1978 bis 1981.* Eds. Bernd Moeller, Hans Patze, and Karl Stackmann. Vandenhoeck & Ruprecht, Göttingen 1983, 70–82.

Schneider, Karin: *Die deutschen Handschriften der Bayerischen Staatsbibliothek München: Die mittelalterlichen Handschriften aus Cgm 4001–5247.* Editio altera. Harrassowitz, Wiesbaden 1996.

Simon, Anne: *The Cult of Saint Katherine of Alexandria in Late-Medieval Nuremberg.* Ashgate, Surrey 2012.

Williams, Ulla and Werner Williams-Krapp. Birgitta von Schweden als Massstab für wahre Heiligkeit. *Studien zur deutschen Sprache und Literatur. Festschrift für Konrad Kunze zum 65. Geburtstag.* Eds. Václav Bok, Ulla Williams, and Werner Williams-Krapp. Verlag Dr. Kovac, Hamburg 2004a, 213–232.

Williams, Ulla and Werner Williams-Krapp: Die Dominikaner im Kampf gegen weibliche Irrtümer: Eberhard Mardachs 'Sendbrief von wahrer Andacht' (mit einer Textedition). *Deutsch-Böhmische Literaturbeziehungen: Germano-Bohemica. Festschrift für Václav Bok zum 65. Geburtstag.* Eds. Hans-Joachim Behr, Igor Lisový, and Werner Williams-Krapp. Verlag Dr. Kovač, Hamburg 2004b, 427–446.

Williams-Krapp, Werner: Die Bedeutung der reformierten Klöster des Predigerordens für das literarische Leben in Nürnberg im 15. Jahrhundert. *Kleine Schriften: Geistliche Literatur des späten Mittelalters.* Mohr Siebeck, Tübingen 2011, 189–208.

Willing, Antje: *Literatur und Ordensreform im 15. Jahrhundert. Deutsche Abendmahlsschriften im Nürnberger Katharinenkloster.* Waxmann, Münster 2004.

Willing, Antje (ed.): *Die Bibliothek des Klosters St. Katharina zu Nürnberg. Synoptische Darstellung der Bücherverzeichnisse.* Akademie Verlag, Berlin 2012.

Zarria, Gabriella: Catherine of Siena and the Italian Public. *Catherine of Siena: The Creation of a Cult.* Eds. Jeffrey F. Hamburger and Gabriela Signori. Brepols, Turnhout 2013, 69–79.

The pictorial hagiography of Saint Radegund and the Capetian religious reform in late thirteenth-century Poitiers

Teemu Immonen

Introduction

In the Médiathèque François-Mitterrand in Poitiers, there are two closely connected medieval liturgical manuscripts MS 250 and MS 252. Both manuscripts contain texts of the Life of Saint Radegund (d. 587), a Merovingian queen turned penitent. They were originally endowed with extensive and nearly identical illustrations depicting scenes from the life of the saint. At some stage, MS 252 was stripped of its illustrations, which are nonetheless known to us from an eighteenth-century copy, MS 251, held in the same library. Both MS 250 and MS 252 come from the church of Sainte-Radegonde in Poitiers, which was the centre of the cult of Saint Radegund and the site of her tomb. Despite their affinity, the manuscripts are separated from each other by approximately two centuries. MS 252, from the late thirteenth or early fourteenth century, is actually a close copy of MS 250, which is dated to the beginning of the twelfth century.

The present article concentrates on the re-interpretation of the pictorial contents of the Romanesque MS 250 in the Gothic MS 252. What requirements did the composition of MS 252 fulfil? These manuscripts belonged to a prominent genre. Illustrated Lives of patron saints were among the most important manuscripts a medieval religious community might possess. The pictorial narratives of such lectionaries conveyed messages of the prestige, devotion, and power of the saint as well as of the guardians of his or her cult. They presented in visual form the legends on which the communities were founded. The re-interpretation of such a pictorial legend was a significant moment in the life of a religious community.

My interest in the recycling of the pictorial contents of MS 250 in MS 252 is primarily functional; I focus on the potential and the limits of manuscript illumination in the propagation of religious (and political) ideology. Only a limited audience can view images of a liturgical manuscript at any one time. I will discuss how and why MS 252 drew on the older manuscript and how its images complemented the pictorial material in the church space for which the manuscript was originally composed. Who were the intended audience of the images? How was the illustrated manuscript including the *Life of Saint Radegund* and composed for the Church of Sainte-Radegonde supposed to promote the cause of its composers, and how did it fit into the context of the intense religious reform of the late thirteenth century? How did the images relate to both earlier and contemporary pictorial material concerning Saint Radegund and composed for the same church?

I will read MS 252 against the background of the significant political, religious, and artistic changes which took place in Poitou in the thirteenth century. At the time, the Capetian dynasty was wresting the area from the hands of their Plantagenet rivals. Poitou began to integrate into France, which was slowly transforming from a cluster of semi-independent dominions into a more coherent unity with a distinct identity. Once the Capetian kings had overrun the Poitou region, it was ruled as an appanage by Alphonse of Poitiers, the brother of Louis IX (1226–1270), but after his death in 1271 it was permanently incorporated into the crown lands. The new rulers called for the local population to associate with the French crown and embrace its ideology.

Christianity in its spiritual as well as official forms was at the core of the Capetian self-understanding and state building. The ruler was closely associated with the ecclesiastic elites of his kingdom. In the coronation ceremony in the cathedral of Rheims, he received the ointment from the archbishop of the city and the symbols of royal power from the abbot of Saint-Denis.

Louis IX was deeply religious and fully committed to the promotion of Christianity through instruction and to the defence of Christendom by whatever means considered appropriate. He went on two crusades, in 1248 and 1270, and he actively sought to convert people of other faiths as well as those whom he considered heretics. In the spirit of the Fourth Lateran Council (1215), the Capetians sought to deepen the religious consciousness of the multitude of believers and fostered the evangelical currents of the contemporary Church. While the Capetian church revival involved the clergy at all levels and included increased training of the lower clergy, the main collaborators of the crown were the bishops and important religious houses.[1] Art in all its forms played an important part in the propagation and formulation of Capetian ideology. Royal patronage was essential for the development of new forms of visual arts and architecture. The major expressions of the so called High-Gothic style – Sainte-Chapelle, the sculptural decoration of Reims Cathedral, the Psalter of Louis IX, and the thirteenth-century tombs of Saint-Denis – were all expressions of royal power.[2]

In Poitiers, the collegial church of Sainte-Radegonde and the cult of the titular saint were part of this process. Capetians supported the church financially and individual members of the college of canons served in the royal administration. During the second half of the thirteenth century, the nave of Sainte-Radegonde was reconstructed and the building received new and extensive pictorial decoration, both

---

[1] For Louis IX, see Jordan 1979; Le Goff 1996. For the Capetian church restoration, see Vauchez 1988, 367–403.

[2] Fundamental is Kimpel and Suckale 1990. A classic exposition of Louis IX's association with art is Branner 1965. For Sainte-Chapelle, see Jordan 2002 and Cohen 2015. For Reims, see Sadler 2012. For the Psalter of Louis IX, see Stahl 2008 and Stirnemann 2011. For the royal tombs in Saint-Denis, see Wright 1974 and Brown 1985.

wall paintings and stained glass. In addition, new liturgical books, MS 252 among them, were produced for the community. How the images on the pages of MS 252 mediated the message of the guardians of the cult is one of the questions I hope to answer here.

Saint Radegund and her cult have received plenty of interest among scholars. For centuries, the saint was venerated as *Mater Patriae* in France. Kings celebrated their victories in her name and people came to visit her shrine in Poitiers in troubled times.[3] There have been many studies of Radegund the Merovingian queen and her hagiographical dossier.[4] MS 250, the above-mentioned illustrated Life of Saint Radegund from the turn of the eleventh and twelfth centuries, has been the focus of a number of noteworthy art-historical studies.[5] The thirteenth-century pictorial decoration of Sainte-Radegonde has also been researched. Meredith Lillich has discussed the late thirteenth-century stained glass windows made for the church that depict scenes of the life of Saint Radegund,[6] while Claudine Landry(-Delcroix) has analysed the church wall paintings portraying Saint Radegund's deeds.[7] Like the stained glass, the wall paintings date from the late thirteenth or early fourteenth century.

The Gothic MS 252, the object of the present study, has received little interest among scholars. The manuscript is occasionally mentioned because its pictures were removed at an unknown time shortly before or

---

[3] Briand 1898; Aigrain 1918; Brennan 1985; 1996.

[4] Robert Favreau has written several important surveys of the religious, artistic, and historical dimensions of the cult and the communities that looked upon themselves as the guardians of the tomb of Saint Radegund, that is, the female monastery of Sainte-Croix in Poitiers and the College of Canons of the church of Sainte-Radegonde which was, in principle, under the tutelage of the nuns. See, in particular, Favreau 1986 and 1994. For the hagiographical dossier, see Martindale (ed.) 1992; McNamara 1992; Jenks 1999; Jones 2014. I have not been able to consult Jennifer C. Edwards' *Superior Women: Medieval Female Authority in Poitiers' Abbey of Sainte-Croix* (Oxford University Press, 2019) as this recent publication only came to my notice after the present book had already gone to press.

[5] For MS 250, see, Ginot 1914–1920; Skubiszewski 1993; Carrasco 1990; Favreau (ed.) 1995; Skubiszewski 1995; Vezin 1995; Lupant 2016.

[6] Lillich 1994.

[7] Landry 1988; Landry-Delcroix 2012.

after the French Revolution. In the late nineteenth century, Xavier de Montault studied MS 252 from a liturgical angle and at the beginning of the twentieth century Émile Ginot examined the manuscript in the context of his survey of the more famous Romanesque MS 250.[8] Ginot concentrated on codicological features, but little has been added on the topic since then. The manuscript is often mentioned in studies which concern the cult of Saint Radegund in general, or individual artistic products of the cult such as the above-mentioned MS 250, the stained glass windows, or the wall paintings.[9] However, questions concerning MS 252 itself have remained in the background.

The lack of interest is understandable considering the loss of the images in MS 252 and the apparent lack of originality of the manuscript, despite its imposing dimensions and careful handwriting. Nevertheless, the dearth of attention is unfortunate as MS 252 may open insights into the use and re-use of images in the Capetian quest for religious and political legitimacy in Poitou at a time when the area was being fully integrated into the kingdom of France. No less importantly, questions concerning the relation of the lost miniatures to the more or less contemporary wall paintings and stained glass windows in the church of Sainte-Radegonde, for which the manuscript was composed, are significant in a wider sense. Our understanding of the functional relations between manuscript illumination and other pictorial media in the Middle Ages is still inadequate because so much has been lost. We know very little about the audiences of medieval illustrated liturgical manuscripts and how their message was conveyed to the congregation in the church.[10] MS 252 can offer us valuable insights into this wider issue.

In the pages that follow, I will first briefly outline the story that MS 252 and MS 250 tell, that is, the life of Saint Radegund, and the

---

[8] de Montault 1894, 188–201: Ginot 1914–1920, 10–11.

[9] See, for example, Landry 1988, 13; Skubiszewski 1995, 118–121; Vezin 1995; Landry-Delcroix 2012, 118–121.

[10] With regard to the relation between manuscript illustration and wall painting, scholars have been interested mainly in stylistic questions, how one affected the other. Questions concerning the congruencies in content have received less interest. Classic studies of the question are: Grabar 1957; Kitzinger 1975; Weitzmann 1984.

development of the saint's cult in the early Middle Ages. The history of the cult sets the stage for the composition of MS 250 in the Romanesque era. I will discuss MS 252 and MS 250 together to clarify the close connection between the two and to point out the differences between them. There follows an analysis of MS 252 in its late thirteenth-century context. I will examine the pictorial representations in the Gothic church of Sainte-Radegonde and analyse their relation, functional as well as artistic, to the images in the contemporary MS 252.

The early medieval cult of Saint Radegund in Poitiers

Radegund was born c. 520 as a Thuringian princess. She became one of the several wives of King Clothar I (d. 561) and the Queen of the Franks after Clothar defeated her father and subjugated her people to Frankish rule. The marriage was not happy and after Clothar had her brother murdered, Radegund fled the court to lead a religious life. Around 550, she moved to Poitiers to pursue a life in solitude outside the walls of the city. From the outset, the queen turned penitent commanded tremendous authority among the Poitevins. Soon a community of religious women grew up around her and between 552 and 557 she founded the abbey of Sainte-Croix on the site. The name of the monastery derived from the relic of the True Cross which Radegund received from the Byzantine emperor Justin II and which was translated to Poitiers in 569.[11]

The prestige of the founder and of the relic of the true cross guaranteed a significant position for the monastery in Frankish society. The abbey enjoyed royal status and attracted princesses and daughters of aristocratic families from near and far. During her life, Radegund never took the position of abbess, serving merely as the spiritual keystone of the community. Before 561 a church dedicated to Mary was erected at some distance from the monastery, outside the Roman walls. It was meant to serve as the nuns' burial church and here Radegund would

[11] The relic of True Cross is still today in the possession of the community of Sainte-Croix.

find her resting place after her death in an odour of sanctity in 587.[12] Later, the burial church was rededicated to Sainte-Radegonde.

After Radegund's death, Venantius Fortunatus, the most prominent literary light of sixth-century Gaul, composed a Life.[13] Venantius, who had been a close friend of Radegund, started to put the work together after he had been elected bishop of Poitiers in 595.[14] Soon after Venantius's death in 609, another Life of Saint Radegund[15] was written by Baudonivia, a sister of the double monastery of Sainte-Croix and a rare example of a female author in Merovingian Gaul. Venantius's and Baudonivia's texts formed the core of the material which shaped the liturgical and more broadly collective memory of Saint Radegund in her own community and in society in general. In addition to the two mentioned authors, Gregory of Tours also wrote about Radegund on several occasions in the *History of the Franks,* as well as in the *Glory of Martyrs* and *Glory of Saints.*[16] Gregory discusses the events that took place in Radegund's monastery both during and after her life.[17]

By the seventh century, the cult of Saint Radegund already incorporated the features which would characterize it throughout the Middle Ages in Poitiers. The tomb of the saint situated in the church of Sainte-Marie-hors-les-Murs, the future Sainte-Radegonde, had become a pilgrimage centre where miracles were reported as having occurred. The literary tradition on which later imaginary of the saint would build had already been formed. Moreover, the Thuringian Princess had already begun to evolve into the holy Queen of the Franks and royal protector of the subjects of the king of France.[18] In Baudonivia's *Life,* we

---

[12] Favreau 1994, 91.

[13] Venantius, *Vita S. Radegundis.* On Venantius, see, for example, Roberts 2009; Williard 2014.

[14] Earlier, Venantius had composed the poem "The Thuringian War" about the bloodshed that had wiped out Radegund's tribe. Venantius, *De excidio.*

[15] Baudonivia, *Vita S. Radegundis.* See, Mayeski and Crawford 2000 which also contains an English translation in Appendix.

[16] Gregory, *Libri historiarum*; Gregory, *Gloria martyrum*; Gregory, *Gloria confessorum.*

[17] See, for example, Glenn 2012.

[18] For the early stages of the cult, see Brennan 1985; Effros 1990; Favreau 1994, 91.

encounter the concept of Radegund as *Mater Patriae* in embryo, as the author claims that the saint acquired the relic of the True Cross from the emperor of Byzantium for the good of the fatherland.[19]

The Carolingians held the cult and the edifices connected to it in high regard.[20] They endorsed both Sainte-Radegonde and Sainte-Croix. Under Carolingian rule, as under the Merovingians, the church maintained a close connection to the royal family. Pepin I, king of Aquitania, was buried there in 838. Rotrudis, the daughter of Charles the Bald (d. 877), used her family ties to become the abbess of the monastery. The church of Sainte-Radegonde was reconstructed at this time and Rotrudis attended the consecration officiated over by Bishop Ingenald of Poitiers in 863. Around this time, the male monastic community of Sainte-Radegonde was substituted by a community of canons, who would remain in charge of the liturgical life of the church thereafter. The relations between the college of canons and the female monastic community in Sainte-Croix would often be strained, as the canons would constantly seek greater independence.[21]

The romanesque cult of Saint Radegund and the illustrated MS 250

In 955, the Carolingian church burned down and the reconstruction work began in earnest only at the beginning of the eleventh century. The new church, however, was also damaged by fire in 1083 and the Romanesque edifice was finally consecrated in 1099.[22] At the time of the construction work, the cult of Saint Radegund and the communities serving the cult were closely connected to the counts of Poitou, one of the leading families in Europe, then at the peak of its power. Empress Agnes (d. 1077), who belonged to the House of Poitiers and married Henry III of Germany, king and subsequently emperor, showed great

---

[19] Brennan 1985.
[20] Favreau 1994, 92.
[21] Kneepkens 1986; Carrasco 1990, 431.
[22] Kneepkens 1986, 335; Carrasco 1990; Lillith 1994.

interest in the female community of Saint-Croix. She pleaded to the pope on their behalf several times in the contest between the monastery and the college of canons of Sainte-Radegonde over the control of the burial church of the saint and her holdings. In 1072, Pope Alexander II did intervene, confirming the ancient rights of the abbess over the college of canons, who were obliged to manage the liturgical services of the convent. Alexander's diploma calmed the situation temporarily but the conflict would go on for centuries with varying intensity.[23]

Despite the discord over administrative questions, both the canons and the nuns appear to have promoted the cult of Saint Radegund energetically. The construction of the new church for the saint was accompanied with the copying of a remarkable illustrated lectionary, MS 250, for the liturgy of the church. The manuscript contained the texts of the main feasts for the *familia* of the saint. Today, the manuscript begins with 20 folios of Gospel readings for the major biblical feasts. These lessons are a later addition, written in a late fifteenth-century hand. The part dating from the eleventh century starts at folio 21. In this section, there is the Life of Saint Radegund written by Venantius Fortunatus (fols. 22–43), followed by the text of Gregory of Tours on Radegund's funeral (fols. 44–46) and Gospel readings beginning with those for Christmas (fols. 47–72). Another hand from the later twelfth century has added documents that contributed to the authority of the cult centre. These are Radegund's own letter to the bishops of Gallia (fols. 73–74), a diploma attributed to King Clothar (fols. 75–76), a forged diploma attributed to Clothar (fol. 78), and a diploma of King Louis the Pious (d. 840) for the monastery of Sainte-Croix (fol. 78).[24] The additions underline the royal associations of the cult of Saint Radegund and the saint's active participation in the ecclesiastical questions of her time.

In its preserved form, MS 250 contains thirty-eight miniatures that illustrate Venantius Fortunatus's Life of Saint Radegund. Ginot was the first to point out that the surviving manuscript is mutilated. Between folios 36 and 37, there were formerly two illustrated pages. Ginot noticed that there were copies of the lost images, together with copies of

---

[23] For the disputes, see Carrasco 1990, Favreau 1994. On the Poitevin society of the time, see Dillange 1995; Treffort 2000; Damon 2008.
[24] For MS 250, see notes 5 and 7 above.

the others, in the eighteenth-century MS 251. He also concluded that in MS 250 the Life of Venantius Fortunatus was originally followed by the Life written by Baudonivia: on the last page of the last booklet containing Venantius's text, there is an author portrait of Baudonivia, but her text does not follow the portrait as would be expected. Ginot hypothesised that this life would also have been decorated with images, although no such images have survived.[25]

Roughly two hundred years after the preparation of MS 250, the canons of Sainte-Radegunde composed a new patron saint *libellus*, MS 252, for Saint Radegund. The obvious intention was to substitute the Romanesque manuscript containing the textual and pictorial narrative of the patron saint of the community with an up-to-date rendering of these texts and images fundamental for the *familia* of the saint. MS 252 is written in a late thirteenth- or early fourteenth-century Gothic hand. Like its Romanesque predecessor, the manuscript contains the Lives of Radegund written by Fortunatus (f. 32r), and Baudonivia (f. 58r). In addition to these Lives, MS 252 contains a third (f. 3r), composed around 1120 by the Metropolitan Archbishop of Tours, Hildebert of Lavardin (d. 1133), soon after the consecration of the new church and the composition of MS 250. Hildebert was an esteemed scholar and ecclesiastic as well as an ardent supporter of the Gregorian reform. He did not make drastic modifications to the story of Radegund, but he changed the emphasis in many places. In his version of the Life of Saint Radegund, Hildebert emphasized chastity and the call to follow the ecclesiastical authorities instead of lay authorities. Where Fortunatus had mentioned Radegund's marriage in passing, Hildebert went to great lengths to point out her aversion to marriage and the bridal bed.[26]

In MS 252, the traditional hagiographies of Saint Radegund and Hildebrand's text are accompanied with a text called *Nova miracula beatae Radegundis* (f. 96r), describing the miracles that took place at the tomb of the saint between 1249 and 1268. It is written in a different hand but also dates to the late thirteenth or early fourteenth centuries. The manuscript was clearly copied in the later thirteenth century, soon

---

[25] Ginot 1914–1920, 22–23.

[26] For the hagiographical text of Hildebert, see, Dalarun 1995.

after the last of the described miracles had taken place.[27] Three more miracles were subsequently added to MS 252. These occurred a little later but they nevertheless attest to the flowering of the cult of Saint Radegund around the turn of the fourteenth century.[28]

Originally, the Gothic MS 252 was illustrated just like its predecessor, the Romanesque MS 250. However, in the vicissitudes of the French Revolution, the illustrated pages were lost. When Abbé Gibault, the conservator of the Municipal Library of Poitiers,[29] purchased the MS 252 from a private person in 1829, the images had gone missing. The existence of the images, however, can be verified from earlier descriptions and by a careful examination of the manuscript. Maurist Dom Léonard Fonteneau spent the years between 1741 and 1769 in Poitiers copying documents concerning the history of the area. His monumental notes, conserved in the Médiathèque François-Mitterrand, also include an important description of MS 252. According to Fonteneau, in the manuscript the *Life* of Fortunatus was illustrated with 28 images and the *Life* of Baudonivia with 13. The *Life* written by Hildebert was preceded by an image where the author offered his work to Saint Radegund.[30] As Ginot has pointed out, one can observe today that folios have been ripped out in the places indicated by Fonteneau.[31]

Fonteneau's description tells us little about the possible congruences between the Romanesque images of MS 250 and the Gothic ones of MS 252. Fortunately, he was not the only religious scholar working on material from Sainte-Radegunde in the second half of the eighteenth century. Towards 1763, the Benedictine monk Antoine-Joseph Pernety (1716–1801) visited Poitiers while collecting material for the preparation of the eighth volume of *Gallia Christiana*.[32] During his visit, Pernety composed a manuscript (today MS 251 in Médiathèque François-Mitterrand) where he drew copies of two closely connected series of scenes from the Life of Saint Radegund by Venantius Fortunatus. It

[27] Ginot 1914–1920, 10–11.
[28] Ginot 1914–1920, 10; Lillich 1994, 77; Moulinier 2001, 3.
[29] For abbé Gibault, see, Gergen 2013.
[30] Fonteneau, vol. 79, p. 59.
[31] Ginot 1914–1920, 11.
[32] Ginot 1914–1920, 12–13.

is clear that the first series faithfully replicates the images from the Romanesque MS 250. In MS 251, every page describing a scene from Venantius's Life in MS 250 in Romanesque style is faced with an image evidently portraying the same scene but composed in a Gothic style. Scholars agree that the Gothic images facing the Romanesque illustrations are copies of those removed from MS 252. Thus, by using the eighteenth-century MS 251, we can reconstruct the general structure of the pictorial decoration of Venantius Fortunatus's Life of Saint Radegund in MS 252 as well as identify the main similitudes and differences from its Romanesque predecessor.[33] So, why is the relation between the two manuscripts meaningful?

MS 250 and MS 252 belonged to a genre called Patron saint *libelli*, luxurious and very expensive, often lavishly illuminated manuscripts containing the lives of the patron saints of a given community or edifice. During the feast day of the patron saint, such manuscripts were solemnly carried to the lectern in the choir where lessons from their pages were read aloud for the community in the Office of Matins in the night. Such lectionaries were of large format for both practical and symbolic reasons. Their size enabled reading in the dim candlelight of the church at night-time. Moreover, the size served to underline the authority of the text that was enunciated from the lectern in the liturgy.[34] The Matins readings were divided into a number of lessons according to the requirements of the different feasts. In the margins of MS 252, the lesson markings are still visible here and there. These Patron saint *libelli* typically belonged to the treasury of the community. Such manuscripts were composed to celebrate and manifest not only the glory of the saint whose life they contained, but also the glory of the community following the saint. The patron saint *libelli* played an integral part in the construction of shared identity in the communities that produced them.

The production of a patron saint *libellus* was most often connected to a significant reconsideration of the communal identity. The illustration of a *libellus* gave visual reading to an ancient text on which the identity

---

[33] Skubiszewski 1995, 128; Vezin, 1995, 118; Landry-Delcroix 2012, 118.

[34] For the physical features of the legendaria, see, for instance, de Montault 1894, 191–192. For the illustrated patron saint *libelli*, see, Wormald 1952; Abou-El-Haj 1997; Hahn 2001.

of the community rested. The pictorial interpretation of the text could add new dimensions to the community's understanding of the contents of their fundamental texts. Interestingly, the composers of MS 252 saw little reason to alter the pictorial narrative of MS 250. The images of the Gothic manuscript diligently portrayed the same scenes as their Romanesque predecessor with few variances. Here and there, the scenes were composed in a slightly different way, but the changes appear to reflect the adjustment of pictorial style from Romanesque to Gothic rather than a change of emphasis in the subject. In the scenes where Radegund is portrayed by an altar, the composer of MS 252 has typically added a cross to the altar.[35] Occasionally, the Gothic composition employs a more markedly biblical iconography than its earlier model.[36]

Radegund often has different headgear in the two manuscripts. For example, in a scene depicting her praying at an altar, whereas in the older version she is portrayed with her head veiled, in the Gothic version her head is bare (5r/6v).[37] A more significant change, however, is the emphasis laid on the royal crown in the newer images. In five images where Radegund is bare-headed or wears a wimple in MS 250, she wears a crown instead in MS 252. The form of the crown is familiar from Capetian royal art.[38] As we will see, Capetian royal emblems were promoted in the contemporary stained glass windows in Sainte-Radegonde as well. Thus, while the composers of MS 252 were on the whole content to update the style of the images to Gothic, they also placed new emphasis on the royal character of Saint Radegund. On the one hand, the pictorial hagiography of MS 252 stressed the continuity with MS 250, and on the other the Gothic imagery of MS 252 included a new focus on Radegund's royalty.

Neither of the prominent features of MS 252 – the conscious adherence to the Romanesque patron saint *libellus* or the dedicated advocacy of the royal image –are likely to be accidents of contemporary

---

[35] See, MS 251, fol. 3r/4v; 5r/6v; 7r/8v; 33r/34v.
[36] See, for example MS 251, fol. 11r/12v (MS 250, fol. 29v), *Radegund Serves the Poor*, the iconography of which in MS 252 alludes more explicitly to the *Last Supper*.
[37] MS 251, fol. 5r/6v.
[38] MS 251, fol. 9r/10v; 13r/14v; 17r/18v; 31r/32v; 37r/38v.

style]. Both approaches are natural in the context of the political changes that took place between the composition of MS 250 in the early twelfth century and MS 252 in the late thirteenth century. Let us take a look at these changes.

The Capetians gain control of Poitou

After the heyday of the cult of Saint Radegund in the early twelfth century, which had seen the construction of the Romanesque church of Sainte-Radegonde, the composition of MS 250, and, soon after that the preparation of a new text for the Life of the saint by Hildebert of Lavardin, Poitiers and the cult of Radegund witnessed a considerable upheaval. In the 1130s, the story of the *de facto* independent duchy of Aquitaine came to an end when Duke William X died without male heirs. William's daughter Eleanor (d. 1204) married first the Capetian king Louis VII of France in 1137 and then, after having divorced Louis in 1152, the Plantagenet king Henry II of England in 1154. The marriages turned Aquitaine into a bone of contention in the rivalry between the two royal families; from the middle of the century to the beginning of the next, Poitou was subordinate to the Plantagenets.

The wide international horizons of the Plantagenets offered a possibility for the cult of Saint Radegund to reach a new audience and followers. Between the twelfth and fourteenth centuries, the cult established a strong foothold in England.[39] In Poitiers, the new rulers also expressed an interest in the cult of Saint Radegund. In the early thirteenth century, work was begun on Sainte-Radegonde, the centre of the cult, with the obvious goal of accentuating the importance of the saint by remodelling the edifice to measure up to the requirements of Angevin Gothic style, the house-style of the Plantagenets. The Romanesque chancel and tower were saved, but the nave was torn down and work was begun on constructing a new one.[40]

[39] For the development of the cult, see Moulinier 2001.
[40] For the Angevin Gothic nave of Sainte-Radegonde, see Mussat 1963, 265–267; Blomme 1993, 263–270.

At this point, the change of fortune in the battle between the Capetians and the Plantagenets interrupted the work on the nave for several decades. In 1242 the Capetians succeeded in driving their rivals out of Poitou. Owing to the importance of the region, King Louis VIII of France (1223–1226) had placed it under the governance of one of his sons, Alphonse, in his testament. Alphonse became count of Poitou in 1241 and governed the county until his death in 1271. Though the count rarely visited his domain in person, his administration effectively tied the region to the kingdom, and Poitou became crown land when Alphonse died without an heir.

Religious reform was important during Alphonse's administration and the count accentuated the role of the Catholic Church in promoting the Capetian cause in the area. Alphonse's actions should be considered in the light of the religious zeal of his brother Saint Louis (Louis IX of France, 1226–1270). The Capetians embraced the cult of Saint Radegund. Under the watchful eye of Louis IX, Vincent of Beauvais (d. 1264) composed his *Speculum maius*, one of the most ambitious encyclopaedic works of the later Middle Ages. In the historical part of the work, *Speculum historiale*, Vincent included a description of the Life of Saint Radegund which drew heavily on the Life written by Hildebert of Lavardin.[41] In Radegund, the Capetian house saw an emblem of a devout, virtuous, and royal French saint threatened by a depraved heretic foreign monarchy.

Alphonse of Poitiers and the cult of Saint Radegund

In Poitiers, the communities associated with the saint, that is, Sainte-Radegonde and Sainte-Croix, became two of the foci of Alphonse's religious reform. Both communities had close connections to the highest echelons of Poitevin society and they recruited from their households. The abbesses of Sainte-Croix belonged to highly influential

---

[41] Moulinier 2001, 3. For Vincent of Bauvais' work, the bibliography is huge. See, for example, Franklin-Brown 2013.

local families, many of which had close connections to other important religious institutions of the city as well.[42] Canons in general played an essential part in Alphonse's administration in Poitou and Sainte-Radegonde belonged firmly to this structure.[43] Towards the end of the 1260s', Alphonse installed his close confidant Guichard of Cambrai in the chapter of the church.[44] In his testament, whose execution Guichart supervised, the count donated to Sainte-Radegonde sixty sous for the annual celebration of his birthday in the church and twenty livres for a chaplain to celebrate a daily mass for him.[45] Later, Alphonse's nephew Peter of Alençon (d. 1284) included Guillaume of Châtelairaut, the prior of Sainte-Radegonde, among the testators of his will.[46] During the same period, Alphonse supported the female community of Sainte Croix as well.[47]

[42] Abbess Jeanne de Plaisance (1264–c. 1269) belonged to a family that would appear prominently on the ecclesiastical scene of Poitiers in the early fourteenth century. One member of the family was a canon and chaplain of Notre-Dame-la-Grande, one of the major churches of the city, in 1304, and another became dean of Saint-Hilaire-le-Grand, another prominent Poitevin community. Jeanne de Plaisance was followed by Jeanne de la Vergne (c. 1269–1284), whose brother Philippe de la Vergne was the schoolmaster of Saint-Pierre, the Cathedral of Poitiers. Briand 1898, 372–375; Favreau 1986, 128.

[43] Robert Favreau has shed light on the college of canons of Saint-Hilaire-le-Grand, who served as the count's representatives in Poitiers. Favreau 1986. See also Landry-Delcroix 2012, 14.

[44] Alphonse addressed a letter to Guichard, "his dear and loyal cleric," in September 1269 (Molinier 1894, doc. 1167, 770) and mentions him as a canon of Sainte-Radegonde in February 1268 (Molinier 1894, doc. 75, 48). See, Lillich 1994, 76.

[45] "De rechief, à l'eglise Sainte Raagon de Poitiers sexante souz chascun an de rente pour nostre anniversaire faire, et vint livres de rente chascun an pour un chapelain tenir, qui chantera chascun jour messe pour nous perpetuement." Berger 1902, 761. See, Lillich 1994, 76.

[46] The testament is edited by Charles du Chagne in Joinville 1668, 181–186. Guillaume is mentioned as "our dear clerk" in 185–186. See, Lillich 1994, 76.

[47] In 14 June 1069, Alphonse produced a document to protect the nuns from external threats. Molinier 1894, doc. 992, 642. For Alphonse of Poitiers' administration in Poitou, see Chenard 2010 and Ripart 2011.

The interest of Alphonse and other Capetians in the church of Sainte-Radegonde was not only administrative or liturgical: they also participated energetically in the visual propagation of the cult of Saint Radegund in the church. The most fervent invigoration of the cult took place in the transition period after the death of Alphonse in 1271. MS 252, which was copied before the end of the thirteenth century, contains a collection of twelve miracles that took place between 1249 and 1268, at the time of the heightened interest of the Capetians in the saint. Two further miracles were added slightly later, at the beginning of the fourteenth century, continuing evidence of the cult's importance during the consolidation of Capetian control in Poitou.[48] Alongside the occurrence of new miracles, the appointments of advocates of the Capetian cause to the chapter, and Alphonse's financial support to the communities, the work on the construction of the western part of the nave was resumed after a hiatus of several decades.

Interestingly, when the Capetians, after some reflection, took up the renovation program of Sainte-Radegonde begun by their adversaries the Plantagenets, they did not eradicate the work of the latter. Rather than restarting from the beginning and building the whole edifice in High-Gothic style, they adopted the construction of the Angevin Gothic nave and brought the works to completion. This does not, however, mean that the Capetians were indifferent to the communicative potential of the edifice housing the remains of the saint. In their battle over the memory of the saint, the Capetians looked elsewhere. While they accepted the Angevin Gothic nave, they set about energetically moulding the pictorial dressing of the cult in the newly created space. Thus, they resorted to the pictorial arts in the propagation of their own message.

In the second part of the century, the building works were complimented with a considerable decorative enterprise. In 1269, two years before his death, Alphonse donated one hundred sous to the church for the making of stained glass windows.[49] Among the images on the windows paid for by the count was an important pictorial Life of Saint

---

[48] The miracles took place in 1304 and 1306. See, Largeault and Bodenstaff 1904, 433.

[49] Arch. nat. JJ 24 D, fol. 10r.. Edited in Ledain 1869, doc. 113, 199. See also, Audouin 1923, doc. 69, 123; Lillich 1994, 76.

Radegund, which is still partly visible in the nave of Sainte-Radegonde today. In addition to the stained glass windows in the nave, the Romanesque choir was decorated with wall paintings. Unsurprisingly, Radegund had a strong presence in the new decoration of the apse as well. There were portraits of the saint and, more importantly, also narrative scenes from her Life, which survive in the wall paintings in the area between the arches and the windows in the apse.[50]

With regard to the pictorial hagiography of the contemporary MS 252 and the earlier MS 250, the narratives in stained glass and wall painting in the church space are extremely interesting. Already at the beginning of the twentieth century, Édouard Rayon recognized that many of the stained glass scenes of the Life of Saint Radegund were more or less faithful copies from MS 250.[51] Similarly, Claudine Landry(-Delcroix) has pointed out the congruencies between the illustrations in the manuscripts and those of both the stained glass windows and wall paintings, even though the last are not modelled directly on the scenes from the former.[52]

Unfortunately, time has not treated the Gothic decoration well. The stained glass windows were severely damaged by Huguenots in 1562 and later reparations often did more harm than good to what was left. What is visible today is largely the work of the nineteenth-century restorer Henri Carot. As a child of his time, Carot freely retouched the surviving scenes and completely repainted those which could not be saved. He also organised the program anew so that few sections remain in their original place. Most of what survived of the original pictorial hagiography of Saint Radegund was assembled in the windows of the bay closest to the apse on the north wall. The windows were heavily restored, which has affected their style. Nevertheless, the iconography of the scenes is still discernible in most places. The paintings in the second

---

[50] For the wall paintings, see Landry 1988; Landry-Delcroix 2012, 118–121.
[51] See Édouard Rayon's Inventaire des vitraux du département de la Vienne from 1925, fols. 211–212 [MH]. For later interpretations of the congruencies between MS 250 and the stained glass scenes, see Verdon 1959, Lillich 1994, 88.
[52] Landry 1988; Landry-Delcroix 2012, 118–121.

bay depicting Radegund's life are Carot's own work. He consulted earlier models but painted the windows following his own personal vision.[53]

The Gothic fresco decoration of the apse has also been retouched heavily by the nineteenth-century restorers. Of the different parts of the choir area, the section above the windows is better preserved. The centre of the decoration was an enormous Christ in Majesty surrounded with the symbols of the four evangelists. Under the feet of Christ, above the gable window, were seated the Madonna and child with angels. On both flanks of the Christ in Majesty there were portraits of saintly nuns and bishops from the story of Saint Radegund. To the left, seen from the nave, there were, first, two of Radegund's disciples, Disciola and Agnes, and then Radegund herself closest to the Madonna and child. To the right, moving from the nave towards the Madonna, there were Medard of Noyon[54], Gregory of Tours, and Fortunatus. The composition was thus Christocentric with a hierarchic presentation of the figures essential for the communal identity serving as mediators between the believers and Christ.

Under the windows, on the wall above the arches of the choir, there are four scenes from the Life of Saint Radegund. On the left hand side, there is first an act of charity and then a miracle. On the right hand side, there is an act of devotion and then Christ appearing to Radegund. At the end of the apse, there is a half-length image of Christ

[53] Lillich 1994, 79–84. In addition to the stained glass pictorial hagiography of Saint Radegund in two bays on the north wall, the remains of the scenes from the Life of the saint have been collected in a window in the first bay from the entrance on the southern wall. These are stylistically different from the above-mentioned ensemble and they have been dated to the first years of the fourteenth century. These scenes depict, for example, miracles that have been added to MS 252 in these same years. The imagery is very similar to that on the earlier stained glass, with Radegund attired in a garment adorned with fleur-de-lis, which also framed the window. The early thirteenth-century stained glass bears witness to the continual interest of the Capetians in the cult and the pictorial tradition concerning the saint in her burial church.

[54] Saint Medard was a bishop who, according to Fortunatus, had consecrated Radegund as deacon when she fled her husband after the murder of her brother. Venantius, *Vita S. Radegundis*, chp. 12, 41.

between the miracle and the apparition.[55] The present scenes are very much a product of the nineteenth-century artists. These paintings were discovered only at that time and in a deplorable condition.[56] Following the conventions of the time, they were heavily painted over. For that reason, it is even more difficult to discern the original iconography or occasionally even the subject matter of the paintings than it is with the stained glass windows. In general, however, scholars date these works to the thirteenth century and contextual evidence strongly supports the view that both the stained glass windows and the wall paintings were produced during the last years of Alphonse's rule and the early part of Philippe III's reign (1270–1285).[57]

In addition to the difficulties regarding the style and details of the surviving images in Sainte-Radegonde, there is the problem that much of the medieval pictorial decoration in the church has been lost. We do not know whether the church had more fresco decoration, and if it did, whether there was a pictorial hagiography of Saint Radegund included in the program, let alone which scenes such a pictorial series would have contained. Furthermore, the choir wall of churches often involved pictorial narratives, but there are no means to detect what kind of pictorial decoration the choir wall of Sainte-Radegonde would have had, whether the Life of the titular saint was included there or not.[58]

The state of MS 252 and MS 250 complicates the discussion of the relationship between manuscript illumination and the media visible in the church space. We are not sure whether the Romanesque MS 250 originally contained illustrations for the Lives written by Baudonivia and, with regard to the 13 illustrations for the Life in MS 252 that Fonteneau reported[59], we know nothing of their contents. At present,

[55] For the wall paintings, see Landry 1988; Landry-Delcroix 2012, 50–53.

[56] M. abbé Auber recounts the story of the discovery of the wall paintings in Auber 1834–1837.

[57] Lillich 1994, 76.

[58] Édouard de Fleury quotes seventeenth-century eyewitness testimonies of a later choir wall of Sainte-Radegonde which contained depictions of miracles that took place during the visit of Jean de Berry to the church in 1412. The choir wall was demolished during the upheavals of the French Wars of Religion. Fleury 1847, 289–293. See also Skubiszewski 2012, 16.

[59] See above, note 29.

we can observe that in the best preserved window closest to the altar in the northern nave wall, six scenes out of sixteen directly copy a model first attested in MS 250. The other ten scenes depict thirteenth-century miracles on the tomb of the saint, miracles that protected the Poitevin community, and Radegund's visions of Christ and Mary. Thus, regardless of the loss of pictorial material in the church and possibly also in the manuscripts, we can see a clear congruence in the material; MS 250 and/or MS 252 contain scenes that are found in the stained glass. On the other hand, due to the loss of material, it is impossible to define with precision the extent to which the manuscript illustrations were translated to other media present in the church.

What of the iconographic contents? Above, we have seen that one of the major differences between MS 250 and MS 252 was the way the latter emphasized Radegund's royal prestige by placing a familiar Capetian crown on the saint's head in several images. The same emphasis is even more markedly visible in the stained glass windows. In them, Radegund is always depicted as a queen wearing a crown and clothed in a garment adorned with fleur-de-lis, the emblem of the Capetian house. Similarly, fleur-de-lis alternating with castles form the frames for the windows. In both manuscript and stained glass illustrations, Radegund is presented as a Capetian queen bringing salvation and protection against both spiritual and corporal afflictions. This was the image with which the Capetian rulers wished to associate themselves.

It is interesting how little the Gothic artists have changed the iconography of the scenes beyond the accentuation of royal prestige through the crown and, at least in the stained glass, the Capetian emblems. (The outline drawings of MS 252 do not allow us to determine how the garments were adorned in the manuscript, or whether or not they were decorated with fleur-de-lis.) The faithful copying of the Romanesque models, linking the Radegund-cult of Alphonse to the earlier twelfth-century cult of the counts of Poitou, may have served to obscure the Plantagenet interlude. The re-use of familiar images would have created a mental continuum, making pre-Plantagenet Poitou as "Capetian" as it was after the dynasty took control in the mid-thirteenth century and removing the "foreign" period from memory.

How then, would manuscript illumination have contributed to the dissemination of the Capetian religious and political message in Sainte-Radegonde? There are no direct answers to this question, but a comparison to other roughly contemporary material offers hints. It appears that the major illustrations of liturgical manuscripts were often reproduced in other media in the church or chapel for which the manuscript was originally copied and in whose liturgical services it was used. For example, the images in an early fourteenth-century English psalter from Peterborough Abbey duplicate the now-lost pictorial cycle carved in the wooden choir stall of the abbey church in the middle of the thirteenth century.[60] In a similar vein, there is an illustrated Bible produced in Canterbury in circa 1140, around the same time when the chapel of Saint Gabriel was decorated with wall paintings in the cathedral of the city. Both decorative programs included certain atypical scenes such as the naming of John the Baptist, thus suggesting a connection between the different pictorial media.[61] Manuel Castiñeiras has suggested that the obviously close relation between the mid-thirteenth-century sculptural decoration of the portal of the abbey church of Santa Maria de Ripoll and the pictorial decoration of the eleventh-century Ripoll Bible might indicate that there was portal decoration contemporary to and congruent]with the Ripoll Bible illustration.[62] In Ravenna, the central panel of the fourteenth-century tympanum at the gate of San Giovanni Evangelista reproduces a contemporary miniature in a contemporary liturgical manuscript composed for the same church.[63]

Perhaps the most interesting point of reference to the relation between MS 252 and the different pictorial material in the church space is the case of Saint Quentin. A sumptuous illustrated *libellus* relating the

---

[60] The motifs and the *tituli* of the carved pictorial cycle have been partly preserved in London, College of Arms, MS Arundel 30, of ca. 1300, and in Gunton 1686, 95–96. See, Sandler 1974, 110–115; James 1987. For the connection between the images and the liturgy, see, Von Daum Tholl 1994.

[61] Camille 1985, 34–35, pointed out the relation between the Bible illustration and wall painting in Canterbury. For the frescoes, see Demus 1970, plate 235, and for the manuscript, Kauffmann 1975, n. 66, p. 93–96.

[62] Castiñeiras 2013.

[63] Ravenna, Istituzione Biblioteca Classense, MS 406, f. 1r. See, Schoolman 2016, 108–110.

saint's life was composed for Saint Quentin at the turn of the eleventh and twelfth centuries, at the same time when a new church was erected over his tomb. Towards the middle of the thirteenth century, the church was rebuilt in a Gothic style and a new pictorial presentation of the saint's deeds was produced; scenes very closely copied from the Romanesque *libellus* were sculpted on the screen of the new Gothic church. It is interesting to note that King Louis IX was present at the consecration of the new church.[64]

From the above examples we can conclude that the pictorial narrative of the illustrated hagiographical patron saint *libelli* was often communicated to the audience in the church through other, more easily visible media and this was often the case with other illustrated liturgical manuscripts also. This is understandable, as dissemination of a pictorial message to a large audience from a manuscript simply was not practical. Why, then, were the images painted in the books at all? They created a connection between the manuscript, the church edifice, and, in the cases of patron saint *libelli*, the tomb of the saint present in the church. The congruence of the images within the book covers and the walls, windows, altar panels, reliquaries, and/or choir walls underlined that they all served to house the essence of the saint. When the images were available in the other media, it was enough for the people to know that they also existed in the manuscript. Thus the illustration merely emphasized the prestige of the manuscript and tied it more directly to the church housing the relics of the titular saint. While this boosted the prestige of the manuscript, it also meant that the illustrated patron saint *libelli* in Sainte-Radegonde or elsewhere probably did not in themselves have much of a role in the propagation of the pictorial message. Rather, they functioned together with the architectural and decorative components of the church for which they were copied.

[64] Branner 1967; Cahn 2003.

Conclusion

MS 252 was clearly part of a larger endeavour to promote the Capetian religious and political agenda in Poitou at the time when the region was becoming increasingly incorporated into the French crown. During the second half of the thirteenth century, the nave of Sainte-Radegonde was reconstructed, the building received an extensive pictorial decoration in both wall painting and stained glass, and new liturgical books, some of them illustrated, were produced for the community. For the Capetians, the cult of Saint Radegund presented a possibility to associate their sovereignty with the prestige of a locally important saint endowed with exceptional royal and devotional qualities. In the promotion of the ideology of the new rulers, the community of Sainte-Radegonde turned to the existing cornerstones of communal identity, that is, to the church building and its liturgical manuscripts as well as to the pictorial messages that decorated them. The new ideology was clothed in old garments with the necessary modifications. In my view, this is the explanation for the close connection between the illustrations of MS 252 and its predecessor MS 250. The Gothic MS 252 was composed by the canons of Sainte-Radegonde on the initiative of the Capetian rulers of the region. The new pictorial reading of the Life of Saint Radegund that the canons created was founded on an old and authoritative tradition, but it transformed the pictorial narrative into a medium serving the aspirations of the Capetian rulers of Poitou and the local elites committed to the Capetian cause.

The feast of Saint Radegund was directly linked to two communities, the canons of the collegial church of Sainte-Radegonde and the nuns of Sainte-Croix. The communities engaged in a prolonged but intermittent dispute over the possessions of Sainte-Radegonde. However, we should not let the economic controversy obscure the fact that the communities were bound together by a common cause, the cult of Saint Radegund. Firstly, Radegund was the founder of both communities and their histories were inseparable from each other. In public, the canons and the nuns appeared together as the guardians of the cult of Saint Radegund.

Secondly, both communities also recruited from the same social stratum and expressed, to a degree, the intentions of this stratum. The same families of elevated social standing produced nuns for Sainte-Croix, which had always been favoured by elites, and canons for the collegial churches of Poitiers. The dispute between the canons of Sainte-Radegonde and the nuns of Sainte-Croix was a controversy involving the internal dynamics of the ecclesiastical elites that appears to have had little effect on the cult of Saint Radegund.

Thirdly, the canons and the nuns came from within the local elites whose cooperation was essential to maintain Capetian power, the administration of their realm, and its unity. The Capetians sought to unify the Church so that it would be a cohesive and stabilizing force within the kingdom. Here, religious and political motives went hand in hand. The Capetians, first Alphonse of Poitiers and then the French sovereigns, relied heavily on the ecclesiastical authority in the organization of civil administration. It is in this light that we should consider the Capetian patronage of the communities of Sainte-Radegonde and Sainte-Croix as well as the royal support for the revitalization of the cult of Saint Radegund. We are dealing, first and foremost, with the construction of an "imagined community" where the saint functioned as the reference point to the people subject to the new power of the Capetian house.

The changes covered the whole array of visual presentation of the cult in Sainte-Radegonde. As regards architecture, the nave of the church was completely rebuilt. Within pictorial arts, the renovation of visual presentation was all-embracing, although the contents themselves appear to have remained close to the earlier renderings. The artists did not necessarily aim to tell a new story; rather, they were stylistically bringing up to date the earlier visual repertory. They were simply transforming the Romanesque visual landscape into a Gothic one with only slight modifications to the iconography and/or the imaginary. It is important to remember that the Gothic style itself was closely connected to the heartlands of the kingdom and the royal ideology. In MS 252, and especially in the stained glass windows made for Sainte-Radegonde, the single most distinguishable feature which underlines the Capetian cause is the new prominence of the crown. The form of the crown is familiar to us from a multitude of thirteenth-century Capetian art works depicting both lay and ecclesiastical rulers, Mary as well as royal saints.

Within this framework, the manuscript illumination itself does not appear to have played a strong role. Rather, it seems to have functioned as a part of the whole, together with the other forms of visual presentation in the church space. The extensive pictorial narrative of the *Life* of the saint on the pages of the liturgical manuscript was not directly available to the multitudes of people visiting the church on the feast day of the saint. The lectionary was placed on a lectern where some visitors may have been allowed to leaf through the manuscript to view its pictorial contents. But this was hardly possible for the majority of the audience, nor did it enable those who had the opportunity to glance through the pictures to engage in deeper contemplation. To affect the audience to any significant degree, the images had to be meditated through other media in the church space, be that stained glass, wall painting, or sculpture.

Sources

Documents

Paris, Archives nationales, Royal chancery Series JJ (Arch. nat. JJ)
  24 D
Paris, Médiathèque de l'architecture et du patrimoine, Archives [MH]
  4 Doc.12, Inventaire des vitraux du département de la Vienne by Édouard Rayon [1925]
Poitiers, Archives départementales de la Vienne
  2 H 1, fonds de l'abbaye Sainte-Croix de Poitiers
Poitiers, Médiathèque François-Mitterrand
  Vol. 79, collection Fonteneau (n. 455–543).

Manuscripts

London, College of Arms
  MS Arundel 30
Poitiers, Médiathèque François-Mitterrand
  MS 40
  MS 250
  MS 251
  MS 252
Ravenna, Istituzione Biblioteca Classense
  MS 406

Printed sources

Audouin, E. (ed.), *Recueil de documents concernant la commune et la ville de Poitiers*. Vol. 1, *1063–1327*. Archives historiques du Poitou, 44. Nicolas, Renault & Cie, Poitiers 1923.

Baudonivia: *Vita sanctae Radegundis*. Ed. Bruno Krusch. Monumenta Germaniae Historica, Scriptores Rerum Merovingicarum, Vol. 2: Fredegarii et aliorum Chronica. Vitae sanctorum. Hahn, Hannover 1888, 377–395.

Berger, Élie (ed.): *Trésor des chartes (layettes) (1261–1270): Inventaire analytique (J///148-J///735)*. Archives nationales: Pierrefitte-sur-Seine 1902. https://www.siv.archives-nationales.culture. gouv.fr/siv/IR/FRAN_IR_000419

Gregory of Tours: *Libri historiarum X*. Eds. Bruno Krusch and Wilhelm Levison. Monumenta Germaniae Historica, Scriptores Rerum Merovingicarum, Vol. 1, 1. Hahn, Hannover 1951.

Gregory of Tours: *Liber in gloria martyrum*. Gregorii Episcopi Turonensis Miracula et opera minora. Editio nova lucisope expressa. Ed. Bruno Krusch. Monumenta Germaniae Historica, Scriptores Rerum Merovingicarum, Vol. 1, 2. Hahn, Hannover 1969, 34–111.

Gregory of Tours: *Liber de gloria confessorum*. Gregorii Episcopi Turonensis Miracula et opera minora. Editio nova lucisope expressa. Ed. Bruno Krusch. Monumenta Germaniae Historica, Scriptores Rerum Merovingicarum, Vol. 1, 2. Hahn, Hannover 1969, 294–370.

Hildebert of Lavardin: *Vita sanctae Radegundis*, Patrologia Latina 171, c. 968–988.

Joinville, Jean de: *Histoire de S. Louis, IX du nom, roi de France*. S. Mabre-Cramoisy, Paris 1668. http://gallica.bnf.fr/ark:/12148/bpt6k5575244j

Ledain, Bélisaire: *Histoire d'Alphonse, frère de Saint-Louis et du Comté de Poitou sous son administration, (1241–1271)*. H. Oudin, Poitiers 1869. http://gallica.bnf.fr/ark:/12148/bpt6k6366852x

Lièvre, Auguste-François and Auguste Molinier: *Catalogue général des manuscrits des bibliothèques publiques de France: Départements / Ministère de l'instruction publique et des beaux-arts*. Vol. 25, *Poitiers, Valenciennes*. Plon, Paris 1894.

Molinier, Auguste (ed.): *Correspondance administrative d'Alfonse de Poitiers*. Vol. 1. Imprimerie nationale, Paris 1894. http://gallica.bnf.fr/ark:/12148/bpt6k29284z

Venantius Fortunatus: *De excidio Thoringiae*. Ed. Bruno Krusch. Monumenta Germaniae Historica, Auctores antiquissimi, Vol. 4, 1: Venanti Honori Clementiani Fortunati presbyteri Italici Opera pedestria. Weidmann, Berlin 1881, 271–275.

Venantius Fortunatus: *Vita sanctae Radegundis*. Ed. Bruno Krusch. Monumenta Germaniae Historica, Auctores antiquissimi, Vol. 4, 2: Venanti Honori Clementiani Fortunati presbyteri Italici Opera pedestria. Weidmann, Berlin 1881, 38–49.

Research literature

Abou-El-Haj, Barbara: *The Medieval Cult of Saints: Formations and Transformations*. Cambridge University Press, Cambridge 1997.

Aigrain, René: *Sainte Radegonde vers 520–587*. Lecoffre, Paris 1918.

Auber, M. l'abbé: Mémoire sur les anciennes peintures à fresque de l'église de Ste-Radegonde. [Décembre 1836]. *Bulletins de la Société des antiquaires de l'Ouest* 1834–1837, 373–379.

Blomme, Yves: *Poitou gothique*. Picard, Paris 1993.

Branner, Robert: *Saint Louis and the Court Style in Gothic Architecture*. Zwemmer, London 1965.

Branner, Robert: The Saint-Quentin Rotulus. *Scriptorium* 21.2/1967, 252–260.

Brennan, Brian: St Radegund and the Early Development of Her Cult at Poitiers. *Journal of Religious History* 13.4/1985, 340–354.

Brennan, Brian: Piety and Politics in Nineteenth-Century Poitiers: The Cult of St Radegund. *Journal of Ecclesiastical History* 47.1/1996, 65–81.

Briand, Emile: *Histoire de Sainte Radegonde, Reine de France, et des Sanctuaires et Pèlerinages et son honneur.* Oudin, Paris and Poitiers 1898.

Brown, Elizabeth A. R.: Burying and Unburying the Kings of France. *Persons in Groups: Social Behavior as Identity Formation in Medieval and Renaissance Europe.* Ed. Richard C. Trexler. Binghamton, New York 1985, 241–266.

Cahn, Walter: Images de la Vie de Saint Quentin. *Art de l'enluminure*, 4, *L'Authentique ou La passion de Saint Quentin* 4/2003, 4–57.

Camille, Michael: Seeing and Reading: Some Visual Implications of Medieval Literacy and Illiteracy. *Art History* 8.1/1985, 26–49.

Carrasco, Magdalena Elizabeth: Spirituality in Context: The Romanesque Illustrated Life of St. Radegund of Poitiers (Poitiers, Bibl. Mun., MS 250). *The Art Bulletin* 72.3/1990, 414–435.

Castiñeiras, Manuel: The Portal at Ripoll Revisited: An Honorary Arch for the Ancestors. *Romanesque and the Past.* Ed. John McNeill and Richard Plant. British Archeological Association, Manley Publishing, Leeds 2013, 121–141.

Chenard, Gaël: Les enquêtes administratives dans les domaines d'Alphonse de Poitiers. *Quand gouverner, c'est enquêter: Les pratiques politiques de l'enquête princière, Occident, XIIIe–XIVe siècles. Actes du colloque d'Aix-en-Provence et Marseille, 19–21 mars 2009.* Ed. Thierry Pécout. De Boccard, Paris 2010, 157–168.

Cohen, Meredith: *The Sainte-Chapelle and the Construction of Sacral Monarchy: Royal Architecture in Thirteenth-Century Paris.* Cambridge University Press, Cambridge 2015.

Dalarun, Jacques: Hagiographie et métaphore: Fonctionnalité des modèles féminins dans l'œuvre d'Hildebert de Lavardin. *Le culte des saints aux IXe–XIIIe siècles: Actes du Colloque tenu à Poitiers les 15–16–17 septembre 1993.* Ed. Robert Favreau. University of Poitiers, Centre d'études supérieures de civilisation médiévale, Poitiers 1995, 37–51.

Damon, Géraldine: Vicomtes et vicomtés dans le Poitou médiéval (IXe–XIIe siècle): Genèse, modalités et tranformations. *Vicomtes et vicomtés dans l'Occident médiéval.* Ed. Hélène Débax. Presses universitaires du Mirail, Toulouse 2008, 223–236.

de Montault, Xavier: *Œuvres complètes.* Vol. 9.6. *Hagiographie (première partie).* Imprimerie Blais, Poitiers 1894.

Demus, Otto: *Romanesque Mural Painting.* Abrams, New York 1970.

Dillange, Marcel: *Les Comtes de Poitou, ducs d'Aquitaine.* Geste éditions, Mougon 1995.

Effros, Bonnie: Images of Sanctity: Contrasting Descriptions of Radegund by Venantius Fortunatus and Gregory of Tours. *UCLA Historical Journal* 10/1990, 38–58.

Favreau, Robert: Heurs et malheurs de l'abbaye XIIe–XVe s.. *Histoire de l'abbaye Sainte-Croix de Poitiers: Quatorze siècles de vie monastique.* Ed. Robert Favreau. Société des Antiquaires de l'Ouest, Poitiers 1986, 117–220.

Favreau, Robert: Le culte de sainte Radegonde à Poitiers au Moyen Âge. *Les religieuses dans le cloître et dans le monde des origines à nos jours: Actes du Deuxième Colloque International du C.E.R.C.O.R., Poitiers, 29 septembre–2 octobre 1988.* University of Saint-Etienne, Saint-Étienne 1994, 91–109.

Favreau, Robert (ed.): *La vie de sainte Radegonde par Fortunat: Poitiers, Bibliothèque municipal, manuscript 250 (136).* Seuil, Paris 1995.

Fleury, Édouard de: *Histoire de Sainte-Radegonde: Reine de France au VIe siècle et patronne de Poitiers.* Henri Oudin, Poitiers 1847.

Franklin-Brown, Mary: The Speculum maius, Between Thesaurus and Lieu de mémoire. *Memory and Commemoration in the Medieval World, c. 500–c. 1400.* Eds. Elma Brenner, Meredith Cohen, Mary Franklin-Brown. Ashgate, Farnham 2013, 143–162.

Gergen, Thomas: Professeur à l'université et directeur de bibliothèque municipale: Le père Gibault de Poitiers et son programme pour l'enseignement universitaire après la Révolution française. *Revista europea de historia de las ideas políticas y de las instituciones públicas* 6/2013, 51–66. http://www.eumed.net/rev/rehipip/06/tg.pdf

Ginot, Émile: Le manuscrit de sainte Radegonde de Poitiers et ses peintures du XIe siècle. *Bulletin de la Société française de reproductions de manuscrits à peintures* 4.1/1914–1920, 9–80.

Glenn, Jason: Two Lives of Saint Radegund. *The Middle Ages in Texts and Texture: Reflections on Medieval Sources.* Ed. Jason Glenn. University of Toronto Press, Toronto 2012, 57–69.

Grabar, André: Fresques romanes copiées sur les miniatures du Pentateuque de Tours. *Cahiers Archéologiques* 9/1957, 329–341.

Gunton, Symon: *The History of the Church of Peterburgh.* Printed for Richard Chiswell, London 1686.

Hahn, Cynthia: *Portrayed on the Heart: Narrative Effect in Pictorial Lives of Saints from the Tenth through the Thirteenth Century.* University of California Press, Berkeley 2001.

James, Montague Rhodes: On the Paintings Formerly in the Choir at Peterborough. *Proceedings of the Cambridge Antiquarian Society* 9/1897, 178–194.

Jenks, Martha Gail: *From Queen to Bishop: A Political Biography of Radegund of Poitiers.* PhD Thesis, University of California, Berkeley 1999.

Jones, Lynn: Perceptions of Byzantium: Radegund of Poitiers and Relics of the True Cross. *Byzantine Images and their Afterlives: Essays in Honor of Annemarie Weyl Carr.* Ed. Lynn Jones. Ashgate, Farnham 2014, 105–124.

Jordan, Alyce A.: *Visualizing the Kingship in the Windows of the Sainte-Chapelle.* Brepols, Turnhout 2002.

Jordan, William Chester: *Louis IX and the Challenge of the Crusade.* Princeton University Press, Princeton, N.J. 1979.

Kauffmann, Claus Michael: *Romanesque Manuscripts, 1066–1190: A Survey of Manuscripts Illuminated in the British Isles.* Harvey Miller, London 1975.

Kimpel, Dieter and Robert Suckale: *L'architecture gothique en France, 1130–1270.* Flammarion, Paris 1990.

Kitzinger, Ernst: The Role of Miniature Painting in Mural Decoration. *The Place of Book Illumination in Byzantine Art.* Ed. Kurt Weitzmann. Princeton University Art Museum, Princeton 1975, 99–142.

Kneepkens, Corneille H.: À propos des débuts de l'histoire de l'église-funéraire Sainte-Radegonde de Poitiers. *Cahiers de Civilisation Médiévale* 29.116/1986, 331–338

Landry, Claudine: Les peintures murales du chœur de l'église Sainte-Radegonde de Poitiers, *Bulletin de la Société des antiquaires de l'Ouest,* 5e série, 12.2/1988, 109–155.

Landry-Delcroix, Claudine: *La peinture murale gothique en Poitou, XIIIe–XVe siècle.* Presses universitaires de Rennes, Rennes 2012.

Largeault, Alfred and H. Bodenstaff: Miracles de Sainte Radegonde (XIII et XIV siècle). *Analecta Bollandiana* 23/1904, 433–447.

Le Goff, Jacques: *Saint Louis.* Galimard, Paris 1996.

Lillich, Meredith P.: *The Armor of Light: Stained Glass in Western France, 1250–1325.* University of California Press, Berkeley 1994.

Lupant, Chrystel: Conception des images et réflexion sensorielle: Approche exploratoire du ms. de la Vie de Sainte Radegonde. *Les cinq sens au Moyen Âge.* Ed. Éric Palazzo. Cerf: Paris 2016, 689–717.

Martindale, John Robert (ed.): Radegundis. *The Prosopography of the Later Roman Empire,* Vol. 3. Cambridge University Press, Cambridge 1992, 1072–1074.

Mayeski, Marie Anne, and Jane Crawford: Reclaiming an Ancient Story: Baudonivia's "Life of St. Radegund," circa 525–587. *Women Saints in World Religions*. Ed. Arvind Sharma. State University of New York Press, Albany 2000, 71–88.

McNamara, Jo Ann: Radegund, Queen of the Franks and Abbess of Poitiers (ca. 525–587). *Sainted Women of the Dark Ages*. Eds. Jo Ann McNamara, John E. Halborg, and E. Gordon Whatley. Duke University Press, Durham NC 1992, 60–105.

Moulinier, Laurence: Un témoin supplémentaire du rayonnement de sainte Radegonde au Moyen Age? La Vita domnae Juttae (XIIe siècle). *Bulletin de la société des Antiquaires de l'Ouest*, 5e série, 15.3 & 4/2001, 181–197.

Mussat, André: *Le style gothique de l'Ouest de la France, 12ᵉ–13ᵉ siècles*. Picard, Paris 1963.

Ripart, François: Les territoires d'Alphonse de Poitiers: Un modèle de principauté avortée?. *Mélanges de l'École française de Rome. Moyen Âge* 123.2/2011, 461–466.

Roberts, Michael: *The Humblest Sparrow: The Poetry of Venantius Fortunatus*. University of Michigan Press, Ann Arbor MI 2009.

Sadler, Donna L.: *Reading the Reverse Façade of Reims Cathedral: Royalty and Ritual in Thirteenth-Century France*. Ashgate, Farnham and Burlington 2012.

Sandler, Lucy Freeman: *The Peterborough Psalter in Brussels and Other Fenland Manuscripts*. Harvey Miller: London 1974.

Schoolman, Edward M.: *Rediscovering Sainthood in Italy: Hagiography and the Late Antique Past in Medieval Ravenna*. Palgrave Macmillan: New York 2016.

Skubiszewski, Piotr: Un manuscrit peint de la Vita Radegundis à Poitiers: Les idées hagiographiques de Venance Fortunat et la spiritualité monastique au XIe siècle. *Venanzio Fortunato tra Italia e Francia*. Provincia di Treviso, Grafiche Zoppelli, Treviso 1993, 195–216.

Skubiszewski, Piotr: Le décor de la "vie de Radegonde" de Poitiers. *La vie de sainte Radegonde par Fortunat: Poitiers, Bibliothèque municipal, manuscrit 250 (136)*. Ed. Robert Favreau. Seuil, Paris 1995, 127–237.

Skubiszewski, Piotr: Préface. *La peinture murale gothique en Poitou, XIIIe–XVe siècle*. By Claudine Landry-Delcroix. Presses Universitaires de Rennes, Rennes 2012, 7–24.

Stahl, Harvey: *Picturing Kingship: History and Painting in the Psalter of Saint Louis*. Pennsylvania State University Press, University Park 2008.

Stirnemann, Patricia: Quand le programme fait fausse route: Les psautiers de Saint-Alban et de saint Louis. *Le Programme, une notion pertinente en histoire de l'art médiéval?*. Ed. Michel pastoureau. Le Léopard d'or, Paris 2011, 165–182.

Treffort, Cécile: Le comte de Poitiers, duc d'Aquitaine, et l'Eglise aux alentours de l'an mil (970–1030). *Cahiers de civilisation médiévale* 43/4.2000, 395–445.

Vauchez, André: Le christianisme roman et gothique. *Histoire de la France religieuse*. Vol. 1, *Des dieux de la Gaule à la papauté d'Avignon (des origines au XIVe siècle)*. Ed. Jacques Le Goff. Seuil, Paris 1988, 283–415.

Verdon, Jean: *Étude iconographique et historique des vitraux consacres à la vie de sainte Radegonde*. Diplome d'etudes superieures, Memoire secondaire. University of Poitiers, Poitiers 1959.

Vezin, Jean: Étude paléographique et codicologique du manuscrit de la Vita Radegundis. *La vie de sainte Radegonde par Fortunat: Poitiers, bibliothèque municipale, manuscrit 250 (136)*. Ed. Robert Favreau. Seuil, Paris 1995, 115–126.

Von Daum Tholl, Susan E.: Life according to the Rule: A Monastic Modification of Mandatum Imagery in the Peterborough Psalter. *Gesta* 33.2/1994, 151–158.

Weitzmann, Kurt: The Genesis Mosaics of San Marco and the Cotton Genesis Miniatures. *The Mosaics of San Marco in Venice*. Vol. 2. *Thirteenth Century*. Otto Demus. University of Chicago Press, Chicago 1984, 105–142, 253–257.

Williard, Hope Deejune: Letter-Writing and Literary Culture in Merovingian Gaul. *European Review of History—Revue européenne d'histoire* 21.5/2014, 691–710.

Wormald, Francis: Some Illustrated Manuscripts of the Lives of the Saints. *Bulletin of the John Rylands Library*, 35/1952, 248–266.

Wright, Georgia Sommers: A Royal Tomb Program in the Reign of St. Louis. *The Art Bulletin*, 56.2/1974, 224–243.

II
MARKING THE BORDERS
BETWEEN 'US' AND 'THEM'

Old errors, new sects:
The Waldensians, Wyclif and Hus
in fifteenth-century manuscripts

Reima Välimäki

Introduction

The Hussite movement, formed around the teachings of Jan Hus (ca. 1370–1415) and other Bohemian reform-minded theologians, and which erupted into radical revolution in 1419, was "a magnificent ride" for Bohemians and a shock to the secular and religious authorities of Europe.[1] Although the Hussites, backed by the victories of their armies, were a new kind of dissident movement, severely threatening the stability of both the state and the Church, heresy was an enemy that the Catholic Church was accustomed to combatting. When the

---

[1] "The magnificent ride" is a description by a contemporary Bohemian chronicle, see *Scriptores Rerum Bohemicarum*, vol. 3, 73; cit. in Fudge 1998, 2. It is also the title of Fudge's book. Much has been written about the Hussite revolution. Fudge's monograph is a good starting point. A classic study in English, and still useful, is Kaminsky 1967. The standard work by Frantisek Šmahel is available in German translation, see Šmahel 2002; a more recent collection of essays is Machilek 2012.

fifteenth-century Catholics engaged in polemical exchange with the Hussite theologians over Eucharist, the authority of the clergy and papacy, freedom of preaching, or indulgences, they could build upon several centuries of canon law, biblical exposition and anti-heretical treatises commenting on these and other matters. Therefore, it is not surprising to find older treatises transmitted in the same manuscripts as the fifteenth-century anti-Hussite and anti-Wycliffite works. Often these earlier texts include anti-Waldensian treatises, in particular works written against the German Waldensians during the persecution of the 1390s.[2]

In this article I explore the common manuscript tradition of the anti-Waldensian, anti-Hussite, and anti-Wycliffite treatises in fifteenth-century Central Europe, and explain the reasons for the inclusion of older, at times outdated material in anti-Hussite compilations. The shared *Überlieferungsgeschichte*[3] of these texts is used to demonstrate the roles that refutations of the old and established heresy Waldensianism played in the attack on the new sects. In other words, the manuscripts illuminate the attempts of fifteenth-century clergymen to describe the new heresies, particularly Hussitism, based on what had already been written. In the manuscript leaves one can find a mixture of prejudice and defamation of enemies, as well as a will to understand the new challengers of the Roman Church in the light of its old antagonists. I propose that the image the late-fourteenth-century polemicists created of the Waldensians influenced the Catholic perception of the Hussites more than has been assumed.

The transmission and rearrangement of the texts in manuscripts is a parallel and complementary process to the borrowings, adaptations and transformation of literary elements, *topoi* at the textual level. An important

---

[2] For an overview on the persecution of German Waldensians at the end of the fourteenth century see esp. Välimäki 2019, 29–37; Modestin 2007, 1–12; Kolpacoff 2000, 247–261. Kieckhefer 1979, 55–73 is a classic, but now outdated.

[3] "The history of transmission", see Driscoll 2010, 93; the *Überlieferungsgeschichtliche Methode* of German philology, which intends to make the different historical layers of the text (*Textgeschichte*) clearly visible, is described in Williams-Krapp 2000. For an English overview of the method, see Garber 2003, 6–7.

strand in the late twentieth- early twenty-first-century scholarship of heresy has been mapping out these *topoi* of anti-heretical literature, studying how they were transferred to new heresies, and unmasking these literary constructions and thus deconstructing imagined sects.[4] Recently, a more pliant understanding of the anti-heretical polemics has emerged, and the polemical texts are again regarded as including some elements derived from the heretics themselves, at least in some cases.[5] The adaptation of literary elements contributed to the purpose of the anti-heretical text, but far from being haphazard, it was often selective and conscious.[6] Just like the writing about heresy, copying old works and compiling texts together was about propagating one's own position and demonizing the enemy, but it can also be seen as a process in which late medieval churchmen discerned and explained the reality of their age, which they experienced as a period of upheaval.

In this article, I suggest that there were two reasons why the Church manuscripts presented the Waldensians, Wycliffites and Hussites together.

1) A genuine wish to understand the Wycliffite/Hussite heresy in relation to the legal and theological tradition of the Church. The treatises produced against Waldensians included lengthy expositions on the points of doctrine under scrutiny in the struggle

[4] The starting point in this field of study has been the classic essay Grund-mann 1976 (1927). Alexander Patschovsky follows this tradition in many of his publications, see esp. Patschovsky 1980; Patschovsky 1991; Patschovsky 1998. In the English-speaking world this approach was introduced above all by Lerner 1972; see also Moore 1976. An important anthology on the 'invention of heresy' is Zerner 1998; see also Brunn 2006; Chiu 2011. A synthesis of the late medieval imagined sects and the transmission of anti-heretical literary topoi to descriptions of witches is Utz Tremp 2008. On Cathars as an invention of the Catholich authors, see esp. Pegg 2001a; Pegg 2001b; Pegg 2016; Moore 2012; Moore 2014.

[5] Biller 2001b. See critique of Biller's reading by Modestin 2013, 224–225; see also Biller 2006; Sackville 2011, 39–40; Sackville 2016; Bruschi 2016; Välimäki 2019, 99.

[6] Sackville 2011, esp. 9, 175, 177; Välimäki 2015, 140–141, 149–150, 152. See also Kelly 2014, 938–939. Kelly points out that not all interrogations on heresy were set up to confirm existing suspicions, as in some one can perceive genuine attempts to uncover new, potentially heterodox opinions.

against Hussitism, above all concerning the authority, dignity and worthiness of priests, the possessions of the Church, and freedom of preaching. Thus they were a natural source of reference when the clergy was trying to understand and refute the new onslaught on its position.

2) The juxtaposition of Waldensians and Wyclif and Hus may also reflect conscious attempts to undermine the position of the Oxford and Prague reformers and represent them as indisputably heretical, reviving in their errors the "old" heresy of the Waldensians. Eleventh- and twelfth-century polemicists had done something similar when they referred to the dissidents of their times by names adopted from patristic sources, such as "Manichees" or "Arians."[7] In medieval polemical literature the heretics were often portrayed as Samson's foxes coupled tail to tail, in other words, essentially the same despite their apparent differences.[8]

The anti-Hussite literature has been extensively studied, and there are detailed accounts of different treatises as well as their manuscript transmission.[9] Here my approach to this substantial body of literature takes a different perspective from earlier studies, as it is based on a survey of the transmission of anti-Waldensian literature written in the 1390s. As stated above, these texts often accompanied younger anti-Hussite works and the texts attacking John Wyclif's tenets. I propose that the threat of the Hussites ensured the popularity of anti-Waldensian literature, the most remarkable example of which are the circa 50 preserved manuscripts of the treatise *Cum dormirent homines*

---

[7] Often the 'medieval Manichees' had little to do with actual heresy, but were simply an academic idea, constructed for the sake of debate, see Chiu 2011, 494. Hussites, of course, were very real at the beginning of the fifteenth century.

[8] Grundmann 1976, 320. The bible verse is Judges 15: 4–5.

[9] See e.g. Hlaváček 1966; Soukup 2009; see the database Soukup, *Repertorium operum antihussiticorum*, on-line database, for a comprehensive account of medieval texts and a bibliography of modern research.

(1395) by the Celestine provincial Petrus Zwicker.[10] On the other hand, the descriptions of Waldensianism, particularly those written in the late fourteenth century, affected the perception of Hussitism more often than frequently assumed. Kathrin Utz Tremp implied an intimate relationship between these two heresies in the minds of fifteenth-century clergy in her introduction to an anthology about the last revival of German Waldensianism under the leadership of Friedrich Reiser, a Waldensian influenced by Taborite teachings. According to Utz Tremp, although we should not regard the "Waldensian-Hussite Internationale" of the fifteenth century as a wholesale invention of the contemporary polemics against heresy, we should pursue the idea that its origins lie more in the perception and representation of fifteenth-century heresy than in any actual exchange between Waldensians and Hussites.[11] The examples presented below demonstrate both this imagination and representation, but also manuscripts whose compilers obviously perceived a notable similarity between the doctrines professed by the Waldensians and the Hussites. It is not out of the question that some protagonists of the Catholic side were aware of real interaction between Waldensian and Hussite communities, a possibility that is discussed below.

This article is a qualitative study of selected manuscripts, not a quantitative analysis of all known fifteenth-century anti-heretical compilations. It does not provide statistics of the number of compilations including both anti-Waldensian and anti-Hussite texts in relation to the complete manuscript tradition of these works. Such a comprehensive analysis will hopefully be possible in the near future, as the library metadata of European manuscript collections is increasingly becoming available in machine-readable formats. This study offers preliminary conclusions as well as a historical and codicological basis for future quantitative studies. The manuscripts analysed are:

---

[10] The manuscripts are listed in Biller 2001b, 263–269. For more detailed and updated manuscript descriptions see Välimäki 2019, 262–289. On Zwicker's treatise, see also Modestin 2013. See also the edition of that text in Gretser 1677.

[11] Utz Tremp 2006a, 16–17; Utz Tremp 2006b, 218.

Library	Manuscript	Dating
Augsburg, Univer-stitätsbibliothek (UB)	MS II. 1. 2° 129	First half of the 15th cent.
Graz, Universtitätsbib-liothek (UB)	MS 336	1444
Munich, Bayerische Staatsbibliothek (BSB)	Clm 5614	1460s (?)
Prague, Národní kni-hovna České repub-liky (NKCR)	XIII. E. 5	1427–1428
	XI. D. 8	After 1480
Salzburg, St Peter	b VIII 9	Late 15th cent.
Vatican city, Vatican Library (Vat.)	Palatinus latinus 677 (Pal. lat.)	ca. 1470
Vienna, Österreichi-sche Nationalbiblio-thek (ÖNB)	MS 1588	1401–1415 /1430–1432
	MS 4511	15th cent. (after 1415)
Wolfenbüttel, Herzog August Bibliothek (HAB)	MS Guelf. 431 Helmst	First quarter of the 15th cent. / 1450–1470
Wrocław, Biblioteka Uniwersytecka (BU)	I F 707	1420

My conclusions are primarily based on codicological evidence, mainly on the transmission of the texts in the same production units[12], but also on occasional notes, titles or other paratextual elements of the manuscripts. In interpreting the medieval manuscripts, it is crucial to bear in mind that the proximity of one text to another is not a sufficient

---

[12] A set of quires that form a codicological unity, often marked by catchwords and a single sequence of quire signature, see Kwakkel 2012, 60–61.

reason to assume that they were originally meant to be together. It is often difficult to say whether different fascicules were first bound together in the Middle Ages or later, and if the former, whether it was done immediately after the composition or decades later. A composite manuscript, typical of late medieval libraries, may include a complicated genesis and complex structure, consisting of several production phases.[13] Among the manuscripts where I have found anti-Waldensian texts together with works refuting Wycliffites, Hussites or both, there are naturally codices that are simply general collections on heresy without any conspicuous programme or even any reason to assume common provenance of different works. In other words, at some point somebody simply decided to bind all the fascicules on heresy inside the same covers. An excellent example of such a later bundle is a codex in the Herzog August Bibliothek Wolfenbüttel that contains in mixed order parts from three different copies of Petrus Zwicker's treatise *Cum dormirent homines*, excerpts from his inquisitor's manual, further excerpts from the thirteenth-century anti-heretical work by the Anonymous of Passau and scraps of fifteenth-century theological treatises, written by eight different hands in Austria and Northern Germany. Parts of the codex were bound together in the fifteenth century, and the rest in the sixteenth or eighteenth century.[14] There are, however, plenty of manuscripts where these texts were either produced at the same time or bound together relatively soon after their production.

As my purpose is to analyse the influence of anti-Waldensian treatises on anti-Hussite literature, it is important to discern the different chronological layers of anti-Hussite works. I follow the chronology of Pavel Soukup, who distinguishes four thematic-chronological groups: 1) the Bohemian polemics of the 1410s; 2) writings from the Council of Constance (1414–1418); 3) the disputations of the Council of Basel in the 1430s, and 4) the documents from the time of Pope Pius II (1458–1464) and Georg of Poděbrady (king of Bohemia 1458–1471).[15]

---

[13] Kwakkel 2012, 58–59.

[14] HAB, MS Guelf. 431 Helmst, f. 1ra–48vb. See the manuscript descriptions Heinemann 1884, 336–337; Välimäki 2019, 277–278 and latest Lesser (forthcoming).

[15] Soukup 2009, 234.

A manuscript produced in Bohemia in the 1420s, at the beginning of the Hussite revolution, can be expected to represent a very different understanding of heresy from a compilation finished in the second half of the fifteenth century, when the radical momentum of the Hussites had already been stayed.

The bohemian fury and the Waldensian pestilence

Before analysing the codicological evidence, it is necessary to present a brief survey of the fifteenth-century perception of the Waldensians, Wycliffites and the Hussites, and possible reasons why a connection was found between the different heresies. First, one should also note that the term "Wycliffite" in continental Europe referred to the proponents (imagined and real) of John Wyclif's condemned ideas, usually Wyclif's Eucharist doctrine (which denied the possibility of transubstantiation), the invalidity of the sacrament delivered by an unworthy priest, or Wyclif's ideas about the Church deprived of its secular power.[16] There were many who had read Wyclif's texts, which spread from England to Bohemia not long after he wrote them, and which were eagerly circulated there.[17] The label Wycliffite was used even before the Bohemian movement was branded as the Hussites, but even after that the term was commonly used to designate the Bohemian heretics.[18] As is often the case with

[16] On Wyclif's thought on these matters, see Penn 2006; Shogimen 2006; Levy 2012, 78–86.

[17] On the transmission of Wycliffite texts from England to Bohemia, see esp. Van Dussen 2012. On Wyclif's influence to the Bohemian reformation, see also Herold 1998; and Soukup 2014, 42–61, who sums up the discussion around the topic. See also Fudge 2010, 151–152, who is more doubtful about the extent of Wyclif's impact to Hus.

[18] Soukup 2017 is the only proper survey on the nomenclature of the Bohemian heretics. According to Soukup, the shift from the 'Wycliffites' to the 'Hussites' was gradual. The latter term was used above all in the polemics of the 1420s. During the negotiations at the Council of Basel in 1430s, a more neutral term, 'Bohemians", was adopted. According to Van Dussen 2012, 118–119, churchmen outside England typically made little distinction between 'Wycliffites' in England and Bohemia.

heresy labels, use of the term was slack, and it is sometimes impossible to know if the suspected "Wycliffites" were genuinely influenced by Wyclif's thought. When Georg von Hohenlohe, the bishop of Passau, accused 'Wiklefiten' in Griesbach and Waldkirchen in 1410–1411, they may have been either Waldensians or dissidents influenced by Jerome of Prague (and thus indirectly by Wycliffite ideas), whom Bishop Georg had imprisoned in 1410.[19]

The fifteenth-century Catholic authors, including some of the most prominent figures of their day, saw a connection between earlier Waldensian heresy and the Wycliffite and Hussite movements they encountered. Aeneas Silvio Piccolomini (later Pope Pius II) wrote in his *Historica Bohemica* (ca. 1457), that the Hussites had "embraced the impious sect and madness of the Waldensians."[20] The historiography linking the Waldensians, Wyclif and Hus had, however, emerged decades earlier. Kondard Justinger (d. 1438) explains in his *Berner-Chronik* how the Bohemians had adopted the Waldensian heresy, whose origins were in the Donation of Constantine. In effect, Justinger accepts the Waldensian historiography that dated the origin of their movement to the lapse of the Church in the times of Pope Sylvester. He also places "Petrus Waldensis", John Wyclif, Jan Hus, and Hieronymus of Prague within the same continuum of heresiarchs.[21]

A little later, the Austrian chronicler and theologian Thomas Ebendorfer appears to have held a special grudge against the Waldensians, and he often presented Hussitism not only as influenced by Wyclif's errors, but as a violent invigoration of Waldensian heresy that had previously remained secret. The *Cronica Austriae* tells us how in 1417 "the heresy of Wyclif started to gather much strength in the Kingdom of Bohemia". A few lines later Ebendorfer explains how the

---

[19] Haupt 1890, 349–350; Schmid 2001. See also Fudge 2010, 148–149, who regards the accused as followers of Jerome.

[20] Piccolomini *Historia Bohemica*, Cap. 35, f. 21ra: "Impiam valdensium sectam atque insaniam amplexi sunt."

[21] Konrad Justinger, Die Berner-Chronik des Conrad Justinger, 288–289. See also Matouš 1997, 368–369; Schäufele 2006, 239; Utz Tremp 2006b, 211; Utz Tremp 2008, 460–461. On the Waldensian's own historiography, see Biller 2001a; Oberste 2005, 401–403; Tolonen 2015; Schäufele 2006, 221–230, 232–246.

Waldensians, "who had remained hidden up to that point, raised their heads" and started to lead people to their errors, first secretly, then by force of arms.[22] He also claims that the Taborite contempt for church buildings and consequently the destruction of churches and monasteries originated in the Waldensian practice of confessing in whatever available place.[23] In the 1450s Ebendorfer wrote that the "Bohemian fury" was in its contempt of Church and sacraments "infected by the Waldensian pestilence,"[24] and in his chronicle of German kings he praised the bravery of King Albrecht II (1438–1439, and duke of Austria from 1404 as Albrecht V) in the war against "Bohemians who are called Hussites, but more properly Waldensians."[25]

How Thomas Ebendorfer became preoccupied with Waldensianism remains a mystery, but he could not refrain from adding a jibe against them even at the end of his sermon collections (*sermones de sanctis*).

[22] Ebendorfer, *Chronica Austriae*, 362: "Quo et anno [1417] invalescere cepit nimis heresis Wickleff in regno Bohemie – – Ibi quoque sumpta occasione Waldenses, qui usque latuerunt, suas cervices erexerunt primum latenter suos inducentes errores, postea vero armata manu defensare et alios ad eosdem visi sunt compellere." Ebendorfer also claimed that the sect of "Adamites" rose at the same time, going around naked, having intercourse "in the manner of dogs" and preaching that the innocent could not commit sin: "Surrexerunt insuper hiis diebus Adamite, qui nudi incedentes vagos coitus canum more <exercebant> predicantes innocentes peccare non posse." Accusations of Adamitism, a form of antinomian heresy, were commonly levelled at radical Hussites. Although long considered to be a real group within the Taborites, these rumours were a fictional construction based on earlier descriptions of the so-called Free Spirit heresy, see Patschovsky 1998, 180–183.

[23] Ebendorfer, *Chronica Austriae*, 363: "multos eciam errores Waldensium assumpserunt, non in ecclesiis, sed ubicumque locorum passim conficiunt, ideo ecclesias et monasteria vastant."

[24] Ebendorfer, *Catalogus praesulum Laureacensium et Pataviensium.*, 227–228: "qui odio inclerum inflammati omnia ecclesiastica sacramenta contaminant, sacras polluunt edes et ad nepharia queque prolapsi, crudelia queque inpares nature perpetrare non verentur, prout Bohemica rabies nostro infelici evo hac Waldense peste infecta luceclarius in suis operibus declaravit."

[25] Ebendorfer, *Chronica regum Romanorum*, 598: "sicut et in bellicis erat imperterritus, prout contra Bohemos vocatos Hussitas, ymoverius Walden(ses)." See also Ebendorfer *Chronica regum Romanorum*, 588.

In a manuscript copied in 1444, according to the colophone based on the sermons he preached at the University of Vienna, the last sermon Ebendorfer had preached was about sin and its satisfaction in life and in eternity. It ends as follows: "Alas, this is against the rustic *Baldenses,* among whom there is no learned man nor anyone declared through miracles, and who without reason deny [the existence] of purgatory. Let us pray to God etc."[26]

Already during the Council of Constance Chancellor Jean Gerson had used the same device in his attack on Wycliffe and his followers, claiming that in their contempt for the ecclesiastical hierarchy they had tried to revive "the old error of Waldensians or the Poors of Lyons."[27] In several other treatises written during the council, Gerson compares Wyclif and Hus to the heresy of the Waldensians.[28] Andreas of Brod, a Prague theologian that remained loyal to the Roman Church, wrote that the Hussite heresy included other heresies, above all that of Wyclif, but also those of the Free Spirits, Adamites, Luciferians and Waldensians. The Hussites also spared the other heretics when they destroyed the innocents and burned the villages.[29]

Even within the Hussite movement itself, divided between the moderate Prague utraquists and the more radical Taborites, Waldensianism was used to denigrate opponents. Master Laurentius

---

[26] Graz UB, MS 336, f. 250rb: "Ecce contra rusticos Baldenses inter quos nullus doctus nec aliquis miraculis declaratus, qui sine racione purgatorium negant etc. Rogemus ergo dominum etc." The colophon is at the same folio: "Finis est horum sermonum de sanctis eximii sacre theologie doctoris magistri Thome de Haselbach anno d. 1444 in quinta feria ante Bartholomei et sunt pronunciati in alma universitate studii Wienensis. Et sunt reportati per Johannem Gareysen protunc eiusdem universitatis studentem."

[27] *De potestate ecclesiastica*: "hic enim fuit error vetus Waldensium et pauperum de Lugduno, qui per Wicleff et sequaces suos renovari quaesitus est, sed juste damnatus." See Gerson, *OEuvres complètes*, vol. 6, 212.

[28] Gerson, *OEuvres complètes*, vol. 6, 286; vol. 8, 132; vol. 9, 449. Daniel Hobbins has suggested that Wyclif's doctrine alarmed Gerson because it targetted the Church's property and thus resembled the two old heresies of the Waldensians and Cathars, see Hobbins 2009, 13. I am, however, inclined to see Gerson's primary point as the threat the Waldensians had caused to the ecclesiastic hierarchy, a threat he perceived as echoed by Wyclif and Hus.

[29] Kadlec 1982, 54–55.

of Březina, belonging to the moderate Prague party and writing the history of the Hussites in the 1420s, lamented that the Taborites denied the existence of Purgatory "with the Waldensians".[30] Another example is a late fifteenth-century Bohemian manuscript. The bulk of it consists of the same Laurentius of Březina's history of the Hussite movement, but it contains also a list of errors titled *Articuli de Pikardis* or *Articuli hereticorum Waldensium et decardorum* [sic].[31] It is indeed an adaptation and partial translation from Latin to Czech of the *Articuli Waldensium* and the *De vita et conversacione*, short descriptions of Waldensian doctrine originating from the circle of Petrus Zwicker in the early 1390s.[32]

There was real co-operation and assimilation between the two heretic groups, though when and where it began has been, and probably will remain, under debate. But at the latest from the second decade of the fifteenth century onwards there were regular contacts between Waldensians and Hussites.[33] When a Hussite priest, Johannes Drändorf, was captured, interrogated and condemned to burn at the stake in Heidelberg, two of his servants were captured at the same time. One of them, Martin Borchard, refused to swear an oath in a way that resembled the Waldensian denial of oaths, and under torture Drändorf

---

[30] Höfler 1856, vol. 1, 397. On Laurentius as a Prague apologist, see Kaminsky 1967, 366–367.

[31] NKCR, XI. D. 8, f. 94r–97v. The text is edited in Höfler 1856, vol. 1, 503–514. In the fifteenth century the name Pikards was used to refer to the radical group of Hussites following Martin Húska. They denied every form of real presence of Christ's body at the Eucharist, and were defamed as immoral antinomians and condemned and persecuted by the moderate Utraquists in Prague as well as by the Taborites. The origin of the name and its usage is best described in Patschovsky 1998, 175–180. For the dating and provenance, see the description at the *Manuscriptorium*.

[32] Välimäki 2019, 168.

[33] In modern scholarship one finds interpretations that either maximize the possible interaction between the two movements, such as Gonnet and Molnár 1974, 211–249; Werner 1963; or that have a tendency to minimize and question every possibility of influence, see Cameron 2000, 144–150; Some of the proponents have also changed their views over time, see Fudge 1998, 37–41; For a moderate approach, see Machilek 2006. See also Doležalová 2013, 310.

confessed that he did not teach this to his servants, but "they knew it well by themselves."[34] Because of this, Franz Machilek has assumed that the two servants had a Waldensian background.[35] Also in the documents from Johannes Drändorf's trial, according to Hermann Heimpel, both the questions of the inquisitors and the answers formed a mixture of Waldensian, Wycliffite and Hussite opinions.[36] The actual trial documents, however, refer only to Wycliffite and Hussite heresy. Waldensianism is not mentioned, and it seems that the inquisitors were not preoccupied with it. The copies of the documents ended up together with anti-Waldensian material, as we will see below.

Hussite theology and the virility of the movement provided fuel for the last upsurge of the German Waldensians. The famous Waldensian-Hussite preacher Friedrich Reiser grew up in a Waldensian family and for a while preached and received confessions in the way of Waldensian brethren. He came into contact with radical Hussites and was subsequently ordained priest by Taborites. Eventually in the 1440s and 1450, after the decline of the Taborite movement, Reiser led a mission in the German regions that had formerly supported Waldensianism, appointing followers of his own and assembling a congregation before he was caught, tried and burned in Strasbourg in 1458.[37] Long before that some Waldensians could describe their beliefs in terms of Hussitism. Konrad Wasen, interrogated in 1430 in Fribourg, explained that "Our faith is like the faith of the Hussites."[38] Wasen, who seems to have been genuinely aware of the Hussites and hopeful about their advance, was an exception among the Fribourgian Waldensians, who were barely influenced by Hussite doctrine by 1430. In fact, as Katherine Utz Tremp has demonstrated, fear of the Hussites preceded the Church's persecution of the Waldensians in Fribourg.[39]

---

[34] Heimpel 1969, 85, 98. See also Machilek 1997, 277; Machilek 2006, 290.
[35] Machilek 1997, 277; Machilek 2006, 290.
[36] Heimpel 1969, 20, 43–51.
[37] The most recent overview on Friedrich Reiser's life and career is Schneider 2006.
[38] "Fides nostra est idem sicut fides Hussitarum." Utz Tremp 2000, nr. 105.
[39] Utz Tremp 2006b, 211–215; Utz Tremp 2008, 460–464.

The question remains as to whether the actual interaction between the Waldensians and the Hussites had any influence on the Catholic descriptions of these heresies. In other words, did the writers quoted above possess knowledge that there were Waldensians joining the Hussite cause? Or was it mere superficial similarity of certain doctrines that led the polemicists and chroniclers to posit this connection? Or was it simply their wish to maliciously slander the Church's opponents? These are the questions I will attempt to answer in the light of the manuscript evidence in the remainder of this article.

The Waldensians, Wycliffites and Hussites on the manuscript leaves

Let us start with a codex that in the fifteenth century belonged to the parish priest Martin of Plana in southern Bohemia. The manuscript was produced in the middle of the Hussite Revolution in 1428, albeit not in Plana but in Eger (the present day Cheb in Western Bohemia, near the Bavarian border), and it is today among the collections of the Czech National Library.[40] Martin certainly belonged to the Roman-minded clergy in Hussite Bohemia. The manuscript contains several early works against Hus and his followers, including, for example, an anonymous treatise against Jacobellus of Mies' (Jakoubek ze Stříbra) articles of communion *sub utraque*, written probably in 1417 (f. 60v–79r) as well as Mařík Rvačka's treatise on the same topic, written at the Council of Constance in 1417 (99v–108v), which is followed by the condemnation of Wyclif's article's from the same council (109r–153r). After Wyclif's articles comes the *Cum dormirent homines* (153v–183v), a treatise by Petrus Zwicker against the Waldensians, written in the same hand as the bulk of the manuscript. Zwicker's treatise is in no way a minor work relegated to the middle of the manuscript, as Martin of

---

[40] NKCR, XIII. E. 5. For the dating and the place of the origin, see the colophons, esp. after the *Cum dormirent homines*, f. 183v. See also the manuscript descriptions, Truhlář 1906, 237; Välimäki 2019, 282 and the online repository *Manuscriptorium*.

Plana listed it among the nine selected works he included in the list of contents, written inside the front cover of the manuscript. Here the *Cum domirent homines* is characterized as "a beautiful and useful refutation of Waldensian heretics."[41]

How was the treatise useful? There are not many marginal notations that would reveal that, but there is one extremely interesting later addition. In the middle of the chapter treating the necessity of obedience to all priests, even to those living in sin, somebody, possibly Martin of Plana, has added a small leaflet written by a later hand.[42] The leaflet is titled "De obedientia" and it is simply a collection of biblical and patristic authorities supporting the position defended by Zwicker in his treatise, that one must be obedient towards one's superiors whatever their conduct. It is especially notable that the addition includes patristic authors, because these are completely absent from Zwicker's treatise, which is characteristically biblical in its argumentation.[43]

There is another short text on Waldensians that has been added to the manuscript, ostensibly after its completion. It has 39 articles of Waldensian errors, but not based on the *Cum dormirent homines*. Ernst Werner edited these and correctly recognised that they have more in common with the description of the Waldensians in Pseudo-David of Augsburg's *De inquisitione hereticorum,* written in the mid-thirteenth century. The 39 articles include some dualist tenets, for example total prohibition of killing animals, that are completely absent in the late fourteenth-century description of Waldensianism.[44] Werner took the colophon to mean that these articles were written in 1428, but it is obvious that they are later; the colophon refers to the completion of *Cum dormirent homines,*[45] and a later hand has written down the articles. Although presenting very different views on Waldensian doctrine,

---

[41] NKCR, XIII. E. 5, front cover, inside: "Item reprobacio pulcra et utilis waldensium hereticorum."

[42] NKCR, XIII. E. 5, f. 159r–v.

[43] On Zwicker's biblicism, see Biller 2001b, 240, 245, 259, 261, 274; Segl 2006, 185; Modestin 2013, 218, 221–222; Välimäki 2019, 64–103.

[44] Werner 1963, 217–219, 275–276.

[45] NKCR, XIII. E. 5, f. 183v: "Anno domini M°cccc xxviii° finita est reprobacio waldensium hereticorum in Egra feria secunda in vigilia Epiphanie domini Amen."

these two texts together demonstrate that the fifteenth-century clergy combatting the Hussites also read, commented on and added to texts on Waldensians.

The thirteenth-century treatise *De inquisitione hereticorum* is not the earliest text on Waldensians that was transmitted together with Hussitica. MS 4511 of the Austrian National Library contains the *De fide catholica contra hereticos sui temporis* by Alan of Lille (f. 113r–158v), a text written in 1199–1202 and considered to be the first full-scale anti-heretical polemic of the high middle ages and a model for later authors.[46] After that comes a more contemporary text, a summary of Zwicker's *Cum dormirent homines.* (f. 159r–160v.) A peculiarity of this manuscript is that the great majority of it is not anti-Hussite, but includes the writings of Hus, above all his extensive *Tractatus de ecclesia.* (f. 1r–100v), and another central figure of the early Hussite movement, Jacobellus of Mies' (Jakoubek ze Stříbra) (*Tractatus de communione sub utraque specie*) (f. 173r–178v). The manuscript belonged to the University of Prague (Carolinum) till it was "borrowed" by Kaspar von Niedbruck in the 1550s and taken to Vienna.[47] The provenance explains the works of Hus, but the inclusion of Alain of Lille and the summary of Zwicker's treatise remain something of a mystery. The binding is fifteenth-century, so the anti-Waldensian works were bound in the middle of the period of Hussite theology in the Middle Ages.[48] Nevertheless, it is an apt reminder that the anti-heretical treatises had long afterlives, and that a

---

[46] Sackville 2011, 13; Vasoli 1963; Wakefield 1967.
[47] ÖNB, Description of MS 4511.
[48] Unfortunately I have not been able to survey the actual manuscript to be able to say anything about its codicological features.

twelfth- or thirteenth-century text could well occupy a place with works of the late fourteenth and fifteenth centuries.[49]

The first example, the compilation in possession of the priest Martin in Bohemia, was compiled in the immediate vicinity of the Hussite armies preparing to advance against their enemies.[50] The alarm they raised was felt far and wide, and its echoes can be found in MS 1588 of the Austrian National Library. Compared to the usual fifteenth-century theological compilations from monastic libraries, where the texts on heresy are usually transmitted, this medium size (247 x 172 mm) manuscript is a luxurious example, written on parchment and in a careful fifteenth-century gothic/bastarda bookhand (or by two different hands). It consists of three fascicles, commissioned by two bishops of Ermland in Eastern Prussia. The first part of the manuscript has a treatise against the Greeks by Bartholomeus Constantinopolitanus, a thirteenth-century Dominican friar, and it belonged to Bishop Heinrich IV Heilsberg von Vogelsang, so it was acquired between 1401 and 1415. The second treatise of the manuscript is *Tractatus contra quattuor*

---

[49] Another example of a compilation containing texts of different age is Vat. Pal. lat. 677. Copied ca. 1470 by an otherwise unknown scribe, Reonaldus Regel de Ingolstadt, it forms one continuous production unit. The texts included are:

1r–40v The Anonymous of Passau (Pseudo-Reinerius Sacconi) "Liber hereticorum"

41r–42v "Articuli magistri Iohannis Wiclef condempnati"

43r–106r "Processus domini petri de ordine celestinorum inquisitoris hereticorum etc."

The first piece is a treatise from the 1260s (Pseudo-Reinerius), followed by Wyclif's condemned articles. The articles are claimed to be those condemned by English clergy in 1382, f. 41r: "Articuli magistri Iohannis Wiclef condempnati in Anglia per xiii episcopos et xxx magistros in theologia. in Conuentu fratrum predicatorum anno domini 1380 [sic]", but the list is in fact a version of the 45 articles condemned at the Council of Constance. The last work is the *Cum dormirent homines treatise* written by the inquisitor Petrus Zwicker in 1395, included with inquisitorial material from the 1390s. The compilation thus combines anti-heretical works of the 1260s, 1390s and 1410s. On the Pseudo-Reinerius redaction of the Anonymous of Passau, see Nickson 1967.

[50] On the offensive phase of the Hussite movement and their military expeditions from 1426 onwards, see Šmahel 2002, vol. 2, 1408–1496.

articulos Hussitarum, written by Peter von Pulkau (Petrus de Pulka) with the help of Bartholomäus Frowein von Ebrach (Bartholomeus de Ebraco) and Giacomo da Chiavari (Jacobus de Clavaro) in Vienna in 1423/1424.[51] It is an important work, but so far unedited. The last treatise is against Waldensians and titled *Contra errores waldensium.* It is the *Refutatio errorum* written by the German inquisitor Petrus Zwicker. To be precise it is the longest and most common redaction of this work, which likewise lacks a complete edition.[52] The last two treatises were copied circa twenty years later than the first fascicule, in 1432 and 1430. They were commissioned by Franz Kuhschmalz, bishop of Ermland (1424–1457).

These manuscripts were perhaps not in one codex in the fifteenth century, for the binding is early modern. But they most certainly were in the same library. In any case it is the last two treatises, acquired most likely by the same bishop from the same source, that are of interest for the present article. Again, it is no wonder that a Prussian bishop, who had also studied in Prague (1412) and in Vienna (1414/1415),[53] ordered a treatise against the Hussites by Viennese theologians. There is even a specific phase in the history of the Hussite wars that may have caused the impetus for the acquisition of a polemical work against Hussites in the lands of Teutonic Order. In 1431–1432 the Polish king Wladislas Jagiello and the Hussites approached each other for talks. They even formed a military union, to the dismay of Catholic princes and especially the Teutonic Order. The fear was not unfounded, as the combined Polish-Hussite army attacked the Order in 1433.[54]

For the *Refutatio errorum* there is no similar obvious reason. Although there were Waldensians on the shores of the Baltic Sea, especially in Brandenburg and Pomerania,[55] there are no traces of persecutions in the diocese of Ermland. An interesting coincidence is that the author

---

[51] On this treatise, see Soukup 2009, 244–245.

[52] On the *Refutatio errorum,* its redactions and its attribution to Petrus Zwicker, see Välimäki 2019, 39–64.

[53] On Franz Kuhschmalz's career, see Karp 2001.

[54] Kras 2004, 276.

[55] Kurze 1968; Kurze 2006; The forthcoming Brill Companion to the Christian Tradition: *The Waldenses,* ed. M. Benedetti and E. Cameron will have a chapter on Waldensians by the Baltic by Peter Biller.

of the treatise, Petrus Zwicker, was born in Wormditt (Orneta), not far from Ermland's diocesan see in Heilsberg. A coincidence is just what it is, however, as Zwicker did his literary work in Austria and possibly at his home monastery Oybin on the border of Bohemia and Upper Lusatia. It must have been interest in the Waldensians that motivated the reproduction of the *Refutatio errorum*. The manuscript in question is no random fascicle that had simply ended up in the library, but a pricy, carefully made copy specifically ordered by the bishop himself.[56] Worth noting also is that even though the Hussites were the pressing danger in the 1420s and 1430s, it was the work on the Waldensians that was first acquired, followed only later by the treatise against the Four Articles.

The trial of Johannes Drändorf in Heidelberg in 1425 was discussed above as one of the possible occasions when former Waldensians joined the cause of the Hussites. The actual trial documents do not mention the Waldensians, but in two manuscripts, one in the University Library of Augsburg and the other in Erzabtei St Peters in Salzburg,[57] the documents were transmitted in a compilation aimed against Wyclif, the Hussites and the Waldensians. The compilations are almost identical in their content, including:

1. *De immunitate clericorum* (unedited).
2. Inquisition against Johannes Drändorf (1425).[58]
3. Errors of John Wyclif condemned at the Council of Constance.[59]
4. Petrus de Alliaco: *Conclusiones de communione sub utraque specie.* (Against Jakoubek ze Stříbra, 1415).[60]

---

[56] ÖNB MS 1588, f. 211v: "Hunc librum scribi fecit dominus *Franciscus episcopus* [diocese invisible, also the name scraped off] Anno domini M° cccc^mo xxx."

[57] Augsburg UB, MS II. 1. 2° 129, f. 121r–152v; Salzburg, St Peter, b VIII 9, f. 284r – 307v. See the descriptions of the manuscripts, Hilg 1999, 127–137; Jungwirth 1910–1912, vol 4. Välimäki 2019, 271, 274.

[58] Edited in Heimpel 1969, 68–96.

[59] Edited in Hardt 1696, vol. 3, 168–211. The manuscripts have a significantly abbreviated version compared to the edited text.

[60] Hardt 1696, vol. 3, 586–592. Again, the text in the manuscripts has been abbreviated.

5. *De efficentia orationis* (continuation to the previous text).
6. Petrus Zwicker: *Processus Petri* compiliation against the Waldensian
heresy, including the polemical treatise *Cum dormirent homines.*[61]

In both manuscripts the compilation is one production unit. The
Augsburg codex is older, probably produced quite soon after the trial of
Drändorf, while the Salzburg manuscript is younger, copied in the 1440s
or after. It is quite likely a copy, albeit not necessarily a direct copy, from
the older manuscript. The inclusion of the anti-Waldensian polemic in
this compilation does not automatically mean that the compiler was
aware that some of Drändorf's followers were probably Waldensians. It
is, however, quite possible that the compiler considered that Zwicker's
treatise was as relevant for the refutation of Drändorf's errors as the anti-
Wyclif and anti-Hussite texts.

The common transmission of anti-Waldensian and anti-Hussite
works did not stop in the 1430s, but continued in the last stage of the
anti-Hussite literature, that is texts produced during the reign of George
of Podébrady. In a theological compilation that once belonged to the
Augustinian canons in Diessen, Bavaria, there is a production unit
including three texts on heresy, written by one scribe, *frater* Johannes
Dorum, in 1469.[62] The first text is an anonymous letter to Jan Hus
against his errors, written in 1414 or 1415 and known as *Eloquenti
viro.*[63] The second is titled "Obuiaciones contra hereticos waldensium"
and it is Zwicker's *Cum dormirent homines.*[64] By contrast, the third text
is contemporary, having the title "Positionis contra Rockizanam".[65] It is

[61] The different versions of the *Processus Petri* have been collated in Välimäki
2019, 106–116.
[62] BSB Clm 5614, f. 247r–297v.
[63] BSB Clm 5614, f. 247ra–60rb. Ed. Hardt 1696, vol. 3, 338–393. For the
dating, see Soukup, *Repertorium operum antihussiticorum,* on-line database.
Ondřej z Brodu (Andreas de Broda) is a possible author, but the authorship
of the work remains contested.
[64] BSB Clm 5614, f. 260va–284ra. There is a colophon at f. 284ra: "Expliciunt
obuiationes sacre scripture errorum waldensium anno d. m. cccc° xliiii°
[1444]". This is either a mistake or the date of the exemplar Johannes Dorum
used. The *Cum dormirent homines* is copied in the same fascicle between the
two works dated 1469.
[65] BSB Clm 5614, f. 284va–297va.

a description of the debate between the Utraquist archbishop of Prague, Jan Rokycana, and the Catholic party of the Bohemian Church, held in 1465 under the auspices of the king of Bohemia, George of Podébrady (the manuscript has the year 1464),[66] which is only four years before the fascicule was finished.

It is notable that the last text is a description of events that were by no means over when the fascicule was copied in 1469. Jan Rokycana was still alive and archbishop of Prague, and the conflict between (moderate) Utraquists and Catholics remained unresolved.[67] The function of the earlier treatises, on their behalf, appears to be to provide doctrinal and/or historical background for the contemporary debates. At the same time they place the Utraquist Jan Rokycana in the continuum of heresiarchs, an impression that was certainly in the interest of the Bavarian Augustinian canons, who were the probable readership of the compilation.

Different sects, same enemy

When the historians and theologians referred to the Waldensian roots of the Hussite heresy, it was often in a rather vague polemical sense. In contrast, the examples above have demonstrated that anti-Waldensian treatises were copied together with anti-Hussite and anti-Wycliffite works at least from the 1420s to the 1460s, and that these compilations were usually theological. They may be polemical, but they nevertheless imply that it was somehow the doctrinal similarity, for example attacks on the position of the clergy, which caused the inclusion of the anti-Waldensian treatises in these collections.

To conclude, I bring up one more example from the beginning of the Hussite revolution in 1420. It demonstrates that at this date a Bohemian Catholic priest hardly distinguished between the Waldensians, the Wycliffites and the Hussites. The manuscript is an anti-Hussite

---

[66] Heymann 1959, 256; see the edition of the text Canisius and Basnage 1725, 753–775.

[67] Heymann 1959, 256.

compilation by a parish priest and bachelor of theology, Jiří of Těchnic (Georgius de Tyechnicz), who also composed some of the texts. The note inside the back cover explicitly states that part of the manuscript has been compiled in 1420 against the "heresiarchs of Constance".[68] However, the compilation starts, not with a text against John Wyclif or Jan Hus, but with Petrus Zwicker's *Cum dormirent homines*. At the start of the treatise, Jiří wrote a short prologue, where he stated that he had considered and read through the careers of heresiarchs, first those of Waldensians, then many others including "Wycliffites, Hussites, Copts, Nicolaytans, Arians" and so on, "whose names it was not possible to include here, and so I accepted the above-mentioned Waldensians and did under their name as much at it seemed [necessary?] to me."[69] After the *Cum dormirent homines* and a short excerpt from the *Refutatio*

[68] Wrocław BU, I F 707, back cover: "Anno domini M° cccc° xx° eciam Collecta contra heresiarchas Constancienses per multos doctores vbi interfui compilacionibus."

[69] Wrocław BU, I F 707, f, 122ra: "Ego tantillus considerans et perlegens omnes cursus heresiarcharum primo Waldensium et aliorum plurimorum hereticorum scilicet wycleficcorum, hussitarum, Coptorum, nicolaytarum, arrianorum, yssmitarum, casiudeopotarum, duplicium, Georgianorum, Machometarum, plurimorum aliorum quos transcuri perlegi quorum hic nomina contineri non possint et sic accepi predicto waldenses feci sub horum nomine quantum mihi videbatur."

errorum several early anti-Wycliffite and anti-Hussite works follow, some of them written by Jiří of Těchnic himself.[70]

Jiří's preoccupation with the Waldensians did not end with the reproduction of the *Cum dormirent homines*. He also wrote a short tract against the Waldensians. It starts with a list of their errors that is based on the *Articuli Waldensium* formulated in the 1390s.[71] After the list Jiří gives his own, short refutation of the Waldensian doctrines, primarily on the question of whether laymen should be allowed to preach. The text proceeds as an imagined disputation between Catholic and heretical proponents. In the middle of the text a revealing lapse takes place. Suddenly, it is no longer a Waldensian but a "wyklephysta" who proclaims that the divine mission (of laymen) must not be proven by miracles, because "according to Gregory [the Great] signs are given to infidels, I have the Scripture for me."[72] For Jiří of Těchnic the Waldensians and the followers of Wyclif and Hus were thus essentially the same.

---

[70] Wrocław BU, I F 707, f. 122ra–153vb, *Cum dormirent homines*; 154ra, *Refutatio errorum*, an excerpt from the first chapter; 154ra–156vb, Jiří of Těchnic, treatise on ecclesiastical privileges (obedience, tithes, interdict), unedited; 156vb–164ra, Mařík Rvačka (Mauritius de Praga) *Tractatus contra Hussitas de sumpcione venerabilis sacramenti ewkaristie sub utraque specie*. Ed. Hardt vol 3, 1696, 779–804; Mansi vol 28, 1785, 432–446; 164rb–169ra, Jean Gerson, *De necessaria communione laicorum sub utraque specie*. Ed. Gerson, *OEuvres complètes*, vol 10, 55–68; 169ra–169vb, Continuation to Gerson's treatise; 169vb–180vb, Jiří of Těchnic, Compilation against the Hussites. Unedited; 181ra–182vb, Jacques de Nouvion (Jacobus de Noviano) *Disputacio cum Hussitis* (1408). Ed. Sedlák 1914; 183vb–191ra, Anonymous treatise against Hussites, unedited; 191ra–193ra, Ondřej z Brodu (Andreas de Broda)?, *Tractatus de corpore Cristi*. Unedited; 193ra–193va, *Epistola wykleph ad apostolicum in extremis directa etc*; 193va–196ra, Various notes on the condemnation of Wyclif's doctrine in Prague; 196rb–199va, Waldensian articles collected by Jiří of Těchnic. Title: *Hy synt articuli Secte waldensium hereticorum*. See also the description in Szymański 2012, 53–55.

[71] Jiří of Těchnic's version of the articles has been edited by Szymański 2012, 55–57.

[72] Wrocław BU, I F 707, f. 197ra: "Sed dixit michi wyklephysta: Etsi miraculis non thouerseo [sic] sicut nec opus est, cum secundum gregorium signa data sunt infidelibus; habeo pro me scripturam."

Altough but one compiler and author, Jiří of Těchnic sheds light on the rest of the compilations where the Waldensians co-existed with Wyclif and the Hussites. The strong presence of anti-Waldensian literature in the fifteenth century demonstrates the considerable imprint that Waldensianism, or more precisely its repression, had left in the spiritual geography of German and Bohemian orthodox clergy. Waldensianism was the background, the old and familiar error and heresy, against which the emerging Hussite radicalism was understood.[73] This was despite Catholic knowledge of the influence of Wyclif's theology on Bohemians from very early on, and of the remarkable doctrinal differences between fourteenth-century Waldensianism and later Hussitism, most notably in the Eucharistic theology.

Without doubt, the Hussites were "hereticated" by relating them to the old heresy of the Waldensians, but in the theological compilations the relationship is far subtler than that. I am confident in proposing that the primary reason for the compilers to include anti-Waldensian polemics in the anti-Hussite compilations was the similarity in doctrine they saw in the two heresies, most importantly in their pronounced anticlericalism. They were certainly convinced of the essential diabolical sameness of all heresies, but that does not preclude a genuine attempt to understand the new dissidents by turning to the available literature.

Conclusions

The texts on the Waldensians transmitted in the fifteenth century with anti-Hussite compilations often formed an integral part of these manuscripts. The list of errors and full treatises written in the fourteenth century, sometimes even earlier, were not haphazardly transmitted remnants among more current works. Instead, the treatises were actively copied, revised and commented on, and used to formulate anti-Wycliffite and anti-Hussite propositions. The anti-Waldensian works

---

[73] There are some exceptions, of which the most remarkable is the Dominican Johannes Nider who compared Hussites to the Cathars, see Chène 2006.

discussed in this article were copied throughout the period when anti-Hussite polemical literature was written, from the time of the Council of Constance to around 1470.

In the beginning of the article, I proposed two reasons why contemporaries might have compared the Waldensians and the Hussites: firstly, a genuine wish to understand the new dissident groups in the light of earlier works on heresy professing similar doctrines, and secondly, a polemical strategy that aimed to stress the heretical nature of the Bohemian reformers by comparing them to the old and infamous sect of the Waldensians. In the material discussed above, the latter, polemical motive seems to dominate at the textual level, especially in the works of Thomas Ebendorfer and Aeneas Silvio Piccolomini. The Hussites were a new sect, but one that revived the old error of the Waldensians. On the other hand, in the anti-heretical compilations another motive seems to be at work. Even though always hostile towards the dissidents, many compilations reveal a more subject-oriented approach to heresy. The texts on the Waldensians were copied and revised because they provided arguments for the theological debates in which the clergy facing the Hussites was involved.

The common *Überlieferungsgeschichte* of the anti-Waldensian, anti-Wycliffite, and anti-Hussite works also shows the full impact made by the late fourteenth-century bishops, theologians, preachers and inquisitors in their campaign against the Waldensians. It is manifested on these manuscript leaves. The persecutors of the late fourteenth century succeeded so well in their warnings against Waldensianism, in their exhortations to act against it, and in their refutations of its doctrine that the effect lasted for several decades, reached far and wide, and even shaped the descriptions of the major heresy of the fifteenth century, the Hussites.

Sources

Manuscripts

Augsburg, Universtitätsbibliothek (UB)
  MS II. 1. 2° 129
Graz, Universtitätsbibliothek (UB)
  MS 336
Munich, Bayerische Staatsbibliothek (BSB)
  Clm 5614
Prague, Národní knihovna České republiky (NKCR)
  XI. D. 8
  XIII. E. 5
Salzburg, St Peter
  b VIII 9
Vatican City, Vatican Library (Vat.)
  Palatinus latinus 677 (Pal. lat.)
Vienna, Österreichische Nationalbibliothek (ÖNB)
  MS 1588
  MS 4511
Wolfenbüttel, Herzog August Bibliothek (HAB)
  MS Guelf. 431 Helmst
Wrocław, Biblioteka Uniwersytecka (BU)
  I F 707

Printed sources

Canisius, Henricus, and Jacques Basnage (eds): *Thesaurus monumentorum ecclesiasticorum et historicorum, sive Henrici Canisii lectiones antiquæ, ad sæculorum ordinem digestæ variisque opusculis auctæ quibus praefationes historicas, animadversiones criticas et notas in singulos auctores*. apud Rudolphum & Gerhardum Wetstenios, Antwerp 1725.

Ebendorfer, Thomas: *Catalogus praesulum Laureacensium et Pataviensium*. Ed. Harald Zimmermann. Monumenta Germaniae Historica. Scriptores Rerum Germanicum Nova Series 22. Hahnsche Buchhandlung, Hannover 2008.

Ebendorfer, Thomas: *Chronica Austriae*. Ed. Alphons Lhotsky. Monumenta Germaniae Historica. Scriptores Rerum Germanicum Nova Series 13. Weidmannsche Verlagsbuchhandlung, Berlin and Zürich 1967.

Ebendorfer, Thomas: *Chronica regum Romanorum*. Ed. Harald Zimmermann. 1–2 vols. Monumenta Germaniae Historica. Scriptores Rerum Germanicum Nova Series 18. Hahnsche Buchhandlung, Hannover 2003.

Gerson, Jean: *Œuvres complètes*. Ed. Palémon Glorieux. Vols. 6, 8–10. Desclée, Paris 1965, 1971, 1973.

Gretser, Jacobus (ed.): [Pseudo]-Petri de Pilichdorf contra Haeresin Waldensium Tractatus [Cum dormirent homines]. *Lucae Tvdensis episcopi, Scriptores aliqvot svccedanei contra sectam waldensivm*. Maxima bibliotheca veterum Patrum, et antiquorum scriptorum ecclesiasticorum. Vol. 25. Anissonios, Lyon 1677, 277F–299G.

Hardt, Hermann von der: *Magnum oecumenicum Constantiense concilium de universali ecclesiae reformatione, unione et fide*. Vol. 3. 7 vols. Gensius, Frankfurt and Leipzig 1696.

Höfler, Karl Adolf Constantin von (ed.): *Geschichtschreiber der husitischen Bewegung in Böhmen.* Vol. 1. Hof- und staatsdruckerei, Vienna 1856.

Justinger, Konrad: *Die Berner-Chronik des Conrad Justinger.* Ed. Gottlieb L. Studer. Druck und Verlag von K.J. Wyss, Bern 1871. http://www.digibern.ch/justinger/BernerChronik_1871/Justinger_Conrad_Berner_Chronik_Gesamtwerk.pdf

Mansi, Giovan Domenico: *Sacrorum conciliorum nova et amplissima collectio: in qua praeter ea quae Phil. Labbeus et Gabr. Cossartius... et novissime Nicolaus Coleti in lucem edidere ea omnia insuper suis in locis optime disposita exhibentur.* Vol. 28. Apud Antonium Zatta, Venice 1785.

Piccolomini, Aeneas Silvio: *Historia Bohemica: a principio gentis, usque ad Georgium Boiebracium.* n.d. Vienna, ÖNB I 137961.

Sedlák, Joannes (ed.): *Jacobi de Noviano, Mgri Parisiensis, disputatio cum Hussitis.* Typ. et Sumptibus Pont. Typ. Benedictinorum Rajhradiensium, Brno 1914.

Scriptores Rerum Bohemicarum. Societas Scientiarum Bohemicae. Vol. 3. 3 vols. Pospissila, Prague 1829.

Databases

Soukup, Pavel: Repertorium operum antihussiticorum, on-line database. (Ref. 6.2.2017) www.antihus.eu

Manuscriptorium. Digital library of Written Cultural Heritage. National Library of the Czech Republic. (Ref. 5.2.2017) http://www.manuscriptorium.com/

Research literature

Biller, Peter: Medieval Waldensians' Construction of the Past. *Proceedins of the Huguenot Society* 25. London 1989, 191–206. In *The Waldenses, 1170–1530: Between a Religious Order and a Church.* Variorum Collected Studies Series. Ashgate, Aldershot 2001a.

Biller, Peter: The Anti-Waldensian Treatise Cum dormirent homines of 1395 and its Author. *The Waldenses, 1170–1530: Between a Religious Order and a Church,* 237–269. Variorum Collected Studies Series. Ashgate, Aldershot 2001b.

Biller, Peter: Goodbye to Waldensianism? *Past and Present* 192.1/2006, 3–33.

Brunn, Uwe: *Des contestataires aux 'Cathares': discours de réforme et propagande antihérétique dans les pays du Rhin et de la Meuse avant l'Inquisition.* Institut d'études augustiniennes, Paris 2006.

Bruschi, Caterina: Converted-Turned-Inquisitors and the Image of the Adversary: Ranier Sacconi Explains Cathars. *Cathars in Question.* Ed. Antonio Sennis. Heresy and Inquisition in the Middle Ages, 4. York Medieval Press, York 2016, 185–207.

Cameron, Euan: *Waldenses: Rejections of Holy Church in Medieval Europe.* Blackwell Publishers, Oxford UK 2000.

Chène, Cathérine: L'hérésie hussite vue par un dominicain observant: le Formicarius de Jean Nider (ca. 1380–1438), mit deutscher Zusammenfassung. *Friedrich Reiser und die 'waldensisch-hussitische Internationale' im 15. Jahrhundert: Akten der Tagung Ötisheim-Schönenberg, 2. bis 4. Oktober 2003.* Eds. Albert de Lange and Kathrin Utz Tremp. Ubstadt-Weiher and Verlag Regionalkultur, Heidelberg and Basel 2006, 317–340.

Chiu, Hilbert: Alan of Lille's Academic Concept of the Manichee. *Journal of Religious History* 35.4/2011, 492–506.

Doležalová, Eva: The Inquisitions in Medieval Bohemia: National and International Contexts. *Heresy and the Making of European Culture: Medieval and Modern Perspectives.* Eds. Andrew P. Roach and James R. Simpson. Ashgate, Farnham and Burlington VT 2013, 299–311.

Driscoll, Matthew J.: The Words on the Page: Thoughts on Philology, Old and New. *Creating the Medieval Saga: Versions, Variability, and Editorial Interpretations of Old Norse Saga Literature.* Eds. Judy Quinn and Emily Lethbridge. Syddansk Universitetsforlag, Odense 2010, 85–102.

Fudge, Thomas A.: *Jan Hus: Religious Reform and Social Revolution in Bohemia.* I.B. Tauris, London 2010.

Fudge, Thomas A.: *The Magnificent Ride: The First Reformation in Hussite Bohemia.* St. Andrews Studies in Reformation History. Ashgate, Aldershot 1998.

Garber, Rebecca L. R.: *Feminine Figurae: Representations of Gender in Religious Texts by Medieval German Women Writers, 1100–1475.* Routledge, New York and London 2003.

Gonnet, Jean, and Amedeo Molnár: *Les Vaudois au Moyen Âge.* Claudiana, Turin 1974.

Grundmann, Herbert: Der Typus des Ketzers in mittelalterlicher Anschauung. *Ausgewählte Aufsätze.* Hiersemann, Stuttgart 1976, 313–327.

Haupt, Herman: Waldenserthum und Inquisition im südöstlichen Deutschland seit der Mitte des 14. Jahrhunderts. *Deutsche Zeitschrift für Geschichtswissenschaft* 3/1890, 337–411.

Heimpel, Hermann: *Drei Inquisitions-Verfahren aus dem Jahre 1425: Akten der Prozesse gegen die deutschen Hussiten Johannes Drändorf und Peter Turnau sowie gegen Drändorfs Diener Martin Borchard.* Vandenhoeck & Ruprecht, Göttingen 1969.

Heinemann, Otto von: *Die Handschriften der Herzoglichen Bibliothek zu Wolfenbüttel. Abth. 1: Die Helmstedter Handschriften.* Vol. 1. Zwissler, Wolfenbüttel 1884. http://diglib.hab.de/drucke/15-4f-10-1b-1/start.htm

Herold, Vilém: How Wyclifite Was the Bohemian Reformation? *The Bohemian Reformation and Religious Practice, vol. 2: Papers from the XVIIIth World Congress of the Czechoslovak Society of Arts and Sciences, Brno 1996.* Eds. Zdeněk V. David and David R. Holeton. Academy of Sciences of the Czech Republic, Prague 1998, 25–37.

Heymann, Frederick G.: John Rokycana : Church Reformer between Hus and Luther. *Church History* 28.3/1959, 240–280.

Hilg, Hardo: *Lateinische mittelalterliche Handschriften in Folio der Universitätsbibliothek Augsburg : cod. II. 1.2° 91-226.* Harrasowitz, Wiesbaden 1999.

Hlaváček, Ivan: Bohemikale Literatur in den mittelalterlichen Bibliotheken des Auslandes: nach den mittelalterlichen Bibliotheksverzeichnissen. *Historica* 13/1966, 113–155.

Hobbins, Daniel: *Authorship and Publicity before Print: Jean Gerson and the Transformation of Late Medieval Learning.* University of Pennsylvania Press, Philadelphia 2009.

Jungwirth, Augustin: *Beschreibung der Handschriften des Stiftes St. Peter in Salzburg.* Handwritten catalogue. Salzburg 1910–1912.

Kadlec, Jaroslav: *Studien und Texte zum Leben und Wirken des Prager Magisters Andreas von Brod.* Beiträge zur Geschichte der Philosophie und Theologie des Mittelalters. New Series, Vol. 22. Aschendorff, Münster 1982.

Kaminsky, Howard: *A History of the Hussite Revolution.* University of California Press, Berkley and Los Angeles 1967.

Karp, Hans-Jürgen. Kuhschmalz, Franz († 1457): *Die Bischöfe des Heiligen Römischen Reiches 1198 bis 1448: ein biographisches Lexikon.* Ed. Erwin Gatz. Duncker & Humblot, Berlin 2001.

Kelly, Henry Ansgar: Inquisitorial Deviations and Cover-Ups: The Prosecutions of Margaret Porete and Guiard of Cressonessart, 1308–1310. *Speculum* 89.4/2014, 936–973.

Kieckhefer, Richard: *Repression of Heresy in Medieval Germany*. Liverpool University Press, Liverpool 1979.

Kolpacoff, Jennifer Mary: *Papal Schism, Archiepiscopal Politics and Waldensian Persecution (1378–1396): The Ecclesio-Political Landscape of Late Fourteenth-Century Mainz*. PhD Thesis, Northwestern University 2000. (Ref. 29.7.2014.) http://search.proquest.com.myaccess. library.utoronto.ca/pqdtft/docview/304614303/abstract/EEB36F63D3BD4B23PQ/2?accou ntid=14771

Kras, Pawel: Dominican Inquisitors in Medieval Poland (14th–15th c.). *Praedicatores, inquisitores I. The Dominicans and the Medieval Inquisition: Acts of the 1st International Seminar on the Dominicans and the Inquisition. 23–25 February 2002*. Ed. Arturo Bernal Palacios. Dissertationes Historicae, 29. Istituto storico domenicano, Rome 2004, 249–309.

Kurze, Dietrich: Waldenser in der Mark Brandenburg und in Pommern im 15. Jahrhundert. *Friedrich Reiser und die 'waldensisch-hussitische Internationale' im 15. Jahrhundert: Akten der Tagung Ötisheim-Schönenberg, 2. bis 4. Oktober 2003*. Eds. Albert de Lange and Kathrin Utz Tremp. Ubstadt-Weiher and Verlag Regionalkultur, Heidelberg and Basel 2006, 219–239.

Kurze, Dietrich: Zur Ketzergeschichte der Mark Brandenburg und Pommerns vornehmlich im 14. Jahrhundert: Luziferianer, Putzkeller und Waldenser. *Jahrbuch für die Geschichte Mittel- und Ostdeutschlands* 16–17/1968, 50–94.

Kwakkel, Erik: Late Medieval Text Collections: A Codicological Typoogy Based on Single-Author Manuscripts. *Author Reader Book: Medieval Authorship in Theory and Practice*. Eds. Stephen Partridge and Erik Kwakkel. University of Toronto Press, Toronto 2012, 56–79.

Lerner, Robert E.: *The Heresy of the Free Spirit in the Later Middle Ages*. University of California Press, Berkeley 1972.

Lesser, Bertram: *Die mittelalterlichen Helmstedter Handschriften der Herzog August Bibliothek. Teil 2: Cod. Guelf. 277 bis 440 Helmst. und Helmstedter Fragmente*. Harrassowitz, Wiesbaden [forthcoming]. (Ref. 14.11.2019) http://diglib.hab.de/?db=mss&list=ms&id=431-helmst&catalog=Lesser

Levy, Ian Christopher: *Holy Scripture and the Quest for Authority at the End of the Middle Ages*. University of Notre Dame Press, Notre Dame 2012.

Machilek, Franz: Deutsche Hussiten. *Jan Hus: zwischen Zeiten, Völkern, Konfessionen: Vorträge des internationalen Symposions in Bayreuth vom 22. bis 26. September 1993*. Eds. Zdeněk Radslav Dittrich and Ferdinand Seibt. Veröffentlichungen des Collegium Carolinum 85. R. Oldenbourg, Munich 1997, 267–282.

Machilek, Franz: Aufschwung und Niedergang der Zusammenarbeit von Waldensern und Hussiten im 15. Jahrhundert (unter besonderer Berücksichtigung der Verhältnisse in Deutschland). *Friedrich Reiser und die 'waldensisch-hussitische Internationale' im 15. Jahrhundert: Akten der Tagung Ötisheim-Schönenberg, 2. bis 4. Oktober 2003*. Eds. Albert de Lange and Kathrin Utz Tremp. Ubstadt-Weiher and Verlag Regionalkultur, Heidelberg and Basel 2006, 277–316.

Machilek, Franz (ed.): *Die hussitische Revolution: religiöse, politische und regionale Aspekte*. Forschungen und Quellen zur Kirchen- und Kulturgeschichte Ostdeutschlands Bd. 44. Böhlau, Cologne 2012.

Matouš, František: Johannes Hus in den Schweizer Chroniken des 15. und 16. Jahrhunderts. *Jan Hus: zwischen Zeiten, Völkern, Konfessionen: Vorträge des internationalen Symposions in Bayreuth vom 22. bis 26. September 1993*. Eds. Z. R. Dittrich and Ferdinand Seibt. Veröffentlichungen des Collegium Carolinum, 85. R. Oldenbourg, Munich 1997, 367–373.

Modestin, Georg: *Ketzer in der Stadt: der Prozess gegen die Strassburger Waldenser von 1400*. Monumenta Germaniae Historica, Studien und Texte, 41. Hahnsche Buchhandlung, Hannover 2007.

Modestin, Georg: The Anti-Waldensian Treatise Cum dormirent homines: Historical Context, Polemical Strategy, and Manuscript Tradition. *Religious Controversy in Europe, 1378–1536.* Eds. Michael Van Dussen and Pavel Soukup. Medieval Church Studies 27. Brepols, Turnhout 2013, 211–229.

Moore, R. I.: Heresy as Disease. *The Concept of Heresy in the Middle Ages (11th–13th C.), Proceedings of the International Conference Louvain May 13–16, 1973.* Eds. Willem Lourdaux and Daniel Verhelst. Mediaevalia Lovaniensia Series I IV. Leuven University Press, Leuven 1976, 1–11.

Moore, R. I.: *The War on Heresy.* Profile Books Limited, London 2012.

Moore, R. I.: The Cathar Middle Ages as an Historiographical Problem. *Christianity and Culture in the Middle Ages: Essays to Honor John Van Engen.* Eds. David C. Mengel and Lisa Wolverton. University of Notre Dame Press, Notre Dame 2014, 58–86.

Nickson, M.: The 'Pseudo-Reinerius' Treatise, the Final Stage of a Thirteenth-Century Work on Heresy from the Diocese of Passau. *Archives d'histoire doctrinale et littéraire du moyen âge* 42/1967, 255–314.

Oberste, Jörg: Le pape Sylvestre en Antéchrist: pauvreté et ecclesiologie dans le débat sur l'hérésie au bas Moyen Âge. *Les Cathares devant l'histoire: mélanges offerts à Jean Duvernoy.* Eds. Anne Brenon and Christine Dieulafait. Domaine historique. Hydre, Cahors 2005, 389–405.

Patschovsky, Alexander: Waldenserverfolgung in Schweidnitz 1315. *Deutsches Archiv für Erforschung des Mittelalters* 36/1980, 137–176.

Patschovsky, Alexander: Der Ketzer als Teufelsdiener. *Papsttum, Kirche und Recht im Mittelalter: Festschrift für Horst Fuhrmann zum 65. Geuburtstag.* Ed. Hubert Mordek. Max Niemeyer Verlag, Tübingen 1991, 317–334.

Patschovsky, Alexander: Der taboritische Chiliasmus: seine Idee, sein Bild bei den Zeitgenossen und die Interpretation der Geschichtswissenschaft. *Häresie und vorzeitige Reformation im Spätmittelalter.* Ed. Frantisek Šmahel. Schriften des Historischen Kollegs. Kolloquien, 39. R. Oldenburg Verlag, Munich 1998, 169–195.

Pegg, Mark Gregory: On Cathars, Albigenses, and good men of Languedoc. *Journal of Medieval History* 27.2/2001a, 181–195.

Pegg, Mark Gregory: *The Corruption of Angels: The Great Inquisition of 1245–1246.* Princeton University Press, Princeton N.J. 2001b.

Pegg, Mark Gregory: The Paradigm of Catharism; or, the Historians' Illusion. *Cathars in question.* Ed. Antonio Sennis. Heresy and Inquisition in the Middle Ages, 4. York Medieval Press, York 2016, 21–52.

Penn, Stephen: Wyclif and the Sacraments. *A companion to John Wyclif: Late Medieval Theologian.* Ed. Ian Christopher Levy. Brill's Companions to the Christian Tradition, 4. Brill, Leiden and Boston 2006, 241–291.

Sackville, L. J.: *Heresy and Heretics in the Thirteenth Century: The Textual Representations.* Heresy and Inquisition in the Middle Ages, 1. York Medieval Press, York 2011.

Sackville, L. J.: The Textbook Heretic: Moneta of Cremona's Cathars. *Cathars in Question.* Ed. Antonio Sennis. York Medieval Press, York 2016, 185–207.

Schäufele, Wolf-Dietrich: *'Defecit ecclesia': Studien zur Verfallsidee in der Kirchengeschichtsanschauung des Mittelalters.* Veröffentlichungen des Instituts für europäische Geschichte, Mainz, 213. von Zabern, Mainz 2006.

Schmid, Alois: Georg von Hohenlohe. *Die Bischöfe des Heiligen Römischen Reiches 1198 bis 1448: Ein biographisches Lexikon.* Ed. Erwin Gatz. Duncker & Humblot, Berlin 2001, 560–561.

Schneider, Martin: Friedrich Reiser - Herkunft, Berufung und Weg. *Friedrich Reiser und die 'waldensisch-hussitische Internationale' im 15. Jahrhundert: Akten der Tagung Ötisheim-Schönenberg, 2. bis 4. Oktober 2003.* Eds. Albert de Lange and Kathrin Utz Tremp. Ubstadt-Weiher and Verlag Regionalkultur, Heidelberg and Basel 2006, 75–86.

Segl, Peter: Die Waldenser in Österreich um 1400: Lehren, Organisationsform, Verbreitung und Bekämpfung. In *Friedrich Reiser und die 'waldensisch-hussitische Internationale' im 15. Jahrhundert: Akten der Tagung Ötisheim-Schönenberg, 2. bis 4. Oktober 2003.* Eds. Albert de Lange and Kathrin Utz Tremp. Ubstadt-Weiher and Verlag Regionalkultur, Heidelberg and Basel 2006, 161–188.

Shogimen, Takashi: Wyclif's Ecclesiology and Political Thought. *A Companion to John Wyclif: Late Medieval Theologian.* Ed. Ian Christopher Levy. Brill's Companions to the Christian tradition, 4. Brill, Leiden and Boston 2006, 199–240.

Šmahel, František: *Die Hussitische Revolution.* Translated by Thomas Krzenck. Vol. 1–3 Monumenta Germaniae historica, Schriften, 43. Hahn, Hannover 2002.

Soukup, Pavel: Zur Verbreitung theologischer Streitschriften im 15. Jahrhundert: Eine antihussitische Sammelhandschrift aus der Erfurter Kartause. *Studia mediaevalia Bohemica* 1/2009, 231–257.

Soukup, Pavel: *Jan Hus: Prediger – Reformator – Märtyrer.* Kohlhammer Verlag, Stuttgart 2014.

Soukup, Pavel: The Waning of the 'Wycliffites': Giving Names to Hussite Heresy. *Europe after Wyclif.* Eds. J. Patrick Hornbeck and Michael Van Dussen. Fordham University Press, New York 2017, 196–226.

Szymański, Jarosław: Hy sunt articuli secte waldensium hereticorum z kodeksu IF 707 Biblioteki Uniwersyteckiej we Wrocławiu. *Historicae viae. Studia dedykowane Profesorowi Lechowi A. Tyszkiewiczowi z okazji 55-lecia pracy naukowej.* Eds. Mateusz Goliński and Stanisław Rosik. Scripta Historica Medievalia, 1. Chronicon, Wrocław 2012, 51–62.

Tolonen, Pekka: Medieval Memories of the Origins of the Waldensian Movement. *History and Religion: Narrating a Religious Past.* Eds. Bernd-Christian Otto, Susanne Rau, and Jörg Rüpke. Religionsgeschichtliche versuche und vorarbeiten, 68. Walter de Gruyter, Berlin and Boston 2015, 165–185.

Truhlář, Josef: *Catalogus codicum manu scriptorum latinorum qui in C.R. Bibliotheca Publica atque Universitatis Pragensis asservantur. Vol. II. Codices 1666–2752 forulorum IX - XV et bibliothecae Kinskyanae.* Societas scientiarum Bohemica, Prague 1906.

Utz Tremp, Kathrin: Einführung. *Friedrich Reiser und die 'waldensisch-hussitische Internationale' im 15. Jahrhundert : Akten der Tagung Ötisheim-Schönenberg, 2. bis 4. Oktober 2003.* Eds. Albert de Lange and Kathrin Utz Tremp. Ubstadt-Weiher and Verlag Regionalkultur, Heidelberg and Basel 2006a, 7–20.

Utz Tremp, Kathrin: Friedrich Reiser und die Waldenser (Hussiten?) in Freiburg im Üchtland. *Friedrich Reiser und die 'waldensisch-hussitische Internationale' im 15. Jahrhundert: Akten der Tagung Ötisheim-Schönenberg, 2. bis 4. Oktober 2003.* Eds. Albert de Lange and Kathrin Utz Tremp. Ubstadt-Weiher and Verlag Regionalkultur, Heidelberg and Basel 2006b, 205–218.

Utz Tremp, Kathrin (ed.): *Quellen zur Geschichte der Waldenser von Freiburg im Üchtland (1399–1439).* Monumenta Germaniae historica, Quellen zur Geistesgeschichte des Mittelalters, 18. Hahnsche Buchhandlung, Hannover 2000.

Utz Tremp, Kathrin: *Von der Häresie zur Hexerei: 'wirkliche' und imaginäre Sekten im Spätmittelalter.* Hahnsche Buchhandlung, Hannover 2008.

Välimäki, Reima: Imagery of Disease, Poison and Healing in the Late Fourteenth-Century Polemics against Waldensian Heresy. *Infirmity in Antiquity and the Middle Ages: Social and Cultural Approaches to Health, Weakness and Care.* Eds. Christian Krötzl, Katariina Mustakallio, and Jenni Kuuliala. Ashgate, Burlington VT 2015, 137–152.

Välimäki, Reima: *Heresy in Late Medieval Germany: The Inquisitor Petrus Zwicker and the Waldensians.* Heresy and Inquisition in the Middle Ages 6. York Medieval Press, York 2019.

Van Dussen, Michael: *From England to Bohemia: Heresy and Communication in the Later Middle Ages.* Cambridge University Press, Cambridge UK and New York 2012.

Vasoli, Cesare: Il 'Contra haereticos' di Alano di Lilla. *Bullettino dell'Istituto storico italiano per il medio evo e Archivio muratoriano* 75/1963, 123–172.

Wakefield, Walter L.: Notes on Some Anti-Heretical Writings of the Thirteenth Century. *Franciscan Studies* 27/1967, 285–321.

Werner, Ernst: Nachrichten über spätmittelalterliche Ketzer aus tschechoslowakischen Archiven und Bibliotheken. *Wissenschaftliche Zeitschrift der Karl-Marx-Universität Leipzig. Gesellschafts- und sprachwissenschaftliche Reihe* 12.1/1963, 215–284.

Williams-Krapp, Werner: Die überlieferungsgeschichtliche Methode: Rückblick und Ausblick. *Internationales Archiv für Sozialgeschichte der Deutschen Literatur* 25/2000, 1–21.

Zerner, Monique (ed.): *Inventer l'hérésie? Discours polémiques et pouvoirs avant l'Inquisition.* Collection du Centre d'études médiévales de Nice 2. Centre d'études médiévales, Faculté des lettres, arts et sciences humaines, Université de Nice Sophia-Antipolis, Nice 1998.

Österreichische Nationalbibliothek (ÖNB). [Description of MS 4511] (Ref. 6.2.2017) http://data.onb.ac.at/rec/AL00177227

Countering the 'heretics': miracle books and Marian devotion in early modern Spain

Thomas Devaney

Introduction

In his *Bautismo del Príncipe de Marruecos*, Lope de Vega recounted a lengthy conversation between a Victorian friar and the titular prince of Morocco, the exiled Muley Xeque.[1] As they strolled from Andújar to the nearby Marian shrine of Nuestra Señora de la Cabeza, the friar pointed out the sights and regaled Xeque with tales of the shrine's history and significance. In describing the crowd of pilgrims who attended the annual *romería*, or pilgrimage to the shrine, he referred to them as a "grand army" in a manner that imagined this shrine as a field of battle against heresy. The friar went on to note that Christians had hidden sacred images, including the Virgen de la Cabeza, in mountain refuges

---

[1] Vega, *Tragedia del rey*, 417–517. Muley Muḥammad al-Shaykh, Muley 'Xeque' or 'Jeque' in Spanish documents, was son of the Sa'dī Sultan Abū 'Abdallah Muḥammad II al-Mutawakkil, who was ousted by Abu Marwān 'Abd al-Malik in 1576. He fled to Spain in the aftermath of the 1578 battle of Alcazarquivir. On his life, see: Gianolio 1795; Oliver Asín 1955; Alonso Acero and Bunes Ibarra 2011.

during the eighth-century Muslim invasion of Iberia because "they feared that the relics would fall into the hands of those barbarians." Relating those actions to the contemporary political situation, he suggested that there was still a pressing need to protect holy images from iconoclasts who would destroy them. For "this is the same thing they do now, those Englishmen that have left our faith, which Spain adores: a thousand times they have taken vengeance on our celestial Lady."[2]

It was no accident that this exchange presented the crowd as crucial to the defence of the faith. Indeed, Lope immediately emphasized the point. After the friar's words, Xeque expressed his surprise that a simple shepherd, and not a king, had been chosen to discover this precious image. But the friar replied that "in our written books," God reveals his "secrets and infinite mysteries to the little people for various purposes." The central role of an unempowered member of the community, a shepherd or child, was common in stories of the discovery of a sacred image. Here, by juxtaposing it with references to past and present threats, Lope offered a militant new vision of customary religious practices while entrusting the safety of both the sacred statue and "our Christian nation in Spain" to the ordinary people attending the *romería*.[3]

In some ways, these sentiments were hardly new. Spanish Catholics had long accorded sacred images a central role in their devotions; the annual pilgrimages or *romerías* to their shrines were important elements in local religious practice. And, as Lope indicated by referring to the eighth-century Muslim invasion, there was a tradition of associating such images, particularly those of the Virgin Mary, with the defence and expansion of the faith.[4] Accounts of the Virgen de la Cabeza,

---

[2] Vega, *Tragedia del rey*, 481. (all translations by the author unless otherwise noted)

[3] Vega, *Tragedia del rey*, 481–2. On the importance of shepherds in early modern Spanish discourse, see Irigoyen-García 2013. Lope explicitly compares the shepherd's discovery of the Virgen de la Cabeza to the annunciation to the shepherds in Luke 2:8–20.

[4] For instance, the *Cantigas de Santa María*, a late thirteenth-century compilation of poem-songs, brought together a number of Marian legends and stories to emphasize the close relationship between Mary and Castilian royal ambitions. See Alfonso X, *Cantigas de Santa María*. For a study of the Virgin Mary as a military symbol, see Remensnyder 2014.

for instance, traced its miraculous discovery by a shepherd to 1227, immediately after Andújar was conquered from Muslims by Fernando III of Castile. And so that statue, like many others, served as both a legitimization of Christian conquest and a symbol of Mary's continued protection of Christian settlers.[5]

Over the course of the sixteenth century, however, holy images acquired additional meanings. The 1492 conquest of Granada and Spanish encounters in the Americas shifted focus away from Islam while the Protestant reformations raised the spectre of a new threat, that of Lutheran "heretics." In response to Protestant critiques that traditional modes of engaging with sacred images amounted to little more than idolatry, the Council of Trent had decreed that, although Catholics should retain their images and give them due honour, the purpose of such images should be educational. The faithful were not to ascribe any divinity or virtue to the image, nor ask any favours of them, nor place any trust in them. Instead images were to remind viewers of the virtues of the person represented, and adorations should be directed not to the image itself but to that person, be it Christ, Mary, or a saint. In attempting to remove all possible taint of superstition, moreover, the Council set firm guidelines for the approval of new images, the validation of reported miracles, and proper conduct for those attending festivals or *romerías*.[6]

The Council of Trent's conclusions did not, of course, represent the perspectives of all Catholics. And one prominent strain of thought, influenced in part by popular practices whose status had become uncertain in the aftermath of Trent, glorified the adoration of images as a means of opposing heresy. While theologians such as the Valencian Jaime Prades drew on late-medieval scholastic thought to outline an understanding of the relationship between images and the divine, spiritual leaders, notably Teresa de Ávila, forcefully argued that images

---

[5] For overviews of Nuestra Señora de la Cabeza's history, see Fe y Jiménez 1900; Torres Laguna 1961; Gómez Martínez 2002; Gómez Martínez 2014.

[6] *Canons and Decrees of Trent*, 215–217. For debates about religious images, see Eire 1986; Duffy 1992; Po-chia Hsia 1998, esp. chap. 10, 'Art and Architecture', 152–164; Michalski 2002; Spicer 2017. On the difficulties of evaluating sanctity in this period, see Lazure 2007; Olds 2012.

could lead one to a closer relationship to God. Both explicitly presented their work as starkly opposed to Protestantism, arguing that, since images bolstered the faith of Catholics, they had the power to contain the spread of Protestant errors. But while Prades and Teresa addressed their writings to relatively narrow audiences, the annual *romerías* at popular Marian shrines—such as Nuestra Señora de la Cabeza, Nuestra Señora de Guadalupe, and Nuestra Señora de la Peña de Francia—attracted huge crowds of pilgrims, who came to see and adore the images housed there.

The means through which many common believers learned about and experienced shrines were also in flux during this period. The printing press had profoundly influenced the development and spread of new forms of religiosity. Widespread literacy and the ready availability of affordable texts (ranging from pamphlet catechisms known as *doctrinas* to *cartillas de leer*, or primers, to well-known masterpieces of Spanish piety) permitted the laity to engage with the faith on a variety of levels.[7] In addition to creating and popularizing new kinds of texts, printing reinvigorated well-established genres. "Miracle books," or compilations of the wondrous healings and other prodigies that had occurred at particular shrines, had been common for centuries. But their popularity increased dramatically in the first half of the sixteenth century. And they remained widespread in later decades, even as Church authorities attempted to impose more stringent requirements for the validation of miracles.[8]

In this chapter, I first examine the context in which Lope de Vega's depiction of pilgrims as an army rallying to the banner of a besieged

[7] While early modern Spanish literacy rates have not been well studied, notarial records suggest that, by the mid-seventeenth century at least, roughly fifty percent of the urban male population could at least write their own name. Bookseller records and library inventories, meanwhile, provide evidence for the popularity of texts or genres as well as their costs. See Nalle 1989; Nalle 1999; González Sánchez 2011; Roldán-Figueroa 2015. Studies of reading practices in individual urban centres include Luengo Pacheco 2002; Weruaga Prieto 2008.

[8] In addition to miracle books devoted to specific shrines, there was also a vast pamphlet literature related to miracles and other wonders, little of which has survived.

Virgin made sense. I do so by considering the political situation at the time and by exploring the writings of Teresa de Ávila and Jaime Prades, both of whom contributed to the development of the notion that the adoration of images might serve to counter Protestantism. I then argue that, especially after the turn of the seventeenth century, miracle books functioned both to ensure the continued popularity of particular shrines and to disseminate this militant understanding of images. Focusing primarily on two images, Nuestra Señora de la Cabeza and Santa María Vulnerata, I suggest that miracle books did more than simply recount tales of marvellous cures and conversions or advertise the advantages of visiting a shrine. At a time when there was a widespread perception that Spain's sacred images were in imminent physical danger, that the threat of Protestantism went beyond the spiritual or the symbolic, they characterized *romerías* as front lines in the battle to strengthen the hearts of the people and to eradicate heresy.

Defining the threat

It is significant that Lope de Vega identified the English as the enemies of the Virgin Mary. For he wrote his *Bautismo* soon after a devastating raid on Cádiz by a combined English–Dutch fleet that took place in 1596 and elicited shocked and indignant responses throughout Spain.[9] Although that attack left many dead and the city in ruins, contemporaries

---

[9] Although Lope's play was published in 1618, most scholars agree that the play was composed sometime between 1593 and 1603. Muley Xeque's movements indicate that he likely visited the shrine in 1593; the title *El príncipe de Marruecos* appears in a list of Lope's comedies included in the 1603 edition of *El peregrino de su patria*. I suggest here, on the basis of his reference to English attacks on the Virgin, that he wrote it after 1596. See Torres 2014. Lope de Vega, moreover, was not the only playwright to engage themes related to the raid. Cervantes' *La española inglesa* told the story of Isabela, a young girl kidnapped from Cádiz and brought to England. Cervantes Saavedra, *La española inglesa*. See also Andrés 2006; Montcher 2011.

emphasized the vandalizing of Cádiz's churches.[10] Pedro de Abreu, for instance, spoke of "the impiety of those perverse and wicked people" who dared to "profane the temples of God, making them into stables for their horses and using them for a thousand shameless acts, mocking the holy things, mistreating the priests with a thousand injuries and insults," and much more. But he reserved his greatest indignation for the raiders' treatment of holy images:

> With their impious and immoral hands, they tore them down from places of devotion where they had been placed with great reverence; they broke them into pieces while ridiculing them, testing the sharpness of their swords on them, they stomped on the resulting pieces and parts with their wicked feet, dragging them on the ground with many insults and indignities: after they had broken them into pieces, they made a bonfire, on which they cooked their food and which, at night, served as a light for the guards.[11]

Abreu's account portrayed the assault on Cádiz as directed against Catholics, not Spaniards. Although the raid was primarily motivated by economic and political considerations (for instance, Spanish aid to the Earl of Tyrone in Ireland), this redefining of the conflict as a religious war served several rhetorical purposes: it reminded readers of the sufferings of Catholic martyrs in England, it united the Spanish population in a common identity and common goal, it emphasized the futility of seeking peace with the enemies of God, and it assured Spanish Catholics that God was on their side.[12]

---

[10] For contemporary accounts of the raid on Cádiz, see Calderón Quijano 1985; Abreu, *Historia del saqueo*. For overviews of the raid as well as extended discussion of later discourses regarding *La Vulnerata*, see Sánchez 2002; Cruz 2008.

[11] Abreu, *Historia del saqueo*, 257–258.

[12] There is a vast scholarly literature on Anglo-Spanish relations during this period. The articles collected in Brownlee 2009 provide a useful starting point. See also Elliott 2002. Scully 2003, using the Battle of Armada as chief example, argues that religious goals took precedence over political ones throughout much of the late sixteenth century.

All this was vividly illustrated by reactions to the defamation by English soldiers of a statue of the Virgin Mary that had been housed in the Cathedral of Cádiz. As a miracle book dedicated to the image recounted several decades later,

> the English heretics… tore the Holy Image from its Throne and, in order to abuse it more publicly, took it to the city's public plaza, where they worshipped it falsely with mockery and taunts, insulting it in all ways. Finally, drawing their swords with diabolic intent, they stabbed it repeatedly, destroying the arms up to the elbows and, having disfigured its beauty, marked its countenance with seven wounds. They did all this without sparing the Baby Jesus from their frenzied anger; they had already knocked it from her arms.[13]

After the raid, the image was recovered and briefly placed in a private chapel. In August 1600, however, it was moved again and ensconced in the chapel at the Jesuit English College of Saint Alban in Valladolid during a ceremony attended by Felipe III and his wife Margarita. To underscore the symbolism of housing the Virgin in this college, where boys were trained to face potential martyrdom in England, there was another ceremony on 7 September, the birthday of Queen Elizabeth I of England. In contrast to England's earthly Virgin Queen, the Spanish honoured Mary as the Virgin Queen of heaven and, highlighting the wounds inflicted on the statue, rechristened it as La Vulnerata ("the injured one").[14] Its damaged arms and face were left unrepaired in order, as Anne J. Cruz suggests, to serve "as a graphic reminder to the Spanish people of the deep and unrelenting hatred held by the English against their religious beliefs."[15]

If this episode thus marked a turn toward the use of sacred images as ideological weapons that united Spaniards against the English, the Vulnerata was, in many ways, an ideal symbol. Yet, alone, it could

---

[13] Demendiola 1667, 1ʳ–2ᵛ. The story is also related in the *Recibimiento que se hizo en Valladolid a una imagen de Nuestra Señora*, a contemporary pamphlet published in Madrid.

[14] Ortíz 1600, 24ᵛ. Williams 1986, 4, 9, 62.

[15] Cruz 2008, 50.

not take on all this rhetorical work. For the story of the sack of Cádiz and the brutalizing of the Vulnerata was a story of failure, of Spain's inability to protect its people, its wealth, and its icon. The ceremonies in Valladolid associated the damaged Virgin with the royal family, yet contemporaries such as Abreu placed much of the blame for the disaster on Felipe II's neglect of Cádiz's harbour defences. Other targets for ire included Cádiz's chief magistrate, Antonio Girón y Zúñiga (accused of cowardice and a series of bad decisions), the Duke of Medinia Sidona (who failed to bring troops to relieve the city), and the wealthy townspeople (who hid their riches in order to avoid sharing with their less-privileged neighbours).[16] All those with the power to protect Cádiz and its holy treasures had failed in their duty. The Vulnerata, then, represented not only English hatred of Catholics, but also reminded all who saw it that Spain had been unable to defend its shores and relics.

It is from within this context that we should consider Lope's account of Nuestra Señora de la Cabeza. Here was a miraculous image of the Virgin cherished and kept safe, not by king or nobles, but by the devotion of the common people. This is not to say that Lope adopted an anti-authoritarian tone; the whole of the play, in fact, linked divine and monarchical power. Rather, by referring to a "thousand" English attacks on the Virgin, the playwright extended the trauma of the Vulnerata's brutalization to other Marian sites. In suggesting that the English would destroy all Marian images if they could, moreover, he transformed the Vulnerata's symbolic meaning into a threat that ordinary people might *act* upon. Their veneration of holy images maintained the vitality of Spanish Catholicism, ensuring that God remained on their side and countering Protestant efforts to undermine *"nuestra Santa Fé."* Such veneration, of course, was already popular, as were the miracle books and other devotional texts that promoted the shrines. These texts permitted the ideas Lope had proposed to be disseminated to a wide audience.

In 1614, for instance, Gaspar Salcedo de Aguirre published his *Relación de algunas cosas insignes que tiene este reyno y obispado de Iaén.*[17] This compendium of holy sites within the diocese of Jaén aimed to

---

[16] Abreu, *Historia del saqueo*, 85, 212–3; Cruz 2008, 45–7.
[17] Aguirre (1614) 2012.

prove the antiquity of Christian belief in the region and to justify local devotional practices, many of which did not accord well with post-Tridentine orthodoxy. When recounting the *romería* to Nuestra Señora de la Cabeza, the same event that Lope had described, Aguirre told of both the image's miraculous discovery just after Fernando III had taken the territory from the Muslims and of the contemporary *romería*. He noted that, when the hordes of pilgrims arrived, they found a sanctuary that looked more like a stronghold than a church. This "very large and very well fortified" shrine boasted ramparts that were fourteen feet thick "in order to resist the furious combat of the winds."[18] Before these walls, the crowd of pilgrims "seems like a numerous army with their many small and large tents." Their impressive number was, for Aguirre, "a great argument for the health of the faith in Spain. So many people gather at a lonely mountain in order to adore an image, and do so at such cost and with such danger from the storms and inclement weather." All this, moreover, was happening "in a time in which the heretics try so hard to eradicate the veneration of images."[19]

Images and the struggle against heresy

Despite the boldness with which various authorities and authors embraced the narrative of Santa María Vulnerata's disfigurement or the idea of the adoration of images as an expression of the Church Militant, many contemporaries were uncertain about the place of image veneration within orthodox Catholic practice. The Council of Trent's decrees regarding images and their adoration challenged a number of traditional practices. And, although local authorities sometimes attempted to implement these and other new rules, some reformers, concerned that the behaviour and beliefs of the common people had not changed, attempted to "educate" the masses in the fundamentals

---

[18] Aguirre (1614) 2012, 61–62. Construction on the shrine began in the late sixteenth century and was completed in 1611. On the shrine, see Lázaro Damas 1996.

[19] Aguirre (1614) 2012, 63–64.

of their faith.[20] The means for doing so ranged widely, encompassing all the media available for reaching early modern audiences. Even Lope de Vega, for instance, felt it necessary to paraphrase the Council's directives in his play. When the Muslim prince, Muley Xeque, asked about Nuestra Señora de la Cabeza's miracles, the Victorian friar responded emphatically that the image could do nothing, for it was only an image. The faithful prayed to the Virgin that she intervene on their behalf with God, who then acted through Mary to perform miracles.[21] Such efforts to instruct the populace in contentious points of faith were complemented by attempts to impose new, orthodox meanings on existing practices. Miracle books, despite (or perhaps because of) their uncertain status in relation to doctrine, were important tools for redefining the meanings of sacred images and of *romerías*. And while they might endorse an orthodox perspective on images and their role in miracle-making, they could also disseminate an understanding of images as powerful weapons in the arsenal of a Church struggling against the perceived heresy of Protestantism.[22]

This latter idea had its roots in the Spanish reform movements of the mid-sixteenth century. Spiritual authorities such as Francisco de Osuna, Ignatius Loyola, Juan de Ávila, and Teresa de Ávila argued for affective forms of devotion that built on and intensified medieval traditions.[23] While all of them emphasized the importance of images and visualization techniques in facilitating practices of self-examination, meditation, and mystical prayer that might bring an individual to a more complete union with God, Teresa was the most overt about how images might counter heresy. Her perspective, though not representative

---

[20] Since the agendas, means, and experiences of "Counter Reformation" or "Catholic Reformation" have been well studied elsewhere, I do not address these here. For a synthesis of recent research on the topic, see Bamji, Janssen, and Laven 2013.

[21] Vega, *Tragedia del rey*, 482.

[22] On miracle writing in the seventeenth century, see Carrasco 1986; Crémoux 2007; Civil 2011.

[23] For emotional norms as a means of creating confessional identity, see Karant-Nunn 2007; Karant-Nunn 2010. On emotions in sixteenth-century Spanish devotional practice, see Carrera 2007a; Carrera 2007b.

of all contemporary strands of thought, gives a sense of the meanings according to images at the time.

In her autobiography, written as the Council of Trent was drawing to a close, she reflected on the role images had played in her own life. In her youth, she lamented, she had been unable to use her imagination to effectively envision Christ and the Passion and so had relied on images. As she put it,

> I was so little able to put things before me by the help of my understanding that, unless I saw a thing with my eyes, my imagination was of no use whatever. I could not do as others do, who can put matters before themselves so as to become thereby recollected. I was able to think of Christ only as a man. But so it was; and I never could form any image of him to myself, though I read much of his beauty, and looked at pictures of him. I was like one who is blind or in the dark... This is why I was so fond of images.[24]

When, after years of dedicated prayer and striving, she had an Augustinian moment of conversion, it was inspired by an image, a statue of the wounded Christ. Since the passions that the contemplation of such images had aroused in Teresa had aided her spiritual progress, it is not surprising that she both pitied and disdained those "heretics who, through their own fault, have lost this blessing; it is clear enough that they do not love our Lord—for if they loved him, they would rejoice at the sight of his picture, just as men find pleasure when they see the portrait of one they love."[25]

Teresa brought these experiences to bear when she founded her first convent of Discalced Carmelites, St Joseph in Ávila, in 1562. At St Joseph, she consciously created a physical environment meant, through

---

[24] Teresa de Ávila, *Libro de la vida*, 9.7.

[25] Teresa de Ávila, *El libro de la vida*, 9.7. She expresses the same idea in her *Camino de Perfección*: "Wherever I turn my eyes, I would want to see [his image]. In what better or more pleasing thing we can use our eyes, then in looking at he who loves us so much and who has in himself all good things. Unfortunate are those heretics who through their own fault have lost this consolation among others." Teresa de Ávila, *Camino de Perfección*, 33.11.

a combination of austere architecture and carefully chosen images, to facilitate similar meditative practices among her followers. Those practices would be necessary if the nuns were to fulfil the mission Teresa envisioned for them. Although the nuns would be enclosed inside the walls of the convert and dedicated to constant prayer, she intended that the convent (and the many other communities she later founded) would serve a missionary purpose. In her *Camino de Perfección*, she linked the founding of St Joseph with her feelings about the "harm being done in France and the havoc caused by those Lutherans and how much that unfortunate sect was growing." Distraught at the souls being lost to heresy and frustrated that the limits imposed on women prevented her from taking direct action, she nonetheless resolved to do "what little I could do, which is to follow the evangelical counsels with all the perfection in my power and endeavour that those few people here with me do the same."[26] Their prayers would help the Church to rescue souls endangered by false beliefs or impious deeds.

The nuns' influence would affect the outside world, in other words, and be just as critical to the Church's health as were the efforts of Franciscan or Jesuit missionaries.[27] Teresa was clear about the association between religious imagery and efficacious prayer. In her autobiography, for instance, she recounted a moment when "I knew that a person to whom I was under great obligation was about to commit an act highly offensive to God… [but] I did not know what to do in order to change his purpose." In her distress, she went to a hermitage "in which there is a picture of Christ bound to the pillar; and there, as I was imploring our Lord to grant this favour, I heard a voice of great gentleness, speaking as if in a whisper." Although frightened at first, Teresa soon "became conscious of an inner calmness, a joy and delight… I saw by this that my prayer was granted, and so it was."[28] Images, for Teresa, woke love for God in people's hearts; that love made their prayers more sincere and encouraged God to grant their petitions.

[26] Teresa de Ávila, *Camino de Perfección*, 1.2. She expressed much the same sentiment in *Libro de la Vida*, 32.6.

[27] On Teresa's goals for her Carmelite foundations, see Bilinkoff 1994. On the decorative scheme of these convents, see Wilson 2010.

[28] Teresa de Ávila, *Libro de la vida*, 39.3–4.

As we have already seen, Teresa explicitly contrasted this love with Protestant practices. In a note written at Ávila in the early 1570s, she recalled reading in a book that it was an "imperfection" to possess ornate images. This confirmed her existing inclination that, given her vow of poverty, it would be best to own only paper images. And so she immediately decided to remove the painting she kept in her cell. But then she heard Christ's voice telling her to reconsider this decision, that

> love is better [than poverty] and I should not reject anything that awakened me to it, nor take such a thing from my nuns... that what the devil did among the Lutherans was to remove all the means for awakening love, and so they were lost. 'My Christians, daughter, must do, now more than ever, the opposite of what they do.'[29]

While Teresa lamented the spiritual danger faced by all those she considered to not be truly Christian, including Muslims, Catholic heretics (such as the *alumbrados*), and the unconverted peoples of the Americas, she returned again and again, in both her treatises and letters, to prayer as a means of saving the "Lutherans." The veneration of images was central to her thinking on this, precisely because Protestant reformers opposed it. By means of their prayers, Teresa and her nuns worked to save souls. Because they used art to facilitate those prayers, those prayers were an especially potent counter to the iconoclastic Lutherans.

Teresa herself was the object of Inquisitorial scrutiny, as a descendent of converted Jews, as an influential female foundress, as the recipient of mystical visions, and as a suspected *alumbrado*.[30] As Christopher Wilson has pointed out, her devotion to images functioned to distance her not only from Protestants but also from the *alumbrados*, who objected to the veneration of sacred images. It was, in other words, a means through

---

[29] Teresa de Ávila, *Relaciones*, 30.

[30] *Alumbrados*, or "illuminated ones," believed that individuals could comprehend the mysteries of God with the help of the Holy Spirit and thus without the need for human intermediaries. This position led some *alumbrados* to reject the sacraments, authority of priests, and other outward signifiers of Christianity. For overviews of *alumbradismo*, see Márquez 1980; Hamilton 1992; Pastore 2004; and Fowler 2016.

which Teresa established that her religious experiences were orthodox. In this, she was ultimately successful, with her canonization in 1622 defining her as an exemplar of female devotion.[31] As Erin K. Rowe has pointed out, though efforts to elevate Teresa to the status of co-patron saint of Spain failed due to the opposition of partisans of Santiago, many also saw her as an exemplar of *Spanish* devotion, a holy warrior poised to defend Spain and lay low her enemies.[32] And her passionate endorsement of the contemplative power of sacred imagery helped to establish those images as central aspects of a post-Tridentine Catholicism that was moving away from a defensive stance regarding "superstitious" practices to a confident assertion that religious images were an essential part of one's spiritual life.

That confidence is apparent in Jaime Prades's *Historia de la adoracion y uso de las santas imágenes, y de la imagen de la fuente de la salud*, first published in 1596 (just prior to the fateful English attach on Cádiz). Noting that he had written this book "in order to combat the deprecation and abrogration of holy images" and as "a light against the heretics of Béarn, France, Germany, and England," Prades argued that both the doctrine of the Incarnation and the clear holiness of archetypal images, such as the Mandylion of Edessa and the Veil of Veronica, provide a theological basis for the essential purpose of holy images: to make visible what is otherwise invisible. Building on medieval scholastic theories which distinguished between grades of holiness, he went on to contend that images representing holy figures merited the same degree of veneration that should be given to the person represented. Thus one should treat an image of Christ as if it were Christ himself.[33] This was, in the post Tridentine world, contested territory.

But Prades sharply distinguished between Christian devotions involving images and the Hebrew prohibitions against idolatry. For he made clear that the image was a representation of something external to

---

[31] Wilson 2010, 54–55. On the posthumous debates over Teresa's orthodoxy, see Ahlgren 1996, 114–144.

[32] Rowe 2006.

[33] Prades 1597, 5–8, 10. On the grades of holiness (*latria, dulia,* and *hyper-dulia*) and their application to images, see Thomas Aquinas, *Summa Theologiæ*, II–II, 84.1 and III, 25.1–6.

itself; it could never be the thing itself. As the products of human hands, images could never be considered works of God. And so, Christians are allowed images "not to adore them thinking there is some deity in them." Rather, the external reverence that Catholics offer to images gives life to their internal faith; the faithful confess and make offerings *to* God *through* the holy images. And, he continued, the clearest proofs of the truth of this are the various miracles and apparitions associated with sacred images throughout Spain and the world. Using the example of the Virgen de la Fuente de la Salud de Traiguera, he emphasized that such miracles occured without human intervention, but "through the will of God alone."[34] The distinctions here are subtle; one could understand how well-meaning believers might fall into error and come to believe in the divinity of the images themselves. Even if such was contrary to Church orthodoxy, they "do not err by adoring images because they worship them with the faith of the Church, and with the intention that it had and has when it suggests that we adore them to honor God."[35]

As Darío Velandia Onofre has argued, Prades's doctrinal flexibility, as well as his use of scholastic theology and his recourse to justification by miracles, suggests an attempt to balance post-Tridentine doctrine with deeply-rooted popular devotions. By framing the debate in terms of a shared opposition to Protestant practices, Prades sought to establish, from the start, a common ground between the two perspectives. This approach was echoed by several subsequent authors. Martín de Roa (in 1622), Juan Acuña de Adarve (1637), and Alsonso Andrade (1669) all composed treatises on the veneration of images; all built upon the theological framework Prades had established while representing themselves as defending traditional practices and as anti-Protestant. In his prologue to the reader, for instance, Acuña de Adarve upheld the miraculous nature of images as well as the anitiquity of devotions to those images. He also maintained that he sought "to challenge the

---

[34] Prades 1597, 6–10, 41, 49.
[35] Prades 1597, 107.

calumnies and errors of the heretic Calvin and his successors, who have tried to slander the images of Christ Our Lord."[36]

Miracle books and popular devotions

Like Teresa de Ávila, Prades and his successors had, despite their care in navigating the theological currents of the time, advocated an attitude toward images that was remarkably in tune with traditional popular practices. As William Christian has demonstrated, sacred images played key roles in local devotions.[37] Although petitioners visited the shrines housing such images year round, the annual *romerías* were moments when whole communities came together along with many pilgrims to adore the image, seek healing, and petition God's favour (through the intercession of the person depicted on the image). In doing so, they engaged emotionally with the images in a manner similar to what Teresa had recommended. There are, of course, stark differences between the experience Teresa described—a dedicated and solitary process of self-interpretation in which the power of images lay in their ability to bring an individual into a state of closeness to God—and the ephemeral unleashing of passions in a frenzy of devotion that characterized many *romerías*. But, in both cases, emotional displays facilitated by the sight of holy images served to purge sins, move God, and open hearts.

Miracles were at the heart of these emotional responses, providing the individual with hope that he or she might now or one day benefit from God's grace and generosity. To the community, miracles demonstrated the truth of the faith and God's continuing intervention in the world. Both miracles and pilgrimage had been part of the Christian tradition since its beginnings, and the custom of composing miracle books that recorded wondrous events at specific shrines dates to late antiquity and became common in the twelfth and thirteenth centuries. But the

---

[36] Velandia Onofre 2017, 188, 191–93; Acuña de Adarve, *Discursos de las efigies y verdaderos retratos*, "Al lector." See also: Roa 1623; and Andrade, *Veneración de los santos imágenes.*

[37] Christian 2004. See also Christian 1981.

sixteenth and seventeenth centuries, amid the theological and political upheavals of the Reformations, saw massive increases in reports of miracles, the foundation of new shrines, and the production and publication of miracle books, leading one historian to describe early modern Europe as among "the golden ages and places of miracles in Christian history."[38] This was not happenstance. As Philip Soergel has argued, in his study of contemporary Bavarian miracle books, clerics and local authorities consciously identified pilgrimage as a primary means of reinvigorating Catholic devotion while establishing doctrinal unity. As did their counterparts in Spain, Bavarian authors presented pilgrimage in explicitly anti-Protestant terms; one theologian contended that pilgrimage was a "spiritual medicine for heretical poison."[39]

The proliferation of long- and medium-distance pilgrimage meant that more travellers were learning of and about shrines from miracle books. The books had several purposes. On one level, they were promotional works—especially important tools for new or previously-obscure shrines, such as Nuestra Señora de la Cabeza or San Ginés de la Jara near Murcia—that detailed the miracles a sacred image had worked as well as the beauty of the natural setting, the grandeur of the shrine, the piety and enthusiasm of the pilgrims, and the goods to be purchased at the fairs that often accompanied annual *romerías*. They were educational texts through which one might learn the history of the image and of local ecclesiastic institutions as well as biblical or hagiographical stories. And they were instruments for advancing the priorities of the official Church. The relative newness of many shrines meant that their meanings were still evolving and malleable. Their popularity meant that nudging these meanings was a way for Church authorities to reach large numbers of believers at a moment when they were emotionally open to such influence.

In some ways, miracle books were ideal tools for this. While visitors from nearby might rely on word-of-mouth reports and local traditions, those coming from afar depended on the texts for knowledge of what to expect and how they should behave, think, and feel. The books, therefore,

---

[38] Harline 2003, 4–5; Soergel 1993. This was not solely a Catholic phenomenon, as explored in Soergel 2012.

[39] Soergel 1991, 125–27.

established behavioural norms that shaped pilgrims' experiences while situating a particular shrine within a larger interpretive framework. In the case of Nuestra Señora de la Cabeza, for instance, both Lope de Vega and Gaspar Salcedo de Aguirre explicitly linked the legends of the statue's discovery in the immediate aftermath of Fernando III's thirteenth-century conquest of the region to the Church's current challenges. Just as the Virgin had miraculously appeared to herald the Christians' victory over the Muslims of Granada, so too would she now lead them against the Protestants.

Yet neither pilgrimages nor miracle books could be completely controlled by the institutional Church. Although most shrines were nominally under the authority of the relevant bishop and local pastoral staff gave sermons and conducted the official rites, *romerías* typically were not directed from the top down. Instead, confraternities, whose members included laymen of nearly all social classes, played central and influential roles in all aspects of the events while local customs and practices provided a framework that was often at least as important as formal doctrine. Miracle books, which were not official Church publications, had many of the same limitations. They were, it is true, subject to the same censorship processes undergone by all books published in Catholic countries, and the Council of Trent's decrees on the authentication of miracles affected the ways in which these texts were composed. The need to avoid reports of unverified miracles, for instance, meant that the typical number of miracles included in a book declined dramatically, from scores or hundreds to just a few exemplars.[40] And those few were described with care and often with explicit reference to eyewitnesses and verification proceedings.

At the same time, however, the authors of these books, although they might hold positions in the Church hierarchy, often deviated from a narrow interpretation of official doctrine to privilege the same local traditions and beliefs that the Council of Trent hoped to restrain. In doing so, they used stories of miracles to argue for the essential orthodoxy of those local practices. Antonio Daza's *vida* of Juana de la Cruz Vázquez y Gutiérrez, a Franciscan tertiary and abbess of the monastery

---

[40] See Taylor 2007.

of Santa María de la Cruz de La Sagra sometimes considered to be the spiritual mother of Teresa de Ávila, was first published in 1610 and then reprinted dozens of times in the seventeenth century (including a 1625 English translation intended for use by missionaries). Daza opened by tracing the long struggles between orthodoxy and deviance, arguing that Catholics of every era, having to contend with heresy, had done so through adherence to traditional and received practice. Protestantism was merely the latest manifestation of a false mode of thinking. He explicitly challenged the efforts of the Calvinist theologian Theodor Beza and others who, he wrote, ridiculed "the devoted piety with which the faithful venerate blessed things" such as holy water, rosaries, candles, and images. They did so in order to "provoke the common people, and prepare them to believe the errors of the ancient heretics which for many years have lain buried in hell, one of which is to condemn the ceremonies and ancient rites of the Church."[41]

Among the many miracles Daza recounted was the story of a miraculous image held at the monastery of Santa María de la Cruz, to which the nuns were especially devoted. Since the image was very old and in disrepair, they remade its head and face and then carried it to Sister Juana, who was sick, and left it in her cell. That night, Juana saw visions of Mary and Christ coming to bless the renovated image, and the nuns' devotion to their image was redoubled. This, Daza noted, was the kind of thing that God had often done "according to the necessity of the times." But, "the heretics who, in these times, are doing so many injuries to holy images, will react poorly to this marvel, which the Lord worked for their confusion and to confirm the ancient usage of the Church."[42]

Similarly, Gabriel de Talavera told of a family from Escurial who came to the shrine of Nuestra Señora de Guadalupe to seek a cure for their crippled and mute daughter. They arrived in town to find "an innumerable mass of people, some coming on account of the fame of the miracles, others in order to see the chastisement that would be given to some heretics from the town."[43] The Virgin, of course, healed the

---

[41] Daça (1610) 1614, 1v–4r., 17r. The English translation was published by the Jesuit English College at Saint Omers.
[42] Daça (1610) 1614, 67v–68r.
[43] Talavera 1597, 240v.

girl, allowing those who had to come to see heretics punished to also witness a miracle. In doing so, she also signalled her approval of the heretics' chastisement. Talavera later laid out his rules for understanding the qualities of miracles. Fifth was an admonition to be not overly sceptical about miracles, for such doubt implied that God was incapable of marvels. It was the devil, he said, who had "taught his disciples, the heretics, to give no credence to great miracles." In this, he went on, heretics were little different from the Pharisees who "had testified that the great deeds that our Redeemer worked were actually caused by the power and force of the devil."[44] Popular religious practices, in other words, did not challenge orthodox doctrine. They proved the piety of the people. They were a visible, essential difference between the faithful and the heretical. And the miraculous healings and other wonders that occurred during *romerías* demonstrated divine approval for these practices.

The miracle books, then, combined a range of perspectives: "elite" and "popular," official and local, reformed and traditional. These creative interactions between individual authors and Church doctrine were paralleled by the active engagement of audiences. Reading was not a passive process of determining and accepting the author's intent; readers were expected, even encouraged, to take notes, skip from place to place in a book, judge, and recombine ideas in a way that blurred the lines between the processes of writing and reading. One "performed a reading" by drawing upon memories of other texts to complete or extend an author's meaning. Indeed, as Fernando Bouza has argued, readers might become "almost co-authors of what they read." Miracle books, whose established rhetorical patterns and lists of marvels invited readers to make comparisons and to find patterns, were particularly amenable to such inventive readings. A reader might draw on memories of shrines visited, miracles witnessed or related, and sermons heard to develop their own interpretations of a holy image.[45]

---

[44] Talavera 1597, 459ᵛ. The comparison to the Pharisees refers to Matt 12:24.
[45] Bouza 2004, 50; Crémoux 2003. The relationship of author to audience has been well studied by, among others, Roger Chartier. See, for instance, Cavallo and Chartier 2003.

Literary consumption, however, was not limited to solitary reading. Although printing vastly expanded the audience for miracle books (and for other books in early modern Spain), the common practice of reading texts aloud in social settings meant that they were not limited to the literate. Examples abound of references to familial and social reading of texts; even the punctuation of most texts was based on oral and not grammatical grounds. Cervantes told of harvesters listening to chivalric tales and the priest reading the story of the "*Curioso impertinente*" aloud in the inn, for instance, while Teresa de Ávila recalled reading saints' lives with her brother and listening to books of chivalry with her mother and other siblings. Luisa de Carvajal's uncle, to give another example, habitually read to the family and others from "the Holy Scriptures and the Holy Doctors of the Church."[46] Authors expected that readers would make meanings through this process of reading socially, just as one might do when reading privately. As Álvaro de Hinojosa y Carvajal commented in a note to readers that prefaced his 1611 *Libro de la vida y milogros de S. Inés*,

> It is said, pious reader, that the lioness gives birth to an unpolished off-spring, with vaguely-formed limbs, and that later, licking it, she shapes it little by little, in that way giving it new form with her tongue. This, my book, is a part of my mind that today comes into the world, to everyone's eyes coarse and formless, but *the tongue of the benevolent reader* will do the work of the merciful mother, giving it new form (emphasis added).[47]

These reading practices applied to all books, but were especially potent when used with religious texts. And much of what people were reading was devotional; Sara Nalle has calculated, using inventories from urban booksellers, that nine-tenths of the available texts were

---

[46] Bouza 2004, 51–52; Cervantes Saavedra, *El ingenioso hidalgo don Quijote de la Mancha*, 32–33; Teresa de Ávila, *Libro de la vida*, 1.4, 2.1; Carvajal y Mendoza, *Historia de su vida espiritual*, 69–70, in *This Tight Embrace* 2000, 73.

[47] Hinojosa y Carvajal 1611, "Al lector."

religious.[48] In one sense, the reading aloud of a religious text (either alone or with others) was a devotional exercise akin to Teresa's use of images. Indeed, text and image were often combined in meditative prayer; one would read a passage, then contemplate an image that complemented or completed the meaning of the text.[49] Such reading, like other forms of devotional practice, could bring one to greater spiritual knowledge. It might also, however, place a layperson in the position of interpreting Scripture or developing opinions regarding doctrinal matters without clerical intervention. In the context of late sixteenth-century religious reforms, the free reading of texts was viewed as dangerous, a practice that might easily lead one into error or heresy. The *Index Librorum Prohibitorum* was intended to protect the morals of the faithful by blocking access to texts with known errors. But, given contemporary reading habits, censorship could not prevent people from drawing false conclusions even from approved books.

But, even as social reading allowed the illiterate to experience religious texts and encouraged interpretive discussion, the practice served also to control the meaning of a book by establishing the reader-speaker as an intermediary between text and audience. So a local priest, for instance, could guide his parishioners' interpretations of a book even as he read it to them. Much of this would be straightforward, a matter of clarifying obscure points and directing conversation toward safe ground. But miracle books also provided fertile material for impromptu sermons on critical matters. When reading, to give just one example, the prologue of the *Historia y Milagros de Nuestra Señora de la Peña de Francia*, a reader-speaker could direct listeners toward the author's comments on the importance of maintaining tradition, which was necessary

> so that the prophecy made by the virginal mouth of the most holy Virgin be fulfilled: that all generations would know her as blessed, and also that the wicked and wretched heretics of our times be confounded, considering how just is their condemnation, in neither receiving nor approving those things which have been received from the holy hands

---

[48] Nalle 1999, 130.
[49] Bouza 2004, 51.

of the Apostles, and approved by the holy Councils, and are used by the Catholic Church.[50]

These words offered opportunities to discuss the origins of local traditions, to condemn Protestant innovations, or to uphold the Catholic Church's doctrinal authority.

Reading aloud, therefore, was not simply a continuation of medieval practices but a self-conscious effort to control the meanings of books, particularly religious books, in a society increasingly influenced by textual culture. Yet, even though reader-centred meaning creation was socially mediated, it still functioned to reduce the inherent authority of the text itself. This process of social interpretation was emotional. The ultimate purpose of miracle books was not the intellectual edification of audiences. Rather, the ideas they conveyed, whether construed freely or through the mediation of an authoritative reader, were meant to be put into action. Miracle books were advertisements of a sort; their intent was to inspire a powerful desire to visit a shrine, to give offerings, and to view the holy image as a link between heaven and earth.

While the hope for miraculous cures continued to be an important attraction, their appeal was enhanced by texts that presented the holy images as being in imminent danger from heretics and suggested that ordinary believers played a central role in the defence of the faith and of the Virgin and Christ, all of whom were besieged by Protestants. Juan Crisóstomo Enríquez's *vita* of Ana de San Bartolomé invited readers and listeners to follow her example. Ana, who had been one of Teresa de Ávila's companions, later worked to expand the Discalced Carmelite order into France. She did so, according to Enríquez, because "[s]he saw that each day the heretics crucified Christ anew, scourged him, crowned him with thorns and blasphemed, and remembering what he ordered her when he told her to help him, wanted to help him carry that new cross, no less heavy that what the Jews had put on his sacred shoulders."[51] How could any pious believer do less?

---

[50] *Historia y Milagros de Nuestra Señora de la Peña de Francia*, "Prologo."
[51] Enríquez 1632, 275.

Miracle books mediated between "official" doctrine and popular practice. Like other texts, they were both within and without the control of the Church. In this way they resembled the shrines, miracles, and *romerías* they described. Castigating Protestant "heretics" for their hatred of the Virgin permitted authors to publicly argue for the orthodoxy of image veneration and thus win the support of Church officials who might be hesitant about the propriety of pilgrims' beliefs and behaviour. The rhetorical links between popular shrines, the holiness of the Virgin, image adoration and anti-English and anti-Protestant propaganda proved to be remarkably durable, as the cases of both the Vulnerata and Nuestra Señora de la Cabeza demonstrate. This was, in part, because they benefitted local constituencies as well as the Spanish monarchy and the institutional Church.

After its installation in 1600, the maimed Vulnerata had remained in the English College of Saint Alban in Valladolid. But, by 1671, the College found itself in need of a new, larger chapel. Unable to count on financial support from the Spanish government, the rector, Manuel de Catalayud, traveled across Spain to raise funds. He focused his efforts on Cadíz and was so successful that he was able to commission a series of eight paintings by Diego Díaz Ferreras to decorate the new chapel. These paintings presented the story of the Vulnerata in a manner that emphasized the statue's political value.[52] The first two images of the series depict the residents of Cadíz venerating the image. The second is especially poignant, as pious Gaditanos kneel and beg the intercession of the Virgin even while the English attackers kill and burn. The removal of the Virgin from the church and its subsequent humiliation and disfigurement feature prominently in the next three paintings, all of which emphasize the brutality of the invaders and the helplessness of the locals. The final images return to the theme of the Virgin's adoration. But these scenes are dominated by members of the royal lineage, including Felipe III and Carlos II, whose veneration of the statue linked Virgin and crown across the generations.

The Jesuits also claimed Santa María Vulnerata. Just a few years earlier, Catalayud's predecessor as rector of Saint Alban, Gregorio

---

[52] All eight images are reproduced in Cruz 2008, 52–59.

Demendiola, had published a miracle book devoted to the statue. His *Historia y Milagros de Nuestra Señora la Vulnerata* began with the attack on Cadíz and the statue's mutilation.[53] After then describing the Vulnerata's subsequent *translatio* to Valladolid, he listed the various miracles, mostly healings, worked through its intercession. All these were typical features of miracle books. But Demendiola devoted the second half of his book to a history of the English College, an institution dedicated to training missionaries who would combat Protestantism in England. With a dramatic retelling of Henry VIII's break with the Church and the persecution of English Catholics, he set the stage for stories of Saint Alban alumni and associates who had been martyred in England. The most detailed of these told of Luisa Carvajal y Mendoza, who was closely associated with Juan de Sigüenza, then rector of the College. She had helped to dress the Vulnerata prior to its installation in Valladolid and, inspired by the statue and by reports of tortured and martyred missionaries, travelled to England in 1605 to seek her own martyrdom. There she engaged in various activities with the Catholic underground and, after a period of imprisonment, died of illness in 1614.[54] Although Demendiola did not quite go so far as to describe her as a martyr, his account linked her to the male martyrs of Saint Alban, who had also been devoted to the Vulnerata. In juxtaposing a traditional account of a miraculous image with a history of Saint Alban's efforts to bolster Catholicism in England, Demendiola made clear that, for the missionaries, the statue was no mere political symbol, but a means through which the Virgin inspired people to take action in defence of the faith.

Militant overtones persisted also in representations of the *romería* of Nuestra Señora de la Cabeza. In 1677, Manuel Salcedo Olid, a prominent local figure, published a book extolling the miracles of the

[53] Demendiola 1667.
[54] Demendiola 1667, ff.102r–114r; *This Tight Embrace*, 1–37; Williams 1986, 64–66. See also Muñoz 1632. For an overview of missionary work in England, see Walsham 2003; Walsham 2014.

Virgen de la Cabeza.[55] In addition to detailing the shrine's history and the statue's many miracles, he devoted several chapters to an account of the *romería* that took place each April. Olid peppered his writing with military references that envisioned the *romería* as a battlefield, with serried ranks of pilgrims defending the massive fortified shrine. And so the various confraternities, waving standards and accompanied by musicians, looked "like battalions of light cavalry," while the pilgrims on foot "seemed to be squadrons of a most numerous army." And the banners waving in the breeze "make many happy with their flutterings, and the variety of their colours has the same force as might kings feel at a huge army of soldiers."[56]

Olid took pains to emphasize the *romería*'s orthodoxy. He repeatedly highlighted the antiquity of the Virgen de la Cabeza's veneration, linking it to Saint Euphrasius (one of the "Seven Apostolic Men" who, according to tradition, were ordained by Peter and Paul and evangelized Spain) and recounting its history from the first century to the seventeenth. Such continuity of practice was a convincing argument for orthodoxy in post-Tridentine Spain, as was the extensive list of irreproachable and prominent figures whose visits to the shrine he detailed. Many of these, as he noted, held high position in the military orders and had served in Spain's wars against non-Catholics, not only the English but also the Dutch and the Ottomans. Olid perhaps intended this strenuous defence of the *romería*'s orthodoxy as a means of upholding local practices which had recently been lampooned in a 1664 satirical poem by Fermín de Sarasa y Arce.[57] For Sarasa y Acre, the *romería* was little more than a raucous, irreverent free-for-all. Although Olid described the same features of the event, he inverted Sarasa y Arce's interpretation of them,

[55] Olid 1677. Olid's connection to Nuestra Señora de la Cabeza was long-standing. Twenty-seven years earlier he had published a short text crediting the effigy with the abatement of an outbreak of plague in Andújar. See Olid 1650. On his life and career, see Torres 1994; Fuentes Chamocho 1995.

[56] Olid 1667, 268, 271, 279.

[57] Sarasa y Arce, *Descripción de la fiesta*. A manuscript copy of this and other of his poems is held at the Hispanic Society of America, MS B 2.492. Those related to Andújar have been published, with modern orthography and punctuation, in Antonio Serrano de Haro, "La visita de un poeta a Andújar en 1664," BIEG 162 (1996): 53–65.

arguing that the pilgrims, though boisterous, were inspired by holy zeal. He extolled the great joy the pilgrims took in their devotions and praised their "heroic" piety, a piety he likened to that of the earliest Christians in Spain and which, he claimed, was the foundation of Spain's enduring commitment to Catholicism.

Conclusions

Olid's book, like the other examples discussed here, mobilized martial language to present devotion to a Marian image as a means of contesting Protestantism or other threats to the faith. And, as in those other examples, he did so in the service of a particular agenda. But, of course, authorial intent was only part of the story; readers, intermediaries, and listeners could interpret Olid's *Panegirico historial* in various ways. Like all miracle books, it did more than simply convey information; it was a material object that served as a site for social and emotional engagement, for performance, interaction, and interpretation. These interactions occurred at a variety of levels: between authorities and authors, between authors and readers, and between speakers and listeners. Like all other early modern texts, miracle books remained stubbornly outside the direct control of central authorities.

That, in part, helps to explain the longevity of these ideas. It is notable that the depiction of sacred images as under threat from Protestant "heretics" persisted eighty years after the wounding of the Vulnerata. There were no major raids which involved the destruction of images in Spain after 1596 (although, to be sure, such did occur during attacks on Spanish possessions elsewhere in Europe and in the Americas throughout the seventeenth century). Fears of secret Protestants in Spain were even further in the past; the Lutheran scare of 1559 in Valladolid and Seville had not lasted long and, when Demendiola and Olid wrote, it had been decades since the Inquisition had executed a Protestant in Spanish territory. If concerns about Protestant incursions continued to matter much for most Spaniards of the late seventeenth century, it was as a latent, not pressing, fear. The idea, however, that the veneration of images was a means of countering Protestantism remained useful to a variety of groups.

Bibliography

Printed sources

Alfonso X, el Sabio: *Cantigas de Santa María*. Ed. Walter Mettmann, 3 vols. Castalia, Madrid 1986–1989.

Abreu, Fray Pedro de: *Historia del saqueo de Cádiz por los ingleses en 1596*. Ed. Manuel Bustos Rodríguez. University of Cádiz, Cádiz 1996.

Acuña de Adarve, Juan: *Discursos de las efigies y verdaderos retratos non manufactos del santo rostro y cuerpo de Cristo Nuestro Señor*. Juan Furgolla de la Cuesta, Villanueva de Andújar 1637.

Aguirre, Gaspar Salcedo de: *Relación de algunas cosas insignes que tiene este reyno y obispado de Iaén* (1614), in *Estudio y edición de la Relación de algunas cosas insignes que tiene este Reyno y Obispado de Iaén y dos descripciones geográficas del Dr. Salcedo de Aguirre (1545–1632)*. Eds. María Dolores Rincón González and Cristina Castillo Martínez. University of Jaén, Jaén 2012.

Andrade, Alsonso: *Veneración de los santos imágenes. Origen y Milagros de la de San Ignacio de Munebrega*. Joseph Fernández de Buendía, Madrid 1669.

The Canons and Decrees of the Council of Trent. Ed. and transl. Henry Joseph Schroeder. Tan Books, Charlotte 1978.

Carvajal y Mendoza, Luisa de: *This Tight Embrace: Luisa de Carvajal y Mendoza (1566–1614)*. Ed. and transl. Elizabeth Rhodes. Marquette University Press, Milwaukee 2000.

Cervantes Saavedra, Miguel de: *El ingenioso hidalgo don Quijote de la Mancha*. Obras completas, vol. 1. Eds. Florencio Sevilla Arroyo and Antonio Rey Hazas. Centro de Estudios Cervantinos, Alcalá de Henares 1994.

Cervantes Saavedra, Miguel de: *La española inglesa*. Obras completas, vol. 2. Eds. Florencio Sevilla Arroyo and Antonio Rey Hazas. Centro de Estudios Cervantinos, Alcalá de Henares 1994, 605–644.

Daça, Antonio: *Historia, vida, y milagros, extasis, y revelaciones de la bienaventurada Virgen Santa Iuana de la Cruz*. Luis Sanchez, Madrid (1610) 1614. [English translation: *The Historie, Life, and Miracles, Extasies and Revelations of the Blessed Virgin, Sister Ioane of the Crosse*. John Heigham, Saint Omers 1625].

Demendiola, Gregorio: *Historia y Milagros de Nuestra Señora la Vulnerata, venerada en el Colegio Inglés desta ciudad de Valladolid*. Bartalomé Portoles, Valladolid 1667.

Enríquez, Juan Crisóstomo: *Historia de la vida, virtudes y milagros de la venerable madre Ana de San Bartholome, compañera de la sancta madre Teresa de Iesus*. Lucas de Meerbeeck, Brussels 1632.

Hinojosa y Carvajal, Álvaro de: *Libro de la vida y milogros de S. Inés*. Fructuoso Lourenço Basto, Braga 1611.

Historia y Milagros de Nuestra Señora de la Peña de Francia. Viuda de Ramirez, Salamanca 1614.

Muñoz, Luiz: *Vida y virtudes de la venerable virgen Doña Luisa de Carvajal y Mendoça, su jornada a Ingleterra, y sucessos en aquel reyno.* Imprenta Real, Madrid 1632.

Olid, Manuel de Salcedo: *Panegirico historial de Nuestra Señora de la Cabeza de Sierra Morena.* Iulian de Paredes, Madrid 1677.

Olid, Manuel de Salcedo: *Epílogo de la solemníssima y mvy festiva translación de la milagrosa imagen de N. Señora de la Cabeça, desde su prodigioso santuario de Sierra Morena, a la Yglesia Mayor de la muy Noble y muy Leal Ciudad de Andújar, para que la preserve del contagio con que Dios nuestro Señor aflixe esta Andaluzía, este año de 1650.* Andújar 1650. Facsimile edition. Ayuntamiento de Andújar et al., Baena 1995.

Ortíz, Antonio: *Relación de la venida de los Reyes Católicos, al Colegio Inglés de Valladolid, en el mes de agosto. Año de 1600. Y la collocación y fiesta hecha en el mismo Colegio, de una ymagen de Nuestra Señora maltratada de los herejes, dirigida a la Sereníssima señora Infanta de España doña Isabel Clara Eugenia.* Andrés Sanchez, Madrid 1600.

Prades, Iayme: *Historia de la adoracion y uso de las santas imágenes, y de la imagen de la fuente de la salud.* Felipe Mey, Valencia 1597.

Recibimiento que se hizo en Valladolid a una imagen de Nuestra Señora. En la Imprenta de la Tina, Madrid 1600.

Roa, Martín de: *Antigüedad veneración y fruto de las sagradas Imágenes, y Reliquias.* Gabriel Ramos Bejarano, Seville 1623.

Sarasa y Arce, Fermín de: *Descripción de la fiesta y procesión de la milagrosísima imagen de Nuestra Señora de la Cabeza que está en Sierra Morena, tres leguas distante de esta Ciudad de Andújar, y se celebra el último Domingo de Abril, habiéndome hallado en ella este año de 1664.* Imp. De E. Rasco. Seville 1889.

Talavera, Gabriel de: *Historia de Nuestra Señora de Guadalupe, consagrada a la soberana magestad de la Reyna de los Angeles, milagrosa patrona de este sanctuario.* Thomas de Gúzman, Toledo 1597.

Teresa de Ávila: *El libro de la vida.* Obras completas de Santa Teresa de Jesús. Ed. Tomás Álvarez. Espiritualidad, Madrid 2002, 27–443.

Teresa de Ávila: *Camino de Perfección.* Obras completas de Santa Teresa de Jesús. Ed. Tomás Álvarez. Espiritualidad, Madrid 2002, 443–623.

Teresa de Ávila: *Las Relaciones.* Obras completas de Santa Teresa de Jesús. Ed. Tomás Álvarez. Espiritualidad, Madrid 2002, 1249–1343.

Vega, Lope de: *Tragedia del rey don Sebastián y bautismo del Príncipe de Marruecos.* Obras completas de Lope de Vega: Comedias, vol. 8. Ed. Manual Arroyo Stephens. Turner, Madrid 1993.

Research literature

Ahlgren, Gillian T.W.: *Teresa of Avila and the Politics of Sanctity.* Cornell University Press, Ithaca NY 1996.

Alonso Acero, Beatriz and Miguel Ángel de Bunes Ibarra: Los Austrias y el norte de Africa: Muley Xeque in the Court of Philip II. *De Maŷrit a Madrid: Madrid y los árabes, del siglo IX al siglo XXI.* Ed. Daniel Gil Flores. Casa Árabe and Lunwerg, Madrid and Barcelona, 2011, 98–107.

Andrés, Christian: Visión de Inglaterra y de los ingleses en la obra novelesca de Cervantes. *Edad de oro cantabrigense: actas del VII Congreso de la Asociación Internacional de Hispanistas del Siglo de Oro.* Eds. Anthony J. Close and Sandra María Fernández Vales. Asociación Internacional del Siglo de Oro, Madrid 2006, 97–102.

Bamji, Alexandra, Geert H. Janssen, and Mary Laven (eds.): *The Ashgate Research Companion to the Counter-Reformation.* Ashgate, Aldershot 2013.

Bilinkoff, Jodi: Woman with a Mission: Teresa of Ávila and the Apostolic Model. *Modelli di Santità e Modelli di Comportamento*. Eds. Giulia Barone, Marina Caffiero, and Francesco Scorza Barcellona. Rosenberg & Sellier, Turin 1994, 295–305.

Bouza, Fernando: *Communication, Knowledge, and Memory in Early Modern Spain*. Trans. Sonia López and Michael Agnew. University of Pennsylvania Press, Philadelphia 2004.

Brownlee, Marina (ed.): *Intricate Alliances: Early Modern Spain and England*. Special Issue. *Journal of Medieval and Early Modern Studies* 39.1/2009.

Calderón Quijano, José Antonio: *Versiones inglesas de los ataques anglo-holandeses a Cádiz (1596, 1625)*. Caja de Ahorros de Cádiz, Cádiz 1985.

Carrasco, Rafael: Milagrero siglo XVII. *Estudios de historia social* 36–37/1986, 401–422.

Carrera, Elena: Pasión and afección in Teresa of Avila and Francisco de Osuna. *Bulletin of Spanish Studies* 84/2007a, 175–191.

Carrera, Elena: The Emotions in Sixteenth-Century Spanish Spirituality. *Journal of Religious History* 31/2007b, 235–252.

Cavallo, Guglielmo and Roger Chartier (eds.): *A History of Reading in the West*. University of Massachusetts Press, Amherst 2003.

Christian, William A. Jr.: *Local Religion in Sixteenth-Century Spain*. Princeton University Press, Princeton 1981.

Christian, William A. Jr.: Provoked Religious Weeping in Early Modern Spain. *Religion and Emotion: Approaches and Interpretations*. Ed. John Corrigan. Oxford University Press, Oxford 2004, 33–50.

Civil, Pierre: Retratos milagreros y devoción popular en la España del siglo XVII (Santo Domingo y San Ignacio). *Visiones y revisiones cervantinas: actas selectas del VII Congreso Internacional de la Asociación de Cervantistas*. Ed. Christoph Strosetzki. Centro de Estudios Cervantinos, Alcalá de Henares 2011, 617–628.

Crémoux, Françoise: De l'original au recyclage : le récit de miracle, un micro-genre contradictoire. *L'Original* 3/2003, 133–144.

Crémoux, Françoise: La relación de milagro en los siglos XVI y XVII: ¿un micro género?. *Actas del XV Congreso de la Asociación Internacional de Hispanistas "Las dos orillas": Monterrey, México del 19 al 24 de julio de 2004*. Eds. Beatriz Mariscal and María Teresa Miaja de la Peña, vol. 2. Fondo de Cultura Económica, Monterrey 2007, 99–111.

Cruz, Anne J.: Vindicating the Vulnerata: Cádiz and the Circulation of Religious Imagery as Weapons of War. *Material and Symbolic Circulation between Spain and England, 1554–1604*. Ashgate, Aldershot UK 2008, 39–60.

Duffy, Eamon: *The Stripping of the Altars: Traditional Religion in England, 1400–1580*. Yale University Press, New Haven 1992.

Eire, Carlos: *The War against the Idols: The Reformation of Worship from Erasmus to Calvin*. Cambridge University Press, Cambridge MA 1986.

Elliott, John: Paz y guerra con Inglaterra, 1554–1655. *Reales sitios* 152/2002, 2–17.

Fe y Jiménez, Luisa: *Historia de Nuestra Señora de la Cabeza de Sierra Morena*. Ricardo Fé, Madrid 1900 [facsimile edition: Real Santuario de la Virgen de la Cabeza y el Centro de Estudios Marianos "Historiador Salcedo Olid", Andújar 2001].

Fowler, Jessica: Assembling Alumbradismo: The Evolution of a Heretical Construction. *After Conversion: Iberia and the Emergence of Modernity*. Ed. Mercedes Garcia-Arenal. Brill, Leiden 2016, 251–282.

Fuentes Chamocho, Francisco: Salcedo Olid, primer historiador de la Virgen de la Cabeza. Manuel de Salcedo Olid. *Epílogo de la solemníssima y muy festiva translación de la milagrosa imagen de N. Señora de la Cabeça, desde su prodigioso santuario de Sierra Morena, a la Yglesia Mayor de la muy Noble y muy Leal Ciudad de Andújar, para que la preserve del contagio con que Dios nuestro Señor aflixe esta Andaluzía, este año de 1650.* Facsimile edition. Ayuntamiento de Andújar et al., Baena 1995, 17–21.

Gianolio, Matteo: *Memorie storiche intorno la vita del Real Principe di Marocco Muley Xeque.* Giacomo Fea, Turin 1795.

Gómez Martínez, Enrique: *La Virgen de la Cabeza: leyenda, historia y actualidad.* Jabalcuz, Torredonjimeno 2002.

Gómez Martínez, Enrique: Evolución histórica de la romería de la Virgen de la Cabeza. *Boletín del Instituto de Estudios Giennenses* 209/2014, 219–238.

González Sánchez, Carlos Alberto: *New World Literacy: Writing and Culture across the Atlantic, 1500–1700.* Bucknell University Press, Lewisburg PA 2011.

Hamilton, Alastair: *Heresy and Mysticism in Sixteenth-Century Spain: The Alumbrados.* James Clarke, Cambridge MA 1992.

Harline, Craig: *Miracles at the Jesus Oak: Histories of the Supernatural in Reformation Europe.* Doubleday, New York 2003.

Irigoyen-García, Javier: *The Spanish Arcadia: Sheep Herding, Pastoral Discourse, and Ethnicity in Early Modern Spain.* University of Toronto Press, Toronto 2013.

Karant-Nunn, Susan C.: Catholic Intensity in Post-Reformation Germany: Preaching on the Passion and Catholic Identity in the Sixteenth and Seventeenth Centuries. *Politics and Reformations, Histories and Reformations: Studies in Honor of Thomas A. Brady, Jr..* Eds. Peter Wallace, Peter Starenko, Michael Printy, and Christopher Ocker. Brill, Leiden 2007, 373–96.

Karant-Nunn, Susan C.: *The Reformation of Feeling: Shaping the Religious Emotions in Early Modern Germany.* Oxford University Press, Oxford 2010.

Lázaro Damas, Maria Soledad: El sanctuario de la Virgen de la Cabeza en el siglo XVI: Historia de un proyecto artístico. *Boletín del Instituto de Estudios Giennenses* 162/1996, 1437–1468.

Lazure, Guy: Possessing the Sacred: Monarchy and Identity in Philip II's Relic Collection at the Escorial. *Renaissance Quarterly* 60/2007, 58–93.

Luengo Pacheco, Ricardo: *Libros y lectores en Plasencia (siglos XVI–XVIII).* Universidad de Extremadura, Cáceres 2002.

Márquez, Antonio: *Los alumbrados: Orígenes y filosofía, 1525–1559,* 2nd ed. Taurus, Madrid 1980.

Michalski, Sergiusz: *The Reformation and the Visual Arts: The Protestant Image Question in Western and Eastern Europe.* Taylor & Francis, London 2002.

Montcher, Fabien: La española inglesa de Cervantes en su contexto historiográfico. *Visiones y revisiones cervantinas: actas selectas del VII Congreso Internacional de la Asociación de Cervantistas.* Eds. Christoph Strosetzki. Centro de estudios cervantinos, Alcalá de Henares 2011, 617–628.

Nalle, Sara T.: Literacy and Culture in Early Modern Castile. *Past and Present* 125/1989, 65–96.

Nalle, Sara T.: Printing and Reading Popular Religious Texts in Sixteenth-Century Spain. *Culture and the State in Spain, 1550–1850.* Eds. Tom Lewis and Francisco J Sánchez. Garland, New York 1999, 126–156.

Olds, Katrina: The Ambiguities of the Holy: Authenticating Relics in Seventeenth-Century Spain. *Renaissance Quarterly* 65/2012, 135–184.

Oliver Asín, Jaime: *Vida de don Felipe de África, príncipe de Fez y de Marruecos (1566–1621)*. Instituto Miguel Asin, Madrid and Granada 1955 (repr. University of Granada, Granada 2009).

Pastore, Stefania: *Un'eresia spagnola: spiritualità conversa, alumbradismo e inquisizione, 1449–1559*. L. S. Olschki, Florence 2004.

Po-chia Hsia, Ronnie: *The World of Catholic Renewal, 1540–1700*. Cambridge University Press, Cambridge MA 1998.

Remensnyder, Amy G.: *La Conquistadora: The Virgin Mary at War and Peace in the Old and New Worlds*. Oxford University Press, Oxford 2014.

Roldán-Figueroa, Rady: Literacy, Spirituality of Reading, and Catholic Literary Culture in Sixteenth-Century Spain. *Journal of Early Modern Christianity* 2/2015, 159–88.

Rowe, Erin Kathleen: The Spanish Minerva: Imagining Teresa of Avila as Patron Saint in Seventeenth-Century Spain. *The Catholic Historical Review* 92/2006, 574–96.

Sánchez, Javier Burrieza: Reparando las heridas: el nacimiento de una devoción de 'Contrarreforma'. *Brocar: Cuadernos de investigación histórica* 26/2002, 107–50.

Scully, Robert: "In the Confident Hope of a Miracle": The Spanish Armada and Religious Mentalities in the Late Sixteenth Century. *The Catholic Historical Review* 89/2003, 643–70.

Serrano de Haro, Antonio. La visita de un poeta a Andújar en 1664. *Boletín del Instituto de Estudios Giennenses* 162/1996, 53–65.

Soergel, Philip: Spiritual Medicine for Heretical Poison: The Propagandistic Uses of Legends in Counter-Reformation Bavaria. *Historical Reflections/Réflexions historiques* 17/1991, 125–49.

Soergel, Philip: *Wondrous in His Saints: Counter-Reformation Propaganda in Bavaria*. University of California Press, Berkeley 1993.

Soergel, Philip: *Miracles and the Protestant Imagination: The Evangelical Wonder Book in Reformation Germany*. Oxford University Press, Oxford 2012.

Spicer, Andrew: Iconoclasm. *Renaissance Quarterly* 70/2017, 1007–22.

Taylor, William B.: The Trouble with Miracles: An Episode in the Culture and Politics of Wonder in Colonial Mexico. *Politics and Reformations, Histories and Reformations: Studies in Honor of Thomas A. Brady, Jr.*. Eds. Peter Wallace, Peter Starenko, Michael Printy, and Christopher Ocker. Brill, Leiden 2007, 373–396.

Torres, José Carlos de: Don Manuel Salcedo Olid, Escritor de Nuestra Señora de la Cabeza. *Boletín del Instituto de Estudios Giennenses* 153/1994, 111–120.

Torres, José Carlos de: La Virgen de la Cabeza y Andújar en una comedia de Lope de Vega. *Boletín del Instituto de Estudios Giennenses* 209/2014, 239–264.

Torres Laguna, Carlos de: *La Morenita y su santuario: Historia de la ciudad de Andújar y de su patrona, la Virgen de la Cabeza de Sierra Morena*. Vol. 3. Imprenta Murillo, Andújar 1961.

Velandia Onofre, Darío. Jaime Prades y las imágenes sagradas. La defensa de su adoración y uso. *Hispania sacra* 69/2017, 185–94.

Walsham, Alexandra: Miracles and the Counter-Reformation Mission to England. *The Historical Journal* 46/2003, 779–815.

Walsham, Alexandra: *Catholic Reformation in Protestant Britain*. Ashgate, Farnham 2014.

Weruaga Prieto, Ángel: *Lectores y bibliotecas en la Salamanca moderna (1699–1789)*. Junta de Castilla y Leon, Salamanca 2008.

Williams, Michael E.: *St Alban's College Valladolid: Four Centuries of English Catholic Presence in Spain*. St. Martin's Press, New York 1986.

Wilson, Christopher C.: Teresa of Ávila vs. the Iconoclasts: Convent Art in Support of a Church in Crisis. *Imagery, Spirituality, and Ideology in Baroque Spain and Latin America*. Eds. Jeremy Roe and Marta Bustillo. Cambridge Scholars Publishing, Newcastle upon Tyne 2010, 45–57.

Between pilgrimage and reform. Bernhard of Breidenbach's Travelogue to the Holy Land (1486) as printed paradigm, moral guidebook and mirror of princes[1]

Stefan Schröder

Introduction

Describing the hazards of the seemingly unstoppable Ottoman expansion in his *Die heyligen reyßen gen Jherusalem zů dem heiligen Grab*, Bernhard of Breidenbach[2] (c. 1434/40–1497), dean of the Cathedral of Mainz since 1484, condemned the fatal inactivity of the ruling elite by comparing them to sleeping shepherds failing in their duty to guard their sheep during the dark night and to give them shelter. To underscore the shortcomings of the powerful, he moreover referred to the images of a sailor who sleeps at sea amid a great thunderstorm and

---

[1] This article was written as part of the project 'Historicizing the Crusades: Strategies of Historiographical Writing and Functions of the Past in the Late Middle Ages', funded by the Academy of Finland (project-number 293416)
[2] The spelling of first and last name varies in the sources and research. The present article follows the spelling used in the Neue Deutsche Bibliographie (NDB). See Fuchs 1955.

of guards and watchdogs who give no sign or bark at the moment of danger. Lamenting further about the debauched state of Christianity, Breidenbach addressed the 'most gracious and most Christian King' Maximilian I (1459–1519) personally, and appealed to the sovereign's

> highest and enlightened reason, wisdom and manifold grace that You have received so amply by God to identify, to ponder what is mentioned above and to consider what is part of Your royal commission and what this royal commission demands and claims [when] facing the [current] hardship of Christianity. [… Thinking] of a pious and faithful Christian within his city, who – together with his willing and obedient subjects – is besieged by enemies and sees how the torches of a merciless war are set on fire. What would this pious duke […] do? What tells You, o victorious master, Your own Christian and faithful heart? He would not ask for long, but call his knights and his army, strengthen them with wise and prudent words like the keen duke and knight Judas Maccabaeus. He would sound the attack […] and would to-gether with his reinforced people penetrate the armed forces of the enemy like a feisty lion […].[3]

Breidenbach's forthright review of the current political situation and his direct request to Maximilian to change the situation is surprising in a text that – given the title – was meant to be an account of his pilgrimage to the most important holy sites of Christendom in Palestine and Egypt. The passionate testimony is even more surprising given the fact that Breidenbach's report – known foremost for its marvellous woodcuts illustrating his journey – has been regarded by subsequent scholars as rather dull and lacking in individuality because of its somewhat impassive and scholarly style, especially in the first part.[4] However, the severe and detailed quality of Breidenbach's criticism is remarkable. He seems to be more than just using the general fear of the

---

[3] Bernhard of Breidenbach 2010, 488–491. If not marked otherwise, English translations are mine.
[4] See Herkenhoff 1996, 187.

'Other' – namely the Muslim Turks – to disapprove of conditions at home, a technique often used by writers of (pre-modern) travel reports. As Kristian Bosselmann-Cyran and Frederike Timm have pointed out, Breidenbach's account was not only a travelogue, but also meant to be read as medium of disseminating distinct sociopolitical positions.[5] When looking closely, it becomes clear that he had indeed intended that his pilgrimage account serve as a vehicle in support of reform efforts in the Holy Roman Empire in general and in support of the concepts of his mentor and superior, Archbishop Berthold of Henneberg (1441/42–1504), in particular.

By examining Breidenbach's comprehensive travelogue, this article will reveal further the context and intentions behind his critical remarks. It will consider the political discourse and disputes regarding Imperial Reform during the last years of the reign of Frederick III (1415–1493) and the early years of his designated successor, young Maximilian (1459–1519). Was it not overly risky to express his disapproval with the political situation in such frank terms? How did Breidenbach legitimate his criticism, and what role did it play within the text as a whole? When analysing the narrative, it is evident that parts of it were meant to serve as a mirror by which the rulers could assess their own conduct. Such parts are almost hidden between wide-ranging descriptions of all aspects of the pilgrimage to Jerusalem, including detailed descriptions of other Christian confessions as well as Muslims and Jews and lengthy chapters dealing with the geography and history of the Holy Land. However, they are not unrelated to the rest of the text; rather, they are thoroughly interwoven with Breidenbach's intentions in publishing the report: his attempts at self-fashioning as an ideal pilgrim, experienced clergyman, learned scholar, authoritative author and publisher. Using the still very new technology of letterpress printing, he published his account in 1486 both in Latin (*Peregrinatio in Terram Sanctam*) and in German, followed by a Flemish translation two years later (*Die heylighe beuvarden tot dat*

---

[5] Cf. Bosselmann-Cyran 1994/95; Timm 2006, 336–351. A recent art history study by Ross (2014) verifies and corrects Timm's results at some points and situates Breidenbach's print more fully within the conventions of 15th-century European art, while also considering contemporary cartographical representations, such as Portolan Charts, as possible sources.

heylighe graft in iherusalem).[6] Breidenbach deliberately addressed a wide audience, and therefore, must have taken into account the fact that his socio-political comments were widely read.[7] At the same time, he had to have been aware of the authorities' critical attitude towards the rapidly expanding printing press.[8] The attempts at 'preventive censorship' by Henneberg and others to regulate the uncontrolled and rapid distribution of hundreds of copies of written text forced Breidenbach to find a subtle balance between being perceived as someone disseminating beneficial reform ideas and someone possibly hoping to undermine the social order.

I therefore investigate Breidenbach's critical statements by discussing his report first from the perspective of the genre of Holy Land travelogues and of the printing market in the 15th century (section 2) and second by considering the intentions of Breidenbach and Henneberg in publishing *Die heyligen reyßen gen Jherusalem* (section 3). I then analyse Breidenbach's criticism of the situation in the Holy Roman Empire and his call for a new crusade (section 4) by comparing it to contemporary texts disapproving of the deeds of the ruling elite (section 5), before finally reflecting on the function of Breidenbach's vision of hell, based originally on a source from the 9th century, and his praise of Venice (section 6). Parts four to six show how skilfully the dean of the Cathedral of Mainz drew from and combined elements of both the Carolingian and crusading past with his own travel experiences to promote imperial reforms and remind readers of their Christian values and duties by using the innovative potential of the printed media.

---

[6] For the German text, see the Breidenbach 2010 edition. Complete digitalisations of the Latin (Breidenbach 1486a), German (Breidenbach 1486b) and Flemish prints (Breidenbach 1488) are available via the digital collections of the Bayerische Staatsbibliothek Munich.

[7] Consider furthermore that the twelve editions of the work (as of 1522) included French, Spanish and Polish translations, meaning that his text indeed had some impact on the printing market.

[8] For an introduction to reading and writing and an overview of the impact of printing at the time, see Lyons 2009. For an in-depth analysis of late medieval authorship, publishing and audiences at the advent of the printing press, see Hobbins 2009.

Breidenbach's pilgrimage and the project of publishing an exemplary print

Even after the loss of Acre in 1291 and the end of the crusader states, Jerusalem and the Holy Land remained one of the most attractive destinations for pilgrims from all over Europe.[9] The foremost motivation for pilgrims was to follow in person the holy sites of Christ's life and passion (*imitatio Christi*), which were subsequently part of the Mamluk Empire. By doing so, they were able to acquire numerous indulgences from the Catholic Church in order to gain forgiveness for their sins and reduce their time in purgatory. However, pilgrimages to the Holy Land were long, dangerous and pricy, and thus only noblemen and patricians could usually afford the journey. They found the journey appealing not only because of religious convictions. A pilgrimage to Jerusalem also meant encounters with different cultures, adventure and the chance to see new sights. Having proved his/her piety and bravery by successfully returning from the Holy Land, the pilgrim could increase his prestige and standing at home. To have been in Jerusalem was a sign of distinction, even in comparison to the other main pilgrimage routes to Rome and Santiago de Compostela.

A combination of these motives certainly influenced Breidenbach as well. He referred to the somewhat topical motive of looking back on his life and realising the many follies of his youth. Doing penance in order to achieve salvation by traveling to Jerusalem should mend his ways and set an example for others.[10] Yet, he did not travel alone and he did not travel only for personal redemption. Breidenbach was accompanied by two other noblemen: Count Johann of Solms-Lich, since 1481 head of one of the most noble and wealthiest families in the region, and the knight Philipp of Bicken, bailiff of Hohensolms and Königsberg. It seems that Breidenbach and Bicken as well as three servants, one cook and one translator capable of speaking Italian escorted the count – who

---

[9] For more on travel in the Middle Ages, see Reichert 2001. For more on pilgrimages to the Holy Land and late medieval accounts of such pilgrimages, see Schröder 2009; Meyer 2012.

[10] Breidenbach 2010, 50–51.

in 1483 was only 18 years old – as fatherly friends and protectors. By making a pilgrimage to the Holy Land, Johann may well have been trying to increase his standing despite his young age. This could be achieved not only by visiting the holy sites in person, but also by being made a Knight of the Holy Sepulchre during a solemn ceremony in the church – for many noblemen, this was actually the highpoint of their pilgrimage.[11]

The journey taken by the party lasted in total nine and a half months.[12] They took advantage not only of the 'all-inclusive tour' to Jerusalem, a tour annually promoted by Venetian patricians,[13] but also extended their pilgrimage by traveling further to Saint Catherine's Monastery on Mount Sinai and to Egypt. The added itinerary allowed them to visit more prominent holy sites, such as Mount Horeb and the Garden of Balsam near Cairo (al-Matariyyah), and to collect more indulgences. The journey through the desert – together inter alia with the Dominican Felix Fabri and the Franciscan Paul Walther of Guglingen, who were authors of extensive pilgrimage reports themselves – added considerably more risk and cost, but it included also more adventures and prestige.

Breidenbach's roundtrip journey consisted of many fascinating experiences worthy of being shared with an audience that rarely had the chance to undertake such a journey. By writing in detail about the holy sites, readers could envision Christ's passion as well as the deeds of the apostles and early Christians. By extensively describing cities like

---

[11] On the motives of the many pilgrims of the German high nobility, see especially Nolte 1997. The solemn ceremony for the knighting of Solms-Lich and other pilgrims is described most fully in the pilgrimage report of Felix Fabri 1843–1849 II, 1–18.

[12] For a summary of the journey, see Timm 2006, 66–70; Ross 2014, 9–11.

[13] This particular trip consisted of direct transit from Venice to Jaffa and an approximately ten-day stay in Jerusalem with guided tours to the holy sites, including optional trips to Bethlehem and along the Jordan River. The term 'all-inclusive' should not suggest that the Venetian offer covered all costs and risks. For more on the contracts and relations between pilgrims and the Venetian captains, see Reichert 2008. The year 1483 was exceptional, with two pilgrim galleys departing Venice with around 150 pilgrims. Additional pilgrims might have undertaken the journey at other times of the year using trade galleys from Venice, Genoa or Marseille to Beirut or Alexandria.

Venice, Cairo and Alexandria – important hubs for trade and cultural encounter – readers could learn about the multiple national groups coexisting there and hear about the manifold cultural differences. By meticulously sharing insights about the lengthy passages through the Mediterranean and the desert, by writing about the extreme climate conditions in an alien environment, by portraying an exotic flora and fauna, Breidenbach gave readers the opportunity to participate in the wonders of God's creation and was able to relate the many obstacles that had to be overcome by the pilgrims during their 'rite de passage'.

Such travel accounts satisfied both the religious needs and basic curiosity of a growing audience, making it a popular genre in late medieval times both in handwritten manuscript and in printed form. Many accounts were of course written for a smaller group of relatives, friends and acquaintances, but some authors also had a general audience in mind or were at least aware of the fact that their text could be read (sometimes aloud) by other people and even in later times. The great number of preserved manuscript copies, e.g. of the pilgrimage accounts of Burchard of Mount Sion and John Mandeville, proved the need for and attraction of written descriptions of the Holy Land.[14] Such accounts of pilgrimages to the Holy Land fuelled the expanding market of printed books. Probably the first travelogue printed for the German market was a 14th-century account in Latin by Ludolf of Sudheim, which was reprinted five times within a few years and, in a German translation, three times in 1477 alone by three different printers in Augsburg.[15] Likewise in 1477, a German *editio princeps* of Marco Polo's travelogue was printed, as was Hans Schiltberger's remarkable account of his travels between 1396 and 1427 through the Turkish territories first as a slave and later as a mercenary. In 1480, the printing press of Anton Sorg in Augsburg finally produced the first printing of Mandeville's narrative

---

[14] Burchard of Mount Sion 1873; Mandeville 2011.
[15] The years given for the first printing of his account differs in the literature, ranging from 1468 to 1470 to 1475/1480. Cf. Herkenhoff 1996, 68, 298; Paravicini 1994, 40–41.

in German, followed one year later by a second edition of Marco Polo's travelogue in German.[16]

Nevertheless, imprinters were not the only ones who understood the potential financial and social benefits of publishing travel reports. The Nuremberg merchant and patrician Hans Tucher (1428–1491), who travelled to the Holy Land and Egypt in 1479/80, put much effort into producing an account of his journeys that was finally published in 1482. His aim was to document what he 'has truly seen with own eyes, experienced and investigated' in order to give subsequent pilgrims valuable information for their own journey; thus, he included copies of the contracts made in Venice and Jerusalem laying out the services provided by the Venetian patron and the Mamluk guides as well as lists of items needed along the way and medical recipes.[17] Tucher, however, was not pleased with the *editio princeps* produced by Johann Schönsperger in Augsburg, and so he commissioned a second printing, this time done by Konrad Zeninger of Nuremberg.[18] This printing was done only a few months later and corrected Schönsperger's various mistakes. Yet, apparently to reduce the loss of money and reputation, Schönsperger reprinted the 'improved' (*gerecht gepessert*) edition by Zeninger in the same year.[19]

Aware of the rich tradition of Latin and vernacular reports in manuscripts and printed books, and using the report of Hans Tucher as a source, Breidenbach had apparently planned from the beginning to write an account of his travels after his return and to publish it in printed form. Following Hans Tucher's instruction to take paper and ink on the journey,[20] Breidenbach made notes during the journey and

---

[16] See the full account of printed travelogues translated into German provided by Herkenhoff 1996, 47–67.

[17] Tucher 2002, 340. The narrative was based on his own diary and that of his fellow traveller Sebald Rieter and on letters that Tucher had sent home to his relatives from Jerusalem and other places. For more on the letters, see Herz 1997.

[18] Tucher 2002, 229–236.

[19] Until 1486, three further prints of the book were published, one again by Zeninger and two based on the defective editio princeps, and therefore, were probably not authorised by Tucher. Cf. Tucher 2002, 241–250; Herkenhoff 1996, 166–168.

[20] Tucher 2002, 633.

invited his fellow traveller Felix Fabri to come with him on the return journey to Mainz in order to compose a travel report together.[21] But Fabri declined due to his obligation to return to his Dominican brothers in Ulm. Even still, Breidenbach was able to base his writings partly on the report of Paul Walther of Guglingen.[22] Breidenbach used a great number of additional sources as well, among them such chronicles as the 1475 printing of the *Rudimentum novitiorum*, encyclopedical works like the *Speculum Maius* and *Historiale* by Vincent of Beauvais, and religious tractates like the *Dialogus contra Judeos* by the Jewish convert Petrus Alfonsi.[23] By using all of this material, he aimed to provide a complete description of all relevant aspects concerning the historical and current situation in the Holy Land, a 'general and almost official reference work to the Near East'.[24]

With its thoroughly collected and systematically ordered information, Breidenbach's text offered readers much deeper insights into the pilgrimage and the history of the Holy Land than the earlier printed accounts by Ludolf of Sudheim and Hans Tucher. To achieve this aim, however, Breidenbach needed the help of one further author. He stated in the Latin edition of his work that while acting himself as *auctor principalis*, he was supported by a *vir doctus*.[25] Only from Felix Fabri do we know that this eligible doctor was Martin Rath, a learned Dominican acting as professor of theology at the University of Mainz.[26]

The final person included in Breidenbach's ambitious plans to create a comprehensive pilgrimage account in printed form was his servant Erhard Reuwich. An artist from Utrecht, Reuwich's main mission was not so much to help his patron with the daily necessities during

---

[21] Fabri 1843–1849 III, 389.

[22] Paul Walther of Guglingen 1892.

[23] For an overview of the sources see Timm 2006, 80–97.

[24] Ganz-Blättler 1991, 292: 'allgemeine[s] und geradezu offizielle[s] Nachschlagewerk[] zum Thema Naher Osten.'

[25] Breidenbach 1486a, fol. 7v and 104r. In the German edition, he speaks of his role as *diß wercks angeber*. Cf. Breidenbach 1486b, fol. 137r; Breidenbach 2010, 540–541. Cf. also Timm 2006, 95–96; Ross 2014, 26–27.

[26] Fabri 1843–1849 I, 347, 353. If not the whole book, as suggested by Fabri, then at least the parts on the different national groups living in Jerusalem and especially on the Muslims and Islam were probably composed by Rath.

the journey, but to produce drawings along the way as illustrations for the text. Reuwich carried out this task in a rather remarkable way, by using both sketches based on what he saw as well as templates found in other works or acquired, for instance, in Venice.[27] Reuwich, who was honoured by Breidenbach (only) in the Latin version as *ingeniosum et erudite[m] pictorem*,[28] produced a total of 26 woodcuts. Most impressive is his opening illustration showing a woman dressed in Venetian style surrounded by the heraldic signs of Breidenbach, Solms-Lich and Bicken,[29] followed by a map of the Holy Land and Egypt consisting of a three-block woodcut that has at its centre a view of Jerusalem from the Mount of Olives, and thirdly a four-block woodcut (approximately 26 cm high and 160 cm long) showing a panoramic view of Venice from the lagoon. Reuwich's illustrations of Jerusalem and Venice (as well as of Methoni, Chania and Rhodes) had to be folded out by readers and were innovations never before used in a printed book. As testified by the colophon and his personal signet in the Latin and German editions, Reuwich was responsible for printing the whole report.

These spectacular woodcuts, which were coloured by hand in some later copies, distinguished Breidenbach's report from all other printed travelogues available on the market at the time. As Breidenbach noted in the prologue, he offered a book that *in form vnd maß vorhin villeicht nit mer gesehen* ('in design and dimension has perhaps never been seen before'), followed by the assumption that both text and images perhaps had never been printed together before.[30] Even if it was not the first printed book that contained woodcuts, it was the most technically and qualitatively advanced to date. In this way, the reading experience was

[27] For more detail, see Timm 2006; Ross 2014. They have also been paradig-matically analysed by Niehr 2001.

[28] Breidenbach 1486a, fol. 7v and 156r; Breidenbach 1486b, fol. 180r; Brey-denbach 2010, 724–725. For more on the signet, see Timm 2006, 261–265.

[29] See Timm 2006, 118. The symbolic meaning is not definitely known. In research, the woman is interpreted both as patronesses of the woodcut-ting art and as figures in the iconographic tradition of holding the heraldic signs. See Fuchs 1960, 52. For an example of the second possibility, see the illustration at the end of the printed work showing a woman holding Reuwich's signet.

[30] Breidenbach 2010, 6–10. Cf. Weinmayer 1982, 166.

shifted to a new level. According to Breidenbach, the lively illustrations should explicitly please the worldly eye in order to promote further pilgrimages to the Holy Land.[31] But the representations also enabled readers who could not afford the journey to participate in Breidenbach's experiences as if they were undertaking the journey themselves. It put them in the role of eyewitnesses who could verify the information given in the text as true. The supposedly realistic nature of the details supported Breidenbach's intention to offer a most comprehensive and reliable travel report. It is part of the technique to ensure readers – who could not prove the descriptions true with their own eyes – that the author of the text was neither exaggerating nor telling lies. Felix Fabri, who used Breidenbach's work after its publication for his own writings and testified to its veracity, praised Reuwich by adapting Breidenbach's phrase describing him as a most cunning, clever and well-taught painter, expressed fittingly that Breidenbach had spared no expense in the proper composition of his book.[32]

The Latin *editio princeps* was finally published on 11 February 1486, just five days before the election of Maximilian as king in Frankfurt am Main.[33] As an important member of the delegation of Archbishop Berthold of Henneberg, Breidenbach was personally present and even assisted Henneberg during the election ceremony.[34] During this gathering of all the important policy-makers of the realm, Breidenbach might have had good opportunities to promote his book or even

[31] Breidenbach 2010, 8–9.

[32] Fabri 1843–1849 I, 329. Felix Fabri followed Breidenbach's report especially in his German description of his pilgrimage to Jerusalem. Occasional differences in the chronology of Fabri's Latin report from that of Breidenbach were explained as non-relevant results of finding a coherent structure for the text. See Fabri 1843–1849 II, 18.

[33] In his handwritten travel instructions for Count Ludwig of Hanau-Lichtenberg, Breidenbach indicated that the book would already be available in 1485 and asked the count not to hand these instructions over to others. See Breidenbach 1880, 145.

[34] Fuchs 1960, 43. The reason for the delay might have been due, among other things, to Breidenbach's journey to Rome in 1484 in order to ask the pope's permission and the pallium for Berthold of Henneberg, who was elected Archbishop of Mainz on 20 May 1484. Weinmayer 1982, 168.

distribute some copies.[35] Some mistakes in the printed copy have given rise to the argument that Reuwich worked in great hurry to finalise the book just before the day of the election.[36] The German version followed a few months later, on 21 June, with some changes; a Flemish version was also authorised by Breidenbach and printed by Reuwich in Mainz in 1488.[37]

'Preventive censorship' and legitimation: the dedication to Berthold of Henneberg

Breidenbach clearly sought to use the advantages of the printing press to disseminate his text more widely. In his dedication letter to Henneberg, he acknowledged the growing importance of the letterpress printing and asked rhetorically 'who would not know or not recognise that new inventions (like the art of printing) are seemingly increasing ceaselessly nowadays?'[38] In fact, Breidenbach had been involved in the printing business already since 1480, when he revised and edited the *Agenda Moguntinensis*, a ritual of the church of Mainz; likewise, in 1485 he helped produce (together with Reuwich and the doctor and botanist Johannes de Cuba) the *Gart der Gesuntheit* ('Garden of Health'), a herbarium describing and illustrating almost 400 plants and minerals as well as drugs based on various ingredients.[39]

Yet the possibilities of the new technology were also criticised by others, since it enabled the quick dissemination of heretical or revolutionary thoughts. Both ecclesiastical and profane institutions were thus keen to control the printing press by implementing 'preventive censorship', meaning that – ideally – all books to be printed would be

[35] Breidenbach was also present at Maximilian's coronation, which took place in Aix-la-Chapelle in April of the same year.
[36] Timm 2006, 350.
[37] All other editions are reprints executed probably without the authorisation of Breidenbach.
[38] Breidenbach 2010, 4–5.
[39] For these works, see Fuchs 1960, 36–37; Timm 2006, 301–305; Ross 2014, 44–47.

checked and approved first by a commission of experts installed by the authorities.[40] The edict on censorship, published in 1485 by Archbishop Berthold of Henneberg of Mainz, was one of the first such attempts. He most likely had looked to the example from Cologne, where Pope Sixtus IV in 1479 had extolled in a papal brief the university's efforts at preventing the printing and sale of erroneous and heretical works and had empowered the institution to use, if necessary, all instruments at its disposal to take action against printers and readers.[41]

Though having, in principle, a positive approach to printing – as did many others, among them Nicholas of Cusa and Martin Luther, while Henneberg characterised the printing of his edict as a divine art[42] – his main argument for the necessity of controlling the printing press had to do with the dangers inherent in using the vernacular. According to him, the German vernacular was by no means the appropriate language to communicate and discuss theological matters. He argued that canonical and other very complex ecclesiastical works written by legal experts were almost impossible to understand, even for highly educated and sophisticated men. But in his time, foolish people irresponsibly and naïvely believed that they could easily translate such texts, not seeing that they use improper German for the Latin terms and thus distort the message. This wrongdoing, a result of the desire for profit and fame, was not restricted to theological books, but also to works of

[40] For more on the concept and the medieval and early modern history of 'preventive censorship', see Minnich 2010; Tortarolo 2001.

[41] There are two slightly different redactions of Henneberg's edict, one dates from 1485 and was printed later in the year together with a text by Bishop Rudolf of Scherenberg or Würzburg, while the second one was published in January 1486, just one month before Breidenbach's *editio princeps*. Cf. Pallmann 1884; Fuchs 1960, 42–43; Weinmayer 1982, 171–175; Ross 2014, 19–22. There seems to be no case of a work suspected of heresy printed in Mainz that could have prompted Henneberg to write the edict (but that says nothing about the trade of dubious books printed elsewhere). Yet, Henneberg still complained in a letter 'of the abuses and errors that appear in books and other printed materials at the semi-annual Frankfurt book-fair'. Cf. Minnich 2010, 74; Pallmann 1884, 240–241. For more on the case in Cologne, see Minnich 2010, 69–72; Hemels 1979, 224–225.

[42] Pallmann 1884; Weinmayer 1982, 171. For more on Luther and others, see Widmann 1973.

other disciplines, even in ways that added untrue information and gave misleading titles to the texts of highly renowned authors. German, in his view, was a language too humble to deal with Latin and Greek texts. He furthermore warned that such a practice was even more dangerous in the case of the Holy Scripture, 'because who is there to help laymen, uneducated menfolk and the female sex with access to the books of the Holy Scripture find the true insights?'[43]

It was thus Henneberg's grave concern that translations of texts such as the Bible would inevitably cause a theologically illiterate audience to incorrectly interpret the text. This was on the one hand the result of the dynamics of the printed market, which gave people access to works that were originally written only for highly specialised readers and thus should be studied only in their proper ecclesiastical and scholarly context.[44] Yet on the other hand, the translation of texts reflects the changing literary tastes and capacities of laypeople in late medieval times, which resulted in the imminent question of how religious literature should be received by the laity.[45] In the eyes of the clerical elite, a careful examination of every manuscript to be printed was therefore quite necessary. Printers who violated the edict were threatened with the destruction of the books, heavy fines and excommunication.

Breidenbach's *Die heyligen reyßen gen Jherusalem* might have been the first, or at least one of the first, work to be published after the edict. He surely knew of the edict beforehand. Breidenbach cunningly used the opportunity to add to his work a dedication letter to Henneberg, in which he presented his work as being in line with the archbishop's objectives. Breidenbach picked up Henneberg's central argument by citing Saint Jerome's letter to Paulinus of Nola. In this letter, Jerome had criticised all kinds of people, including the scolding old woman, the doting old man and the wordy sophist claiming to understand and

---

[43] Pallmann 1884, 239; with a German translation by Hille-Coates 2000, 224–225. Similar concerns were expressed in a text written probably in the 1480s by an anonymous cleric from Nuremberg. See Widmann 1973, 31.
[44] See Weinmayer 1982, 172–173.
[45] For contemporary tractates that tackled this question, see Honemann 1992.

write about the Holy Scripture.[46] The printing art of the 15th century now gave such incompetent people the opportunity to publish their opinions. Breidenbach rejected this approach as overly arrogant from a metaphorical standpoint. While admitting that he was far from being educated enough, he would allocate the responsibility for writing about such precious treasures as the Holy Bible only to prudent educated men with their sharp intellect, meaning that only clerical and academically trained scholars should write on that topic, men like Henneberg himself. Alluding to the offering left by the poor widow in the Temple (Mark 12:41–44), Breidenbach saw his book as a small, yet honourable, contribution to the field of religious writings.[47]

Breidenbach further underscored his topical humility by admitting, for rhetorical effect, that his book was actually not worthy of examination, even as he presented a copy to Henneberg and asked the archbishop most humbly not to disdain the book and to have a look at it when he had the time.[48] In this way, Breidenbach was somewhat thwarting his own advertisement strategy of stating that his book was something never seen before and that he had invested a certain amount of labour in producing it.[49] Henneberg's encouragement, however, would help to further improve the text and to eliminate all frivolous mistakes. Breidenbach praised the archbishop at length for his talents, wisdom and admirable deeds,[50] thus presenting Henneberg as the most perfect expert for evaluating *Die heyligen reyßen gen Jherusalem*: 'Nothing that

[46] Breidenbach 2010, 5. Cf. Ross 2014, 25. Jerome's letter 53, *Ad Paulinum in studio Scriptuarum*, was used – which Breidenbach was certainly aware of – as an introduction by Johannes Gutenberg in his famous print of the bible.

[47] Breidenbach 2010, 5. Cf. also Weinmayer 1982, 176–178, who points out that the strategy enabled Breidenbach also to tackle issues that might have been controversial in scholarly circles without getting drawn into such discussions.

[48] Breidenbach 2010, 5 and 15. Regarding humility as a rhetorical topic, see Curtius 1973, 93–95; Simon 1957–1960 I, 108–119.

[49] Cf. footnote 30 and Breidenbach 2010, 10–11. Assuring readers that he had already invested much time, Breidenbach, on the other side, also remarked that his work could not be compared with some hastily and amateurishly produced prints, which are criticised in Henneberg's edict. See Weinmayer 1982, 176.

[50] Breidenbach 2010, 14–17.

ever has come under the file of Your baronial Grace, which is very sharp and rubs off any rust, has not been decently straightened, cleaned and refined after the probation.'[51]

Breidenbach rhetorically gave Henneberg all liberty to proceed with the book as he wished; Breidenbach would accept any verdict.[52] Yet, since Henneberg apparently approved of the book, it went to print and Breidenbach's writing found a wider readership. As he stated himself, a close examination by Henneberg, who was the most trustworthy and qualified person, would increase the credibility of the book's content and attest to its spiritual merits: 'What has been examined by Your baronial Grace and gotten approval, which is also correct and therefore in any case to be endorsed, so that it enjoys even more esteem; [...] whereas things that have been rejected and refused by Your baronial Grace are regarded as meaningless, small and futile.'[53] As Barbara Weinmayer has pointed out, 'preventive censorship' was thus not only used as a means for supressing non suitable ideas, but also to legitimate Breidenbach's book and give it the highest possible recognition.[54]

Promoting imperial reform and remembrance of the glorious crusading past

The archbishop's indirect approval increased the value of *Die heyligen reyßen gen Jherusalem* and enhanced also Breidenbach's reputation as the author of the book. At the same time, Breidenbach's praising of Henneberg's wisdom enhanced the authority of the archbishop. Such praise not only positioned Henneberg as the ultimate authority for

[51] Breidenbach 2010, 10–11. Cf. Weinmayer 1982, 175.
[52] Breidenbach 2010, 12–14.
[53] Breidenbach 2010, 10–11.
[54] Weinmayer 1982, 178. On the receiver's role in dedication letters in legitimating texts, see also Simon 1957–1960, part II, 112–136. The use of Henneberg's heraldic sign for the initial 'R' at the beginning of the dedication letter in the Latin and German version of 1486 is a further sign of approval. In any other case, Henneberg would not have allowed him to use it otherwise.

defining what should be included in the cultural canon and what not,[55] but also recognised his position as the principal head of the electorate of Mainz, making him territorial lord of one of the most prestigious states of the Holy Roman Empire.

Elected as archbishop of Mainz in 1484,[56] Henneberg came to power at a time when the diocese was suffering territorial losses and financial setbacks after the Mainz Diocesan Feud, also known as the Baden-Palatine War of 1461–1463. As a result, the diocese had considerably less power compared with the more prosperous neighbouring states. Moreover, the clash between the archbishop and the citizenry, in which the citizenry were stripped of most of their privileges after 1463, led to further conflicts that weakened the position of the diocese.[57] Yet, being elected archbishop of Mainz still meant having more power than just to preside over the electorate of Mainz and its territories. In Henneberg's time, the archbishop of Mainz was one of the three Arch-Chancellors of the empire, in his case the person responsible for all imperial affairs in the German territories. He furthermore presided over the prince-electors of the Holy Roman Empire, making him accordingly in charge of calling the members to elect a new king and organising the coronation.[58] He was thus one of the most influential political figures in the empire.

Regarding all the roles that put Henneberg alternately in opposition to the king and/or emperor, to other dukes, to his own cathedral chapter or to the population of the city of Mainz, it can be regarded as a clever choice of Henneberg to recommend Breidenbach as his successor as dean of the Cathedral of Mainz in 1484. Profiting from the noble background and influence of his family, Breidenbach could rely on good contacts in the region. Having previously served as treasurer of the city of Mainz, he furthermore had good insights into the city's financial affairs and good connections to the citizenry. He thus seems a perfect candidate for Henneberg to promote as a loyal confidant

---

[55] Weinmayer 1982, 178.

[56] For more on Henneberg's life and further references, see the short overview by Heinz 2015.

[57] For a general introduction, see Dumont & al. 1999.

[58] For more on the different roles of the archbishop of Mainz and his relationship to the chapter, see Heinig 1996.

who could successfully negotiate with the archbishop on the one hand and the members of the cathedral and the city of Mainz on the other. Breidenbach, who proudly referred to his new position in his pilgrimage report,[59] was surely compelled to show gratitude to his promoter. This could be done not only by including flattering praise in his dedication letter, but also by supporting Henneberg in other parts of *Die heyligen reyßen gen Jherusalem*.

Archbishop Berthold of Henneberg is well known in historiography especially for his efforts at reforming the empire.[60] He, for instance, advocated the implementation of a public peace in order to end the many feuds that were causing political and economic instability in the German territories. He thus supported the idea that the right to decide and to use violence should only be in the hands of the king himself (as the king would have seen it as well) or the particular sovereigns of the main German states (in fact needed by the king to maintain the peace) – a position that was contested by other members of the nobility, who saw the right to feud as one of their indispensable aristocratic privileges. Henneberg endorsed a public peace based on Christian teachings, but even more because of the sheer necessity of controlling the electorate of Mainz, with its fragmented territorial possessions.[61] His biggest achievement was the proclamation of the *Ewige Landfrieden* ('Eternal Peace') at the Diet of Worms in 1495, though this by no means put an end to quarrels or warfare. Moreover, together with members of the Diet he also decided to establish an Imperial Chamber Court, which was in line with Henneberg's intention to gain from the emperor more rights and privileges to execute imperial power in place of the prince-electors. This was an accomplishment that actually brought Henneberg – even though he and Maximilian continued to work closely together – in opposition to the Habsburg ruler. The climax of this development was

[59] Breidenbach 2010, 540–541.
[60] In the historiography, Henneberg's politics are described both in very negative and also very positive ways, as one can see, for instance, in Bader 1954, 81–85. Accordingly, the impact and consequences of the imperial reform and the intentions of the many involved persons have been controversially discussed in numerous works.
[61] Roll 1998, 42.

the completion of an imperial government in 1500 that consisted of a committee of 20–22 members responsible for taxation politics, warfare and foreign policy. The emperor was merely given, in this context, the role of an honorary president. This project, however, failed in the end as a result of Emperor Maximilian's I refusal to cooperate and because of internal disputes between the representatives of the estates. Subsequently, the imperial government was dissolved in 1502 and Henneberg's courtly influence was reduced.

Breidenbach's critical comments regarding contemporary politics within the empire to an extent foreshadowed Henneberg's own experiences, who in 1486 was still relatively at the beginning of his term. This should not imply that Henneberg had a clear national agenda from the beginning as to what should be changed and how it could be done. Breidenbach's remarks on high politics should, furthermore, not be seen as distinctively outlining aspects of such a programme. In this respect, his comments are much too general. But they may be seen as giving some hint as to the direction of Henneberg's approach and could have represented an attempt to lay the groundwork for the future and direct the attention of the public to it.

Breidenbach's observations are part of a section subtitled 'a lamentation on the miserable situation of the church in the Occident together with a serious admonition to the princes of the realm to convince them to increase their efforts to save and protect the church'.[62] It is followed by a lamentation on the condition of the Holy Land and especially of Jerusalem and precedes his mourning the overall situation throughout Orient, in which Breidenbach could point to his own eyewitness accounts in order to verify the horrid situation.[63] By using in these passages very impassioned words and moving images in order to create empathy, fear or anger, Breidenbach obviously wanted to motivate the reader to take action. The topic and structure of the text imply that

---

[62] Breidenbach 2010, 484–485.

[63] Some of his observations regarding the fatal state of the East may have had their source in the pilgrimage account of Paul Walther of Guglingen, who included an oration on the need to re-conquer the Holy Land. Yet, the idea for the last section seems to have come from Breidenbach himself or his co-author Martin Rath.

after pinpointing the nature of the situation in the East, Breidenbach also had something to say about the state of affairs in the West. Having witnessed the conditions overseas, he felt duty-bound not to close his eyes to concerns closer to home.

Breidenbach's lamentation consists of five main parts: 1) the huge threat from outer enemies in form of the Turks, 2) the fatal state of his own society as a consequence of the inactivity of the ruling elite, 3) the memory of a golden crusading past, 4) concrete criticism of the lifestyle of the knighthood and 5) an invocation involving the elements of a sermon to unite and rise up against all religious adversaries.

His starting point was the expansion of the Ottoman Empire. He discussed the cities and provinces that had recently been conquered or attacked. This was frequently done in the form of rhetorical questions regarding who was responsible for the cruel assaults, so that Breidenbach each time could provide the identical answer to such questions: the Turks.[64] He thus stressed that the infidels were coming closer and posed an imminent and lethal danger to every single Christian. This passage corresponds to Breidenbach's very detailed description of Islam, probably written by Rath. The pseudo-historical notes on Muhammad and the origin of the new religion, as well as his characterisation of the followers of the prophet, are intensely polemical. Breidenbach/Rath condemned Muhammad as a son of the devil, portrayed his life as a continuous chain of sins, lies and deception, debased his faith as heretical to the core and depicted Muslims as irrational subjects who blindly follow impious doctrines and who persecute, suppress and exterminate Christians in all places. It is a sum of all the negative images of the competing religion created by Christian-Latin authors during medieval times.[65]

---

[64] Breidenbach 2010, 486–489. See also his separate descriptions of the Turkish conquest of Constantinople, Negroponte and Otranto at the end of his report, each time emphasising the cruelty of the Turkish troops. Breidenbach 2010, 668–725.

[65] Breidenbach 2010, 290–409. Concerning Breidenbach's description, see Schröder 2009, 239–291; Schröder 2015. On medieval images of Islam in general, see inter alia Tolan 2002; Di Cesare 2012.

While excluding the pope from his criticisms by admitting that His Holiness without doubt knows more than anyone else,[66] Breidenbach especially blamed the German princes for not completing their responsibilities and for allowing their religious enemies to assemble great power. Similar to the 'mirror of princes' genre, Breidenbach clearly summarised the tasks of a sovereign and emphasised that the power granted by God should be exercised in line with Christian virtues and Christian disciplines: their foremost duties are to protect the church, to comfort widows and orphans, to contain all evil and to accord justice to everyone. Moreover, Breidenbach explicitly determined that they must fulfil such duties in order to ensure their personal salvation. Their faults and their obstinacy were causing great harm and had been judged a disgrace.[67] Referring to the Bible (David, Hiob) and to the ancient philosophers (Boethius), Breidenbach elaborated at length upon a world ruled by deception, falsehood and injustice, one where even the clergy has lost its way.[68] Only after describing a society full of vices that, according to the author, were forcing God to allow for even more disorder so that mankind could finally recognise its sins and change, Breidenbach wrote disapprovingly of the way 'our princes' are always at odds with each other. Instead of fighting the Turks and pushing sharp swords down their throats, the princes were staining themselves with their own Christian blood.[69] He thus condemned the princes for their constant feuding and described how nothing motivates the nobility more than warfare and strife, suggesting that members of the nobility were often driven by their own anger. Breidenbach was referring here not only to the often criticised violent quarrels within the upper class, but also indicated that the fine line between authoritative legal measures and anger-driven violence was repeatedly not maintained. Addressing the princes directly, Breidenbach admonished them to wake up and realise how much could be achieved by turning all their energy and weaponry against the outer enemy. By pointing to absolution as the

[66] Breidenbach 2010, 488–491.
[67] Breidenbach 2010, 494–495. For more on the princes' duties in late medieval texts of this genre related to a German audience, see Rösener 2008.
[68] Breidenbach 2010, 494–503.
[69] Breidenbach 2010, 502–503.

heavenly wage for fighting the infidels, as *miles Christi*, Breidenbach reminded the princes that there would be much better cause to engage in a just war against the Muslims.[70]

The following remembrance of the crusades underscores the possibility of combining the nobility's desire for honour and glory through fighting with the aim of achieving forgiveness for their sins and securing a just place in the afterlife.[71] By referencing the idealised past of the crusading times for his audience, Breidenbach was referring to the most glorious events related to fighting against the Muslims. He mentioned in particular Charlemagne, Roland and Godfrey of Bouillon as three protagonists whose deeds should be recalled and seen as examples to be followed.[72] Charlemagne, with his popular – yet fictive – campaign to reconquer the Holy Land, stands in for the ideal king and greatest warrior who defended Christianity against heathen armies invading both from the West and East. He included the iconic figure of Roland from the well-known *Chanson de Roland* in his discussion because Roland was fighting for a just cause and his heroism in the epic Battle of Roncevaux secured him both an afterlife in paradise and an eternal place in the collective memory, both of eminent concern for the ruling elite. He lastly mentions Godfrey as the most prominent leader of the First Crusade and founder of the Kingdom of Jerusalem, a man who gained an exceedingly positive image in medieval historiography for being the most skilful warrior and the most modest of rulers.[73]

By referring to each of these figures, all men who had been elevated to mythical heights, Breidenbach was picking up on the still current and ever flourishing idea of crusading as a noble cause. On the one hand, remembrance of the various crusades to the Holy Land was kept alive through numerous military campaigns that were equally labelled

---

[70] Breidenbach 2010, 502–507.

[71] Breidenbach 2010, 506–511.

[72] The re-creation of the crusading past and its functions for a late medieval audience is the topic of the project 'Historicizing the Crusades' by the author. For more on the changing images and uses of the crusading past throughout time, see Tyerman 2011; Paul and Yeager 2012.

[73] For more on Charlemagne and Roland, see Stuckey 2008. For more on Godfrey, see Wolfzettel 2004.

as crusades and fought against all kinds of outer and inner enemies of Christianity: the Reconquista in Spain, the wars against the Turks in Eastern Europe, the fights against the 'pagans' in the Baltic North as well as the campaigns against Christian heretics, most notably the Hussites. Each of these campaigns was frequently legitimated by relying on the rhetoric of crusading.[74] On the other hand, the deeds of the first crusaders were actively remembered in a number of tractates written in the aftermath of the fall of Acre as the last Christian stronghold in 1291. These extensively debated texts suggested various ways to organise a new crusade to recapture Jerusalem.[75] Many kings and high noblemen therefore felt obliged to take up the cross and promised to engage themselves personally in holy warfare or at least donate sums of money to the cause. Pope Pius II's efforts at organising a new crusade and the 'Feast of the Pheasant' arranged by Duke Philip the Good in 1454, both of which resulted from the Ottoman's capture of Constantinople, are only the two most prominent examples from the 15th century of such crusading notions.[76]

Remembrance of the crusades was, moreover, maintained in the church's liturgy, sermons and religious practices, in manuscript collections and early prints of crusader chronicles, in vernacular translations and continuations of the heroic stories (namely William of Tyre's *Historia rerum*, the so-called *L'Estoire de Eracles*), in popular narratives like the *Chansons de Geste*, in further crusading romances and in songs and humanistic tractates.[77] Last but not least, the crusading past was inscribed in historiographical works to promote the glorious origin and deeds of a family, city or nation, and was upheld by societies like the Order of the Holy Sepulchre, which originated from a Franciscan tradition to elevate noble pilgrims to knights at the church of the

---

[74] For more on the crusades in later medieval times, see Housley 1992.
[75] See Leopold 2000.
[76] Bisaha 2004; Paviot 2004.
[77] Cf. Linder 2003 (Liturgy); Moodey 2012 (illuminated crusader histories); Handyside 2015 (William of Tyre); *The Canso d'Antioca* 2003 (Chansons de Geste); Manion 2014 (crusading romances); Hankins 1995 (humanistic texts).

Holy Sepulchre in Jerusalem.[78] As a consequence of all these factors, the crusades were embedded in the cultural memory of late medieval Europe.

Part of that cultural memory also entailed remembrance of the long period of decline of the crusader states and the numerous defeats and more negative images of the crusades. Breidenbach, however, for the most part omitted such negative images from his work. He only briefly mentioned the efforts of France's King Philipp II and England's King Richard I, commonly known as Richard the Lionheart, during the Third Crusade in order to show how they, too, had mobilised a great number of knights to reconquer Jerusalem after Saladin's taking of the city in 1187. Yet he said nothing about the failure of their ambitious goals or that Philipp and Richard had left the Holy Land in disagreement.[79] Finally, Breidenbach made vague references to the many glorious deeds of the Bavarian and Austrian dukes, achieved in communion with the most splendid German knighthood, as a means of particularly strengthening the collective identity of the 'German nations'. He explicitly requested that they honour the memory of their ancestors by continuing to engage in fighting the Muslims, thereby proving that the present nobility could live up to the glorious deeds of their forefathers and be worthy of their vaunted origin.[80] Breidenbach thus cleverly appealed to the class consciousness of the nobility, to their dynastic ambitions, which included the construction and maintenance of a positive family history, in order to motivate them.

Breidenbach's final uplifting statement that the weaponry, skills and craftsmanship of the knighthood were currently at a peak was made together with a further criticism of the uselessness of tournaments and other knightly games. As with the feuds, the nobility engaged in such competitions on a regular basis as evidence of their abilities, power, rank and wealth.[81] In late medieval times, splendid tournaments also

---

[78] Paul 2012; Bellomo 2014. On the Order of the Holy Sepulchre, see Feld-kamp 2016.

[79] Breidenbach sees the loss of the Holy Land after 88 years and seven appointed kings of Jerusalem as a consequence of the lack of support from the West.

[80] Breidenbach 2010, 510–511.

[81] Breidenbach 2010, 512–513.

served as a political instrument, both in the field of diplomacy and as a way of strengthening the feeling of belonging to a very exclusive group. Especially Maximilian I – often called the 'last knight' because of his preoccupation with knighthood – spent a great deal of money on tournaments as important aspects of the courtly feasts to legitimate his power.[82] Breidenbach, in contrast, disapproved of such a dangerous, even bloody sport and spoke of pride and folly. Instead of investing so much effort and large sums of money on such tournaments, the knights could better direct all their energies to humiliating the evil infidels and preventing them from mocking Christians by asking 'where is their God?' (Psalm 79).[83] This biblical reference led readers to Breidenbach's final emotional appeal for the nobility to take up the cross in God's name and prove that God had indeed given them a virile and strong heart and that they would always trust in Him. By closing his lamentation on the situation in the West with an 'Amen', Breidenbach highlighted the special significance of his request. By using this basic element of a sermon, he aimed to assure his audience that God approved of his concern.[84]

Breidenbach's demands within the context of contemporary reform tractates

Breidenbach's criticism of feuds and tournaments as well as of the general situation is not new. The appeal for an imperial peace already had a long history. Looking at the local historical tradition, he might even have been aware of the imperial peace of 1235 announced by Emperor Frederick II at Mainz, which became one of the basic 'constitutional' legal texts for the Holy Roman Empire. He might also have been aware of the so-called *Reformatio Friderici*, a decree by Emperor Frederick III in 1442 that, inter alia, had the goal of increasing the security of certain groups, such as peasants, who should not be attacked or their harvests

[82] See Pfaffenbichler 2014.
[83] Breidenbach 2010, 514–515.
[84] Breidenbach 2010, 514–515.

destroyed, thus attempting to put a stop to the common practice of pillage and plunder during feuds.[85] There is also a long, though ambivalent, tradition of criticising tournaments. Representatives of the church in particular saw the costly events as symbols of a debauched courtly lifestyle and an expression of cupidity.[86]

Breidenbach's remarks were also not so innovative when looking at other contemporary writings. Such texts consisted of polemical and satirical poems that strongly condemned members of the nobility for their sinful lifestyle and inability to preserve peace, sometimes even by creating alternative utopian worlds in which violence, war, injustice, simony and taxes did not exist.[87] Other texts originated from religious movements and mythical ideas that promoted the image of moral decay within the institution of the church and announced that the world would soon come to an end.[88] Written partially as a consequence of the Catholic Ecumenical Councils, especially those held in Siena, Basle and Florence in the first half of the 15th century, a third group of texts provided somewhat more concrete suggestions for altering the situation in the empire and the curia and for reducing current miseries. Key concepts in these tractates, often penned by anonymous, not always clerical, authors, were the notions of justice, right, peace and freedom.[89] They mostly understood reform not in the sense of creating a social order based on new principles, but instead claimed that the society they lived in had somehow renounced a primordial ideal. Often the authors used the metaphor of the empire suffering from a serious 'illness' as a result of its disrespect of the law. This was done by depicting a culture in which the clergy mostly lived in simony and both the nobility and commoners were driven by the desire to increase their tangible goods at all cost. Reform thus meant re-establishing the supposedly perfect

---

[85] For more on the imperial peace of 1235, see Mainzer Reichslandfrieden 1977. For more on the decree of 1442, see *Regesten Kaiser Friedrichs III.* 1986, No 41; Koller 2005, 80–81; Bookmann 1979, 524–526.

[86] Cf. Barber and Barker 2000, 139–149; more specifically, Krüger 1985.

[87] For the content and functions of such poems, such as for, instance, the anonymous *König Wenzels Landfriede* (end of 14th cent.) or Michel Beheim's *Lügenlied* (15th cent.), see Kellermann 2012.

[88] See Schäufele 2006.

[89] Annas 2012, 232–233.

structures of a golden era.[90] In most cases, the authors wanted these reforms to be applied via a top-down approach.

Johannes Schele (1385/90–1439), for instance, bishop of Lubeck and participant in the Council of Basel, focused in his *Avisamenta reformacionis in capite et in membris* primarily on the church and the clergy.[91] Divided into 114 sections, he not only argued for the prohibition of all attempts to translate the Bible into the vernacular (§95), but also, similar to Breidenbach, advocated putting an immediate end to all warfare between Christian sovereigns (§51), reminded the authorities of their duties to protect clerics, widows and orphans (§101), forbade nobles from starting feuds without the permission of their superiors (§102), disapproved of vendettas (§102), bemoaned the fact that acts to dishonour somebody often ended up in deadly violence (§103) and, finally, strongly recommended a new crusade to the Holy Land (§114). Peter of Andlau (c. 1420–1480) in the *Libellus de cesarea monarchia* (1460) likewise condemned the injustice and insecurity stemming from the loss of virtues and the increasing arbitrariness of the elites and their feuds.[92] Finally, the *Reformatio Sigismundi* might well have been the reform text best known by a wider audience. Anonymously written in German in the aftermath of the Council of Basel, but giving the (alleged) impression of Emperor Sigismund acting as author, it likewise demanded a public peace and the prohibition of feuds.[93] The text was reprinted several times after 1476, often in combination with the *Reformatio Friderici*, thus increasing its popularity.

---

[90] For more on the metaphor of illness, see Struve 1978. For the meaning of the term 'reform', see Struve 1994, 373, 378; Annas 2012, 225–226. Breidenbach mirrored this notion by mentioning that the world had turned away from its initial system of justice and had become corrupted. Breidenbach 2010, 502–503.

[91] Johannes of Schele 2002. Cf. also Struve 1994, 380.

[92] Peter of Andlau 1998, 150–151, 284–287, 298–303. Cf. Struve 1994, 374.

[93] *Reformation Kaiser Sigismund* 1964, 310–312. See Struve 1994, 370. One later redaction of the text makes reference to the somewhat similar analogy used by Breidenbach that if the powerful are asleep, the little ones (meaning the knights and the cities) have to stay awake even more. See Struve 1978, 109.

It is not unlikely that Breidenbach and Henneberg had some knowledge of these reform tractates, even though a distinct dependency cannot be determined and the publicity and impact of these writings remains in some cases unclear.[94] One can find many differences between the sometimes very detailed proposals and Breidenbach's more general pleas. Although Breidenbach indicates the present injustices and the deficient legal framework,[95] the reform tractates are much more specific, taking the hardships of the average person in the street more into account. Being part of the ruling elite himself and being dependent on Henneberg, Breidenbach was also less harsh than other authors who – as, for instance, the anonymous author of the *Reformatio Sigismundi* – argued for a complete failure by the privileged people and the clergy in particular. Moreover, there is a fundamental dissimilarity between Breidenbach and the *Reformatio Sigismundi* in particular, since the latter viewed a new crusade as a waste of time and energy. Instead of fighting infidels, it would be better to start a campaign against usury, simony and injustice within the German territories.[96] Yet, since the time when the *Reformatio Sigismundi* had been written, the successful Ottoman conquest of Constantinople and other cities after 1453 had completely changed the picture. As a result, the discourse on the 'Türkengefahr' gained much more popularity. It led, inter alia, to frequent rhetorically orations promoting a crusade against the Turks at imperial diets.[97]

---

[94] For different standpoints on the impact of the writings, see Annas 2012, 229. The 'Upper Rhenish Revolutionary', an unknown author of a further reform tractate, provided the story that he was fobbed off by the Arch-Chancellor at Worms in 1495 after trying to show him his work. See Brady 2015, 52–53, who also discusses Henneberg's possible knowledge of Nicholas of Cues' influential text *De concordante catholica*.

[95] See Breidenbach 2010, 498–499, for more hints on the situation at court where legal claims were twisted into unjustness and complaints of the rich generally getting richer while the poor did not know how to survive.

[96] *Reformation Kaiser Sigismund* 1964, 86–88, 77. Cf. Struve 1978, 115–116.

[97] On the image of the Turk in writings of 15th-century Germany, see Höfert 2003. On the speeches, see Helmrath 2004.

Moreover, extra taxes were raised and letters of indulgence were sold in Mainz, as elsewhere in Germany, to finance military campaigns.[98]

More in line with the reform tractates is the fact that Breidenbach assigned a strong and vital role to the king. Breidenbach felt the king should set an example by living a commendable and moral lifestyle and he should the one to take action and implement the reforms. Peter of Andlau in his work *Libellus* addressed Frederick III in person. He used harsh words to create the image of a ruler who had lost much of his power because of his carelessness, idleness and discord: 'How do You want to take account of this when standing in front of God? If You tolerate this situation, Emperor, then You would never have the right to call Yourself Augustus. [...] You now have to rise, You who is sleeping!'[99] Being the first and the noblest person of the empire, the one who stands above all others, the king, or respectively the emperor, was naturally seen as the most powerful and having the best means for finding a solution to the problem. The focus on king and emperor resulted, furthermore, in prophetical tales popular in the 15th century; such tales announced the appearance of a Prince of Peace who would resolve the deplorable situation affecting the empire. This hope and deep yearning for a strong ruler who could implement reforms is mirrored, for example, in the *Reformatio Sigismundi* and later in the tractate of the 'Upper Rhenish Revolutionary'.[100] While the author of the *Reformatio Sigismundi* proclaimed that this Prince of Peace would be a commoner, Breidenbach set his hopes in the newly elected King Maximilian; he hoped the king would dramatically intervene to improve the political situation. By reminding Maximilian of his duties and encouraging him

---

[98] See Ross 2014, 58–60, who points out that despite all crusade propaganda, the German estates, including that of the clergy, were critical of any papal or imperial attempts to establish further taxes to finance military campaigns.

[99] Peter of Andlau 1998, 302–303. For more on the image of the king in Peter of Andlau's work, see also Annas 2012, 237. The metaphor of the sleeping emperor can also be found in a German pamphlet written in 1470 in Vienna. See Schreiner 1987, 246.

[100] *Reformation Kaiser Sigismund* 1964, 326, 342. See Struve 1977, 81–87; Struve 1978, 107–110. For more on the connections with popular vernacular texts that express a yearning for the return of the 'sleeping hero', Emperor Frederick I and Frederick II, respectively, see Kellermann 2013.

Stephan Schröder

to take action, as cited in the introduction of this article, Breidenbach was also explicitly expressing his belief that the whole Christian world was extremely pleased by the election. He thus emphasised the great expectations of the community. Breidenbach's metaphor of the pious leader who would not hesitate to fight and defend his realm, like a latter-day Judas Maccabeus, mirrors not only the pejorative allegory of the sleeping shepherd, but also creates the image of a leader who is active, energetic and eager to gain plenty of fame and honour. This may point to the image of the young Maximilian, whereas his father Frederick III was often criticised for his inactivity, lethargy and lengthy absences from the German territories.[101]

Interestingly, the fact that he personally addressed Maximilian I is only part of Breidenbach's German version. When comparing the Latin, German and Flemish prints of the travelogue, several differences emerge. In the German *editio princeps*, Breidenbach for example omitted some medical instructions for travellers that were printed at the end of the Latin text. The reduction of some theological background information furthermore suggests he was adjusting the German version to fit a non-clerical audience that was less scholarly educated or interested.[102] Yet the additional passage concerning Maximilian in the German edition was a more vital alteration.[103] It resulted from the changed situation between the publishing dates of the Latin version in early February, before the election of Maximilian as king, and of the German edition in June, when Maximilian was already serving as king. Issues like the

[101] Breidenbach 2010, 490–491. For more on the use of Judas Maccabeus as heroic leader in crusader texts, see Lapina 2015. For more on the negative image of Frederick III, see Schreiner 1987; Koller 2005, 238–239.

[102] For more on the differences between the Latin and German editions, see Mozer's introduction in Breidenbach 2010, XXXI–XXXII. For more on differences in the order of the woodcuts, see also Ross 2014, 69.

[103] This alteration was first documented by Timm 2006, 350. That the addition cannot be found in the Flemish edition either might result from Reuwich having used the Latin text as a template. This somehow surprising hypothesis that Reuwich, seen in research as the person who translated the text into Flemish, might have worked with the Latin and not with the German text has yet to be examined more thoroughly. It would mean, however, that Reuwich had a more thorough education than expected.

implementation of an imperial chamber court, the standardisation of coinage and a public peace had already been discussed at meetings following the king's coronation. Maximilian himself had suggested during the negotiations that the electors and further potent dukes should have the right to control and maintain such a peace. However, fearing a loss of influence and power, the minor imperial states as well as Emperor Frederick III rejected this request.[104] The renewed version was, in the end, just a general prohibition of feuds.[105] It is not certain whether Maximilian's offer was meant to be taken seriously and showed his willingness to reform the empire, or if it was just an attempt to bring the electors to his side in order to provide himself with more autonomy from his father. Nonetheless, Breidenbach's modification (perhaps included in agreement with Henneberg) can be seen as an attempt to gain the ear of the king, to use the printing press to create a direct channel of communication. In making Maximilian aware of the pressing need for reform via his printed book, Breidenbach might have aimed both to show that such a policy would be supported by many people and to influence public opinion in order to increase the pressure being put on Maximilian to initiate reforms.

Warnings from hell and Venice as a role model for an ideal Christian society

When closely reading Breidenbach's lamentation, it is possible to think that he made his point clear: a fundamental change in politics was needed in order to stop the increasing immorality and sinfulness of Christian society and to prevent the empire from being torn apart in chaos and Christian Europe from being overrun by the Turks. For Breidenbach, instant change was needed, otherwise it would be too late. It seems, however, that a final distinct hint was compulsory to warn

---

[104] See Hollegger 2005, 64 and also 62–63 regarding Maximilian's generous promises to Cologne, Mainz and the County Palatine of Rhine in the case of supporting his election.

[105] Koller 2005, 212.

his readers of the outcomes if they decided not to act. By including a vision of hell somewhat abruptly after his lamentation, Breidenbach was making it plain that to continue on the current path would have severe, even irrevocable, consequences also for the afterlife. He borrowed this vision of hell, known as the *Visio Karoli Grossi*, inter alia from Vincent of Beauvais's *Speculum historiale*.[106] Originally, the vision was written around 885 in Reims and attributed to Charles III, known as Charles the Fat (839–888), but for some reason the main protagonist in Breidenbach's version is Charles II, known as Charles the Bald (823–877), who served as King of France and, from 875 to 877, also as Holy Roman Emperor.[107]

Charles is shown God's just judgement in a dream in which his spirit is guided through different parts of hell by a shining white figure. Protected by holding a flaxen thread, he is shown the infernal horrors and the manifold kinds of tortures sinners had to endure: the dukes and advisors of his father, Louis the Pious, suffered dreadfully in pits of burning pitch, sulphur, wax and other materials. Others sat in wells of boiling water mixed with melting ores or in furnaces full of pitch and were being attacked by dragons, scorpions and snakes. Confessing that they rightfully deserved their punishment for the deeds done during their lifetimes (selfish behaviour, willingness engage in warfare, cupidity and pride), the dukes and advisors warned Charles that his counsellors awaited the same fate. Finally meeting his father, who was covered up to his hips in a vat of boiling water, Charles was shown that his own soul would face the same treatment if he did not change. Yet there was also hope. Charles was led to a comfortable valley, where he found his relatives Lothair I (795–855) and Louis II (825–875), apparently recovering from the agonies of hell and redeemed from torture by the

---

[106] Breidenbach 2010, 516–527 with footnote 675; Vincent of Beauvais 1964, Lib. 24, Cap. 49–50, 979–980.

[107] Since Vincent, who used William of Malmesbury as his source, also focused on Charles III, Breidenbach might have taken this vision from another text. For more on the vision being one of Dante's inspirations for his description of the inferno, see Levison 1948, 243–245; Gardiner 1989, 129–133; Dutton 1994, 234–251.

intercession of Saint Remigius of Reims, patron saint of the Franks.[108] Without the saint's constant interventions, the Carolingian dynasty would soon have ceased to exist and Charles would already have lost his power. Therefore, they insist on appointing the future Louis III, known as Louis the Blind (863/65–882), as Charles's heir in order to secure the reign of the family. The vision ends with the image of Charles giving the flaxen thread to a child and thus symbolically handing over his power to Louis III.

Breidenbach reproduced this vision not for its last part, which had a distinct political context in backing up the claims of Louis III to the throne, promoting the cult of Saint Remigius and strengthening the bishop's see in Rheims,[109] but to find a suitable parallel between the misdeeds of the great men of the Carolingian Empire of the Franks and the faults of the German princes of the 15th century.[110] Moreover, it is again the king who is depicted as the key figure responsible for altering the socio-political structures of the realm. He is the only one capable of implementing changes by defining and controlling the actions of the clerical as well as the non-clerical elite. It is difficult to determine the impact of the dramatic images depicting a wide variety of the most painful tortures on contemporary readers, especially with respect to the enduring image of the Late Middle Ages in particular as a period of great anxiety.[111] For Breidenbach as well as for other authors, however, hell in this context serves as the ultimate moral sanction. It underscored the importance of his concerns regarding the inner and outer threats that the empire faced at his time.

The vision of Charles II the Bald concludes the first part of Breidenbach's *Die heyligen reyßen gen Jherusalem*, followed by three woodcuts of the Holy Sepulchre, of Jerusalem as the centre of the Holy Land and of the exotic animals that pilgrims encountered on the way.

[108] For this part of the vision and its interpretation as purgatory, see especially Le Goff 1984, 118–122.
[109] The only apparent parallel would be to see the question of succession between Charles the Bald and Louis III as allegory for Frederick III and Maximilian I.
[110] For an overview, see Angenendt 1997, 695–705; Dinzelbacher 1981, 2002.
[111] See the master narrative of Delumeau (1978) as well as Vorgrimler (1993); Dinzelbacher 1996.

Hence, the vision has a meaningful place at the end of a number of more theoretical and academic chapters and before the start of the second part, which tells of Breidenbach's journey to Egypt and back home. With his section 'praise of the history of the impressive city of Venice', Breidenbach also included a meaningful chapter at the beginning of the first part,[112] meaningful because it provided an example to readers of the devastating situation currently being faced by the Christian world. As the preferred place of departure to the Holy Land in the Late Middle Ages, pilgrims usually spent several weeks in the city waiting for the galleys to depart.[113] They had time to acquire all of the things necessary for the trip and to become familiar with the many landmarks of the city, ranging from the numerous magnificent churches with their valuable relics to the Doge's Palace as the place of government and the huge dockyard of the Venetian Arsenal – all of them highlighted in Reuwich's woodcut of Venice.[114] The pilgrims were impressed by the very different scenery and the exotic character of one of the largest and richest cities in Europe. By guiding and hosting especially the noble pilgrims, the Venetians used every opportunity to represent Venice as a strong, liberal and pious city that, according to its myth of origin, was much older and nobler than Rome.[115]

Breidenbach's description was – as were many others – influenced by the literary motive of the *laudes urbium*, a praise of the city that followed a certain scheme with statements on its topography, origin, military and economic strength, architectural features and constitution as well as the culture and vitality of its civil life.[116] In comparison to other travel reports, he gave less information about churches and relics and did not

[112] Breidenbach 2010, 68–81.
[113] For the description of Venice in pilgrimage reports, see Denke 2001; Schröder 2009, 104–126, 205–226.
[114] For the woodcut and its connection to the praise of Venice in the text, see Timm 2006, 123–144, 338; Ross 2014, 65–69.
[115] The Venetian council passed many edicts regarding the stay of pilgrims in the city and the organisation of their passage to the Holy Land. For more on the myth (and counter-myths) of Venice, see Crouzet-Pavan 1984; Fried 2004, 157–166; Muir 1981.
[116] See Curtius 1973, 163–168. For further references, see Schröder 2009, 101–102.

refer in detail to the abundance of goods available in Venice. Instead, Breidenbach repeatedly emphasised the peace and unity of the Venetians, stating that they were able to maintain concord even during turbulent times. He thus displayed the Venetian self-presentation, of performing as one body, which was especially highlighted in solemn processions such as the Feast of Corpus Christi, a procession often observed by pilgrims while waiting for the departure of the pilgrim's galley.[117] Furthermore, he outlined specifics about the Venetian government, such as the office of the 'podestà' and the time restraints placed on the assignments of ambassadors, both established to minimalise personal enrichment.[118] He also pointed to the strict provisions of duties that each office-holder, even the Doge as the symbolic leader of the republic, were given; severe sentences were meted out in cases where such duties were violated.[119] The aim of the regulations was to prevent one family or faction from gaining too much influence, which ultimately could fundamentally change the fine-balanced distribution of power. Breidenbach interpreted these efforts as visible signs of the great virtues of the Venetians. He praised their piety and steadfastness, their benevolence and love, their wisdom, reason and prudence as well as their sense of justice, and he stated that they do not tolerate muggers, other criminals or any sect that contradicts God's laws.[120]

Breidenbach's purpose was certainly not to promote the Venetian constitution, with its political system of a mixed government consisting of democratic, aristocratic and monarchic elements, and suggest that it should serve as a model for the Holy Roman Empire.[121] At first glance, the power allocated to the Doge might have some parallels with Henneberg's plans of establishing an imperial government, but the city's

---

[117] Breidenbach 2010, 68–69, 70–71, 76–77.
[118] Breidenbach 2010, 74–75. Elected as a 'podestà' and appointed by a single city, a Venetian nobleman acted as head of the magistrate for a certain period of time. At the end of his term, he had to return to Venice and could not immediately be re-elected to office in the same city. For the example of Venice, see Rösch 1989.
[119] Breidenbach 2010, 74–77, 80–81. For more on the promissione ducalis, see Muir 1978.
[120] Breidenbach 2010, 76–77, 80–81.
[121] See Riklin 2006 (esp. chapter 6).

constitution stood in contradiction to Breidenbach's idea that the king should be a strong and powerful ruler implementing reforms. In his description, the Venetians are represented as the counterparts of the selfish and imprudent German princes. Even though Breidenbach's eulogy on Venice is put at the very beginning of the travel journal and is not explicitly linked with the lamentations at the end of part one of *Die heyligen reyßen gen Jherusalem*, it was meant to hold up a mirror to his audience, to make them aware of the alarming state of affairs at home as well as the overall dangerous geo-political situation. Omitting, for instance, its manifold trade interests and close diplomatic relations with the Ottomans, Breidenbach instead portrayed Venice as a state guarding Christianity and capable of constantly fighting against the Turks.[122] By idealising their deeds, Breidenbach's intention might have been to encourage the German knights to take some pointers from their fellow believers living south of the Alps.[123]

Conclusion

The themes of reform and reformation have been evoked in several ways in this article. The analysis of Breidenbach's *Die heyligen reyßen gen Jherusalem* reflects on the changing book market in the 15th century, where the printing press allowed for new ways of communication and of addressing audiences. Breidenbach recognised early on the new possibilities offered by it and created a book that impressed a wide range of readers with its woodcuts. At the same time, he was aware of the concerns expressed by the authorities and clergy about an uncontrollable marked that inevitably would lead to the publishing of non-authorised and heretical works. Through his dedication letter to Henneberg, Breidenbach elegantly addressed such concerns and turned them to his

---

[122] Breidenbach 2010, 76–79.
[123] A further example of a heroic Christian resistance is the example of the siege of Rhodes by the Turks in 1480, which Breidenbach described at length based on the chronicle of Guillaume Caoursin. See Breidenbach 2010, 690–723.

advantage. Together with his superior, who surely approved this letter before it was printed, Breidenbach created an incunabula that set the standard for other authors and could be seen as exemplary.

The rapid distribution of his work via the divine art of printing also gave Breidenbach the opportunity to use this medium for political propaganda. The intended audience, addressed broadly through versions in Latin, German and Flemish, was deliberately confronted with a harsh criticism of the ruling elite, pointing to the inability of elites to unite and fight against the Turks and outlining the increasing injustice and self-interest that were destroying the Christian foundations of society. By remembering the glorious crusader past and pointing to a Carolingian vision of hell, Breidenbach adapted past events and narratives to serve the current needs of society. His exhaustive analysis of the errors of Islam and the noble example of Venice furthermore gave readers numerous examples of good and evil so that they could critically reflect on their existence and the need to act before risking slavery or death at the hands of the Turks or – even worse – cruel punishment in the afterlife. To publish such a negative assessment of the situation in German territories was only possible with the protection of Henneberg, who was himself an important member of the elite. Creating in his report the image of himself as an ideal pious pilgrim and as an erudite expert on the Holy Land and the world overseas, Breidenbach was further able to ground his criticism by referencing his own first-hand experiences from the journey. He actively used his role as a pastor to educate and to give advice to his readers. By erecting strict cultural borders against all non-Catholic stances, he sought to strengthen the Christian belief in a crucial period of time characterised by him as chaotic and hostile. The text thus presents a specific worldview that defined what was at stake and what should be done both on the individual level and the collective level to ensure a secure future. Last but not least, Breidenbach's text demonstrates that pre-modern pilgrimage reports are much more than random sequences of certain memories from a traveller.

The new technology of the printing press seemed ideal for sharing Breidenbach's viewpoints with a broad clerical as well as non-clerical audience. The timing of the publication as well as its structure and content in evaluating the situation in the empire suggest that Breidenbach and

Henneberg hoped to influence public opinion and strengthen the faction that was arguing for reform. That Henneberg himself later became one the most prominent figures in the struggle for reform attempts was, however, certainly not only due to Breidenbach's travelogue. Maximilian's election as King of the Germans in 1486 represented the perfect opportunity to announce what ought to be changed in order to subvert both inner and outer threats to the empire. Yet the hope that Maximilian would hear their plea and institute basic changes remained unfulfilled. Henneberg's efforts were surely important in the long run, but after the failure of the imperial government in 1502, his position at court was weakened. Authors of later reform works were disappointed by Maximilian and severely criticised his politics.[124]

Despite Breidenbach's elaborate lamentations and severe criticism of contemporary politics, the travelogue itself seemed to be perceived by readers predominantly as a description of a pilgrimage to the Holy Land. Felix Fabri used Breidenbach's text for his own writings and also often criticised the conditions at home, but nowhere in it did he comment directly on Breidenbach's lamentation. Likewise, later pilgrims such as Konrad Grünemberg and Arnold of Harff used pieces of the text as well as Reuwich's magnificent woodcuts for their own travel reports without referring to Breidenbach's points of disapproval.[125] Based on the limited knowledge that we have on the reception of Breidenbach's report, it seems that his critiques were hidden too well within the manifold other topics of his descriptions, or else simply not taken into account by the readers, who were more interested in learning about the journey to Jerusalem itself. Some later editors and translators of Breidenbach's work even decided to shorten or omit parts of the text. Breidenbach's lamentation on the fatal state of the Occident is missing, for example, in the French translations by Jean de Hersin in 1488 and in the print done in 1522; in the Spanish version of 1498, it was partly condensed but

---

[124] See Märtl 1987.

[125] Reuwich's depiction of the pilgrim's galley was even used by the printer of the second letter of Christopher Columbus, which reported on his western route to India. A copy of the Spanish edition of Breidenbach's text from 1498 was part of the library of Ferdinand Columbus, Christopher's son. See Reichert 1998.

also revised and commented on by the translator, Martin Martinez de Ampies.[126] Especially after Henneberg's death in 1504, the dedication letter was also sometimes left out. Times had changed and it was apparently regarded as necessary to make adjustments to Breidenbach's *Die heyligen reyßen gen Jherusalem* for the intended audiences in other countries and in the early 16th century.

Bibliography

Printed sources

The Canso d'Antioca: an Occitan epic chronicle of the First Crusade. Eds. Carol Sweetenham and Lina M. Paterson. Ashgate, Aldershot and Hants 2003.

Bernhard of Breidenbach: *Peregrinatio in terram sanctam.* Erhard Reuwich, Mainz 11 February 1486. [GW 05075; HC *3956]

Bernhard of Breidenbach: *Die heyligen reyßen gen Jherusalem zů dem heiligen Grab.* Erhard Reuwich, Mainz 21 June 1486. [GW 05077; HC 3959]

Bernhard of Breidenbach: *Die heylighe beuarden tot dat heylighe grafft in Jherusalem.* Erhard Reuwich, Mainz 24 May 1488. [GW 05081]

Bernhard of Breidenbach: *Le saint voiage et pelerinage de la cité saincte de Hiérusalem.* Gaspar Ortuin, Lyon 18 February 1489. [GW 05079]

Bernhard of Breidenbach: *Viaje dela tierra sancta.* Paul Hurus, Zaragoza 16 January 1498. [GW 05082]

Bernhard of Breidenbach: *Le grand voyage de Hierusalem, lequel traite des pérégrinations de la sainte cité de Hierusalem du Mont Sainte Catherine de Sinay et autres lieux saints.* Reynault, Paris 1522.

Bernhard of Breidenbach: Die Reiseinstructionen des Bernhard von Breitenbach 1483. *Deutsche Pilgerreisen nach dem Heiligen Lande.* Eds. Reinhold Röhricht and Heinrich Meisner. Weidmann, Berlin 1880, 120–145.

Bernhard of Breidenbach: *Peregrinatio in Terram Sanctam. Frühneuhochdeutscher Text und Übersetzung.* Ed. Isolde Mozer. De Gruyter, Berlin and New York, 2010.

Burchard of Mount Sion: Descriptio Terrae Sanctae. *Peregrinatores medii aevi quatuor.* Ed. J. C. M. Laurent. Hinrichs, Leipzig 1873 (2nd ed.), 1–100.

Fabri, Felix: *Fratris Felicis Fabri Evagatorium in Terrae Sanctae, Arabiae et Egypti peregrinationem.* Ed. Konrad Dietrich Hassler. Bibliothek des Literarischen Vereins Stuttgart 2–4. Literarischer Verein, Stuttgart 1843–49.

---

[126] Breidenbach 1489; Breidenbach 1498; Breidenbach 1522. The latter edition was based on the French translation of Nicolas de Huen of 1489 which still included this passage. For further alterations, especially concerning the woodcuts, see Davies 1911, IX; Bosselmann-Cyran 1994/95, 112.

Mainzer Reichslandfrieden, 1235, August 15. *Quellen zur deutschen Verfassungs-, Wirtschafts und Sozialgeschichte bis 1250*. Ed. Lorenz Weinrich. Ausgewählte Quellen zur deutschen Geschichte des Mittelalters 32. Wissenschaftliche Buchgesellschaft, Darmstadt 1977, 462–485.

Mandeville, John: *The Book of John Mandeville with Related Texts*. Ed. Iain Macleod Higgins. Hackett Publishing Company, Indianapolis 2011.

Peter of Andlau: *Kaiser und Reich – Libellus de cesarean monarchia*. Ed. Rainer A. Müller. Bibliothek des deutschen Staatsdenkens 8. Insel Verlag, Frankfurt am Main and Leipzig 1998.

Paul Walther of Guglingen: *Fratris Pauli Waltheri Guglingensis Itinerarium in Terram Sanctam et ad Sanctam Catharinam*. Ed. Matthias Sollweck. Bibliothek des Literarischen Vereins Stuttgart 192. Literarischer Verein, Tübingen 1892.

Johannes of Schele: Sequuntur avisamenta reformacionis in curia et extra in utroque statu, ecclesiastico et seculari, secundum Johannem episcopum Lubicensem, qui infrascripta hinc inde collegit. *Quellen zur Kirchenreform im Zeitalter der grossen Konzilien des 15. Jahrhunderts. Zweiter Teil*. Eds. Jürgen Miethke and Lorenz Weinrich. Ausgewählte Quellen zur deutschen Geschichte des Mittelalters 38b. Wissenschaftliche Buchgesellllschaft, Darmstadt 2002, 202–237.

Reformation Kaiser Sigismund. Ed. Heinrich Koller. MGH Staatsschriften des späteren Mittelalters 6. Anton Hiersemann, Stuttgart 1964.

Regesten Kaiser Friedrichs III. 1986 (1440–1493) Band 4: Die Urkunden und Briefe aus dem Stadtarchiv Frankfurt am Main. Ed. Paul-Joachim Heinig. Böhlau, Vienna et al. 1986.

Tucher, Hans: *Die 'Reise ins Gelobte Land' Hans Tuchers des Älteren (1479–1480). Untersuchungen zur Überlieferung und kritische Edition eines spätmittelalterlichen Reiseberichts*. Ed. Randall Herz. Wissensliteratur im Mittelalter 38. Dr. Ludwig Reichert Verlag, Wiesbaden 2002.

Vincent of Beauvais: *Speculum quadruplex sive Speculum maius naturale, doctrinale, morale, historiale*. Vol. 4, *Speculum historiale*. Akademische Druck- u. Verlagsanstalt, Graz 1964.

Research literature

Annas, Gabriele: Gehorsamkeyt ist tod, gerechtigkeyt leyt not, nichts stet in rechter ordenung. Zum Begriff der "Gerechtigkeit" in Schriften zur Reichsreform des 15. Jahrhunderts. *Gerechtigkeit im gesellschaftlichen Diskurs des späteren Mittelalters*. Eds. Petra Schulte, Gabriele Annas and Michael Rothmann. Zeitschrift für Historische Forschung, Beiheft 47. Dunckler-Humblot, Berlin 2012, 223–254.

Angenendt, Arnold: *Geschichte der Religiosität im Mittelalter*. Wissenschaftliche Buchgesellschaft, Darmstadt 1997.

Bader, Karl Siegfried: Kaiserliche und ständische Reformgedanken in der Reichsreform des endenden 15. Jahrhunderts. *Historisches Jahrbuch* 73/1954, 74–94.

Barber, Richard and Juliet Barker: *Tournaments. Jousts, Chivalry and Pageants in the Middle Ages*. The Boydell Press, Woodbridge 2000.

Bellomo, Elena: Rewriting the Past: The Conquest of the Holy Sepulchre in the Memory of Italian Communal Cities. *Jerusalem the Golden. The origins and impact of the First Crusade*. Eds. Susan B. Edgington and Luis García-Guijarro. Brepols, Turnout 2014, 275–290.

Bisaha, Nancy: Pope Pius II and the Crusade. *Crusading in the Fifteenth Century: Message and Impact*. Ed. Norman Housley. Palgrave Macmillan, Houndsmill 2004, 39–52.

Bookmann, Hartmut: Zu den Wirkungen der "Reform Kaiser Siegmunds". *Deutsches Archiv für Erforschung des Mittelalters* 35/1979, 514–543.

Bosselmann-Cyran, Kristian: Einige Anmerkungen zum Palästina- und Ägyptenkompendium des Bernhard von Breidenbach (1486). *Kairoer Germanistische Studien* 8/1994–1995, 95–115.

Brady, Thomas A.: Maximilian I and the Imperial Reform at the Diet of Mainz, 1495. *Maximilians Ruhmeswerk. Künste und Wissenschaften im Umkreis Kaiser Maximilians I.* Eds. Jan-Dirk Müller and Hans-Joachim Ziegeler. De Gruyter, Berlin 2015, 31–56.

Crouzet-Pavan, Élisabeth: Récits, images et mythes: Venise dans l'Iter Hiérosolomytain (XIV^c–XVe siècles). *Mélanges de l'École Francaise de Rome, Moyen Age – Temps Moderne* 96.1/1984, 489–535.

Curtius, Ernst Robert: *Europäisches und lateinische Mittelalter.* Francke, Bern and Munich 1973 (8th ed.).

Davies, Hugh William: *Bernhard von Breydenbach and his Journey to the Holy Land, 1483–4: A Bibliography.* J. & J. Leighton, London 1911.

Delumeau, Jean: *La peur en Occident, XIVe–XVIIIe siècles: une cité assiégée.* Fayard cop., Paris 1978.

Denke, Andrea: *Venedig als Station und Erlebnis auf den Reisen der Jerusalempilger im späten Mittelalter.* Historegio 4. M. Hennecke, Remshalden 2001.

Di Cesare, Michelina: *The Pseudo-Historical Image of the Prophet Muhammad in Medieval Latin Literature. A Repertory.* Studien zur Geschichte und Kultur des islamischen Orients 26. De Gruyter, Berlin and Boston 2012.

Dinzelbacher, Peter: *Vision und Visionsliteratur im Mittelalter.* Hiersemann, Stuttgart 1981.

Dinzelbacher, Peter: *Himmel, Hölle, Heilige: Visionen und Kunst im Mittelalter.* Wissenschaftliche Buchgesellschaft, Darmstadt 2002.

Dinzelbacher, Peter: *Angst im Mittelalter: Teufels-, Todes- und Gotteserfahrung: Mentalitätsgeschichte und Ikonographie.* Schöningh, Paderborn and München 1996.

Dumont, Franz, Ferdinand Scherf, and Friedrich Schütz (Eds.): *Mainz – Die Geschichte der Stadt.* Philipp von Zabern, Mainz 1999 (2nd ed.).

Dutton, Paul Edward: *The Politics of Dreaming in the Carolingian Empire.* University of Nebraska Press, Lincoln et al. 1994.

Feldkamp, Michael F.: *Vom Jerusalempilger zum Grabesritter: Geschichte des Ritterordens vom Heiligen Grab.* Patrimonium, Aachen 2016.

Fried, Johannes: *Der Schleier der Erinnerung: Grundzüge einer historischen Memorik.* Beck, Munich 2004.

Fuchs, Reimar Walter: Bernhard von Breidenbach (Breydenbach). *Neue Deutsche Bibliographie.* Vol. 2. Ed. Bayerische Akademie der Wissenschaften. Duncker & Humblot, Berlin 1955, 571.

Fuchs, Reimar Walter: Die Mainzer Frühdrucke mit Buchholzschnitten 1480–1500. *Archiv für Geschichte des Buchwesens* 2/1960, 1–129.

Ganz-Blättler, Ursula: *Andacht und Abenteuer: Berichte europäischer Jerusalem- und Santiago-Pilger (1320–1520).* Jakobus-Studien 4. Narr, Tübingen 1991.

Gardiner, Eileen: *Visions of Heaven and Hell Before Dante.* Italica Press, New York 1989.

Handyside, Philip: *The Old French William of Tyre.* Brill, Leiden 2015.

Hankins, James: Renaissance Crusaders: Humanist Crusade Literature in the Age of Mehmed II. *Dumbarton Oaks Papers* 49/1995, 111–207.

Heinig, Paul-Joachim: Zwischen Kaiser und Konzil: Die "Reformdiskussion" in der Mainzer Kirche. *Die Reform von Kirche und Reich zur Zeit der Konzilien von Konstanz (1414–1418) und Basel (1431–1449).* Eds. Ivan Hlaváček and Alexander Patschovsky. Universitätsverlag Konstanz, Konstanz 1996, 109–133.

Heinz, Stefan: Der Staatsmann. Erzbischof Berthold von Henneberg (1441/42–1504). *Schrei nach Gerechtigkeit: Leben am Mittelrhein am Vorabend der Reformation.* Eds. Winfried Wilhelmy and Anja Lempges. Schnell & Steiner, Regensburg 2015, 46–49.

Helmrath, Johannes: The German "Reichstage" and the Crusade. *Crusading in the Fifteenth Century: Message and Impact.* Ed. Norman Housley. Palgrave Macmillan, Houndsmill 2004, 53–69 and 191–203.

Hemels, Joan: Mahnmal statt Jubiläum: Nährboden und Grundlage kirchlicher Zensur vor und nach 1479. *Communicatio Socialis* 12/1979, 221–244.

Herkenhoff, Michael: *Die Darstellung außereuropäischer Welten in Drucken deutscher Offizinen des 15. Jahrhunderts.* Akademie Verlag, Berlin 1996.

Herz, Randall: Briefe Hans Tuchers d. Ä. aus dem Heiligen Land und andere Aufzeichnungen. *Mitteilungen des Vereins für die Geschichte der Stadt Nürnberg* 84/1997, 61–92.

Hille-Coates, Gabrielle: Bibelsprachen – Heilige Sprachen: Zur Legitimierung des Hauptsprachenmodells im Spannungsfeld von Latein und Volkssprache im Mittelalter. *Muster und Funktionen kultureller Selbst- und Fremdwahrnehmung: Beiträge zur internationalen Geschichte der sprachlichen und literarischen Emanzipation.* Eds. Ulrike-Christine Sander and Fritz Paul. Wallstein, Göttingen 2000, 204–238.

Hobbins, Daniel: *Authorship and Publicity before Print: Jean Gerson and the Transformation of Late Medieval Learning.* University of Pennsylvania Press, Philadelphia 2009.

Höfert, Almut: *Den Feind beschreiben. "Türkengefahr" und europäisches Wissen über das Osmanische Reich (1450–1600).* Historische Studien 35. Campus, Frankfurt am Main 2003.

Hollegger, Manfred: *Maximilian I (1459–1519).* Kohlhammer, Stuttgart 2005.

Honemann, Volker: Der Laie als Leser. *Laienfrömmigkeit im späten Mittelalter. Formen, Funktionen, politisch-soziale Zusammenhänge.* Ed. Klaus Schreiner. Oldenbourg Verlag, Munich 1992, 241–251.

Housley, Norman: *The Later Crusades, 1274–1580: From Lyons to Alcazar.* Oxford University Press, Oxford 1992.

Kellermann, Karina: Vom Spiel mit den Normen zur Normierung: Die narrative Konstruktion von Gegenwelten in Zeitklage und politischer Polemik des Spätmittelalters. *Text und Normativität im deutschen Mittelalter: XX. Anglo-German Colloquium.* Eds. Elke Brüggen, Franz-Josef Holznagel, Sebastian Coxon and Almut Suerbaum. De Gruyter, Berlin and Boston 2012, 353–367.

Kellermann, Karina: "Kaiser Friderich ist komen!" Der Wiederkehrmythos und die frühe Vision eines 1000 jährigen deutschen Reiches. *Gründungsmythen Europas im Mittelalter.* Eds. Michael Bernsen, Matthias Becher and Elke Brüggen. Gründungsmythen Europas in Literatur, Musik und Kunst 6. V & R unipress, Bonn University Press, Göttingen 2013, 177–199.

Koller, Heinrich: *Friedrich III.* Wissenschaftliche Buchgesellschaft, Darmstadt 2005.

Krüger, Sabine: Das kirchliche Turnierverbot im Mittelalter. *Das ritterliche Turnier im Mittelalter. Beiträge zu einer vergleichenden Formen- und Verhaltensgeschichte des Rittertums.* Ed. Josef Fleckenstein. Veröffentlichungen des Max-Planck-Instituts für Geschichte 80. Vandenhoeck & Ruprecht, Göttingen 1985, 401–422.

Lapina, Elizabeth: *Warfare and the Miraculous in the Chronicles of the First Crusade.* The Pennsylvania State University Press, University Park, Pennsylvania 2015.

Le Goff, Jacques: *The Birth of Purgatory.* Chicago University Press, Chicago 1984.

Leopold, Antony: *How to Recover the Holy Land: The Crusade Proposals of the Late Thirteenth and Early Fourteenth Centuries.* Ashgate, Aldershot 2000.

Levison, Wilhelm: Die Politik in Jenseitsvisionen des frühen Mittelalters. *Aus Rheinischer und fränkischer Frühzeit.* L. Schwann, Düsseldorf 1948, 229–46.

Linder, Amnon: *Raising arms: Liturgy in the struggle to liberate Jerusalem in the late Middle Ages.* Brepols, Turnhout 2003.

Lyons, Martyn: *A History of Reading and Writing in the Western World.* Palgrave Macmillan, New York 2009.

Manion, Lee: *Narrating the Crusades: Loss and Recovery in Medieval and Early Modern English Literature.* Cambridge University Press, Cambridge 2014.

Märtl, Claudia: Zum "Traum" des Hans von Hermannsgrün. *Zeitschrift für Historische Forschung* 14/1987, 257–264.

Meyer, Carla: New Methods and Old Records: Awareness and Perceptions of the Near East in Hans Tucher's Account of his Journey to the Holy Land and Egypt. *The Medieval History Journal* 15.1/2012, 25–62.

Minnich, Nelson H.: The Fifth Lateran Council and Preventive Censorship of Printed Books. *Annali della Scuola Normale Superiore di Pisa. Classe di Lettere e Filosofia, Serie 5,* 2.1/2010, 67–104.

Moodey, Elizabeth J.: *Illuminated Crusader Histories for Philip the Good of Burgundy.* Brepols, Turnhout 2012.

Muir, Edward: The Doge as primus inter pares: Interregnum Rites in Early Sixteenth-century Venice. *Essays Presented to Myron P. Gilmore.* Vol. 1, *History.* Eds. Silvio Bertelli and Gloria Ramakus. Villa I Tatti 2. La Nuova Italia, Florence 1978, 145–160.

Muir, Edward: *Civic Ritual in Renaissance Venice.* Princeton University Press, New Jersey 1981.

Niehr, Klaus: Als ich das selber erkundet vnd gesehen hab: Wahrnehmung und Darstellung des Fremden in Bernhard von Breydenbachs Peregrinationes in Terram Sanctam und anderen Pilgerberichten des ausgehenden Mittelalters. *Gutenberg-Jahrbuch* 76/2001, 269–300.

Nolte, Cordula: Erlebnis und Erinnerung. Fürstliche Pilgerfahrten nach Jerusalem im 15. Jahrhundert. *Fremdheit und Reisen im Mittelalter.* Eds. Irene Erfen and Karl-Heinz Spieß. Franz Steiner Verlag, Stuttgart 1997, 65–92.

Pallmann, Heinrich: Des Erzbischofs Berthold von Mainz ältestes Censuredict. *Archiv für Geschichte des deutschen Buchhandels* 9/1884, 238–241.

Paravicini, Werner (ed.): *Europäische Reiseberichte des späten Mittelalters: Eine analytische Biographie.* Vol. 1, *Deutsche Reiseberichte.* Kieler Werkstücke D 5. Peter Lang, Frankfurt am Main et al. 1994.

Paul, Nicholas: *To Follow in Their Footsteps: The Crusades and Family Memory in the High Middle Ages.* Cornell University Press, Ithaca and London 2012.

Paul, Nicholas and Suzanne Yeager (eds.): *Remembering the Crusades: Myth, Image, and Identity.* Rethinking Theory. Johns Hopkins University Press, Baltimore 2012.

Paviot, Jacques: Burgundy and the Crusades. *Crusading in the fifteenth century Message and Impact.* Ed. Norman Housley. Palgrave Macmillan, Houndsmill 2004, 70–80.

Pfaffenbichler, Matthias: "wie der jung [...] kunig in allen ritterspilen, auch in teutschen und welschen stechen ubertreffenlichen was" – Maximilian I. und das höfische Turnier. *Kaiser Maximilian I.: Der letzte Ritter und das höfische Turnier.* Eds. Sabine Haag et al. Publikation der Reiss-Engelhorn-Museen 61. Schnell & Steiner, Regensburg 2014, 129–139.

Reichert, Folker: *Erfahrung der Welt: Reisen und Kulturbegegnung im späten Mittelalter.* Kohlhammer, Stuttgart et al. 2001.

Reichert, Folker: Zur Illustration des Columbus-Briefes "De insulis inventis" Basel 1493 (GW 7174). *Gutenberg-Jahrbuch* 73/1998, 121–130.

Reichert, Folker: Pilger und Patrone: Aspekte einer gespannten Beziehung. *Venezia incrocio di culture: Percezioni di viaggiatori europei e non-europei a confronto. Atti del Convegno Venezia, 26–27 gennaio 2006.* Eds. Klaus Herbers and Felicitas Schmieder. Centro Tedesco di Studi Venezani. Ricerche 4. Edizioni di storia e letteratura, Rom 2008, 21–31.

Riklin, Alois: *Machteilung: Geschichte der Mischverfassung.* Wissenschaftliche Buchgesellschaft, Darmstadt 2006.

Rösch, Gerhard: Die Festlandspolitik Venedigs im 13. und 14. Jahrhundert. *Geschichte in Wissenschaft und Unterricht* 40/1989, 321–332.

Rösener, Werner: Fürstenhof und Sakralkultur im Kontext spätmittelalterlicher Fürstenspiegel. *Fürstenhof und Sakralkultur im Spätmittelalter*. Eds. Werner Rösener and Carola Fey. Formen der Erinnerung 35. Vandenhoeck & Ruprecht, Göttingen 2008, 21–40.

Roll, Christine: "Sin lieb sy auch eyn kurfurst…". Zur Rolle Bertholds von Henneberg in der Reichsreform. *Kurmainz, das Reichserzkanzleramt und das Reich am Ende des Mittelalters und im 16. und 17. Jahrhundert*. Ed. Peter Claus Hartmann. Geschichtliche Landeskunde 47. Steiner, Stuttgart 1998, 5–43.

Ross, Elizabeth: *Picturing Experience in the Early Printed Book: Breydenbach's Peregrinatio from Venice to Jerusalem*. The Pennsylvania State University Press, University Park, Pennsylvania 2014.

Schäufele, Wolf-Dietrich: *"Defecit Ecclesia": Studien zur Verfallsidee in der Kirchengeschichts-anschauung des Mittelalters*. Veröffentlichungen des Instituts für Europäische Geschichte Mainz. Abt. für Abendländische Religionsgeschichte 213. Philipp von Zabern, Mainz 2006.

Schreiner, Klaus: "Correctio principis". Gedankliche Begründung und geschichtliche Praxis spätmittelalterlicher Herrschaftskritik. *Mentalitäten im Mittelalter. Methodische und inhalt-liche Probleme*. Ed. František Graus. Vorträge und Forschungen 35. Thorbecke, Sigmaringen 1987, 203–256.

Schröder, Stefan: *Zwischen Christentum und Islam: Kulturelle Grenzen in den spätmittelalterli-chen Pilgerberichten des Felix Fabri*. Orbis mediaevalis. Vorstellungswelten des Mittelalters 11. Akademie Verlag, Berlin 2009.

Schröder, Stefan: The Encounter With Islam Between Doctrinal Image and Life Writing: Ambrosius Zeebout's Report of Joos van Ghistele's Travels to the East 1481–1485. *Fear and Loathing in the North: Muslims and Jews in Medieval Scandinavia and the Baltic Region*. Eds. Jonathan Adams and Cordelia Heß. De Gruyter, Berlin and New York 2015, 83–106.

Simon, Gertrud: Untersuchungen zur Topik der Widmungsbriefe mittelalterlicher Geschichts-schreiber bis zum Ende des 12. Jahrhunderts. *Archiv für Diplomatik* 3–4/1957–1958 and 5–6/1959–1960, 52–119 and 73–153.

Struve, Tilman: Utopie und gesellschaftliche Wirklichkeit: Zur Bedeutung des Friedenskaisers im späten Mittelalter. *Historische Zeitschrift* 225/1977, 65–96.

Struve, Tilman: Reform oder Revolution? Das Ringen um eine Neuordnung in Reich und Kirche im Lichte der "Reformatio Sigismundi" und ihrer Überlieferung. *Zeitschrift für die Geschichte des Oberrheins* 126/1978, 73–129.

Struve, Tilman: Kontinuität und Wandel in zeitgenössischen Entwürfen zur Reichsreform des 15. Jahrhunderts. *Sozialer Wandel im Mittelalter: Wahrnehmungsformen, Erklärungsmuster, Regelungsmechanismen*. Ed. Jürgen Miethke. Thorbecke, Sigmaringen 1994, 365–382.

Stuckey, Jace: Charlemagne as Crusader? Memory, Propaganda, and the Many Uses of Charlemagne's Legendary Expedition to Spain. *The Legend of Charlemagne in the Middle Ages: Power, Faith, and Crusade*. Eds. Matthew Gabriele and Jace Stuckey. The New Middle Ages. Palgrave Macmillan, New York 2008, 137–152.

Timm, Frederike: *Der Palästina-Pilgerbericht des Bernhard von Breidenbach und die Holzschnitte Erhard Reuwichs: Die Peregrinatio in terram sanctam (1486) als Propagandainstrument im Mantel der gelehrten Pilgerschrift*. Hauswedell, Stuttgart 2006.

Tolan, John V.: *Saracens: Islam in the Medieval European Imagination*. Columbia University Press, New York 2002.

Tortarolo, Edoardo: Zensur als Institution und Praxis im Europa der Frühen Neuzeit: Ein Überblick. *Die Praktiken der Gelehrsamkeit in der Frühen Neuzeit*. Eds. Helmut Zedelmaier and Martin Mulsow. Niemeyer, Tübingen 2001, 277–294.

Tyerman, Christopher: *The Debate on the Crusades, 1099–2010*. Issues in Historiography. Manchester University Press, Manchester 2011.

Vorgrimler, Herbert: *Geschichte der Hölle.* Wilhelm Fink, München 1993.

Weinmayer, Barbara: *Studien zur Gebrauchssituation früher deutscher Druckprosa: Literarische Öffentlichkeit in Vorreden zu Augsburger Frühdrucken.* Münchener Texte und Untersuchungen zur deutschen Literatur des Mittelalters 77. Artemis, Munich 1982.

Widmann, Hans: *Vom Nutzen und Nachteil der Erfindung des Buchdrucks aus der Sicht der Zeitgenossen des Erfinders.* Gutenberg-Gesellschaft, Mainz 1973.

Wolfzettel, Friedrich: Gottfried von Bouillon: Führer des ersten Kreuzzugs und König von Jerusalem. *Mythen Europas: Schlüsselfiguren der Imagination.* Vol. 2, *Mittelalter.* Eds. Inge B. Milfull and Michael Neumann. Pustet, Regensburg 2004, 126–143.

III
ACTION AND COUNTERACTION:
BOOK CENSORSHIP AND VIOLENCE

The role of pamphlets in church controversies in late medieval England

Eva Schaten

Introduction

On 31 October 1517, Martin Luther published a hand-written list of 95 Latin propositions, according to legend by posting them on the doors of the Castle Church in Wittenberg. Although this episode cannot be verified through contemporary sources, it remains one of the most iconic moments in European history.[1] In publishing a list of controversial doctrines in this manner, Luther would, however, have followed a strong medieval tradition. The doors of churches and town halls had been used

[1] It cannot be conclusively said whether Martin Luther actually posted his list according to the popular belief, although, in the light of a recently discovered letter by his secretary, this seems likely. For a thorough discussion of the available evidence, see the essays collected in Ott and Treu 2008. It would have been in accordance with the academic traditions in Wittenberg to post a list of conclusions as invitation to a *disputatio* – the posting itself would have been executed not by the scholar himself, but by the beadle. See Treu 2008 and Moeller 2008. This opinion is supported by Pettegree 2015, 70–72, who also assumes that in accordance with Wittenberg customs, the 95 theses would have been printed.

as bulletin boards for centuries, displaying official announcements as well as more controversial items. The practice was also widespread in medieval England, where dissenting writings frequently appeared posted on church doors in a manner similar to Luther's famous *Ninety-Five Theses*. These early religious pamphlets may not have had the same impact and achieved the same level of distribution as Luther's famous theses, but they illustrate that long before the Reformation period and its printed pamphlets, it was possible to gain access to the public opinion and to find a large audience for church criticism.

The following study will discuss church controversies of late medieval England that involve the use of pamphlets and examine the role they played in these conflicts. The first controversy is also the most famous: the publication of the famous *Twelve Conclusions of the Lollards* during the Parliament of 1395. This incident will serve to illustrate how the provocative posting of a pamphlet could turn into a turning point in the history of a religious movement, especially in its perception by the authorities. This is a unique event, however, as the roles of pamphlets in religious controversies are diverse. How a pamphlet could be used to strive for support from the laity will be shown in two examples from fourteenth century London, the first during the Blackfriars Council of 1382 and the second during a controversy about the Dominican order in 1314. Pamphlets were often used as supporting medium in sermon controversies, as will be shown in the discussion of incidents involving the Augustinian friar Peter Pateshull in 1387 and the Mendicant Controversy of 1464. The controversies mentioned so far involve vernacular pamphlets and a possible lay audience, but similar publication methods were also used in academic controversies among the clergy. This aspect will be discussed in two incidents involving bishops: the anti-mendicant campaign of Bishop FitzRalph in the 1350s and the earliest pamphlet controversy from the late thirteenth century, involving Archbishop Pecham and the "infamous folio".

Pamphlets in the late medieval manuscript culture

Pamphlet is a term used in historical research to describe a variety of written items, with diverse physical attributes. As it is normally used in connection with short printed tracts, a format popularized in the Reformation period, the use of the term for late medieval manuscripts is controversial.[2] However, as there is a strong tradition that connects pamphlets circulating during medieval church controversies to their printed successors during the Reformation, the term is chosen here to describe not only a format, but also a genre.[3] While the length and format of early modern printed pamphlets were determined by the mechanics of printing and their commercial trading,[4] the manuscript culture knew no such constraints. Late medieval hand-written pamphlets were of varying length and contained a short text or list, hand-written on one or two sheets, which may have been sewed together to create a roll.[5] In the records of late medieval England, a variety of English, Latin, and French nouns was used to describe such small writings: bills or *billae*, *schedulae* or *scripturae*, but also letter, *escrowes* (scrolls), and, quite frequently, libels, if they contained slanderous accusations. Whether the multitude of descriptions for small writings indeed reflects a multitude of formats and layouts cannot be verified today, as very few of them survive as a physical object.[6] This does not mean that the texts published in this way disappeared. Posted pamphlets were noticed and read on site, but also taken down, copied, and circulated – or confiscated by the

---

[2] For a definition of the early modern pamphlet, see Raymond 2006, especially 4–26.

[3] For the tradition leading from medieval controversies to Reformation pamphlets, see Scase 2010.

[4] Raymond describes printed pamphlets as a "short, quarto book", with an extent of one to twelve sheets, which made them cheap to produce, as they could easily be sold unbound. Raymond 2006, 5, 81–83.

[5] There are other terms in use to describe these short writings, such as broadside, see Justice 1994, and bills; see the research by Wendy Scase, for example Scase 2007.

[6] Surviving pamphlets, seditious bills, and petitions show that the roll format was a popular format for lists of demands; see the numerous examples in Scase 2007.

authorities as evidence. Many were copied into chronicles, court records, or commonplace books. Some of these texts had a considerable afterlife, proving that pamphlet posting was a very effective way of publication in the manuscript culture, especially considering that texts published by posting were occasional literature, connected to current events, and in most cases ephemeral.[7] The number of copies is unknown for most incidents, yet chronicle reports seem to indicate that more than one copy was posted at a single location. Reports from medieval Bohemia point to a veritable mass production, resulting in 80–300 copies of some Hussite pamphlets, even though this is not supported by surviving manuscripts.[8]

Religious pamphlets in the manuscript culture were no commercial product (at least, there is no record of trading). They were meant to circulate, handed around and be copied privately. The point of publication was the posting or handing out of one or several copies in a public place, especially church doors, a practice that became more frequent in the last quarter of the fourteenth century, coinciding with the general rise in literacy.[9] The religious pamphlets of medieval England correlate to Hruza's definition for Hussite manifestos: they are texts, whose intended function is to transmit subjective thoughts to a wider public, with the intention to influence the audience's opinion and acts.[10] Pamphlets were "expressions of social division, they challenged behaviour deemed abusive in similarly abusive language."[11]

---

[7] Bill-posting as method of publication has been described as "evanescent," not meant to make a lasting impact; Hanna 2005, 32.

[8] Šmahel 1992, 263.

[9] Justice 1994, 29. Numerous examples are given in Scase 1998.

[10] "Als Manifeste kann man Texte bezeichnen, deren intendierte kommunikative Funktion aus der Vermittlung von subjektivem Gedankengut an ein größeres Publikum, das in seiner Meinung und in seinem Handeln beeinflußt werden sollte, bestand." Hruza 1999, 82.

[11] Hanna 2005, 33.

The *Twelve Conclusions of the Lollards*

This is observable in the famous example of the *Twelve Conclusions of the Lollards*, posted in early 1395 at St Paul's Cathedral and Westminster Abbey during a session of Parliament. The authors describe themselves as "pore men, tresoreris of Cryst and his apostlis," who wish to inform the lords and commons of Parliament about "certeyn conclusionis and treuthis for þe reformaciun of holi chiche of Yngelond."[12] The list of conclusions included a rejection of orthodox doctrines such as priesthood instated through ritual, celibacy, transubstantiation, exorcisms, and pilgrimages. Behind this campaign were members of the Lollard movement, although their exact identity is unknown.[13] This movement, which was famously described as "premature Reformation",[14] originated in the last quarter of the fourteenth century and was inspired by the writings and teaching of the Oxford scholar John Wycliffe.

The list posted in 1395 is one of the earliest documents connected to the Lollard movement. No original has survived, but the contents are known, primarily from a refutation written soon after the event by the English Dominican prior Roger Dymmok, who quoted each of the twelve points in full before refuting them.[15] Dymmok gives the

---

[12] Hudson 1978, 24–29.

[13] "Lollardi in hoc Parliamento, nacti occasionem ex regis absencia, cum suis fautoribus in omnem maliciam efferebantur, figentes publice super hoscia Sancti Pauli et Westmonasterii abhominabiles cleri accusaciones, et hactenus inauditas conclusiones. ... Et ut euidencius demonstrem pessimos illorum conceptus, conclusiones hic inseram quas fixerunt super oscia supradicta sub isto prohemio..." [followed by text of the bill] Walsingham 2011, 13.

[14] See Hudson 1988.

[15] Dymmok's refutation is edited in Dymmok 1922. The *Twelve Conclusions* are also printed in Hudson 1978, 24–29. Refutations, also called confutations, were a tool normally employed in academic debates; see Clasen 1960, 176. They were a popular tool used by orthodox theologians to counter heretical writings. The citation of the original passages had the side effect of preserving a number of texts that otherwise would have vanished, as was the case with the English text of the *Twelve Conclusions*. Refutations were directed towards a scholarly audience and written exclusively in Latin, even if the refuted text was in the vernacular.

conclusions in both an English and a Latin version.[16] The fact that the document was posted publicly is not mentioned once, but repeatedly. The posting during Parliament meant a large presence of secular lords and clergy, who would have been both literate and influential, guaranteeing an audience. For Dymmok, this is the most offensive part of the affair: as the posting happened during Parliament he took it as an insult to the King, to whom he dedicated his work.[17] The form of address used for the Twelve Conclusions even resembles the one used for parliamentary petitions.[18] All in all, the publication method, time, and place, as well as the format, of the *Twelve Conclusions* was the "most provocative way of publication."[19]

The role of the Twelve Conclusions for the history of the Lollard movement was pivotal: their publication was, as one historian put it, "the quintessential and crucial literary-political gesture of Lollardy."[20] The publication embodied the final step in the development of the movement from the academic environment, where it had begun in the wake of John Wycliffe, into the wider world, carried now by laymen and -women. This step was made out in the open, visible to the inhabitants of London and Westminster and the high clergy and knights assembled for Parliament. The posting re-opened a conflict that had lain dormant for some years and it had far-reaching consequences.[21] The convocation of the province of Canterbury, which sat at the same time as Parliament, made an appeal to the King "to exert the secular arm" against the Lollard sect.[22] This was a demand to make the crime of heresy subject to capital punishment, an important step in the

---

[16] The Latin version also survives in a slightly different version in Shirley 1858, 360–369.

[17] See Dymmok 1922, xxxiii and Scase 2005, 288.

[18] Scase 2007, 88.

[19] Scase 2007, 94.

[20] Scase 2005, 283.

[21] There is neither secular nor ecclesiastical legislation concerning Wycliffism between 1382 and 1395 apart from royal proclamations against unlawful conventicles, which may or may not have been connected to the emerging Lollard movement; see Calendar 1902, Richard II, Vol. IV: 1389–1392, 530–531 and Rymer 1726, VII, 746.

[22] Scase 2005, 286. See Bray 2005, IV, 159–160.

development of anti-heresy legislation in England. Behind this motion was the Lord Chancellor Thomas Arundel, then Archbishop of York. A few years later, Arundel would become Archbishop of Canterbury under Henry IV and orchestrate the church's campaign against the Lollard movement, which included the introduction of capital punishment for heresy in 1401 and the prohibition of the English Bible translation in 1407. But the starting point for this new phase of persecution was the posting of the Twelve Conclusions in 1395.[23]

Pamphlet posting at the Blackfriars Council

The pamphlets posted in 1395 were not the first writings connected to Wycliffism that circulated in this manner. At the Provincial Council held in the Blackfriars priory in London in 1382, doctrines taken from John Wycliffe's teachings had become the subject of a formal condemnation for the first time. They were classified as heretical or erroneous.[24] On 18 June, almost four weeks after the condemnation, Wycliffe's Oxford pupils, Nicholas Hereford, Philip Repingdon, and John Aston were summoned to appear before the Council for an interrogation. They were expected to make a statement as to whether they believed in the doctrines recently condemned.[25] While it seems as

[23] 1395 saw a marked increase in anti-Lollard legislation. In July, the chancellor of Oxford received the order to "remove and expel from the university all Lollards there dwelling, and all others notoriously suspect of heresy ..." Calendar 1902, Richard II, Vol. V: 1392–1396, 434. On the same day, an examination of John Wycliffe's *Trialogus* by all doctors of theology at Oxford was ordered; Calendar 1902, Richard II, Vol. V: 1392–1396, 437–438. This was reinforced by a papal bull, sent on 17 September of that year, which ordered the archbishops of Canterbury and York to make enquiries about those commonly called Lollards. A similar bull was sent to the English king; Bliss 1903, 513–516, see also Hudson 1988, 92 and McHardy 1997.

[24] Printed from the register of Archbishop Courtenay in Wilkins 1737, III, 157–158. The condemned list did not mention the author's name, however, and John Wycliffe as a person was never brought to trial for heresy during his lifetime.

[25] The chain of events is described in Kelly 1999, 11–17.

if Archbishop Courtenay and the assembled clergy had the high ground and the Oxford scholars were powerless victims, the actual situation was rather different. When Wycliffe had been interrogated by Courtenay on two earlier occasions, riots had been narrowly avoided, as the townsfolk alternately took the side of the Archbishop and Wycliffe.[26] Only one year before, the Peasants' Revolt of 1381 had devastated the City of London and Courtenay's predecessor Simon Sudbury had been beheaded by the rebels. So in 1382, the fear of another uprising was always present and not unjustified. The involvement of the lay population in the proceedings against John Wycliffe had to be avoided to prevent another violent altercation. Archbishop Courtenay evidently took steps to confine the discussion to the walls of the Blackfriars priory and restrict the audience to educated clergy. His examination of Hereford, Repingdon, and Aston relied on established procedures in cases of academic dissent and was held in Latin. This was appropriate insofar that all three were clergymen, Oxford masters of theology, and high-standing members of the academic community. Their expected behaviour would have been the submission to correction, acknowledgement of the judgement of the council and refusal to further believe in doctrines now proven to be wrong. The alternative would have been a potential conviction of heresy. Courtenay probably expected a quick process, with a complete retraction by the three men, as had been the outcome in similar cases.[27]

The suspects did not play along, however: John Aston refused to make his answers in Latin, because, as he said, the present members of the laity would not understand him. He refused to observe the linguistic boundary set by the Archbishop and deliberately provoked the council. He was pronounced a heretic and sent to prison.[28] His Oxford colleagues Nicholas Hereford and Philip Repingdon appeared before the council on 18 June, but also refused to submit themselves to correction.

---

[26] Walsingham 2003, 84–86 and 197.

[27] A recent precedent for this procedure was the condemnation of 30 doctrines in 1368, most of which were taken from the writings of the Oxford theologian Uthred of Bolton. The list was likewise anonymous and as Uthred made no effort to affirm his opinions after the condemnation, he was neither punished for heresy nor lost any privileges. For this case, see Knowles 1963.

[28] Wilkins 1737, III, 164.

Presented with the condemned propositions and asked about their stance on them, they demanded a copy of the list to prepare a defence, which was granted to them. Appearing again at the next session of the council on 20 June, they brought a written reply to the accusation. The reply was again subject to an examination and six of the points made by Hereford and Repingdon in their defence were declared heretical.[29] However, their sentence was adjourned for a week until 27 June.[30]

The proceedings had taken part in the sheltered, scholarly, Latin environment of an ecclesiastical council. Faced with the verdict, Wycliffe's pupils tried to gain the support of the lay population, who had some years previously shown to be capable of disrupting the proceedings against John Wycliffe himself.[31] On 19 June two *Confessions* were published, both on the subject of the Eucharist: one was written communally by Hereford and Repingdon and the other by John Aston, while still under arrest.[32] The manner of publication of these short texts is not recorded in detail, but a later source says that Aston's pamphlet was distributed in the streets and squares of London, both in an English

[29] Shirley 1858, 319–325, 326–328.
[30] Wilkins 1737, III, 160–161, 163; Kelly 1999, 13, 16.
[31] In February 1377, Wycliffe had been summoned to appear before the archbishop. The hearing was disrupted by a mob of angry Londoners showing their contempt for Wycliffe's patrons John of Gaunt and Henry Percy. A year later, a similar hearing at Lambeth Palace was disrupted again by a group of citizens, who were this time in support of Wycliffe. See Lahey 2009, 17–19.
[32] The two *Confessions* have a very similar introductory and closing phrase, which implies that the three prisoners must have consulted with each other while composing them. Both *Confessions* survive in Bodl. MS Bodley 647, f. 70r–v and are edited from there in Aston 1987, 328–330 (all quotations from this edition). There is another copy of both texts in Henry Knighton's chronicle; Martin 1995, 276–281. Knighton's source for the two documents was likely Philip Repingdon himself, who was likewise a canon of Leicester. Repingdon's name is deleted in the address, while Aston's and Hereford's remain. Aston's bill in a Latin translation is also found in Shirley 1858, 329–330.

and a Latin version.[33] The one by Hereford and Repingdon, who also described themselves as being in the archbishop's prison, was probably published in a similar way. So instead of keeping the whole affair within the walls of the Blackfriars monastery, with a clerical audience and confined to Latin, Archbishop Courtenay received the response he had demanded in English and addressed not to the clergy, but to "alle cristen men" and "alle men and alle wymen to whom þis confession comes to here." Yet while the three men were not ready to bow to the authority of the council and submit themselves to correction, they also did not intend to implicate themselves further by publishing unorthodox views. The statements about the Eucharist in both *Confessions* are of "sacramental orthodoxy".[34] Other controversial topics are not mentioned. The purpose of this pamphlet campaign was a defence against an unjustified excommunication, not to further publish Wycliffite thoughts or provoke a further examination for heresy.

The two *Confessions* could not be condemned as erroneous: although their authors were considered suspects of heresy, the texts themselves were orthodox. They also did not qualify as treasonous, as they contained no political criticism or a call for rebellion. Therefore, no legal instrument for suppression was available. The only answer the council *could* make was the excommunication of the three suspects as heretics, which was pronounced on the 20 June 1382. This verdict and the reasons behind it were published in a manner similar to the one used by Aston: the clergy distributed copies of the verdict in the streets and squares. This was not the normal procedure to announce an excommunication and might have been an "ill-advised step," as it further increased the public interest.[35]

---

[33] "Magistrum quoque Johannem Astone nolentem ad earum aliquam quomodolibet respondere, damnavit ibidem, et tradidit custodiae seculari. Qui damnatus in excusationem sui erroris, et commotionem populi contra archiepiscopum et clerum sibi in hac parte faventem; talem scripsit confessionem in Anglico et Latino, et eam in plurimis schedulis fecit distribui per vicos Londoniarum et plateas" Shirley 1858, 329.

[34] Cole 2008, 174. Cole presumes that the two texts were copied into Bodl. MS Bodley 647 along with strongly Wycliffite texts as "propaganda against [Hereford and Repingdon] as turncoats." See also Larsen 2011, 200.

[35] Aston 1987, 298; see also Kelly 1999, 18 and Larsen 2011, 201. The notice of excommunication is printed in Shirley 1858, 331.

If anyone in London had been so far unaware of the proceedings at the Blackfriars Council, they now heard about the conflict through an official announcement. Hereford and Repingdon immediately made an appeal in protest of the excommunication. This appeal again was written on a piece of paper and posted to church doors in London, this time at St Paul's Cathedral and St Mary-le-Bow, a peculiar to the archbishop of Canterbury and the seat of the ecclesiastical court for the Province of Canterbury. The text of the appeal does not survive, but the answer made by Archbishop Courtenay does, dated 1 July 1382.[36] Unsurprisingly, he did not grant the appeal, which he called frivolous and therefore false and malicious. For a publication, he again mimics his adversaries: The answer was to be posted in the same spots as the appeal, but also on other church doors.

The process against the three Oxford men at the Blackfriars Council as Archbishop Courtenay intended it, was to be conducted in a formal and established manner, based on the inquisitorial method, in Latin, and according to academic precedence.[37] The outcome was very different: The laity became involved by the use of the English language, as insisted on by John Aston, and the flurry of pamphlets posted on various church doors, which guaranteed that the population of London was kept up to date on the proceedings. However, there were no direct consequences of this involvement of the public and there was no demonstration of support or a release of John Aston from prison. Instead, in the course of 1382, all three men eventually returned to orthodoxy and made recantations. Philip Repingdon even became a bishop later in life.[38]

A pamphlet campaign of Dominican apostates in 1314

The search for publicity also was the driving force behind a pamphlet campaign in the early fourteenth century, which likewise concerned the Blackfriars priory and aimed at exposing intramural proceedings to a

[36] Wilkins 1737, III, 165.
[37] Kelly 1999, 12.
[38] For their recantations, see Bray 2005, IV, 53–54.

larger audience – it was also ultimately unsuccessful. In 1314, a group of apostate Dominicans, who had recently left the London priory, began to accuse their order of misconduct. These accusations had first been made at the Dominican general chapter held at London on 11 June 1314, but went unheard. An attempt was made to silence the critics,[39] who instead decided to leave the monastery and change their approach from internal criticism to public whistle-blowing. They devised a pamphlet campaign, intending to catch the attention of the population of London, other clergymen, and the ecclesiastical authorities. Their method of publication was a combination of public reading and posting. In the *Letter-Book of London*, the incident is described as follows:

> [The apostates] have published defamatory writings, and have caused the same in public places within the city aforesaid to be read and recited, and have left copies of the same in those places fixed upon the walls.[40]

Two versions of the published text survive, both in Latin (there is no evidence for a vernacular version): One copy is part of a chronicle, the continuation of the *Flores Historiarum* written at Westminster, whereas another can be found among the state papers in the Public Record Office. The pamphlets had apparently been taken down and transmitted to the authorities. They were not destroyed but treated as evidence, copied, and filed, with identification of the persons involved.[41] The accusations voiced in this manner were directed at the system of punishment within the Dominican order: Friars who had offended the rules were held in small cells within the convent, where many allegedly died from the foul air and discomfort. The main culprit was the master general of the Dominican Order, Berengarius de Landora.

---

[39] Röhrkasten 2004, 528–529.
[40] Riley 1868, 111–113. The original is written in French and calendared in Sharpe 1903, fol. xxvb. See also Hanna 2005, 33.
[41] Laud 1890, 161–167. The copy among the State Papers (PRO E135/1/12) is edited in Little 1890. See also "Reference E135/1/12" in Discovery Catalogue, The National Archives, Kew (http://discovery.nationalarchives.gov.uk/details/r/C3408176, accessed 7/12/2016). The two versions are not identical and present several variant readings.

Unfortunately for the apostates, the king took the side of the Dominicans: In his early youth, Edward II had been educated by Dominicans and remained close to this order his whole life. So in a letter patent dated 18 September the mayor and sheriffs of the city of London were ordered to take countermeasures and arrest all vagabond Dominican friars.[42] Moreover, a prohibition was to be made

> ... that any person shall, on pain of heavy forfeiture to us, write any such manner of writings containing defamation of the said Order, or publish the same, or give aid to those writing or publishing the same, either secretly or openly.[43]

A Latin note following the writ on the Patent roll confirms that its contents had been published: it had been read aloud at St Paul's Cathedral, in the presence of members of the clergy and "many persons then writing there", which is an allusion to professional scribes transacting their business within the church.[44] This choice of location probably implied a warning to the scribes not to copy the apostates' writings. The official reaction indicates that the pamphlets were taken as a serious threat to the reputation of the Dominican order. Publicly voiced criticism by members of the order could not be ignored, as it had a high credibility.

Further details about the affair in London are not known. But the campaign made waves beyond the local level. Archbishop Reynolds of Canterbury was concerned that through the pamphlets the controversy would spread to Oxford, as is evident from his letter sent to the chancellor of that university.[45] Reynolds speaks of *libelli famosi* that were circulated by the apostates and warns the chancellor not to prohibit

---

[42] "Mandate directed to the mayor and sheriffs of the city of London, for the arrest of all vagabond friars of the Order of Preachers in their city. They are strictly to prohibit the publication of defamatory writings by such apostates." Calendar 1898, 176.

[43] Riley 1868, 111–113.

[44] Riley 1868, 113, n17.

[45] Edited in Little 1890, 112.

the circulation within the university.[46] On the same day, the 1 October 1314, an order was sent by the royal chancery to the sheriff of Oxford, who was also told to arrest all vagabond Dominicans and deliver them to their order for punishment. Also, "he is to forbid within his bailiwick the publication of scurrilous writings against the order, and to arrest the apostates publishing such, and all persons aiding them."[47] These documents might imply that the apostates left London and tried to find a more sympathetic audience. Blackfriars Hall at Oxford had strong ties with the London convent, but other members of the university might have been more supportive, as the university was at that time engaged in a heated dispute with the Dominicans over the granting of degrees.[48] The importance of pamphlets as medium for transmitting a controversy beyond the local level was recognized by the archbishop.

Even if the king did not support their protest, and the apostates were arrested for their efforts, their publication strategy was successful. The public condemnation of their action in St Paul's Cathedral guaranteed the highest degree of publicity. The initial attempt of voicing the criticism had been made behind closed doors at the general chapter, but after the apostates had left the priory, a pamphlet campaign had been the only available communication channel for further dissemination – and one that certainly had made a deep impact.

The sermon of Peter Pateshull

Another friar, who had left his monastery and started to publish complaints about his order, was the Augustinian Peter Pateshull. In 1387, he purchased a license to become a so-called papal chaplain, which was a privilege that freed him from his order.[49] Pateshull left

---

[46] The term 'libelli famosi' goes back to the Codex Justinianus. It was taken over into the Canon Law and used throughout the Middle Ages as legal term for defamatory and slanderous writings. See Werner 2007, 57.

[47] Calendar 1898, 186.

[48] See Gelber 2004, 39–42 and 66–71.

[49] Hudson 2004.

the Augustinian priory, but remained in London and began to preach about the immorality of the mendicant orders. In one of his sermons, he even urged the assembled crowd of about a hundred people to destroy their religious houses immediately. A riot was narrowly avoided by the intervention of another Augustinian, Thomas Ashburn. The chronicler Thomas Walsingham gives an account of the following events:

> Meanwhile the Lollards, who still had friar Pateshull with them, urged him, inasmuch as he had just been distracted while preaching, to compose a document in which to describe all the charges he had made, and more if he knew of any. He immediately fell in with their evil schemes, and composed the document, in which he accused certain of his own friars of the murder of various of their own brethren. In order that his words should be the more believable, he gave the names of those murdered and specified those who were tortured. ... When he had completed the document (*cartam*) he pinned it upon the doors of the church of St Paul's in London, so that the friars might suffer even greater discomfiture. ... Many of the 'hooded' knights who read this document declared with assurance that everything which was written in it was true. They therefore took some extracts from it so that they could satisfy their own malice at some future time.[50]

This time, the publication of a pamphlet took place after the conflict, and it was also the endpoint of this particular controversy: After an order for arrest was made, Peter Pateshull fled the city and was never heard from again.[51]

Pateshull published his pamphlet to support and supplement his sermon. Transferring a sermon into writing to preserve it for a wider

---

[50] Walsingham 2003, 819–821.

[51] There is an order for arrest, made out on 18 July 1387 for one William Pateshull; see Calendar 1900, 386. Although there is no indication that Pateshull was influenced by John Wycliffe's ideas – his animosity against the friars seems to have come from personal experience – his preaching and publishing certainly was in accordance with the anti-clerical sentiments of the growing Lollard movement. The 'hooded knights' mentioned by Walsingham were certainly members of the movement, named for their habit of not removing hats in the presence of the sacrament. See Capgrave 1983, 191.

audience was no unusual practice in late medieval England.[52] There are several sermons known to have circulated on their own in pamphlet format, concerning a current controversial topic. They were not intended as model sermons or preaching aids, but part of a specific controversy, with the intention to enhance the range of the sermon.[53] Pateshull, as well as the hooded knights, had an interest in enlarging the controversy and the transfer to writing would result in a further circulation of Pateshull's complaints, so very valuable to church critics as an insider's view. At this time, John Wycliffe had been dead for four years and his immediate pupils had recanted. Pateshull's pamphlet – which presumably was written in English – could potentially add to the growing corpus of Wycliffite literature.[54] Again, after the scandal created by his sermon, he no longer had access to the pulpit as communication channel. Although it had not been his first choice, a written publication of his statements by posting pamphlets was the only available method of dissemination.

The London mendicant controversy of 1464

The mendicant controversy of 1464 is another example for pamphlets as part of a religious dispute and as supplementary medium to sermons.

[52] This has to be set apart from the usual model sermon collections or cycles intended as preaching aids such as the English Wycliffite sermons and John Mirk's *Festial*. For these, see Spencer 1993, 269–320.

[53] See, for example, William Ive's sermon of 1464 (see below, fn. 59) and the sermons delivered by the Cistercian William Rymyngton, later chancellor of Oxford, at the York convocations in 1372 and 1373. These have been described as "some of the fiercest denunciation of fellow-clergy to be found in all English sermon literature" Owst 1961, 271. The sermons survive in a single manuscript, now Paris, Bibliothèque de l'Université, MS 790 and are edited from this manuscript in O'Brien 1968. Another better known example is the sermon "Redde rationem," preached in 1387 by Master Wimbledon, which survives in numerous English and Latin copies. For the latest research and an updated manuscript listing, see O'Mara 2010.

[54] Anne Hudson suggests the expansion of Pateshull's oeuvre to include antifraternal poems, which have strong ties to the Lollard movement. See Hudson 2006.

In September 1464, the controversy broke out in London, when a Carmelite friar named Henry Parker preached a Sunday sermon at St Paul's Cross.[55] Parker declared that, according to scripture, Christ and his apostles had been beggars, living of alms. In his opinion, this was the preferred way of living for all priests and the secular clergy should follow the mendicant friars in this aspect.[56] This led to discussions among the audience, as it "made men to groge [be angry] and to muse passing soore."[57] The secular clergy took these murmurings seriously enough to make an answer. On the following Sunday, another sermon was held at St Paul's Cross, this time by Dr William Ive, a prominent London theologian who held a prosperous living in the city.[58] Ive transmitted his sermon to writing, in which he accused the friars of erring against the church, in a Latin version under the title *Lectiones de mendicitate Christi*, which survives in a single copy.[59]

Three months later, on 9 December, another doctor of divinity, the Carmelite Thomas Halden, answered Ive's sermon and defended the mendicant position, again on a Sunday at St Paul's Cross.[60] Halden's sermon was followed by a public *disputatio* in the Carmelite schools, the favoured way to dissolve theological disputes, on the following Wednesday, which was attended by many theologians and

[55] The history of this controversy is recounted in Du Boulay 1955. In the appendix, Boulay edits a Latin account of the episode from LPL MS 22, which is a version of the Latin Brut chronicle. The author of this chronicle had access to the ecclesiastical archives and included the text of the papal bull related to the controversy. See Du Boulay 1955, 169–171. There is also a lengthy English account of the events in the continuation of the so-called *Gregory's Chronicle*, which is edited from the unique manuscript BL MS Egerton 1995 in Gairdner 1876.

[56] Du Boulay 1955, 171.

[57] Gairdner 1876, 228.

[58] Gairdner 1876, 228. It has been suggested, that either William Ive himself or his colleague and friend Thomas Eborall is the author of the continuation of Gregory's chronicle, which would make this an eyewitness account. See Thomson 1972.

[59] Bodl. MS Lat. theol. e.25, fols. 1–26; see Walker 2004. There is no edition of this sermon yet.

[60] For a reconstruction of the events from the available sources, see Du Boulay 1955, 159–161.

clerks. As the *disputatio* ended with a proclaimed confirmation of the mendicancy of Christ, the controversy now entered into a new round. On Sunday, 16 December, another sermon was held at St Paul's Cross by the Cambridge graduate Edward Story, the rector of All Hallows the Great. Story reassured the public that there was nothing wrong with the church and the "begging" mentioned in the bible was a matter of interpretation. It was clear that after this, the Carmelites would not be granted access to the pulpit at St Paul's Cross again, as the secular clergy had a clear interest to end the public discussion of the topic of clerical possession. The Carmelites now reverted to the tested method of publishing pamphlets:

> But that same Sonday the fryers set uppe byllys at every chyrche dore that the doctor sayde nott trought [truth], but the trought shulde be schewyd ande sayd by Docter Master John Mylverton, the pryor of the same place.[61]

To match the publicity generated by a Sunday sermon at St Paul's Cross, the Carmelites used pamphlets to notify the population *and* scheduled the sermon for Sunday afternoon, which was an unusual time, but it had an advantage: the sermon at St Paul's Cross would have been finished by then. This attempt at raising public interest was highly successful and Carmelite prior John Milverton faced a large crowd for his sermon.[62] The text of his sermon is not known, but Milverton certainly reinforced the arguments previously brought up by his brothers. The population of London, upon hearing this sermon, was greatly agitated and calls for disendowment grew louder. An uprising was narrowly avoided, yet John Milverton and one of his brothers had

---

[61] Gairdner 1876, 229.
[62] The Latin chronicle from LPL MS 22 states that the people after midday flocked to the church of the Carmelites: "Statim post meridiem confluxit populus ad Carmelitas, et eo forte alacrius quo preter morem ab illo tempore sermo futurus erat." Quoted after Du Boulay 1955, 172.

to flee the country to escape excommunication.[63] During the Carmelite controversy the pamphlets distributed by the Carmelites were used to draw an audience for a sermon scheduled at an unusual time and day. They did not seem to have contained any theological content other than an advertisement for the sermon. The role of the pamphlets was to distribute information and to draw a crowd, in an attempt to match the publicity generated by a sermon controversy at St Paul's Cross.[64]

The anti-mendicant campaign of Richard FitzRalph

This venue had also been at the heart of another controversy about apostolic poverty, raging a century earlier. The Irish bishop Richard FitzRalph of Armagh (d. 1360) was a strong opponent of the mendicant orders. His battle against their privileges and ideals lasted from 1350 until his death ten years later. As a prominent theologian, he was able to take this issue to the highest level of ecclesiastical authority and addressed the papal curia several times. One episode in his long battle against the mendicants took place in London and sheds further light on the relationship between sermons and written pamphlet.[65] Between June 1356 and March 1357, Bishop Fitzralph had preached a series of sermons against the mendicants and their ideal of apostolic poverty in London, notably at St Paul's Cross. The friars of London, especially the Franciscans, who were the direct target, were not prepared to leave his accusations unanswered and composed a list of 20 propositions taken from Fitzralph's teachings, which they considered to be erroneous. This

---

[63] Milverton and Holden travelled to Rome to appeal to the Pope, who arrested them and examined them for heresy. Milverton remained in papal prison until 1468, when he was forced to recant after running out of money. He was reinstated to his office as principal and returned to England. Copsey 2004.

[64] For the importance of the sermons held at St Paul's Cross, see Horner 1998.

[65] For this and the following, see Walsh 2010. See also Szittya 1986, 123–151.

list, named *Appellacio*, was delivered to Fitzralph's lodgings.[66] The bishop answered these accusations point by point in a vernacular sermon two days later, on 12 March 1357. This final sermon was also transferred into writing and circulated independently, giving another example of an occasional sermon addressing a current controversial topic, which was published as a pamphlet.[67]

In this case, the sermons circulating in pamphlet form were not meant for the lay population. Although Fitzralph preached in the vernacular, he wrote his ideas down in Latin – they were meant to circulate within the academic community and among theologians abroad and contributed to scholarly debate. Although his arguments could also be translated into the other vernaculars, as T. P. Dolan points out, Fitzralph did not write his sermons for a lay audience, using instead complex arguments and cross-referencing more suited for academic discourse.[68] His intended audience clearly was one of fellow clergymen, highly educated, and able to follow complex arguments.

Archbishop Pecham and the "infamous folio"

The example of Bishop Fitzralph and the London mendicants shows that religious pamphlets were therefore not always meant for a large audience and not always appealed to the lay population. They could also be utilized as weapon in a personal conflict with a limited audience. Such was the case with our last example of Archbishop Pecham and the "infamous folio", which was part of the Thomism controversy in the late thirteenth century. The Oxford Prohibitions of 1277, which were directed against the philosophy of Thomas Aquinas, had already

---

[66] Only one manuscript copy is known from a codex assembled by a Peterhouse fellow in the second quarter of the fifteenth century: SS MS 64, 4r–v; see Walsh 1975, 224–225.

[67] The text of the sermon survives in two manuscripts: SS MS 64, 58r–71v and SJC MS 65, 88r–96v. See Szittya 1986, 129.

[68] Dolan 1989, 31.

initiated a "tract war" between adherents and opponents of Thomism.[69] Their renewal by Pecham in a sermon at Oxford in October 1284 revitalized the controversy with the Dominican order at Oxford as main opponent.

One result was the circulation of a pamphlet in the spring of 1285 that slandered the archbishop. In a letter dated 1 June 1285 Pecham informed Bishop Sutton of Lincoln, that this piece of writing had come to his attention.[70] He describes it as "maledicta pagina et infame folium," which had been published with the express intention to hurt him.[71] This description indicates that the pamphlet in question was written on a single sheet of parchment. Pecham further calls it acephalous in the beginning, spiteful in the middle, and disgraceful in the end – with 'acephalous' indicating the absence of an author's name.[72] Pecham advises the bishop of Lincoln to be vigilant and watch out for the traces of this pamphlet and as a good shepherd lead those of his flock who had strayed back into the path of truth.[73] There is no order to collect copies of the pamphlet, or to destroy them, and no instructions are given to punish those in whose possession it was found. The archbishop was not able to inhibit the circulation of the pamphlet and, since it was anonymous, he could not accuse the author directly: Pecham answered in the only possible way, by writing a lengthy refutation, packed with scriptural quotes, which he sent to Bishop Sutton.

No more details about the authorship and the manner of publication of the infamous folio are known. A circulation beyond the academic community is likely, as the bishop of Lincoln, in whose diocese the University of Oxford was located, was the recipient of Pecham's letter. A few years earlier, the attempt of the Bishop to conduct a visitation at Oxford and punish scholars had led to a quarrel, which had to be resolved by Archbishop Pecham, who decided in favour of the University:

---

[69] For the chain of events, see Ehrle 1970, 77–82 and Larsen 2011, 45–51.

[70] The letter is edited in Ehrle 1970, 71–76.

[71] "... maledicam paginam et infame folium ausus est in nostri praeiudicium publicare." Ehrle 1970, 72.

[72] "Cuius folii est acephalum principium, malignum medium et finis fatuus et deformis." Ehrle 1970, 72.

[73] Ehrle 1970, 76.

the bishop had no power over members of the academic community, who were to be disciplined by the chancellor only.[74] Therefore, Pecham's motive behind the letter could not have been to eradicate opposition at Oxford, as Bishop Sutton had no jurisdictional power within the University. The purpose of Pecham's letter was rather to restrict further dissemination of the 'infamous folio' in other parts of Lincoln diocese. The circulation of a pamphlet was of considerable concern for someone as high in the church hierarchy as the Archbishop of Canterbury, which again shows the power of pamphlets and the helplessness of the authorities, when faced with this type of dissent.

Conclusion

As the incidents discussed above show, circulating or posting pamphlets was an effective way to distribute dissident propaganda in late medieval England: this type of publication was difficult to suppress or control and had a high potential for at least annoying the authorities, but also could elicit a fierce reaction. Especially the posting of pamphlets on church doors, normally the space for official announcements, can be considered as infiltrating an exclusive channel of communication, or even as "visual violence."[75] The posting of the *Twelve Conclusions* during Parliament, which led to anti-Lollard legislation and a renewal of persecution, is a case in point.

Pamphlets were used to transfer inner-church conflicts from the enclosed world of the ecclesiastical councils and monasteries into the eyes of the laity, but were also involved in more personal conflicts, as was the case with Archbishop Pecham and his fight against the "infamous folio". In most cases, however, the main motive behind posting a pamphlet was the need for publicity to support the cause. Arousing the interest of the lay population could be an important factor, as the people of London had shown repeatedly that they were willing to resort to physical

[74] Larsen 2011, 51.
[75] Van Leeuwen 2004, 79.

violence to demonstrate their support for a dissenting cause. This was the motive behind the posting of the *Confessions* by John Aston, Philip Repingdon, and Nicholas Hereford during the Blackfriars Council, who hoped for sympathy towards the Wycliffite cause exhibited earlier by the Londoners, and the pamphlet campaign by the Dominican apostates in 1314. Both efforts were in vain, yet illustrate how pamphlets could be used to draw attention to controversies behind the closed doors of monasteries.

Bearing in mind the limited available communication channels for religious dissidents in late medieval England, a pamphlet campaign seems to have been the preferred method of spreading – or answering – controversial ideas. This very useful method of dissemination was theoretically available to anybody who could pay a scribe, but the majority of identifiable pamphleteers were literate clergymen, who were able to draw up and copy lists of conclusions or demands. As has become apparent in most of the examples presented here, there is a close connection between pamphlets and oral communication. As the example of the Carmelite controversy of 1464 has shown, the publication of a pamphlet was often preceded or followed by a sermon or a *disputatio* of similar content, making it mainly an auxiliary medium. A pamphlet such as the one distributed by the Augustinian friar Peter Pateshull in 1387, reinforced the presented arguments of the sermon, made them available for further study, and widened the possible range of coverage, both geographical and chronological. With the help of pamphlets, inner-church controversies could become wider movements and exceed the original limited scope of publicity offered by a sermon or *disputatio*. Quite often, texts originally published on pamphlets had a considerable afterlife and were copied and read for centuries – Martin Luther's theses would be the most famous example of this lasting effect.

Bibliography

Manuscripts

Cambridge, Sidney Sussex College (SS)
MS 64
London, British Library (BL)
MS Egerton 1995
London, Lambeth Palace Library (LPL)
MS 22
Oxford, Bodleian Library (Bodl)
MS Bodley 647
MS Lat. theol. e.25
Oxford, St John's College (SJC)
MS 65
Paris, Bibliothèque de l'Université
MS 790

Printed sources

Bliss, W. H. and J. A. Twemlow (ed.): *Calendar of Papal Registers Relating To Great Britain and Ireland*. Vol. 4, *1362–1404*. His Majesty's Stationery Office, London 1903.

Bray, Gerald (ed.): *Records of Convocation*. 20 vols. Boydell Press, Woodbridge 2005–2006.

Calendar of the Close Rolls preserved in the Public Record Office. Various publ., London 1902–.

Calendar of the Patent Rolls, Edward II/2, AD 1313–1317. Her Majesty's Stationery Office, London 1898.

Calendar of the Patent Rolls, Richard II/3, AD 1385–1389. Her Majesty's Stationery Office, London 1900.

Capgrave, John: *Abbreviacion of Cronicles*. Ed. Peter J. Lucas. Early English Text Society, Original Series 285. Oxford University Press, Oxford 1983.

Dymmok, Roger: *Liber Contra XII Errores et Hereses Lollardorum*. Ed. H. S. Cronin. Wyclif Society, London 1922.

Gairdner, James (ed.): *The Historical Collections of a Citizen of London in the 15th century*. Camden Society, London 1876.

Laud, Henry (ed.): *Flores Historiarum*. Vol. 3, *AD 1265 to AD 1326*. Rolls Series 95/3. Her Majesty's Stationery Office, London 1890.

Little, A.G.: A Record of the English Dominicans, 1314. *English Historical Review* 5/1890, 107–112.

Martin, G. H. (ed. and transl.): *Knighton's Chronicle, 1337–1396*. Clarendon Press, Oxford 1995.

McHardy, Alison: *De heretico comburendo*, 1401. *Lollardy and the Gentry in the Later Middle Ages*. Eds. Margaret Aston and Colin Richmond. Sutton Publishing, Stroud 1997, 112–126.

Riley, Henry (ed.): *Memorials of London and London Life*. Longmans, Green and Co., London 1868.

Rymer, Thomas (ed.): *Foedera, conventiones, literæ, et cujuscunque generis acta publica, inter reges Angliæ [...]*. 20 vols. 2nd ed. J. Tonson, London 1726.

Sharpe, Reginald (ed.): *Calendar of Letter-Books for the City of London: E, 1314–1337*. His Majesty's Stationery Office, London 1903.

Shirley, Walter (ed.): *Fasciculi Zizaniorum Magistri Johannis Wyclif cum Tritico.* Longman, Green and co., London 1858.

Walsingham, Thomas: *The St Albans Chronicle: The Chronica maiora of Thomas Walsingham.* Vol. 1, *1376–1394.* Ed. and transl. John Taylor, et al. Clarendon Press, Oxford 2003.

Walsingham, Thomas: *The St Albans Chronicle: The Chronica maiora of Thomas Walsingham.* Vol. 2, *1394–1422.* Ed. and transl. Wendy Childs, et al. Clarendon Press, Oxford 2011.

Wilkins, David (ed.): *Concilia Magnae Britanniae et Hiberniae, a synodo Verolamiensi, A.D. 446 ad Londinensem, A.D. 1717.* 4 vols. Gosling et al., London 1737.

Research literature

Aston, Margaret: Wyclif and the Vernacular. *From Ockham to Wyclif.* Eds. Anne Hudson and Michael Wilks. Blackwell, Oxford 1987, 281–330.

Clasen, P. Sophronius: Collectanea zum Studien-und Buchwesen des Mittelalters. *Archiv für Geschichte der Philosophie* 42.2/1960, 159–206, 247–271.

Cole, Andrew: *Literature and Heresy in the Age of Chaucer.* Cambridge University Press, Cambridge 2008.

Copsey, Richard: Milverton, John (d. 1487). *Oxford Dictionary of National Biography.* Oxford University Press, Oxford 2004 [http://www.oxforddnb.com/view/article/18805, accessed 10 Dec 2016].

Dolan, Terry P.: English and Latin Versions of Fitzralph's Sermons. *Latin and Vernacular: Studies in Late-Medieval Texts and Manuscripts.* Ed. A. J. Minnis. Brewer, Cambridge 1989, 27–37.

Du Boulay, F. R. H.: The Quarrel between the Carmelite Friars and the Secular Clergy of London, 1464–1468. *The Journal of Ecclesiastical History* 6/1955, 156–174.

Ehrle, Franz: John Pecham über den Kampf des Augustinismus und Aristotelismus in der zweiten Hälfte des 13. Jahrhunderts. *Gesammelte Aufsätze zur englischen Scholastik.* Ed. Franz Pelster. Ed. di Storia e Letteratura, Rome 1970, 59–86.

Gelber, Hester Goodenough: *It could have been Otherwise: Contingency and Necessity in Dominican Theology at Oxford, 1300–1350.* Brill, Leiden and Boston 2004.

Hanna, Ralph: *London Literature, 1300–1380.* Cambridge University Press, Cambridge 2005.

Horner, Patrick: Preachers at Paul's Cross: Religion, Society, and Politics in Late Medieval England. *Medieval Sermons and Society: Cloister, City, University.* Ed. Jacqueline Hamesse. Fédération Internationale des Instituts d'Etudes Médiévales, Louvain-la-Neuve 1998, 261–282.

Hruza, Karel: Schrift und Rebellion: Die hussitischen Manifeste aus Prag von 1415–1431. *Geist, Gesellschaft, Kirche im 13.–16. Jahrhundert.* Ed. František Šmahel. Filosofia-Verlag, Prague 1999, 81–108.

Hudson, Anne (ed.): *Selections from English Wycliffite Writings.* Cambridge University Press, Cambridge 1978.

Hudson, Anne: Pateshull, Peter (fl. 1387). *Oxford Dictionary of National Biography.* Oxford University Press, Oxford 2004 [http://www.oxforddnb.com/view/article/21543, accessed 3 April 2016].

Hudson, Anne: Peter Pateshull: One-Time Friar and Poet? *Interstices: Studies in Late Middle English and Anglo-Latin Texts in Honour of A.G. Rigg.* Eds. Richard Firth Green and Linne Mooney. University of Toronto Press, Toronto 2006, 167–183.

Hudson, Anne: *The Premature Reformation: Wycliffite Texts and Lollard History.* Clarendon Press, Oxford 1988.

Justice, Steven: *Writing and Rebellion: England in 1381.* University of California Press, Berkeley, Los Angeles and London 1994.

Eva Schaten

Kelly, Henry Ansgar: Trial Procedures against Wyclif and Wycliffite in England and at the Council of Constance. *Huntington Library Quarterly* 61.1/1999, 1–28.
Knowles, David: The Censured Opinions of Uthred of Boldon. *The Historian and Character and Other Essays*. Cambridge University Press, Cambridge 1963, 129–170.
Lahey, Stephen: *John Wyclif.* Oxford University Press, Oxford 2009.
Larsen, Andrew: *The School of Heretics: Academic Condemnation at the University of Oxford, 1277–1409.* Brill, Leiden 2011.
Moeller, Bernd: Thesenanschläge. *Luthers Thesenanschlag – Faktum oder Fiktion.* Eds. Joachim Ott and Martin Treu. Evangelische Verlagsanstalt, Leipzig 2008, 9–32.
O'Brien, Robert: Two Sermons at York Synod of William Rymyngton. *Citeaux* 19/1968, 40–67.
O'Mara, Veronica: Thinking Afresh about Thomas Wimbledon's Paul's Cross Sermon of c. 1387. *Leeds Studies in English* 41/2010, 155–171.
Ott, Joachim and Martin Treu (ed.): *Luthers Thesenanschlag – Faktum oder Fiktion.* Evangelische Verlagsanstalt, Leipzig 2008.
Owst, G. R.: *Literature and Pulpit in Medieval England.* Blackwell, Oxford 1961.
Pettegree, Andrew: *Brand Luther: 1517, Printing, and the Making of the Reformation.* Penguin Books, New York 2015.
Raymond, Joad: *Pamphlets and Pamphleteering in Early Modern Britain.* Cambridge University Press, Cambridge 2006.
Röhrkasten, Jens: *The Mendicant Houses of Medieval London, 1221–1539.* LIT Verlag, Münster 2004.
Scase, Wendy: 'Strange and Wonderful Bills': Bill-Casting and Political Discourse in Late Medieval England. *New Medieval Literatures* 2/1998, 225–247.
Scase, Wendy: Antifraternal Traditions in Reformation Pamphlets. *The Friars in Medieval Britain: Proceedings of the 2007 Harlaxton Symposium.* Ed. Nicholas John Rogers. Shaun Tyas, Donington 2010, 239–264.
Scase, Wendy: *Literature and Complaint in England, 1272–1553.* Oxford University Press, Oxford 2007.
Scase, Wendy: The Audience and Framers of the Twelve Conclusions of the Lollards. *Text and Controversy from Wyclif to Bale.* Eds. Helen Barr and Ann Hutchinson. Brepols, Turnhout 2005, 283–301.
Šmahel, František: Reformation und Receptio: Publikum, Massenmedien und Kommunikationshindernisse zu Beginn der hussitischen Reformbewegung. *Das Publikum politischer Theorie im 14. Jahrhundert.* Eds. Jürgen Miethke et al. Oldenbourg, Munich 1992, 255–268.
Spencer, H. Leith: *English Preaching in the Late Middle Ages.* Clarendon Press, Oxford 1993.
Szittya, Penn: *The Antifraternal Tradition in Medieval Literature.* Princeton University Press, Princeton 1986.
The National Archives: *Discovery Online Catalogue.* Kew, Surrey 2016 [http://discovery.nationalarchives.gov.uk/]
Thomson, J. A. F.: The Continuation of Gregory's Chronicle: A Possible Author?. *The British Museum Quarterly* 36/1972, 92–97.
Treu, Martin: Urkunde und Reflexion: Wiederentdeckung eines Belegs von Luthers Thesenanschlag. *Luthers Thesenanschlag – Faktum oder Fiktion.* Eds. Joachim Ott and Martin Treu. Evangelische Verlagsanstalt, Leipzig 2008, 59–67.
Van Leeuwen, Jacqueline: Over slapscheten en levereters: Pamfletten en strooibriefjes in de laatmiddeleeuwse Vlaamse stad. *Madoc* 18/2004, 77–85.
Walker, Simon: Ive, William (d. 1486). *Oxford Dictionary of National Biography.* Oxford University Press, Oxford 2004; online edn, Jan 2008 [http://www.oxforddnb.com/view/article/14498, accessed 26 March 2016].

Walsh, Katherine: Archbishop Fitzralph and the Friars at the Papal Court in Avignon, 1357–1360. *Traditio* 31/1975, 223–245.

Walsh, Katherine: Fitzralph, Richard (b. before 1300, d. 1360). *Oxford Dictionary of National Biography*. Oxford University Press, Oxford 2004; online edn, May 2010 [http://www.oxforddnb.com/view/article/9627, accessed 10 Dec 2016].

Werner, Thomas: *Den Irrtum liquidieren: Bücherverbrennungen im Mittelalter*. Vandenhoek and Ruprecht, Göttingen 2007.

Physical and verbal violence: persecuted Protestant communities during the reign of Mary I (1553–1558)

Gabriele Müller-Oberhäuser

Introduction

When the news of the death of the young English king Edward VI on 6 July 1553 gradually reached the continent, a general feeling of apprehension among religious reformers rapidly spread in continental Europe as their correspondence attests. In a letter to Henry Bullinger John Calvin wrote on 7 September 1553 from Geneva: "We have good reason to feel anxiety – yea, even torment – regarding that nation [England] ... the Church of God will be in a manner buffeted by manifold tempests. Let us, therefore, ... commend this very troubled state of affairs to God."[1] Similar letters from the following months clearly indicate the growing concern of reformers for the processes of religious change in England after Mary I's accession to the throne. They especially lamented the sad condition of Protestant English bishops in prison and the fate of Protestant exiles in England, now forced to leave the country and wander again through Europe looking for a refuge and

[1] Calvin vol. 2 2007, 426.

a new home.[2] Things obviously went from bad to worse as time went on. So on 20 October 1555 Sir John Cheke, the eminent classical scholar and humanist, former tutor to Edward VI and at that time already an exile in Europe, wrote to Calvin from Strasbourg that the three prominent Anglican bishops Thomas Cranmer (Canterbury), Nicholas Ridley (London), and Hugh Latimer (Worcester) were expected to be burned soon or had already been burned (actually Ridley and Latimer had already been burned together on 16 October 1555 in Oxford, while Cranmer was to be burned in the following year, on 21 March 1556, the three forming the group of the 'Oxford Martyrs').[3] All in all, Cheke gave a rather dismal, if not desperate summary of the situation in his country, deplored as "our wretched and now greatly ruined England."[4] So the early fears and anxieties from autumn 1553 had proved to be more than justified from the reformers' point of view, and in the history of the English Reformation Mary's reign from 1553 to 1558 came to be regarded as one of severe religious persecution of individual reformers as well as of the developing Protestant communities of clergymen and of laypersons – a persecution that earned her the epithet 'Mary the Bloody'.

This article concentrates on the topic of violence in religious persecutions during Mary's reign, on physical as well as on non-physical violence exerted by the use of language, and – from a book historian's point of view – on the role of written communication in manuscript and print in religious controversies and conflicts. Against the background of an outline of the historical context of Mary's Re-Catholization process (1), the main focus will be on violence against Protestant individuals and communities, but also on violence against objects that represented their beliefs, their books (2); the third and last part will offer a closer look at Edmund Bonner, the bishop of London, and his role in Mary's restoration policy, with special regard to the relationship between the use of verbal and physical violence in examinations and interrogations in heresy trials.

[2] Anderson 1973, 50–52.
[3] Loades 1970, esp. 167–191.
[4] *Original Letters* vol. 1 1846, 149.

The historical context: Mary I and the restoration of Roman Catholicism in England

Henry VIII's breach with Rome and the establishment of the Church of England under a royal supremacy in 1534 led to a rather unstable religious development of the Henrician Reformation till his death in 1547. It was characterised by an earlier phase with only tentative and hesitant attempts at religious reform during the 1530s, with the dissolution of the monasteries on the one hand and with Henry's English Bible, his Great Bible, of 1539, on the other hand, and by a later, more conservative phase after 1539, represented by the Six Articles of Faith with their emphasis on the traditional concepts of the Eucharist, on celibacy and confession.[5]

It was not until Edward, his son and a minor of just nine years, succeeded him in 1547 that the first determined attempts at a religious reform towards Protestantism were made, mainly promoted by his Council that was dominated by his Protestant and well-educated uncle Edward Seymour, Lord Protector, and by Thomas Cranmer, the Archbishop of Canterbury, whose efforts culminated in the two editions of the Book of Common Prayer of 1549 and of 1552.[6] The boy king Edward, often seen as the second Josiah, represented to many hopeful religious reformers in Europe the epitome of a truly godly king; his realm was appreciated as *the* model of a successful reformation in a unified country, a hope for others in Europe as it had come into being without bloody wars, and thus presenting a well-governed truly Christian state based on the principles of the gospel. In particular after the Augsburg Interim of 1548, Edward's comparatively peaceful England offered shelter and protection, hospitality and often also permanent positions of different sorts to exiles from continental Europe, and Thomas Cranmer's invitations and generous hospitality proved to be an incentive to new networks of highly influential reformers in England, to Martin Bucer from 1549 to 1551 in Cambridge and to Peter Martyr from

---

[5] Bernard 2005; Dickens 1964, 109–196.
[6] MacCulloch 1999; Loach 1999.

1447 to 1553 in Oxford.[7] Equally important were special rights that were granted to Stranger Churches in order to establish new religious communities of exiles, a generosity also guided by the hope that these actively reforming communities might in the long run help and support the young and only gradually developing English church. All this was, of course, immediately threatened, all these hopes were destroyed when the young king died at the age of only fifteen and Mary I succeeded her half-brother in July 1553, as the daughter of Catherine of Aragon and a stout and fully committed Roman Catholic, who was determined to stop and put religious reform in reverse in order to restore the ties with Roman Catholicism. This trend towards restoration was even more strengthened by her marriage in July 1554 to prince Philip of Spain (the future king Philip II), the son of Charles V, a marriage with a foreigner and a Habsburg prince that was most unpopular in England and even provoked strong resistance.[8]

The process of restoration and reconciliation with Rome envisaged by Mary I proved to be rather difficult and equally slow in the beginning as England was under an interdict and in a state of schism, and also Parliament was reluctant to follow her. So it took her till the end of 1554 and her third Parliament before an official reconciliation with Rome was finally achieved.[9] In her efforts she was mainly supported by Stephen Gardiner, the bishop of Winchester, and Lord Chancellor.[10] An even more important ally was the Catholic reformer Reginald Pole who had lived in mainland Europe on the continent since the 1530s, when he had to leave England. In November 1554 he returned to England as cardinal-legate and archbishop of Canterbury. Under the influence of the first two periods of the Council of Trent (1545–1548, 1551–1552) and in contact with Fray Bartolomé Carranza he turned out to be one of the most energetic motors of the process of restoring Roman Catholicism in England.[11]

[7] MacCulloch 1996, 351–409, esp. 380–383.
[8] Loades 1989, 222–273; Edwards 2011, 226–265.
[9] Edwards 2011, 224–225; Loach 1994; Duffy 2009; Loades 1965.
[10] Redworth 1990, 289–329.
[11] Mayer 2000, 252–301; Mayer 2012, 1–13; Duffy 2009, 29–56; Edwards 2012, 141–160, 159.

As legal expression of the changes involved in this process we find several important statutes and proclamations under Mary and Philip. As the main objective was to undo the Reformation that had been started under Edward VI, the new policy needed an adequate legitimation. On the one hand acts that had been passed by her predecessors had to be repealed, as can be seen in an act repealing the acts against Rome by Henry VIII (1 & 2 Philip & Mary c. 8, 1555),[12] which abolished Henry's act of supremacy and included an explicit acceptance of the pope's supremacy as a precondition for papal absolution and the end of the interdict. On the other hand, Mary I re-enforced the old heresy laws of Lollard times, together with the restitution of the ecclesiastical courts that were needed for heresy trials in *(An) act for the renewing of three Statutes made for the punishment of Heresies* (1 & 2 Philip & Mary, c. 6, 1554),[13] referring to letters patent and acts by Richard II, Henry IV, and Henry V.[14] And it is with these acts that a new (or rather old) legal basis was created for a religious restoration that the well-known severe persecutions, heresy trials, torture and executions by burning started at the beginning of 1555. As part of the attempts at guaranteeing the success of the process, the communication systems in a well-established print culture of the sixteenth century also became a target of intensified surveillance. But to be effective, the old heresy laws of the late Middle Ages had to be adjusted to the changed communication situation in the middle of the sixteenth century, as it was no longer mainly a matter of wandering Lollard preachers as in Richard II's time or of a fight against an astonishing Lollard manuscript production in the English language as in Henry IV's and Henry V's time. In Mary's statutes and proclamations we therefore normally find the whole range of oral and written communication, including printed books, under supervision.[15]

---

[12] *Statutes of the Realm* (SR) 2009 (1819) vol. 4., 246–253; see also *Tudor Constitutional Documents* 1948, 121–129, esp. 125–129.

[13] *SR* 2009 (1819) vol. 4, 244; *Tudor Constitutional Documents* 1948, 124–125.

[14] *SR* vol. 2 2009 (1810): 5 Richard II, Stat. 2, c. 5 (1382), 25–26, 2 Henry IV, c. 15 (1400–1401): *De haeretico comburendo*, 125–128, and 2 Henry V, Stat. 1, c. 7 (1414): *Suppression of Heresy Act*, 181–184.

[15] Loach 1986; Loades 1991.

Mary I's mistrustful attitude to the press, which in her opinion had to be controlled by any means can, for example, be seen in her proclamation of 18 August 1553. In a paragraph on false rumours, unlicensed preachers, and plays, we also find printers explicitly mentioned, as

> printers of false fond books, ballads, rhymes, and other lewd treatises in the English tongue concerning doctrine in matters now in question and controversy touching the high points and mysteries of Christian religion; which books, ballads, rhymes, and treatises are chiefly by the printers and stationers set out to sale for her grace's subjects of an evil zeal for lucre and covetousness of vile gain.[16]

For Mary I all printers were mainly interested in profit and had no regard for the contents of their products – a view that is in definite contrast to facts as quite a large group of printers, most of them situated in London, had been committed Protestants during Edward's reign so that profit at least for many of them had not been their only or even their main concern. But most of them had to leave England in 1553 anyway and printed on the continent, for example in Wesel or Emden, and in the English language, thus being able to smuggle their books into England. Or they took the risk of printing on secret presses in the country, which was more dangerous. That Mary I's main strategy was to control book production in England (she was less effective in preventing books from coming into England from the continent!) is underlined by the fact that she made use of the London-based Stationers' Company, the central institution of the English book trade, which she turned into a useful instrument of control and literary censorship by also granting a charter to the Company in 1557.[17] Thus the Stationers' Company could from this time on operate in support of the government's attempts at controlling the trade in searching printing shops, confiscating copies and even in destroying censored books, and this was not just in cases of

---

[16] *TRP* vol. 2, 6.
[17] Clegg 2003, 13–14, 20–23, 27–28; Blagden 1960, 19–33.

internal (mainly economically based) conflicts within the trade but for more general religio-political reasons.

Mary I's royal proclamations give evidence of her continuous attempts at controlling both, oral as well as literary communication. So right from the beginning of her reign in August 1553 religious controversy, unlicensed plays, and printing were forbidden. On 10 April 1554 orders were given that seditious bills had to be destroyed, and on 13 June 1555 a proclamation was published with the title *Enforcing Statute against Heresy, Prohibiting Seditious and Heretical Books*, including a list of titles of authors of forbidden books.[18] These books had either to be delivered to the authorities or to be burned. A proclamation of June 1555 was directed against both sources of unwanted books, against foreign import and against clandestine presses in England producing heretical books. The threat of severe punishment is unambiguous in a proclamation of 6 June 1558 that answers to threats of a revolution and danger to Queen Mary:

> whosoever – – be found to have any of the said wicked and seditious books, or finding them do not forthwith burn the same without show-ing or reading the same to any other person, shall in that case be reputed and taken for a rebel, and shall without delay be executed for that offence, according to the order of martial lawe.[19]

With this legal basis in mind, we can turn to the question of violence against persons (based on heresy laws) and books (based on censorship regulations) in the religious field.

Religious persecution: 'burning books' – 'burning heretics'

The relationship between books as material objects as well as carriers of messages, of texts and pictures, and the agents, the individuals and groups communicating by the use of these books, can be manifold, in

[18] *TRP* vol. 2 1969, 5–8, 41–42, 57–60.
[19] *TRP* vol. 2 1969, 90–91, 91.

particular when it comes to censorship and religious persecution in the sixteenth century. As we know from the history of literary censorship, a book could be burned when the author could not be found (or when he was already dead), as a substitute, and as an act intended to kill the 'brainchild' of the author, to kill – execute – his creation, as part of his thinking, beliefs and identity. Authors as well as book owners and readers could be burned with their books (some of them had to throw them into the fire themselves), but always it was a gesture of high symbolic value, most of the time taking place as part of a solemn public spectacle in front of an audience to whom it was addressed and whose orthodoxy it was supposed to strengthen.[20]

Literary censorship and the role of books in heresy procedures

Burning books as "the visible symbol of repression"[21] is not a particularly prominent feature of censorship during Mary's reign and there is nothing new in its forms and functions,[22] nor is it especially characteristic of her censorship policy when we take into account the long history of book burning in general and in England in particular: John Wyclif's books were burned in Oxford in 1411, and looking at the early Tudors we find Henry VIII who had Martin Luther's (Latin) books burned at St Paul's Cross in 1521.[23] Generally speaking, we do not find many cases of burned books during Mary I's reign in the sources, but as a possible explanation some scholars have put forward the idea that the brutal executions of so many Protestants may have overshadowed the relevance of 'mere' symbolic executions of books. But some examples, mainly taken from John Foxe's *Acts and Monuments,* can illustrate different types of book burnings.

a) Bones and books burned: Paul Fagius, professor of Hebrew, and Martin Bucer, regius professor of divinity, had died of natural causes

[20] Werner 2007, 107–125; Rafetseder 1988.
[21] Da Costa 2014, 414.
[22] Cressy 2005; Loades 1964.
[23] Meyer 1958.

during the reign of Edward VI and had been buried in Cambridge, but both were posthumously condemned as heretics under Mary I. Their bodies were dug out, chained to the stake in coffins and then publicly burned in the marketplace in Cambridge on 6 February 1557, and "a great sort of bookes that were condemned with them, were cast into the same [the fire]."[24] Both, bones and books, had to play their roles in a posthumous symbolic execution, in a ritual that was put on stage as a major civic spectacle for the members of the audience that were supposed to understand the message in terms of Catholic orthodoxy.

b) Books burned together with the martyr: This is the case with two laymen, William Wolsey, a constable and radical Protestant, and Robert Pygot, a painter, who were burned together with some books in 1555. When books were thrown into the fire which looked like (banned) New Testaments to them, according to John Foxe they both cried out: "Oh geue me one of the[m]" so that they could each clasp a book close to their breast, while reciting Psalm 106.[25] With the same expressive gesture of the clasped book close to the heart we also find a man called John Hullier, a curate, who was burned at the stake in 1556:

> there was a co[m]pany of bookes which were cast into the fire, and by chaunce a Communion-booke fell betwene his handes, who receyuing it ioyfully opened it, & read so long as the force of the flame & smoke caused him that he could see no more – – holding his handes vp to heaven, & the booke betwixte his armes next his hart, thanking God for sending him it.[26]

"By chance" is here interpreted as God's Providence, with the book (probably the Book of Common Prayer) representing God's help and consolation in tribulation close to death. Holding the book close to his heart is also a gesture of complete identification with the contents of these highly esteemed books from the victim's point of view, though

---

[24] Foxe 1570, 2190–2191 [2150–2051], 2190 [2150] (all quotations from *TAMO*, the online edition 2011); the page numbers in brackets refer to the original pagination; see also Dickens 1964, 233.
[25] Foxe 1583, 1740 [1716].
[26] Foxe 1583, 2028 [2004].

the book had been (wrongfully) condemned by the authorities. And not only this gesture of clasping the book close to one's heart but also the act of even reading the book in the middle of the flames can also be understood as a sign of resistance and steadfastness in Foxe's dramatic narration of the death of this martyr.

c) Books used as evidence in heresy trials: John Bonsaye of Beverley, a layman, owned banned books in 1556. As he had spoken publicly against transubstantiation, he was examined, and the books he owned, written by Protestant authors Thomas Becon, Roger Hutchinson and Nicholas Grimald, were used against him as evidence in the interrogations. In the end he decided to abjure to avoid execution and had to do penance as a consequence, among other things in walking bare-footed and bare-legged on a Saturday in the market place, "to cast the said iij bookes in the fier and see theme godelie burned."[27] He had to carry a paper with the inscription: "This man hath kept hereticall and sediciouse bookes contrarie to the lawes."[28] To Arthur George Dickens, Bonsaye with his books represents the type of the well-informed and literate Protestant who by his reading was able to form his own religious opinions and to participate in religious debates.[29] The public burning of his precious, but condemned books in front of the repentant book owner and of all the witnesses around symbolises his *purgatio* and his re-integration into the orthodox community, and it has, of course, biblical models (Acts 19, 19).

Executions: burning 'heretics' in Marian England

Against the already-mentioned background of a rather gradual development of the reconciliation process with Rome in 1553–1554 and the urgent problem of legitimising heresy trials and executions by statutes, the first heresy trials and executions of those individuals who did not recant, but remained 'obstinate', could not start before

[27] Dickens 1982, 139–141, 141.
[28] Dickens 1982, 141.
[29] Dickens 1957, 13.

January/February 1555, and they started with the first execution by fire in Smithfield on 4 February 1555 with the vicar and translator of the Bible, John Rogers, the so-called proto-martyr of the Marian reign.[30] Looking at the following executions this also means that all the trials and executions during the reign of Mary I took place within only four years, between February 1555 and November 1558, when Mary died and her Protestant half-sister Elizabeth ascended the English throne.

All in all about 300 Protestants were burned in Marian England, the majority of them being laypersons.[31] In London which had been one of the strongholds of early Protestantism during Edward's reign,[32] more than 100 persons, mainly men, were burned publicly in Smithfield, often in small groups. Most of them had been questioned and tried by Edmund Bonner, the bishop of London,[33] and about forty of them had been sent to him from Essex for examinations. Bonner interrogated and condemned in person 90 suspects; in the other cases he at least signed the final condemnations. In comparison, only two executions for heresy are known during Edward's reign.[34] There is also evidence that Bonner saw about 450 suspects in his ecclesiastical court, but obviously they were not all executed, which means that they had accepted Bonner's instruction after having recanted. As (often incomplete and fragmentary) sources we sometimes have official documents like the Bishops' Registers,[35] though they often only give the final verdict, but also correspondence and sometimes unedited manuscripts written and circulated by the accused as eye witnesses, some of them later published in print. In chronicles at least some dates and names of those executed can be found, e.g. in Charles Wriothesley's, Windsor Herald, *Chronicle of England During the Reign of the Tudors from A.D. 1485 to 1559* and in the *Diary* of Henry Machyn, citizen of London, from A.D. 1550 to A.D. 1563.

---

[30] Chester 1981. The appendix offers the opportunity of comparing Rogers' own account (293–337) with Foxe's version in the 1563 edition (338–369).
[31] For a chronological list see Freeman 2011 (Appendix); Freeman 2011 (Burning Zeal), 174 (fig. 10.1).
[32] Brigden 1989.
[33] Alexander 1987; Loades 2011.
[34] MacCulloch 2002, 141; MacCulloch 1996, 474–475.
[35] Smith 1981, esp. 145.

But the most comprehensive narrative of the persecutions is that written by John Foxe. Our modern understanding of the religious persecutions under Mary I mainly (and often exclusively) depends on John Foxe's *Acts and Monuments*, better known under its more popular title as *The Book of Martyrs*.[36] Together with the English Bible and the Book of Common Prayer Foxe's martyrology, written in retrospective and under the safe conditions of the Elizabethan age, forms the third pillar of English Protestantism and of the Anglican Church as it represents a new Protestant vision of history (and not only of English history!) leading to a truly Protestant nation under Elizabeth I. Foxe had already started in the middle of the sixteenth century to collect material and reports about the horrible events in England when he stayed in continental Europe during Mary's reign, working only from a distance and therefore without any direct knowledge, first in two editions in Latin still printed on the continent[37], then later, after his return to England under Elizabeth I and closer to witnesses, in the form of four massive editions in English printed by John Day during the author's lifetime in 1563, 1570, 1576 and 1583.[38] Based on an ever increasing amount of sources in the form of letters and of eye witness reports about torture and executions or as written reports of prisoners themselves that had been smuggled out of prison before their death,[39] Foxe offers the most comprehensive account of the persecutions during the 1550s; in many cases no other sources are available, and consequently John Foxe's *Acts and Monuments* is all we have.[40]

---

[36] Foxe 2011 (online variorum edition *TAMO*); Freeman 2011 (*TAMO*).

[37] *Commentarii Rerum in Ecclesia Gestarum* and *Rerum in Ecclesia Gestarum*.

[38] 1563 (STC 11222), 1570 (STC 11223), 1576 (STC 11224), 1583 (STC 11225), all accessible in *Early English Books Online* (*EEBO*); see also King 2006, 80–133.

[39] Ahnert and Ahnert 2015; Ahnert 2003.

[40] For the debate on the reliability of John Foxe as a historian and his textual strategies see e.g. Collinson 1994; Collinson 2011; Freeman 2000.

Physical and non-physical violence: 'bloody Bonner, the butcher'

It is well known that there is a striking ambivalence about the use of physical violence in a Christian world, in particular with regard to killing human beings for their religious beliefs. Typical issues were (and are) the legitimacy of physical violence, of force, of hurting or even killing on religious grounds, but also the relationship between the power of the sword and the power of the word with its emphasis on persuading and convincing others in matters of religion, including the topic of religious tolerance and the concept of civilised and polite conduct and interaction, also (and even more so) in situations of controversies and conflict. In using the example of Edmund Bonner, the concept of violence that has traditionally been understood to refer primarily to physical acts will be extended to include aspects of non-physical violence, thus taking into account more recent debates on violence. In the following discussion, such violence is in particular observable in the forms of language deliberately used to hurt by intimidating, humiliating, insulting and threatening suspects in heresy examinations.

Edmund Bonner, bishop of London, and religious persecution under Mary I

Born about 1500, Edmund Bonner studied both laws in Oxford, and in 1527 he started a career as diplomat and administrator under Henry VIII, first in the service of Cardinal Thomas Wolsey as the cardinal's chaplain, and later, after Wolsey's fall 1530, in the service of Thomas Cromwell.[41] He was appointed bishop of Hereford in 1538 and bishop of London in 1540. In close contact with Cromwell, the main organizer and motor of the first steps towards the Reformation in England, he supported Henry's anti-papal policy and his claim for supremacy; and

---

[41] Alexander 1960; Carleton 2006.

throughout the 1540s, till the death of Henry in 1547, he acted as one of Henry's more conservative bishops. It was during these years that he also participated in heresy trials leading to executions, of which the most notorious one was that of Anne Askew in 1545–1546.[42] Under Edward VI he was removed from office and spent most of these years (from 1549 to 1553) in prison as he had refused to accept the Edwardian Book of Common Prayer and to preach according to the Protestant doctrine of the sacraments.

With the accession of Mary I to the throne in 1553 he was pardoned and re-instated as bishop of London. It came to be his main task to put into effect the Catholic restoration in the diocese of London, and in particular in his Church, St Paul's. Part of this task was the determined fight against heresy and the Protestant communities in London in continuation of his activities in the 1540s under Henry VIII. With regard to the high number of executions by burning in London that were the result of the trials conducted in his court, and on the basis of reports about the way he proceeded in interrogations, he became the arch-villain of the Marian persecutions, abused as 'bloody Bonner, the butcher'. This extremely negative image has been put in a new perspective in some respect in more recent research, where the active role of Stephen Gardiner at least in the beginning of Mary's reign is emphasised.[43] But also Queen Mary I herself seems to have played an active role, probably also encouraged by her Spanish confessors who had come to England with Philip of Spain. We have evidence that already at the beginning of 1554 Mary I had pushed Bonner to speed up ("her graces commaundemente to be putte in spedye execution") in a letter of seven pages with articles addressed to the bishop of London that she also had printed and distributed to make her demands public.[44] And last but not least, there was Cardinal Reginald Pole, who brought with him ideas of the Catholic Reformation from Rome. So the search for the villain seems to be a rather complex affair. But obviously Bishop Bonner was the man who had to do the 'dirty' work, as he was responsible for implementing order in his diocese, which contained many Protestants.

[42] Askew 1996.
[43] Riordan and Ryrie 2003.
[44] Mary I 1554 (*EEBO*, STC 9182), title page.

However, there is also the other side of his personality, namely Edmund Bonner the preacher and the author of catechisms and sermons for the clergy, where he concentrated on the process of re-education by sermons and books, as a bishop who saw himself as the good shepherd who cared for his flock, feeling responsible for their souls and their salvation. But it is really John Foxe who shaped the image of Bonner as bloody butcher for future generations as the fat, gluttonous, cruel cannibal, "with belly blowen and head so swolne",[45] a sadist who drank the blood of his victims and who took pleasure in watching the pain und sufferings of those in his hands: "This Cannibal in three yeares space / Three hundred Martirs slew: / They were his food, he loued so blood, / he spared none he knew."[46] And the persuasive power of the woodcuts in the English editions picturing his brutal behaviour in examinations underlines the message of the text.

Violence and language: Bonner's examinations and trials

The main interest in research on martyrdom has always been more on the side of physical violence exerted by the authorities in form of public and spectacular executions with all their horror, with weeping relatives and friends and last speeches from the stake, adding up to what has been called the 'theatre of martyrdom'.[47] Compared to these dramatic narratives, aspects of verbal violence[48] used in heresy trials, and in particular in the preliminary processes of examinations and interrogations, seem to have been (with a few exceptions)[49] rather neglected. On the basis of the study of reports by victims and John

---

[45] Foxe 1563, 1770 [1689].

[46] Foxe 1563, 1770 [1689].

[47] Nicholls 1988, esp. 49–51, 52; Dailey 2012, 53–97.

[48] For discussions of the complex relationship between language and violence see Krämer 2007, 34–36; Liebsch 2013, 7–12; Nunner-Winkler 2004.

[49] Covington 2002; Covington 2010; Covington 2014; for general aspects of trials in ecclesiastical courts see Helmholz 2003.

Foxe's *Acts and Monuments* a few aspects of Bonner's examinations can be summarized.

Examinations by Bonner as reported by victims and narrated in Foxe's *Acts and Monuments* were often quite long and numerous, and several of the accused had to go through a great number of interrogations, again and again on the same essential topics, as Bonner tried to find out whether the accused had changed his or her mind meanwhile and was finally willing to recant. Bonner took his role seriously, as he, the good pastor, felt responsible for the soul of his sheep, and he was quite ambitious in the confrontation with the accused. In accordance with the general attitude of the church, a suspect who stayed 'obstinate' was a failure for him. So he took great efforts in convincing first of all the well-educated and also university-trained leaders, often clergymen, of the Protestant lay communities, as a 'victory' in these verbal duels would not only be a greater triumph for him, but a recantation by one of the leaders would also be more effective in its impact on the Protestant communities. The verbal means Bonner used ranged from soft luring and mild persuasion and promising rewards to threatening the steadfast opponent with torture and even death. On the basis of modern pragma-linguistics and concepts of dialogue structures this special type of dialogue in the tradition of inquisitorial encounters can be analysed in more detail, as an interrogation with fixed roles in a hierarchical frame defined by inequality, with a clear-cut power structure as to the turn-taking system, that means, as to who alone can ask questions and who is required to answer but never allowed to ask back, as well as in the choice of topics by the more powerful speaker. In the context of heresy suspicions it is always a dialogue with a decision to be taken at the end by only one person, and therefore a dangerous verbal exchange under risk for only one of the persons involved, where finally his or her life is at stake. We have to take into account that in analysing these examinations the focus is on written reports of oral discourse, and therefore they reflect different degrees of literariness, in particular when written by well-educated protestants with knowledge of dialogue genres and dramatic conventions. The reports were mainly written from the point of view of the victims as a sort of legacy to their communities, possibly also for posterity, but always written down in order to bring to light and to make known to the outside world what had happened in these interrogations, to act as witnesses to the cruelty of the opponent, to reveal and expose the actions of the aggressors against peaceful and godly people, and also to warn and prepare others who might have to share the same fate in the future. In a way written communication of this type can be understood as the basis for forming textual communities and for strengthening individual as well as social identities under the aspect of shared suffering, of experienced violence wrongfully committed against God's godly people. Though the dominant type of dialogue is the interrogation or examination structured by question and answer sequences, we find interesting features of the turn-taking system as to the length of utterances of the speakers and the tendency to longer monologues. This is for example the case when Bonner takes on the role of an instructor and teacher so that the verbal exchange resembles a didactic dialogue, or when he turns into a preacher and introduces elements of a sermon in order to impart theological knowledge and Catholic doctrine. But with well-educated and even learned suspects, laypeople and clergymen, he often meets with problems, so for example in 1555 with John Philpot, Archdeacon of Winchester,[50] where elements of a *disputatio* can be observed, thus introducing a highly competitive element into the exchange of arguments. Bonner, who by his education and training is actually more of an administrator than a theologian, sometimes even seems to be at a loss and has to send for books from his library to support his arguments.[51]

When one person has to go through several interrogations, we can often observe a gradual development and change in the strategies of the speakers involved. Together with flattery and persuasion Bonner offers very open definitions to win acceptance, but gradually, when it is clear that this does not work, he puts pressure on the interrogated person and requires an answer without any evasion, vague phrasing or ambiguity. "Speak plainly", "Speake, yea or nay"[52], or the accused is summoned to give a determinate or resolute answer.[53] There is no longer

[50] Foxe 1583, 1819 [1795]–1854 [1830].
[51] Foxe 1583, 1827 [1803], 1835 [1811].
[52] Foxe 1583, 1838 [1814].
[53] Foxe 1583, 1547 [1523], 1558 [1534], 1616 [1592].

room for strategic ambiguity and for blurred distinctions as the borders between orthodoxy and heresy have to be unambiguously marked. The most essential religious issues are selected, summarized in short apodictic sentences by Bonner in order to serve as final touchstones, often centered on the eucharist, where complex arguments are no longer accepted, where the doctrine in the way Bonner phrases it has to be accepted or denied with a simple 'yes' or 'no' (a or b, not a yet b). The more advanced the process of interrogation is, the more radical Bonner becomes; he even tends to run out of patience and to lose control. Instead of the polite 'you' of the beginning it is then the condescending 'thou', and in the end it is just a matter of calling the accused names like 'heretical knave', 'varlet', 'traitor', or 'syrrhar'.

An equally important factor is the situational context of the verbal encounter, as to time, place and number of persons present, and that goes together with different degrees of formality or informality of the speech situation. Many of the interrogations by Bonner take place in a more informal setting, that is, in Bonner's own palace in Fulham, and he often uses the terms 'talk', even 'private talk', or 'private conference' for these preliminary examinations which represent a special subtype of interrogations. Notorious was Bonner's coal-house, an annex close to his palace that was used for storing coals. This annex he had turned into a small prison where the accused sometimes had to stay for rather a long period of time. The 'talks' in his palace normally took place with only a few witnesses, sometimes with archdeacon Nicholas Harpsfield or a few clerics of his household as a sort of semi-public, but very often they were just verbal exchanges between Bonner and the accused. In contrast to this rather informal situation, the last and official phase usually took place in the consistory at St Paul's, with more examiners present, some of them bishops of other dioceses, with witnesses and a notary to keep the records of the procedure and to write down the final verdict. From the reports that were smuggled out of the prisons and from eyewitnesses[54] we know that the informal talks must have been the worst for the suspects as they were completely in the hands of Bonner. As he was obviously a choleric, he tended to lose his temper when he

---

[54] Freeman 2004; Greengrass 2013.

realised that all his efforts to convince the accused were of no avail, that he had failed. And then – frustrated – he even turned to physical violence.

In his coal house he had stocks which he used for punishing obstinate persons, as witnessed by John Philpot, who met a man from Essex there. This man had already recanted, but had later repented his recantation, and that had enraged Bonner so much that "he fell vpon him like a lion",[55] hit his face blue and black and tore out part of his beard. There was also a man called Thomas Tomkins, a weaver, who remained equally steadfast; so Bonner made him hold his hand into the flame of a candle to give him a foretaste of burning at the stake.[56] Another man, Thomas Hinshaw, a young apprentice, angered him so much that "the fat-panched Bonner" used rods to lash him.[57] It was one of his steadfast partners in these encounters that even dared to criticize Bonner and other examiners present directly for the use of "vnrighteous force" in threatening him with torture and death in matters of belief where persuasion and arguments should be the appropriate 'weapons': *fides est suadenda, & non imponenda*,[58] as John Philpot put it. He saw his examiner's use of language as violence comparable to physical violence as well as a preliminary to physical violence, thereby acting like people at their wits' end "which haue none other argument to stand by, but violence."[59] Thus the victim, the suspect and defendant John Philpot, re-interprets the use of verbal and physical violence practised by the more powerful persons in the controversy as an indicator of intellectual failure and weakness instead of strength and superiority as would be expected of a bishop and of those who assisted him in the examinations of suspects.

While the focus in research on interrogations in heresy trials has up to now mainly been on their legal and institutional contexts or on the quality and development of the theological arguments brought forward by the speakers, a closer look at the micro-structure of this special

[55] Foxe 1583, 1822 [1798].
[56] Foxe 1583, 1557 [1533]–1559 [1543].
[57] Foxe 1583, 2967 [2043]–2068 [2044], 2068 [2044].
[58] Foxe 1583, 1841 [1817].
[59] Foxe 1583, 1847 [1823].

type of dialogue from a more pragma-linguistic point of view would be profitable. As to the special question of verbal violence that can be observed in these exchanges that are often marked by warnings, threats and insults as dominant speech acts on the side of the interrogator, the discourse on the use and abuse of language within the dialogue uttered by both speakers offers further insights into the mechanisms of adversarial dialogue. In criticising *alter ego*'s or in defending one's own language use, speakers tend to refer to leading social values and norms determining language use, as for example charity and politeness (courtesy or civility); and they also refer to the traditional *vitia linguae* inherited from the Middle Ages that form a strong contrast to positive concepts of verbal social interaction: "That is spoken vncharitably, my Lord"[60] is John Philpot's accusation within the Christian context of a verbal exchange on matters of faith. The (assumed) lack of theological competence of his interrogators in general and of Edmund Bonner in particular, is substantiated by their "vaine words"[61] and their "rayling judgment"[62], reproaches uttered by suspects that refer to both, weak theological arguments and to intimidating and aggressive verbal form and style, thus leading to a complete failure of the interrogators' efforts to persuade others. Adverbs indicating the quality of utterances are an obvious indicator of this discourse on language use in confrontational dialogues, as, for example, "to speak mildly", "to speak gently", "to speak charitably" with their appeal to positive values in contrast to an uncharitable use of language, often found in combination with adverbs like "maliciously", "untruely", or "falsely". They form part of a more general process of negotiating the use and abuse of language within a shared speech situation in a face-to-face interaction dominated by the context of heresy examinations and thus marked by mortal danger for the less powerful speaker.[63]

---

[60] Foxe 1583, 1850 [1826].
[61] Foxe 1583, 1844 [1820].
[62] Foxe 1583, 1829 [1805].
[63] A more detailed study of dialogues and the use of violent language in religious controversies in sixteenth-century England is in preparation.

Conclusion

After a short phase when the Reformation was implemented under Edward VI, the process of re-Catholization during the reign of Mary I was connected on the one hand with the use of words to support a process of re-education by sermon and by books, but on the other hand also with the re-introduction of the traditional concept of heresy, which led to persecution, danger, and even execution for those who resisted this process. As to the role of the communication system in the process of re-Catholization, the power of the printing press was required to be checked by the traditional instruments of literary censorship, with lists of heretical and dangerous books, possibly leading to their confiscation and to the public spectacle of book-burning, sometimes together with the burning of their owners. A legal basis in the form of statutes and proclamations for these practices directed against people and books seems to have been important so as to avoid the impression of despotism and arbitrariness. In the processes of persecution Protestants, clergymen as well as laypersons, as individuals and as members of religious communities, experienced various forms of violence, not only physical violence by torture and eventually also execution by fire, but also by verbal attacks in (pre-)examinations in the context of heresy trials. But while books that had been indispensable for them in developing new individual and social religious identities were banned and destroyed by fire, they were able to use forms of written communication in manuscript and in print to reach others, not only to make their suffering known to the world outside prison, but even more to impart knowledge by representing in detail confrontational verbal exchanges on matters of faith to strengthen others. Their reports of physical suffering and verbal exchanges initially smuggled out of prison as manuscripts finally rose above the death of the individuals and found their lasting literary form in print in John Foxe's influential narratives of their martyrdom in his *Acts and Monuments*.

Bibliography

Printed sources

Askew, Anne: *The Examinations of Anne Askew*. Ed. Elaine V. Beilin. Oxford University Press, New York and Oxford 1966.

Calvin, John: *Letters of John Calvin*. Ed. Jules Bonnet. 4 vols. Presbyterian Board of Publication, Philadelphia 1858. Repr. Wipf & Stock Publishers, Eugene OR 2007.

Early English Books Online (EEBO) http://eebo.chadwyck.com.

Foxe, John: *Commentarii Rerum in Ecclesia Gestarum*. V. Rihelius, Strasbourg 1554.

Foxe, John: *Rerum in Ecclesia Gestarum*. N. Brylinger and J. Oporinus, Basel 1559.

Foxe, John: *The Unabridged Acts and Monuments Online or TAMO* (Variorum edition) (HRI Online Publications, Sheffield 2011), http//www.johnfoxe.org.

Mary I: A copie of a letter wyth articles sente from the Queenes Maiestie vnto the Bysshoppe of London [...] at her graces commaundement to be putte in spedye execution. John Cawood, London 1554 (STC 9182). Early English Books Online http://eebo.chadwyck.com (2 February 2017).

Original Letters Relative to the English Reformation. Ed. Hastings Robinson. Cambridge University Press, Cambridge, 1846–1847.

Statutes of the Realm: From Original Records and Authentic Manuscipts. Ed. Alexander Luders, Thomas Edlyne Tomlins et al., 11 vols. London 1810–1828, online edition *The Making of the Modern World*. Gale 2009, Gengage Learning Princeton University Library (http://galenet.galegroup.com).

Tudor Constitutional Documents A.D. 1485–1603 with an Historical Commentary. Ed. J.R. Tanner. Cambridge University Press, Cambridge 1948.

Tudor Royal Proclamations. Vol. 2, The Later Tudors (1553–1587). Ed. Paul L. Hughes and James F. Larkin. Yale University Press, New Haven and London 1969.

Research literature

Ahnert, Ruth: *The Rise of Prison Literature in the Sixteenth Century*. Cambridge University Press, Cambridge 2013.

Ahnert, Ruth and Sebastian E. Ahnert: Protestant Letter Networks in the Reign of Mary I: A Quantitative Approach. *Journal of English Literary History* 82/2015, 1–32.

Alexander, Gina M. V.: *The Life and Career of Edmund Bonner, Bishop of London, until His Deprivation in 1549*. Ph.D. Diss. University of London 1960.

Alexander, Gina M. V.: Bonner and the Marian Persecution. *History* 60/1975, 364–391.

Anderson, Marvin W.: Peter Martyr, Reformed Theologian (1542–1562): His Letters to Heinrich Bullinger and John Calvin. *Sixteenth Century Journal* 4/1973, 41–64.

Aston, Margaret and Elisabeth Ingram: The Iconography of the Acts and Monuments. *John Foxe and the English Reformation*. Ed. David M. Loades. Scolar Press, Aldershot 1997, 66–142.

Bernard, George W.: *The King's Reformation. Henry VIII and the Remaking of the English Church*. Yale University Press, New Haven 2005.

Blagden, Cyprian: *The Stationers' Company. A History, 1403–1959*. Allen & Unwin, London 1960.

Brigden, Susan: *London and the Reformation*. Clarendon Press, Oxford 1989.

Carleton, Kenneth: Bonner, Edmund (d. 1569), Bishop of London. *Oxford Dictionary of National Biography*. Oxford University, 2004; online edition May 2006 http://www.oxforddnb.com (4 February 2013).

Chester, Joseph Lemuel: *John Rogers: The Compiler of the First Authorised English Bible, the Pioneer of the English Reformation, and Its First Martyr*. Longman, London 1861.

Clegg, Cyndia Susan: *Press Censorship in Elizabethan England*. Cambridge University Press, Cambridge 2003.

Collinson, Patrick: Truth and Legend: The Veracity of John Foxe's Book of Martyrs. *Elizabethan Essays*. The Hambledon Press, London 1994, 151–177.

Collinson, Patrick: John Foxe as Historian. *The Unabridged Acts and Monuments Online or TAMO (HRI Online Publications, Sheffield 2011)* http//www.johnfoxe.org (5 February 2013).

Covington, Sarah: The Heresy Examinations of John Philpot: Defiance, Bold Speaking and the Making of a Martyr. *Reformation* 77/2003, 79–133.

Covington, Sarah: The Villainous Tribunals: Reading the Judicial Examinations in the Acts and Monuments. *Acts of Reading: Interpretation, Reading Practices, and the Idea of the Book in Foxe's Actes and Monumentes*. Ed. Thomas P. Anderson and Ryan Netzley. University of Delaware Press, Newark 2010, 176–207.

Covington, Sarah: The Tribunals of Christ and of Man: Law and the Making of Martyrs in Early Modern England. *Mortality* 19/2014, 134–150.

Cressy, David: Book Burning in Tudor and Stuart England. *Sixteenth Century Journal* 36/2005, 1–18.

Da Costa, Alexandra: Functional Ambiguity: Negotiating Censorship in the 1530s. *The Library*, 7th Series 15/2014, 410–423.

Dailey, Alice: *The English Martyr from Reformation to Revolution*. University of Notre Dame Press, Notre Dame 2012.

Dickens, Arthur G.: *The Marian Reaction in the Diocese of York*. St Anthony's Press, London and York 1957.

Dickens, Arthur G.: *Lollards and Protestants in the Diocese of York*. Oxford University Press, Oxford 1959.

Dickens, Arthur G.: *The English Reformation*. Schocken Books, New York 1964.

Dickens, Arthur G: *Reformation Studies*. Hambledon Press, London 1982.

Duffy, Eamon: *Fires of Faith: Catholic England under Mary Tudor*. Yale University Press, New Haven and London 2009.

Edwards, John: *Mary I: England's Catholic Queen*. Yale University Press, New Haven and London 2011.

Edwards, John: Fray Bartolomé Carranza's Blueprint for a Reformed Catholic Church in England. *Reforming Reformation*. Ed. Thomas F. Mayer. Ashgate, Farnham, Surrey 2012, 141–160.

Freemann, Thomas S.: Fate, Faction, and Fiction in Foxe's Book of Martyrs. *Historical Journal* 43/2000, 601–623.

Freeman, Thomas S.: Publish and Perish: the Scribal Culture of the Marian Martyrs. *The Uses of Script and Print, 1300–1700*. Ed. Julia Crick and Alexandra Walsham. Cambridge University Press, Cambridge 2004, 235–254.

Freeman, Thomas S.: John Foxe: A Biography. *The Unabridged Acts and Monuments Online or TAMO (HRI Online Publications, Sheffield 2011)* http//www.johnfoxe.org (5 June 2013).

Freemann, Thomas S.: Burning Zeal. Mary Tudor and the Marian Persecution. *Mary Tudor. Old and New Perspectives*. Ed. Susan Doran and Thomas S. Freeman. Palgrave Macmillan, Basingstoke 2011, 171–205.

Freeman, Thomas S.: Appendix: Foxe's Marian Martyrs. *Mary Tudor: Old and New Perspectives.* Ed. Susan Doran and Thomas S. Freeman. Palgrave Macmillan, Basingstoke 2011, 225–271.

Greengrass, Mark: Scribal Networks and Sustainers in Protestant Martyrology. *Archives Internationales des Idées/International Archive of the History of Ideas* 209/2013, 19–35.

Helmholz, R. H.: Judges and Trials in the English Ecclesiastical Courts. *Judicial Tribunals in England and Europe, 1200–1700.* Vol 1: *The Trial in History.* Ed. Maureen Mulholland and Brian Pullan. Manchester Unversity Press, Manchester and New York 2003, 102–116.

King, John N.: *Foxe's 'Book of Martyrs' and Early Modern Print Culture.* Cambridge University Press, Cambridge 2006.

Krämer, Sybille: Sprache als Gewalt oder: Warum verletzen Worte? *Verletzende Worte: Die Grammatik sprachlicher Missachtung.* Ed. Steffen K. Herrmann. Transcript, Bielefeld 2007, 31–48.

Liebsch, Burkhard: What Does (Not) "Count" as Violence: On the State of Recent Debates About the Inner Connection Between Language and Violence. *Human Studies* 36/2013, 7–24.

Loach, Jennifer: The Marian Establishment and the Printing Press. *English Historical Review* 101/1986, 135–148.

Loach, Jennifer: Mary Tudor and the Re-Catholisation of England. *History Today* 44/1994, 16–22.

Loach, Jennifer: *Edward VI.* Yale University Press, New Haven and London 1999.

Loades, David: The Press Under the Early Tudors: A Study in Censorship and Sedition. *Transactions of the Cambridge Bibliographical Society* 4/1964, 29–50.

Loades, David: The Enforcement of Reaction, 1553–1558. *Journal of Ecclesiastical History* 16/1965, 54–66.

Loades, David: *The Oxford Martyrs.* B.T. Batsford LTD, London 1970.

Loades, David: *Mary Tudor. A Life.* Blackwell, Cambridge, MA 1989.

Loades, David: *Politics, Censorship and the English Reformation.* Pinter, London and New York 1991.

Loades, David: Foxe and Queen Mary. *The Unabridged Acts and Monuments Online or TAMO (HRI Online Publications, Sheffield 2011)* http//www.johnfoxe.org (5 February 2013).

Luborsky, Ruth Samson: The Illustrations: Their Pattern and Plan. *John Foxe. An Historical Perspective.* Ed. David Loades. Ashgate, Aldershot 1999, 67–84.

MacCulloch, Diarmaid: *Thomas Cranmer: A Life.* Yale University Press, New Haven and London 1996.

MacCulloch, Diarmaid: *The Boy King: Edward VI and the Protestant Reformaion.* University of California Press, Berkeley and Los Angeles 2002 (orginally published as *Tudor Church Militant. Edward VI and the Protestant Reformation.* Allen Lane, London 1999).

Mayer, Thomas F.: *Reginald Pole: Prince & Prophet.* Cambridge University Press, Cambridge 2000.

Mayer, Thomas F.: Introduction. *Reforming Reformation.* Ed. Thomas F. Mayer. Ashgate, Farnham, Surrey 2012, 1–13.

Meyer, Carl S.: Henry VIII Burns Luther's Books, 12 May 1521. *Journal of Ecclesiastical History* 9/1958, 173–187.

Nicholls, David: The Theatre of Martyrdom in the French Reformation. *Past & Present* 121/ 1988, 49–73.

Nunner-Winkler, Gertrud: Überlegungen zum Gewaltbegriff. *Gewalt: Entwicklungen, Strukturen, Analyseprobleme.* Ed. Wilhelm Heitmeyer and Hans-Georg Soeffner. Suhrkamp, Frankfurt a.M. 2004, 21–61.

Rafetseder, Hermann: *Bücherverbrennungen: Die öffentliche Hinrichtung von Schriften im historischen Wandel*. Böhlau, Vienna 1988.

Redworth, Glyn: *In Defence of the Church Catholic: The Life of Stephen Gardiner*. Basil Blackwell, Oxford 1990.

Riordan, Michael and Alec Ryrie: Stephen Gardiner and the Making of a Protestant Villain. *Sixteenth Century Journal* 34/2003, 1039–1063.

Smith, David M.: *Guide to Bishops' Registers of England and Wales: A Survey from the Middle Ages to the Abolition of Episcopacy in 1646*. The Royal Historical Society, London 1981.

Werner, Thomas: *Den Irrtum liquidieren: Bücherverbrennungen im Mittelalter*. Vandenhoeck & Ruprecht, Göttingen 2007.

Wood, Rufus: Supplementing the Word: Spiritual Endurance and Bodily Suffering in Foxe's *Acts and Monuments: Writing and Reform in Sixteenth-Century England. Interdisciplinary Essays*. Ed. John Blakeley and Mike Pincombe. Edwid Mellen Press, Lewiston NY 2008, 1–24.

———

Abbreviations
EEBO   Early English Books Online
SR   Statutes of the Realm
STC   Short Title Catalogue
TRP   Tudor Royal Proclamations

Concepts of violent language in inner-Protestant controversies in Elizabethan England

Sarah Ströer

Introduction

In terms of religious conflict and controversy, the Elizabethan era (1558–1603) is one of the most interesting in English history.[1] The country went a unique path in terms of religious policies that started with the break from Rome during Henry VIII's reign (r. 1509–1547). Under Edward VI (r. 1547–1553), Henry's son, the country turned towards Protestantism in doctrine until Mary I, upon her succession (r. 1553–1558) reinstated Catholicism. Elizabeth I, daughter of Henry VIII and Anne Boleyn, was a Protestant and upon her accession to the throne in 1558 steered the country towards Protestantism once again. However, Elizabeth's Religious Settlement was not radically Protestant. It reinstated a version of the Protestant Book of Common Prayer which still allowed for "a Catholic understanding of the real presence of Christ"[2]

---

[1] For an overview of the recent historiography on the "English Reformation" see Wenig 2000, 3–8. For a concise account of the Reformation in England Heal 2003; for the later decades see MacCulloch 2001.

[2] Haigh 1993, 240.

during the communion, and vestments and church ornaments remained in use. A large portion of the Elizabethan protestant clergy understood these issues as elements of Roman Catholicism remaining in the English Church, and they expected the Settlement to be provisional with further reform of the Church to follow. Elizabeth, on the other hand, viewed the matter of religious policy as settled. The reform-minded part of the clergy and similar reform-minded groups of lay people, which existed especially in London, fuelled the inner-protestant controversies during Elizabeth's reign. The three most important of these were the Vestments Controversy of the 1560s, the *Admonition* controversy of the 1570s, and the Marprelate Controversy of 1588/89.

In all three controversies printed material and the style of language contained within it was used as a "weapon" by reform-minded circles in the "fight" for further reformation of the English Church. In assessing this issue, it is important to distinguish between a modern perspective that all too quickly describes acts of aggression as violence and a contemporary perspective that focusses on the self-perception of the participants of these controversies. Unfortunately, this self-perception is at most times difficult to assess. The Marprelate Controversy, which will be considered in detail below, has proven to be valuable since the texts by the reformers as well as the official answers by the bishops discuss the role of language use and book production in theological controversies.

Language and violence in theological controversies

The Marprelate Controversy was arguably the most prominent Elizabethan inner-protestant controversy. Named after the tracts' fictitious author Martin Marprelate, this controversy took place between October 1588 and September 1589. In seven tracts, six of them pamphlets between 30 and 56 pages, and one broadsheet, a group of lay reformers attacked the leading and high ranking clergy of the English Church. The tracts have attracted much scholarly attention and have been studied, among other issues, for their literary style and use of rhetorics,[3] and for their materiality and use of the printed page.[4] Authorship has still not been established for certain, but research today is focused on other aspects and regards the tracts as a collaborative effort.[5] Three men were probably at the centre of the Marprelate "project": John Penry, a Welsh polemicist, Job Throkmorton, a country gentleman who sat in the 1586/87 parliament and held pro-puritan speeches, and Robert Waldegrave, a London printer who printed puritan and Presbyterian material during the late 1570s and early 80s.[6] Scholars largely concur that Marprelate "attacked" the bishops in his tracts and some scholars have commented on his use of metaphors of physical harm, such as Evelyn Tribble in her study *Margins and Marginality*.[7] However, there is no study that analyses the issue of how and to what end notions and concepts of violent language were expressed in the Marprelate tracts and in the answers to the tracts. This article is based on my recently finished PhD thesis "Violent Language and Its Use in Religious Conflicts in Elizabethan England: Discourses on Values and Norms in the Marprelate Controversy (1588/89)" which aimed to close some of these gaps and analysed and discussed in detail the contemporary notions of violence and language.

Considering modern theories and scholarship, the relationship between language and violence can take several shapes. Language can be seen as inducing or provoking physical violence. On the other hand, language is often seen as the anti-thesis to violence, and discussion and debate are viewed as the tools to stop conflicts from escalating into physical violence. Furthermore, language can describe and define acts of violence, and finally, language itself can be a medium for violence. All these notions, and especially the last one, presuppose a pragmatic

---

[3] For an early study of Marprelate's style see Coolidge 1959, 526–532. For Marprelate's use of rhetoric in his satire see Anselment 1970, 103–119, as well as Anselment 1979, esp. 33–60. See also Kendall 1986.

[4] Tribble 1993, Clegg 1997, 170–197, and Lander 2006, 80–109.

[5] For studies that focus on the authorship of the tracts see McGinn1966 and Carlson 1981.

[6] Cross 2015; Collinson 2015; Mann 2016.

[7] Tribble 1993, 102, 109.

perspective on language and language use which assumes that speaking and writing, and indeed printing, are actions that individuals perform. Such a pragmatic perspective has become widespread in a large portion of linguistic research since the 1950s due to the influence of natural language philosophy and speech act theory.[8] Understanding speaking, writing, and printing as actions means drawing attention to the effects of language use. One of these effects can be harm done to people, things, or causes. In modern English, this is often expressed metaphorically by language relating to physical harm and thus it seems commonplace that humans use language to harm other humans. However, philosophical, linguistic, and psychological research into why humans are able to do this has produced complex results. The most important theoretical contribution to the issue of linguistic vulnerability has been made by the philosopher Judith Butler in her 1997 book *Excitable Speech*. She has argued that humans are vulnerable to harm done via language because of the role language plays in constituting the social existence of individuals: "One 'exists' not only by virtue of being recognized, but, in a prior sense, by being *recognizable*."[9] Thus, since language is constitutive of human social existence, it can also alter this social existence which can at times be perceived as harmful or hurtful.

In a historical perspective the question is what kind of specific notions about the relationship between language and violence were present and whether these were the same as the concepts suggested as universal by modern theories. The Elizabethans held complex notions about how and why language, and especially language in print, was a dangerous tool that could be used to do harm to people, to causes, even to the stability of the country. On the following pages, this article will consider some of these notions and concepts and their historical contexts. It will present and discuss some of the narratives, metaphors, similes and argumentative structures that were available to Elizabethans to write about language and violence in the context of theological controversy.

---

[8] Austin 1972; Searle 1969; Searle 1979; Collavin 2011.
[9] Butler 1997, 5. Emphasis is in the original.

The book and language as weapons in Elizabethan inner-Protestant controversies

The first Elizabethan inner-Protestant controversy took place in the 1560s and began with the issue of the necessity of clerical vestments. One of the central issues causing opposition to the policy of the Established Church after the Religious Settlement of 1559 was the fact that clerics were requested to wear the surplice during church services. Reform-minded protestant ministers believed the surplice to be a sign of Roman Catholicism and thus regarded it as unnecessary. In the early 1560s the issue caused some agitation, with ministers being deprived of their positions for refusing to wear the surplice, especially in London.[10] In 1566, the first printed tracts against vestments appeared anonymously. These tracts were answered shortly afterwards, also anonymously, but this reply is generally attributed to Matthew Parker, who lamented that the London ministers had "publiquely by prynt diuulged and dispearsed"[11] their tracts. Making a theological discussion public seems to have been Parker's main reason for answering the tract.

The first tract by the reform-minded ministers was printed by Henry Denham, a member of the Stationers' Company. This London organization of printers oversaw and regulated the trade of printing. In 1566, a system of licensing was established that required members of the company to enter every book they printed into the Company's Registers. By doing so, they obtained a license to print this work; printing without a license was punishable by fines.[12] Denham printed the tract without such a license, making it illegal, and he was indeed fined 20s. The supposed author of the first tract, Robert Crowley, was deprived of his benefice in 1566 by the High Commission, but he was allowed to return in 1575.[13] In this case of controversy, there were consequences for both the author and printer of the controversial material, but neither

10 Collinson 1967, 70–77.
11 [Parker] 1566, sig *3.
12 Clegg 1997, 15; Loades 1991, 99.
13 Clegg 1997, 50.

suffered prosecution by the State. In this early stage of inner-protestant religious controversy in Elizabethan England, the reform-minded circles still enjoyed some freedom to express non-conforming ideas, even if they were sanctioned. Part of the reason for this relative freedom certainly was that the non-conforming ideas expressed in the Vestments Controversy were not nearly as radical as those expressed in the later cases of controversy. Nevertheless, in the Vestments Controversy printed material was used as a means to express theologically non-conforming ideas, addressing a wider public rather than an academic readership. However, it is important to emphasize that the language employed by the reformers was not seen as problematic; the mode of publication and distribution mainly caused legal concerns that were dealt with by the Stationers' Company. While the content was controversial and at times brought forward as harsh critique, the pamphlets were not expressedly critized as harmful.

Inner-Protestant controversy took a more radical turn in the 1570s when the doctrine of Presbyterianism spread in reform-minded circles. The debated issues centred upon the basic structure of church government of the English Church, especially concerning the hierarchical structure of the church and the role of the bishops. Presbyterianism favoured a more democratic approach to church government based on the four offices of the primitive church described in the Acts of the Apostles and after the example of the Genevan churches.[14] The Presbyterians vehemently opposed the traditional and hierarchical structure of the English Church, the office of bishop in general, and the fact that the English bishops held worldly power. The *Admonition* controversy, which took place between 1572 and 1575, was named after the first two tracts that appeared after the 1572 parliament, in which reform bills had once again failed. The first *Admonition to the Parliament* appeared anonymously but is generally attributed to John Field, a young London clergyman who was to become the leader of the Presbyterian movement, and Thomas Wilcox, also a prominent Presbyterian.[15] The *Admonition* was a harsh critique of the current government of the English Church,

---

[14] Lake 1988, 1–2.
[15] Collinson 2008; Collinson 2004.

employing much stronger language than the tracts in the Vestments controversy did. While the London ministers of the 1560s largely meant to explain their position and theological reasons for refusing to wear the surplice, the *Admonition to the Parliament* was meant by the reformers and understood by the authorities as an attack. Employing anti-Catholic discourse, Field and Wilcox, for example, characterized the bishops as cruel tyrants and called the Book of Common Prayer "an unperfecte booke, culled & picked out of that popishe dunghill, the Masse book full of abhominations."[16] The controversy continued with a second tract by the reformers, and the Establishment answered with a sermon held by Thomas Cooper, then Bishop of Lincoln, at Paul's Cross and with a reply in print, the *Answer to a Certen Libel Intituled, An Admonition to the Parliament* by John Whitgift, Master of Trinity, Cambridge at the time. Whitgift's *Answer* started the second phase of the controversy, and he was answered by Thomas Cartwright, also in a more traditional form of detailed refutation.

The reactions by the Establishment to these Presbyterian works were slightly different than those to the tracts of the Vestments controversy. In this case, not only the Church in the form of the High Commission took action against the controversial material but also the State. Soon after the publication of the first *Admonition* the two authors, Field and Wilcox, were detained, and in October 1572 they were sentenced to one year in prison.[17] The Queen also reacted by royal proclamation, by which she sought to suppress the distribution of the two *Admonitions*. First and foremost, the proclamation was a reaction to the non-conforming content of the works which was feared to "make division and dissention in the opinions of men"[18] and thus to endanger the religious unity of the country. There is already an uneasiness about the powers of language inherent in this fear, but it is not yet called *sedition* as it would be in the reactions to the Marprelate tracts.

---

[16] [Field] 1572, 21.
[17] Clegg 1997, 51.
[18] Elisabeth I 2009.

Case study: Concepts of violent language in the Marprelate controversy

The first Marprelate tract, commonly known as the *Epistle* appeared from a secret press that was hidden in a private manor in October 1588. The authors used a pseudonym rather than choosing to write anonymously. This pseudonym, Martin Marprelate, was developed into a kind of stage persona, who seems to address the bishops reverently but in fact employs irony and sarcasm as well as dramatic and satirical literary elements to attack them. As will be illustrated below, Marprelate tells anecdotes about several members of the leading clergy and insults them implicitly and explicitly. The *Epistle* was a reaction to *A Defense of the Government in the Church of Englande for Ecclesiasticall Matters* by John Bridges, a lengthy defence of the existing church government against Presbyterian works of the 1580s. Bridges used jokes and ridicule in the *Defense*, and the first Marprelate tracts were a critique of Bridges' style.[19] The second tract, known as the *Epitome*, appeared in November 1588 and afterwards the tracts seem to have attracted the attention of church officials and of the Queen. The search for the secret press, the printer of the tracts and their author began in the winter of 1588/89 but remained unsuccessful for some time.[20] In mid-January the *Admonition to the People of England* by Thomas Cooper, Bishop of Winchester, appeared. This work was the first printed response to the tracts. Cooper condemned both content and style of the tracts and presented the language Marprelate used as dangerous. The third Marprelate tract called *Certain Mineral and Metaphysical Schoolpoints*, a broadsheet, appeared at the end of January, followed by a proclamation by the Queen and the first of several sermons against the tracts in February. In March 1589 the fourth Marprelate tract appeared, this time a longer pamphlet in quarto format similar to the first two tracts, called *Hay Any Work for Cooper*, which focussed on Thomas Cooper as the new prime target.

Until this point the tracts had been printed by Robert Waldegrave. After printing *Hay Any Work for Cooper* Waldegrave left the Marprelate

---

[19] Vivier 2014, 3–35 for the relationship of Marprelate and Bridges.
[20] Black 2008, lviii.

project, and it took until July until a new printer could be recruited. With the fifth and sixth tracts, *Theses Martinianae* and *The Just Censure and Reproof of Martin Junior*, two new personas were introduced. In the fifth tract the original Martin's son claims to publish his father's work, which he found in a lane; in the *Just Censure* the older brother reprimands his younger brother for having acted rashly. After the sixth tract the printer and his assistants decided to go to Lancashire to print the next tract, but due to a mishap they were discovered by the authorities and detained and questioned.[21] In September 1589 a last tract, *The Protestation of Martin Marprelate*, appeared, which apparently was printed by amateurs, possibly by John Penry and Job Throkmorton themselves.

For reasons that are hard to identify, remarkably few individuals were punished in the aftermath of the controversy. The printers John Hodgkins, Valentine Simmes, and Arthur Tomlin were held first in Bridewell and then in the Tower.[22] There are extant documents that prove that they were interrogated several times, possibly under torture, and finally confessed in December 1589 to having printed the second set of the Marprelate tracts.[23] Hodgkins was even sentenced to death "on the charge that printing the *Theses Martinianae* violated the statute 23 Elizabeth, chapter 2", the Act against seditious words against the Queen.[24] However, he was pardoned after signing a submission. His assistants were eventually freed as well. Several of the supporters – individuals who had for example allowed the press to be hidden on their property – were sentenced to fines, which were remitted in the end. John Penry was able to flee to Scotland, as well as Robert Waldegrave. Job Throkmorton was indicted for being Marprelate but then released on a technicality.[25]

As mentioned, the Marprelate tracts do not just react to the *Defense* and to the *Admonition* on a thematic level, criticizing the existing church government and calling for further reform. The tracts also contain

[21] Black 2008, lv.
[22] Black 2008, lv.
[23] Arraignment of John Hodgkins.
[24] Black 2015.
[25] Black 2008, xlv–xlvi.

anecdotes about several members of the high-ranking clergy, especially some of the bishops, and attack a number of individuals personally. Furthermore, all of the Marprelate tracts, as well as the *Admonition*, contain reflections on language use and its role in religious controversy and thus provide illustrative material regarding contemporary concepts of violent language.

The Marprelate tracts contain a plethora of creative insults, irreverent language, ridiculing anecdotes, and ambiguous threats. Thus, for example, Marprelate employs an anti-Catholic discourse in characterizing the bishops as cruel tyrants, calling them "petty antichrists, petty popes, proud prelates, intolerable withstanders of reformation, enemies of the gospel, and most covetous wretched priests."[26] Such anti-Catholic insults were common *topoi* in reformation polemics.[27] Marprelate also attacks John Bridges by questioning his academic abilities, as for example when he muses that his books "seem to proceed from the brains of a woodcock, as having neither wit nor learning."[28] He calls Thomas Cooper, the Bishop of Winchester, "choleric and peevish"[29], claims Richard Cosin is lacking in grace and is disposed of jesting, and accuses John Aylmer of bowling on Sundays and of having stolen cloth belonging to two London dyers.[30]

Thomas Cooper in his *Admonition* strongly condemns this irreverent language and presents it as dangerous. In the paratext to the *Admonition*, "To the Reader", Cooper makes use of an illustrative metaphor regarding the effects of slander: "The darts, I confesse, of deceitfull and slaunderous tongues, are verye sharpe, and the burning of the woundes made by them, will as hardly in the hearts of many bee quenched, as the coales of Iuniper."[31] Cooper here alludes to Psalm 120.3–4: "What doth a deceiptfull tongue vnto thee? what good bryngeth it thee / [So much] as sharpe arrowes of a strong man [in thy sydes:] with Iuniper coales

---

[26] Marprelate 1588, Epistle, 10.
[27] On anti-Catholic discourse see Lake 1989, 72–106; Wiener 1971, 27–62.
[28] Marprelate 1588, Epistle, 14.
[29] Marprelate 1588, Epistle, 8.
[30] Marprelate 1588, Epistle, 8;13.
[31] Cooper 1589, sig. Aij r–v.

[powred on thy head.]"[32] Cooper claims that Marprelate's language use has done harm by invoking the images of the sharp dart, a weapon, and the burning wound it produces. *Dart* here can refer to any pointed missile. It has to be understood as a ranged weapon, which is released on an incentive of the bowman or thrower and then exists and issues damage on its own. The damage is done after careful aiming with some delay in time. Cooper uses the dart as a metaphor for words by referring to tongues as well, but it can also be understood as a metaphor for a printed tract, which is prepared and aimed and then released. This metaphor stresses the effect of Marprelate's language by the emphasis on the physical wound. Thus, Cooper implies that the effects of slanderous language are analogous to such a physical wound. However, he presents the wounds made by slander as located in the "hearts of many", in other words, in the spiritual body rather than in the physical. Here, there is a concept of effective and harmful language present, of language that has been actively used and has produced effects, not physically or even socially, but on the spiritual bodies of "many".

A second metaphor related to a concept of violent language is that of the tongue as a snake and the effects of language as venomous. This image is one of the central metaphors of Christian speech ethics and can also be traced to the psalter. Psalms 58.4 for example claims that the wicked "have venom like the venom of a serpent" and psalm 140.3 that "they make their tongues sharp as a snake's, and under their lips is the venom of vipers." This metaphor also employs notions of physical effects via the metaphor of venom that the speakers of violent language "inject" into their victims. Thomas Cooper refers to the image of the serpent and venom a number of times in the *Admonition*. In the letter to the reader when he explains his motivation for answering the Marprelate tracts he writes: "I must needs therfore looke for any hurt, that venemous, scoffing, and unbridled tongues can worke toward me."[33] Cooper here presents Marprelate's language use as an aggressive action, which was intended to do him harm and is in fact able to do harm.

---

[32] The Holie Bible 1568. This edition was commonly known and will be referred to below as the Bishops' Bible.

[33] Cooper 1589, sig. Aij r.

In a number of instances throughout his tracts, Martin Marprelate employs metaphors of physical harm in connection to works of theological controversy or the language contained within it, as well. In the first tract, for example, Marprelate comments on the previous Admonition controversy from the 1570s. John Whitgift, then master of Trinity College, Cambridge and Archbishop of Canterbury by the time of the Marprelate tracts, had left Cartwright the last word in the second phase of this controversy:

> Well fare old mother experience yet, the burnt child dreads the fire: his grace will carry to his grave, I warrant you, the blows which Master Cartwright gave him in this cause: and therefore no marvel though he was loth to have any other so banged as he himself was to his woe.[34]

Marprelate uses the words "blows" and "banged" to describe what Cartwright's books did to Whitgift. Both have the general meaning here of "to hit", and "hit" as a noun respectively, implying violent action, which is only intensified by the phrase "as he himself was to his woe." Cartwright's books or his arguments "hit" Whitgift and caused him woe. By these physical metaphors, Marprelate implies that Cartwright's books had done harm to Whitgift. However, he does not emphasize the effects of this harmful language but rather focusses on the action done by Cartwright. In the *Epistle*, Marprelate compares the controversy to a physically violent fight, in which weapons are used, from which one can run like a coward and from which one will appear as the winner. He presents printed words, and the argument contained in them as weapons, implying that they are effective and one can act with them, maybe even harm people or causes.

Some of the other Marprelate tracts also contain similar metaphors of printed works "hitting" their addressees. In the beginning of *Hay Any Work for Cooper* for example, Marprelate uses a notion of hitting as punishment when he promises John Bridges to "lay on load" on him. Literally, this expression means "to deal heavy blows"; figuratively it

---

[34] Marprelate 1588, Epistle, 8.

can mean "to speak with emphasis of exaggeration".[35] This is one of the instances in which Marprelate issues threats that can be understood literally as physical violence or figuratively as writing of further books. Already the first tract, the *Epistle*, contains a revealing passage in which Marprelate issues threats towards John Bridges and towards the bishops: "…yet you shall answer my reasons, or else I will so course you, as you were never coursed since you were a simoniacal dean."[36] *To course* means to pursue or hunt with foxes but was also used figuratively as to pursue or persecute. Marprelate extends this threat of hunting further in the *Epistle* to comprise the bishops as well. If the bishops will not answer him in print, he will "kindle such a fire in the holes of these foxes, as shall never be quenched as long as there is a lord bishop in England."[37] He very assertively says "you shall answer", "you shall not deal" and threatens with "or else" and "unless." Here, again, Marprelate's threat can be understood in a literal way as a threat of physical violence or in a figurative way as threatening to publish more material on the bishops.

The hunting metaphor is open to a range of interpretations. What Marprelate most likely actually means by his threats becomes more explicit in the *Epistle* as well. Marprelate refers to his own activity of publishing anecdotes about the bishops as his most feared quality and threatens that "[i]f you do not leave your persecuting of godly Christians and good subjects, that seek to live uprightly in the fear of God, and the obedience of her Majesty, all your dealing shall be made known unto the world."[38] Marprelate threatens to continue publishing stories about the bishops. In the light of this passage, his more metaphorical threats can be understood as meaning the same: making known publicly – by printing further tracts – more about the bishops. Marprelate seems to be aware that the danger the authorities perceive him to be is grounded in his ability to address a wide and public readership by his use of cheap print and non-academic style.

While in the early Marprelate tracts comparisons of controversy to physical action or even fighting are numerous, the relationship of

[35] load, n., OED Online 2015.
[36] Marprelate 1588, Epistle, 19.
[37] Marprelate 1588, Epistle, 19.
[38] Marprelate 1588, Epistle, 33.

language and violence changes in the last tract, *The Protestation of Martin Marprelate*. In this tract, the use of language in controversy and scholarly disputation are presented entirely positively, as the peaceful alternative to physical violence, and ultimately as the only way to resolve conflict and find the truth. The theme of the "free disputation" for the puritans to discuss their agenda is present already in the first tract when Marprelate uses formulaic expressions reminiscent of formal petitions and expresses faith that a free disputation will establish the truth about theological controversial questions. [39] The last tract that was published, the *Protestation*, can then be read as a challenge to a disputation. Marprelate emphasizes the puritans' allegedly peaceful language use against the alleged physical violence the authorities have used in their reactions to the earlier tracts and asserts that

> one sound syllogism – brought in for the proof of their unlawful callings shall more dismay and sooner induce me to give over my course that a thousand warrants, a thousand pursuivants, a thousand threats, and a thousand racks.[40]

Marprelate further argues that the bishops are responsible for the physical violence that certain members of the Marprelate project suffered or were feared to suffer and positions himself and the puritans as reasonable academics who use the only means to establish the truth: language and argumentation.

In the Marprelate tracts, language appears as exceedingly powerful and effective in the context of religious controversy. Such a concept of language as a "weapon" that is employed in order to "win" an academic argument is common for the era and can be traced to the figure of the orator in Cicero and Quintilian and is also present in the Bible.[41] Academic training in the Elizabethan universities was largely based on classical rhetoric and dialectic and students were trained in the use of rhetorical figures, in composition of texts, and the most effective forms

---

[39] Marprelate 1588, Epistle, 9.
[40] Marprelate 1589, The Protestation, 198.
[41] Rebhorn 1995, 42.

of argumentation.[42] Furthermore, formal disputations constituted an integral part of university education. These practices permeated the elite culture of Elizabethan England to such a degree that Joshua Rodda in his study on religious disputations has called this elite culture "discursive"[43] and Peter Mack describes it as a "culture of debate".[44] University educated Elizabethans believed that rational argumentation would always bring the truth to light. On the other hand, it was believed that a skilled orator was able to persuade anyone of anything and this was often expressed in martial language as for example in Henry Peacham's style manual *The Garden of Eloquence* who compares rhetorical figures to "martiall instruments both of defence & invasion" and then even explicitly calls them "weapons alwaies readie in our handes, wherewith we may defend our selues, inuade our enemies, reuenge our wrongs, ayd the weake, deliuer the simple from dangers, co[n]serue true religion, & confute idolatry?"[45] However, this concept of effective language use, even if it was expressed in physical and martial metaphors, does not automatically constitute a concept of violent language. The power wielded by language use is in this context largely evaluated as legitimate.

But the authorities perceived the Marprelate tracts as dangerous. On the one hand, the content, that is the arguments for a Presbyterian church government, were thought to undermine religious unity. On the other hand, the reactions to the Marprelate tracts show that the way Marprelate used language was understood as dangerous as well. Uncontrolled language was largely believed to be the sign of an unchristian and unstable character. Furthermore, the concept of sedition began to emerge at the end of the sixteenth century, grounded on the belief that language had the power to incite civil war and unrest.[46] David Cressy points out that during the sixteenth century no precise legal definition of sedition existed, but cases of seditious words were tried by the Court of Star Chamber.[47]

[42] Mack 2002.
[43] Rodda 2014, 8.
[44] Mack 2002, 9.
[45] Peacham 1593, [sig. AB iv r].
[46] sedition, n, *OED Online* 2016. Manning 1980, 101.
[47] Cressy 2010, 43.

The concept of language being able to incite civil unrest occurs in Thomas Cooper's *Admonition*, for example when he warns that "if this outragious spirit of boldnesse be not stopped speedily, I feare he wil prove himself to bee, not onely *Mar-prelate*, but *Mar-prince, Mar-state, Mar-law, Mar-magistrate*, and all together, vntill hee bring it to an Anababtisticall equality and communitie."[48] By warning that Marprelate's behaviour might lead to an "Anababtisticall equality and communitie" Cooper implies that he fears an overthrow of the hierarchical structure of society altogether. It is likely that Cooper here alludes to the events that had taken place in Münster some fifty years previously, where the Anabaptists managed to establish an Anabaptist kingdom and community of goods within the city. On the one hand, Cooper's warning refers to the presbyterian form of church government. On the other hand, however, Cooper also argues that language use is a sign of someone's state of mind and that Marprelate's language use will lead to uproars and civil wars:

> [i]t hath also in all Histories bene obserued, that loose boldnesse of minde tovvard the Superiours, is ioyned always with contempt: and contemptous boldnesse is the very roote and spring of discord, dissentions, vprores, ciuill vvarres, and all desperate attempts, that may breed trouble and danger in the State.[49]

Cooper does not use the term *sedition* itself but the argument he makes indicates a concept of language use being able to incite physical violence. The invocation of the dangers of Anabaptism was a common strategy in anti-puritan writing and already employed in the *Admonition* controversy in the 1570s by John Whitgift. However, Cooper here makes an explicit connection between language use and the danger it poses to the stability of the state.

---

[48] Cooper, 1589, 36. The prefix "mar-" derives from the verb *to mar* and means "To hamper or hinder; to impair or damage. mar,v. *OED Online*, 2016.
[49] Cooper 1589, 36.

Conclusion

How notions of harm and violence done by language were and are expressed in any time or context reveals underlying norms and values of language use. They show how the limits of legitimate language use were debated and negotiated. That concepts of violent language and harm done by language existed in Elizabethan England is obvious. This article has shown how such notions were expressed in one of the most infamous theological, inner-protestant controversies, the Marprelate controversy. Language, as has been stressed, was thought to be an effective tool of argumentation and persuasion, and thus was used accordingly in the inner-Protestant religious controversies. The three controversies that were considered here show that language was seen as powerful and potentially dangerous – so much so that authors and printers were punished not solely for the content of what they produced but also for the style of the language used and the manner of publication. It could also be shown that the Marprelate tracts diverge to some extent from a notion of language as the tool with which truth will established. In the tracts language was used as a weapon, directed not against the opponents' arguments but against the opponents themselves. The bishops reacted accordingly, critizing such language use as harmful and unchristian.

The metaphors and comparisons used in the texts of the Marprelate controversy have shown that both sides viewed their language as effective and powerful. Furthermore, both sides made use of physical imagery in connection to language use, the metaphors of hitting with arguments, comparisons of language to weapons and its effects to physical wounds. It has also been shown that there existed a notion of language as the anti-thesis to physical violence, of argumentation and debate as the peaceful alternative.

It is not surprising that in the context of theological controversy religious aspects, metaphors and concepts were central, and it has been shown that they were used especially by the bishops in their reactions and condemnations of Marprelate's language. In the introductory remarks of this article it was mentioned that modern research usually understands harm done by language as psychological or social harm.

Language thus has the power to alter one's sense of self or one's social identity. Elizabethan England had notions of lanuage being able to do harm to reputation, honour, or one's "good name" – an aspect that unfortunately could not be expanded here. More importantly in the current context is the fact that there existed a notion of language doing spiritual harm to the recipient and to some degree even to the speaker of such language. The centrality of biblical metaphors in the discourse of violent language in the sources demonstrates that the danger of this language use was understood in religious terms. Such language did harm "in the hearts" of the addressees and the speakers and writers of such language were seen as uncharitable and unchristian.

What is maybe more surprising is the deep uneasiness about the political implications of harmful language that the sources demonstrate. Embedded in religious themes and theological notions of providence and an apocalyptic worldview that believed the end of days to be imminent, there is a fear present of the effects the "boldness" of the Marprelate tracts might have on the people who read them. Such anxieties over the power of language, the power of print to incite unrest, rebellion, and pysical violence, the power of language to harm people or causes, the notion that a person's language use reveals his or her character are all central to any consideration of the role of language use and print to the religious culture of the era.

Bibliography

Sources

"Arraignment of John Hodgkins," *The Marprelate Press: A Documentary History*, February 2015, University of Massachusetts Amherst, accessed 27 June 2016, http://people.umass.edu/marprelate/documenttwenty.html.

C[ooper], T[homas]: *An Admonition to the People of England*. C. Baker, London 1589. STC 5682. *Early English Books Online*. Accessed 3 November 2016 http://eebo.chadwyck.com/search/full_rec?SOURCE=pgimages.cfg&ACTION=ByID&ID=99853729&PAGENO=1.

Elizabeth I: By the Queene. The Queenes Maiestie Consydering that notwithstanding that by Great and Matrure Deliberation of the Wysest of the Realme, a Godly & Good Order of Public Prayer and Administration of the Sacraments hath ben set Foorth and Allowed by Parliament, 1573. *Censorship and the Press, 1580–1720.* Vol. 1, *1557–1639.* Ed. Cyndia Susan Clegg. Taylor & Francis, London 2009, 41–42.

[Field, John:] "An Admonition to the Parliament." *Puritan Manifestoes. A Study of the Origin of the Puritan Revolt.* Eds. Walter Howard Frere and Charles Edward Douglas. Society for Promoting Christian Knowledge, London 1907, 1–57.

The Holie Bible. Conteynyng the Olde Testament and the Newe. R. Iugge, London 1568. STC 2099. *Early English Books Online.* Accessed 6 October 2016 http://eebo.chadwyck.com/search/full_rec?SOURCE=pgimages.cfg&ACTION=ByID&ID=99857223&PAGENO=1.

Marprelate, Martin: *The Martin Marprelate Tracts. A Modernized and Annotated Edition.* Ed. Joseph Black. Cambridge University Press, Cambridge 2008.

[Parker, Matthew:] *A Brief Examination for the Tyme, of a Certaine Declaration, Lately Put in Print in the Name and Defence of Certaine Ministers in London.* R. Iugge, London 1566. STC 10387, Reel number 341:31. *Early English Books Online.* Accessed 1 September 2016 http://eebo.chadwyck.com/search/full_rec?SOURCE=pgimages.cfg&ACTION=ByID&ID=99837469&VID=1792&PAGENO=1.

Peacham, Henry: *The Garden of Eloquence Conteining the Most Excellent Ornaments, Exornations, Lightes, Flowers, and Formes of Speech, Commonly Called the Figures of Rhetorike.* H. Jackson, London 1593. STC 19498. *Early English Books Online.* Accessed 20 September 2016 http://eebo.chadwyck.com/search/full_rec?SOURCE=pgimages.cfg&ACTION=ByID&ID=99849547&PAGENO=1.

Research literature

Anselment, Raymond: *'Betwixt Jest and Earnest' Marprelate, Milton, Marvell, Swift & the Decorum of Religious Ridicule.* Toronto University Press, Toronto 1979.

Anselment, Raymond: Rhetoric and the Dramatic Satire of Martin Marprelate. *Studies in English Literature, 1500–1900* 1/1970, 103–119.

Austin, John Langshaw: *How to Do Things with Words.* 2nd ed. Oxford University Press, Oxford 1972.

Black, Joseph: Introduction. *The Martin Marprelate Tracts: A Modernized and Annotated Edition.* Ed. Joseph Black. Cambridge University Press, Cambridge 2008.

Black, Joseph: Introductory Matter to the Arraignment of John Hodgkins. *The Marprelate Press: A Documentary History.* University of Massachusetts Amherst 2015. Accessed 27 June 2016 http://people.umass.edu/marprelate/documenttwenty.html.

Carlson, Leland H.: *Martin Marprelate, Gentleman: Master Job Throkmorton Laid Open in His Colors.* Huntington Library, San Marino CA 1981.

Clegg, Cyndia: *Press Censorship in Elizabethan England.* Cambridge University Press, Cambridge 1997.

Collavin, Elena: Speech Acts. *Handbooks of Pragmatics.* Vol. 1, *Foundation of Pragmatics.* Eds. Wolfram Bublitz and Neal R. Norrick. De Gruyter Mouton, Berlin 2011, 373–395.

Collinson, Patrick: *The Elizabethan Puritan Movement.* Cape, London 1967.

Collinson, Patrick: Field, John (1544/5?–1588). *Oxford Dictionary of National Biography.* January 2008. Accessed 23 May 2016 http://www.oxforddnb.com/view/article/9248.

Collinson, Patrick: Throckmorton, Job (1545–1601). *Oxford Dictionary of National Biography.* May 2015. Accessed 22 Aug 2016 http://www.oxforddnb.com/view/article/27391.

Collinson, Patrick: Wilcox, Thomas (c.1549–1608). *Oxford Dictionary of National Biography*. 2004. Accessed 23 May 2016 http://www.oxforddnb.com/view/article/29390.

Cooligde, John S.: Martin Marprelate, Marvell and Decorum Personae as Satirical Theme. *PMLA* 5/1959, 526–532.

Cressy, David: *Dangerous Talk: Scandalous, Seditious, and Treasonable Speech in Pre-Modern England*. Oxford University Press, Oxford 2010.

Cross, Claire: Penry, John (1562/3–1593). *Oxford Dictionary of National Biography*. May 2015. Accessed 22 August 2016 http://www.oxforddnb.com/view/article/21894.

Haigh, Christopher: *English Reformations: Religion, Politics, and Society under the Tudors*. Oxford University Press, Oxford 1993.

Heal, Felicity: *Reformation in Britain and Ireland*. Oxford University Press, Oxford 2003.

Kendall, Ritchie D.: *The Drama of Dissent: The Radical Poetics of Nonconformity, 1380–1590*. The University of North Carolina Press, Chapel Hill 1986.

Lake, Peter: *Anglicans and Puritans? Presbyterianism and English Conformist Thought from Whitgift to Hooker*. Unwin Hyman, London 1988.

Lake, Peter: Anti-Popery: the Structure of a Prejudice. *Conflict in Early Stuart England: Studies in Religion and Politics 1603–1642*. Eds. Richard Cust and Ann Hughes. Addison-Wesley Longman Limited, London 1989, 72–106.

Lander, Jesse M.: *Inventing Polemic: Religion, Print, and Literary Culture in Early Modern England*. Cambridge University Press, Cambridge 2006.

Loades, David: The Theory and Practice of Censorship in Sixteenth-Century England. *Politics, Censorship and the English Reformation*. Pinter Publishers, London 1991, 96–108. (orig. 1974)

MacCulloch, Diarmaid: *The Later Reformation in England, 1547–1603*. Palgrave, Basingstoke and New York, 2001.

McGinn, Donald J.: *John Penry and the Marprelate Controversy*. Rutgers University Press, New Brunswick NJ 1966.

Mack, Peter: *Elizabethan Rhetoric: Theory and Practice*. Cambridge University Press, Cambridge 2002.

Mann, A. J.: Waldegrave, Robert (c.1554–1603/4). *Oxford Dictionary of National Biography*. May 2015. Accessed 22 Aug 2016 http://www.oxforddnb.com/view/article/28441.

Manning, Roger B.: The Origins of the Doctrine of Sedition. *Albion: A Quarterly Journal Concerned with British Studies* 2/1980, 99–121.

Rebhorn, Wayne A.: *The Emperor of Men's Minds*. Cornell University Press, Ithaca and London 1995.

Rodda, Joshua: *Public Religious Disputation in England, 1558–1626*. Ashgate, Farnham 2014.

Searle, John: *Expression and Meaning: Studies in the Theory of Speech Acts*. Cambridge University Press, Cambridge 1979.

Searle, John: *Speech Acts: An Essay in the Philosophy of Language*. Cambridge University Press, Cambridge 1969.

Tribble, Evelyn B.: *Margins and Marginality: The Printed Page in Early Modern England*. University Press of Virginia, Charlottesville 1993.

Vivier, Eric D.: John Bridges, Martin Marprelate, and the Rhetoric of Satire. *English Literary Renaissance* 1/2014, 3–35.

Wiener, Carol Z.: The Beleaguered Isle: A Study of Elizabethan and Early Jacobean Anti-Catholicism. *Past and Present* 51.1971, 27–62.

Wenig, Scott A: *Straightening the Altars: The Ecclesiastical Vision and Pastoral Achievements of the Progressive Bishops under Elizabeth I, 1559–1579*. Peter Lang Publishing, Bern and New York 2000.

Authors

Thomas C. Devaney (Associate Professor, University of Rochester) is a scholar of late medieval and early modern cultural history. Currently, he is engaged in a project examining the emotional and sensory experience of local pilgrimage in early modern Iberia.

Meri Heinonen, PhD, has studied the gendered and bodily aspects of medieval German mysticism and the relationships between religious mentors and their female protégées in later medieval German culture. Recently she has been interested in the Dominican reform and the impact of libraries on the lives of medieval nuns.

Teemu Immonen, PhD, is a researcher at the Department of Cultural History, University of Turku. His main scholarly interests concern the history of Romanesque illuminated manuscripts, the cults of saints as well as medieval reform movements.

Gabriele Müller-Überhäuser is Professor Emerita of Book Studies and English Philology at the English Department of the University of Münster. Her research interests focus on English book history of the later Middle Ages and the Reformation, especially on the history of censorship in the religious field, verbal violence in manuscript and print, and the history of reading.

Päivi Räisänen-Schröder, PhD, is Adjunct Professor at the Department for Church History at the University of Helsinki. Her research interests focus on early modern religiosity in a broad sense, e.g. lived religion, gender, the history of reading, and the history of the Reformation as well as the Radical Reformation.

Marika Räsänen (Phd, Adjunct Professor) is currently a Senior Lecturer at the Department of Cultural History, University of Turku. Her research interests include religious material and devotional culture in late medieval and early modern Europe.

Eva Schaten, MA, is a doctoral student in the English Department and works as administrator in the Faculty of Catholic Theology at the University of Münster. Her research interests include censorship in the late medieval manuscript culture and the history of magic.

Stefan Schröder, PhD, Adjunct Professor (docent) and Academy Research Fellow (University of Helsinki, Department of Church History), is a historian specializing in late medieval cultural and religious history. His research interests include the cultural encounter between Christianity and Islam in the Middle Ages, medieval travel reports and maps, the transmission of knowledge and cultural memory.

Sarah Ströer, PhD, has studied discourses of language and violence in Elizabethan religious controversy at the "Religion and Politics" Cluster of Excellence at the University of Münster. Her research interests include book history, religious history and discourse analysis.

Reima Välimäki, PhD, is a Postdoctoral Researcher at the University of Turku, Turku Institute for Advanced Studies and the Department of Cultural History. His research interests include medieval heresy and inquisitions, polemical treatises, as well as medievalism and history politics.